World Trade Law in Practice

Markus W Gehring
Jarrod Hepburn
Marie-Claire Cordonier Segger

Authors
Markus W Gehring, Jarrod Hepburn, Marie-Claire Cordonier Segger

Publisher
Sian O'Neill

Editor
Carolyn Boyle

Marketing manager
Alan Mowat

Production and design
John Meikle, Russell Anderson

Publishing directors
Guy Davis, Tony Harriss, Mark Lamb

World Trade Law in Practice
is published by
Globe Law & Business
Globe Business Publishing Ltd
New Hibernia House
Winchester Walk
London Bridge
London SE1 9AG
United Kingdom
Tel +44 20 7234 0606
Fax +44 20 7234 0808
Web www.gbplawbooks.com

Printed by Antony Rowe Ltd

ISBN 0-9548706-8-9 / 978-0-9548706-8-3

Table of contents

Preface

John H Jackson[1]
Institute of International Economic Law, Georgetown University

International economic law has an important and potentially profound relationship to the challenges and opportunities faced by countries and people in the world today. In these times, it is commonplace to see comments about the extraordinary and growing interdependence of international economic activities and the stresses these developments cause for existing economic and governmental institutions. But although commonplace, such phenomena are not trivial. Evidence of the stresses caused by globalisation has become apparent, and we are beginning to see economic and political fallout from financial and other crises. We are also seeing effects upon transatlantic relations, particularly in the context of certain World Trade Organisation (WTO) cases, such as those concerning bananas, beef hormones and biotech products. Political leaders in the context of this growing interdependence often feel helpless in the face of external trade and monetary pressures, and some succumb to the temptation to play upon similar frustrations of their constituents.[2] It is essential that both practising professionals today and law students, the practitioners of tomorrow, gain an understanding of the rules of international economic law in context. In today's economy, this is an important, even crucial, subject for school teaching and scholarship, and a vital activity for legal professionals. This book, *Word Trade Law in Practice*, explains international economic law in practical terms and is a valuable contribution to such endeavours.

Several characteristics make legal practice and studies in this field particularly challenging and rewarding. First of all, international economic law has an extraordinarily broad scope of application. Virtually every type of government regulation of economic activity – including antitrust or competition policy, securities regulation, labour law, immigration law, insurance, banking, bankruptcy, trade and goods, trade and services, capital flows, monetary policy, labour adjustment policies for unemployment and exchange rate effects – is influenced by and linked to international economic law. So the subject is really not a narrow one. Indeed, in some ways it embraces a very large proportion of the subjects that we think of more broadly as general international law. Second, national governments increasingly find they cannot effectively regulate many of these activities without some type of

1 This preface is based on Professor Jackson's Hersch Lauterpacht Memorial Lectures delivered in November 2002 at Cambridge University, and his lecture at the Lauterpacht Research Centre for International Law 2006, Cambridge University.

2 John H Jackson, "International Economic Law: Jurisprudence and Contours" in American Society of International Law (ASIL), *Proceedings of the 93rd Annual Meeting*, (Washington, DC: ASIL 2000), p 98.

cooperation or coordination with other national governments or national institutions. In some cases, one can focus on economic regulation as the subject; in other cases, transactional activity can be the focus. Although I view this field as a question of economic regulation rather than transactions, a great part of the subject is transactional, and this is perhaps very relevant to the active professional who has to figure out how to do things. A third characteristic, which is integral, is the linkage between the national or municipal law and international law. One cannot successfully approach this subject without looking to the intertwining of those two levels of law. I think this is also true of general international law, incidentally; but it is certainly accentuated in the context of international economic law.[3]

As the countries of the world become increasingly interdependent, nation-state governments cannot regulate effectively on many subjects. As a result, national governments cannot meet the expectations of their constituents and cannot deliver upon their promises to their constituents. This imposes a considerable amount of tension on governments and makes governing much more difficult. Within this context, there is a worry that there will be a 'race to the bottom' and that there will be a tendency for governments to redress their insecurity by using barriers of one type or another. For example, it leads to what some economists analyse as the prisoners' dilemma: when one country raises barriers, another is likely to do so, and soon all countries will be hurt. What is the solution? The solution is cooperative institutions at the international level. These institutions should be based on rule orientation, as opposed to power orientation. These rules should be well formulated and effective. In other words, they should cause certain kinds of behaviour and inhibit other kinds of behaviour.[4]

Given this need, what are the characteristics needed for a successful international cooperative institution? A few characteristics can be suggested. First, the system must be rule oriented. Second, it must include reliable and effective dispute settlement procedures. Third, it must be structured around international 'regulatory' institutions. Fourth, it must have credibility and legitimacy. Fifth, it must be transparent. And sixth, it must provide meaningful mechanisms for full participation of stakeholders.[5] With its focus on the practical aspects of WTO law, this book also underlines the need and opportunities for such participation.

Of course, important questions arise as to whether these characteristics are being developed and enhanced in the evolution of the WTO. The WTO system is not without challenge and criticism (some of it severe, and even including 'physical' street protests). Clearly the WTO system is not perfect and certain criticisms exist. First, there are questions related to institutional structure and WTO governance; second, concerns about the impact of the WTO on power allocation among various participants (eg, government and non-government entities, rich and poor countries, producers and consumers, labour and human rights issues); third, worries that the

---

3 John H Jackson, *supra* note 1 p 99–100.
4 John H Jackson, "The Perils of Globalization and the World Trading System", *Fordham Int'l LJ* 24, no 1/2 (2000), p 371, 374
5 *Ibid*, p 377.

WTO is overreaching because it increasingly addresses issues of sovereign state internal regulation and governance; fourth, worries that the WTO does not go far enough in addressing issues (including internal government issues) to redress important governmental distortions of world markets, which distortions (eg, agricultural export and domestic subsidies) particularly disadvantage poorer countries; and fifth, unmet challenges to the effectiveness of the WTO in accomplishing its mission, such as the proliferation of preferential (non-most favoured nation) agreements such as free trade agreements.[6]

The WTO system, including its very important dispute settlement mechanism, is unique in international law and international relations, and has proven sufficiently powerful as to address many important questions of world trade law. The jurisprudence is impressive by any objective observation of other existing tribunals in the real world, national and international. One of the persistent themes of this jurisprudence is the 'devilish detail' of balancing the values of nation-state sovereignty with the contemporary world need for cooperation and multilateral activity of nations and other participants in the globalised economy. This book addresses this detail in a comprehensive yet clear way, and can serve as a valuable tool for the student and practitioner alike in developing an understanding and ability to apply the rules of the increasingly complex and essential body of world trade law.

John H Jackson is university professor of law at the Georgetown University Law Center and director of the Law Center's Institute of International Economic Law. He joined the Georgetown faculty after a distinguished career as Hessel E Yntema professor of law at the University of Michigan. He has advised the US and other governments and international organisations on international trade law, and from 1973 to 1974 was general counsel of the Office of the United States Trade Representative. In June 2003, Professor Jackson was awarded the honorary degree of doctor iuris honoris causa *by Hamburg University Faculty of Law and was also appointed to the WTO Consultative Board. The board released a report entitled "The Future of the WTO: Addressing Institutional Challenges in the New Millennium" in January 2005. He has published widely in the area of international trade law, including* The Jurisprudence of GATT and the WTO: Insights on Treaty Law and Economic Relations *(Cambridge University Press, 2000).*

6 John H Jackson, "The Changing Fundamentals of International Law and Ten Years of the WTO", *J Int'l Econ L* 8, no 1 (2005), p 3, 6.

A rapidly changing field – the scope of world trade law

1. Introduction

In a globalised economy, world trade law enters the practice of most international legal questions, from company mergers (and related due diligence) to the drafting and negotiation of sales contracts. A basic understanding of world trade law is necessary for most legal practitioners, along with solid information on where to find further resources. However, most books on world trade law are either weighty academic tomes or detailed technical studies. The purpose of this book is to provide a short, accessible introduction to the aspects of world trade law that are most likely to be encountered in international legal practice, along with practical information on how a practitioner can represent the interests of a client in world trade matters.[1]

It is hoped that *World Trade Law in Practice* will serve as the short guide to world trade law for corporate counsel and new associates in law firms who do not have an extensive grounding in international law. It may also be of use to students and scholars of business, international relations and law who are not specialised in the field. This book presents the international law applicable to world trade law in a simple, step-by-step way, with short sections explaining key concepts and procedures, accessible discussions of key cases, and a careful selection of recommended resources.

As such, this book provides, in its introductory chapters, explanations of key concepts and the legal forums that are available to a firm with a case. A second series of chapters explains how a lawyer might be called upon by a firm or business association to use the relevant law. The book then continues with a series of chapters discussing the substantive rules and where to find more information, each starting with a case study which takes the lawyer through the general steps of tracking the legal issues and using the dispute settlement mechanisms mentioned in the previous section, including what the client could realistically hope to achieve. The book finishes with a concluding section on sustainable development aspects of trade law and other emerging issues, as well as a short discussion on future directions for the field.

1 As such, the specific topics presented have been screened in the interest of brevity, accessibility and relevance to legal practice. For instance, although important and politically sensitive, areas of trade law such as agriculture and textiles are not covered herein. Useful discussions of such issues can be found online at www.wto.org. A short but comprehensive introduction to the study of world trade law can be recommended: J Jackson, *The World Trading System: Law and Policy of International Economic Relations* (MIT Press, 1997).

As such, Section 1, "Introduction", starts with this overview of the book, followed by a short historic overview of World Trade Organisation (WTO) law and an explanation of the general structure of WTO law and the WTO dispute settlement mechanism. The second chapter explains key concepts found in all levels of world trade law, while the third explains the participation of private parties such as business and associations in trade policy and negotiations. Section 2, "A case in world trade law", begins with a chapter on national enforcement of world trade law primarily drawn from the European Union, the United States and Canada. It follows with a chapter which discusses the private initiation of WTO disputes and explains the Section 301 procedure in the United States and the EU Trade Barriers Regulation. The final chapter explains the limited participation of private parties in WTO disputes.

Section 3, "The practice of world trade law - important law (and remedies) to know", explains the most relevant substantive areas of world trade law: tariffs and import/export, technical and sanitary standards and labels, subsidies, dumping, services and IP rights.

Section 4, "The future of world trade law", first explains the new debates and emerging law about sustainable development concerns such as market access for renewable resources, the globalisation of health, human rights and labour standards and the promotion of trade in environmental goods and services. The following chapter, on other emerging issues in world trade law, explains the trade law on investment, competition, trade facilitation and public procurement. Finally, the last chapter provides a short conclusion to the book.

The book has been written from the perspective of a lawyer whose client might have a case in the WTO, the European Union or the North American Free Trade Agreement. The structure makes it a good 'primer' for a lawyer trained in domestic litigation and issues who needs a quick overview of the international law with references for where to go for further information, or a business, law or international relations student seeking to understand and apply world trade law.

2. A short history of world trade law

Trade law is one of the oldest areas of international law. Most very early 'international' treaties granted trade concessions and allowed products to be traded from one ancient city state to another. As such, there is no right to free trade in international law. This can be contrasted with, for instance, the freedom of the high seas, and means that it is every country's sovereign decision to allow trade with another country or not.

It is useful to provide context to the concepts behind 'free trade', drawing on the thoughts and history behind world trade law. Early works by economists such as Adam Smith, David Ricardo and John Stuart Mill suggested that countries could benefit economically from free trade between them, as it allows each to build on its respective comparative advantages. The advent of free trade treaties brought a moderate degree of liberalisation, but by the 1860s many countries quickly returned to protectionist policies in response to fears of British economic dominance. After a period of relative stability based on the gold standard, countries began to exercise their sovereign right to determine trade relations, leading to a period of high protectionism after the depression of the late 1920s and 1930s. Several important countries sought to raise barriers and isolate themselves from the world economy, in order to protect their own industry. However, most countries returned to multilateralism in the late 1930s by developing reciprocity in their trading relationships, granting tariff concessions between countries on a mutual basis.

This multilateralism also formed the basis for the allied post-war economic discussions, which eventually led to the negotiation of the Charter for an International Trade Organisation (the so-called Havana Charter), which included provisions mandating cooperation in many areas such as trade, labour and competition. However, this comprehensive economic agenda failed, largely because the US Senate did not approve the treaty. Nevertheless, one part of the Havana Charter, the General Agreement of Tariffs and Trade (GATT), was enacted provisionally in 1947 and formed the basis for almost 50 years of operation. GATT 1947 focused specifically on trade in goods and did not include any other area of international trade or economic regulation. This narrow scope was part of its success in attracting many countries as contracting parties and achieving significant tariff reductions in seven rounds of trade negotiations. After significant tariff reductions, the GATT 1947 contracting parties recognised that other barriers – outside the purview of 'trade in goods' – were becoming more important and impeded exports. Thus, during the late 1970s, in the Tokyo Round of trade negotiations, additional agreements were adopted, dealing with technical barriers to trade, food standards, dumping and subsidies.

In 1994, after nearly a decade of deliberations and negotiations, GATT 1947 was replaced by the Agreement Establishing the World Trade Organisation (WTO) and its subsequent agreements, one pillar of which remained GATT.

3. Today's world trade law

Today's world trade law is based on several levels of international trading regimes and can be found in two major sets of agreements:

- law concerning the WTO; and
- international trade law stemming from bilateral or regional trade agreements.

The WTO, despite unsuccessful attempts to renegotiate some of its rules and a shift of focus within the international community towards regional trade agreements, is still at the heart of the international trade regime. At the time of publication, the WTO has 149 extremely diverse member states, with some important international economic actors such as Russia involved in membership negotiations. Arguably, the exponential increase in trade in goods during recent decades was due to the stability and predictability of the international trading system. The Uruguay Round of negotiations leading to the creation of the WTO also saw the inclusion of new issues such as trade in services and trade-related IP rights, and aimed to bring agriculture and textiles back under GATT disciplines.

Fundamentally, the WTO is a member-driven organisation with a comparatively small Secretariat. The WTO's mandate is to:

- administer the WTO agreements;
- provide a forum for trade negotiations;
- settle trade disputes;
- monitor national trade policies;
- facilitate technical assistance and training for developing countries; and
- promote cooperation with other international organisations.

In addition to the development of the WTO regime, there has been rapid growth in regional trade agreements and bilateral agreements which exist parallel to the ambit of the WTO but must conform to principles embedded therein. According to GATT rules, regional trade agreements should serve as 'building blocks', not 'stumbling blocks', to facilitate the functioning of the world trading system. For the practitioner, this means that a multilayered analysis of agreements governing trade is crucial; it is not sufficient only to analyse the implications of WTO law while ignoring preferential rules enshrined among trading partners in regional trade agreements or national rules which implement international trade law regimes.

The WTO agreements and dispute settlement outcomes – the latter having at least strong persuasive power or *de facto* precedent character – largely determine international trade rules with relevance for both the private and public sector. These WTO agreements also contain guidelines governing international commercial conduct and guard against trade distorting behaviour such as unlawful subsidising practices and 'dumping' (ie, product sale in a foreign country below the sales price in the country of origin or below cost plus distribution price).

The WTO agreements are broadly organised into three pillars – goods, services and IP rights. The goods pillar is the largest, including agreements on many different aspects of international goods trade. There are also plurilateral agreements signed only by a subset of the WTO membership, and various cross-cutting accords.

Pillar 1: trade in goods General Agreement on Tariffs and Trade (GATT)	• Agriculture • Sanitary standards • Textiles • Technical standards • Trade-related investment measures • Anti-dumping measures • Customs valuation methods • Pre-shipment inspection • Rules of origin • Import licensing • Subsidies and counter-measures • Safeguards
Pillar 2: trade in services General Agreement on Trade in Services (GATS)	• Movement of natural persons annex • Air transport annex • Financial services annex

	• Shipping annex • Telecommunications annex
Pillar 3: IP rights Agreement on Trade-Related Aspects of Intellectual Property Rights (TRIPs)	
Cross-cutting agreements	• Dispute Settlement Understanding • Trade Policy Review Mechanism
Plurilaterals	• Agreement on Trade in Civil Aircraft • Agreement on Government Procurement

Of course, such a brief overview of the WTO treaty framework provides only the beginnings of an accurate picture of WTO law. The main commitments of WTO members are contained in individual detailed country schedules attached to GATT (tariff schedules) and GATS (services schedules). These two documents are comprehensive listings of all the products for which the WTO member in question has accepted a commitment to a binding tariff at a particular level. For example, the tariff for microwave ovens for imports into the United States is bound at 4% according to value, and the United States has completely liberalised architectural services in cross-border supply.

4. The settlement of disputes in world trade law

Trade disputes were a common phenomenon in the later years of GATT 1947. Indeed, the animosity and absence of middle ground in some disputes between the United States and the European Union triggered a new approach to dispute settlement in the WTO. Instead of a positive vote to adopt a dispute settlement decision, as was required by the contracting parties of GATT 1947, the WTO now operates in reverse, so that decisions under its dispute settlement mechanism can be dismissed only by the unanimous vote of all members. This negative consensus means that even the party that won the case must agree for a report to be dismissed in the formal adoption meeting of the Dispute Settlement Body (which is identical to the General Council but acts under a different chairperson). This system makes the WTO's Dispute Settlement Understanding (DSU) highly effective and contributes to its objective to represent "a central element in providing security and predictability to the multilateral trading system" (Article 3.2 of the DSU). The requirement to settle disputes formally rests with the WTO members, which often devote significant time to the use of other pre-juridical techniques such as consultation and other arbitration-like elements of the dispute settlement mechanism. If these preliminary attempts to defuse a trade-related conflict fail to satisfy either party, the DSU process is set in motion and carried out first by a WTO panel (composed of three trade experts chosen *ad hoc* to hear the case and determine the facts), and second by the WTO Appellate Body (a standing body of nine trade law experts, of whom three are called upon to hear legal appeals to the panel's determination).

The following diagram explains the flow of the DSU process:

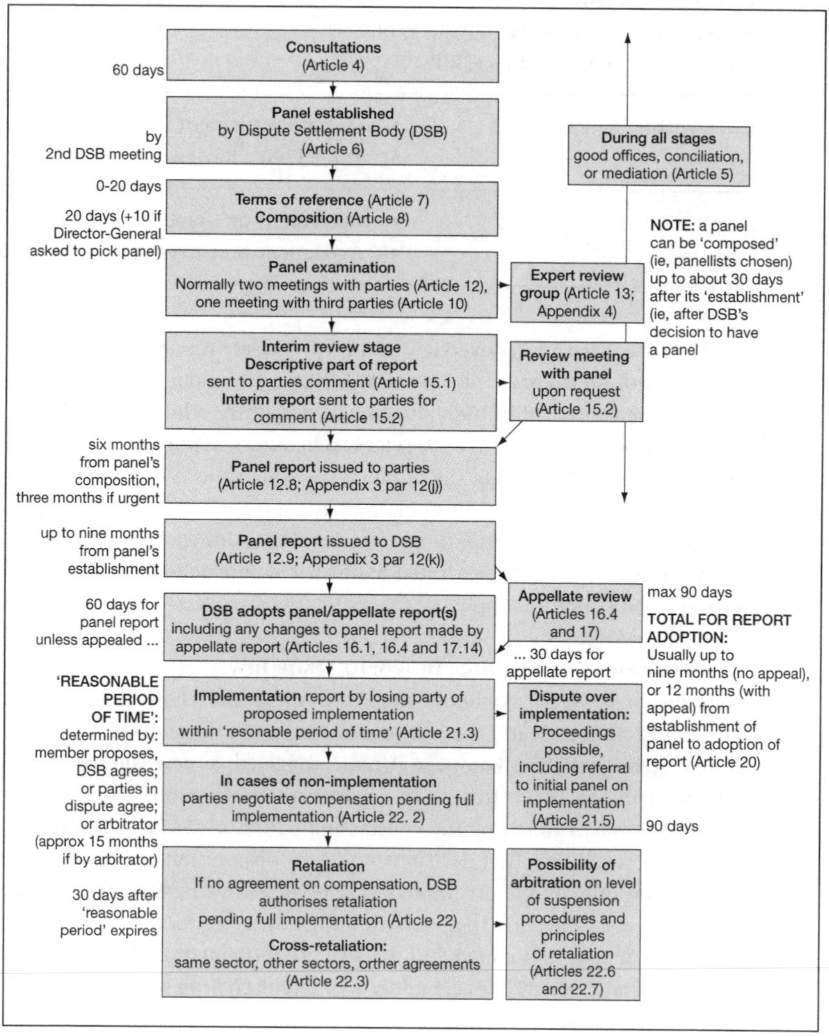

Source: WTO, *Understanding the WTO* (Geneva: WTO, 2005), p 59.

Besides the negative consensus, formal rules on implementation strengthen the dispute settlement mechanism. If a dispute settlement decision is not implemented by the losing party, the Dispute Settlement Body can authorise retaliation (eg, suspension of trade concessions such as preferential tariffs) if the parties to the dispute cannot agree themselves as to compensation. Even cross-retaliation – that is, suspension of trade concessions for products unrelated to the dispute – can be authorised (with the United States adopting a carousel approach, whereby the affected products change over time). In light of its effectiveness, the DSU has been the target of increased public scrutiny and questions surrounding its legitimacy. Especially in politically charged trade disputes, the selection of panel and Appellate Body members has been extremely contentious. Given that the WTO agreements regulate a wide range of issues, disputes arise on a myriad of topics. For instance, cases have involved topics ranging from the use of genetically modified organisms (*EC – Approval and Marketing of Biotech Products*), enforcement of domestic IP laws (*Denmark – Measures Affecting the Enforcement of Intellectual Property Rights*), environmental safeguards (*US – Shrimp/Turtle*), domestic legislation (*US – Section 211 Appropriations Act*) and customs duties (*India – Measures Affecting Customs Duties*).

As mentioned above, the WTO regime aims to enhance trade liberalisation and negotiates trade concessions in trade rounds. The 1994 Uruguay Round led to the conclusion of the current WTO agreements. More recently, the Doha Development Round commenced in 2001 but, despite meetings in Cancun (2003), Geneva (2004) and Hong Kong (2005), significant disagreements in negotiating positions remain. The areas of agriculture, negotiations on market access, export subsidies and domestic support have been particularly divisive, with stark material differences between some industrialised countries and developing country WTO members.

5. The future of world trade law

The creation of the WTO in 1995 encouraged many developments in world trade law by providing an official forum for debate. Recent years have seen the emergence of increased debate in the WTO's Committees on Trade and Environment and Trade and Development, as well as increased discussion of the links between trade and other fields such as public health, foreign investment and competition. Sustainable development is an ever-more integrated part of global debate; more countries (and regions) are engaging in environmental and sustainability impact assessment of new trade negotiations; and the decisions of WTO panels and the Appellate Body are playing a growing role in setting the agenda of world trade. The scope of trade law has now moved well beyond its purely commercial origins and proposals exist to take it further, as is discussed in the last part of this book.

Key concepts in world trade law

Four principles provide the foundations of world trade law. These principles were set out in the General Agreement on Tariffs and Trade 1947 (GATT), and were later extended to all three pillars (goods, services and IP rights) of the World Trade Organisation (WTO). The key concepts of international law on trade, including these, are set out below in brief, and are important to understand in order to gain a grasp of the more detailed legal rules in this field.

1. Tariffs and tariffication

GATT 1947 focused on the maxim of 'tariffs only' – that is, all other trade measures (quotas, import restrictions and even technical barriers) should be converted into tariffs ('tarifficated'), charged at the border and bound by negotiated tariff schedules (see Articles II and XI:1 of GATT). Tariffs are the trade instrument of choice because they are relatively transparent and much easier to negotiate, since their economic value can be calculated. The international system for classification of tariffs is also uniform and harmonised, as established in the Brussels Convention on Nomenclature for the Classification of Goods in Customs Tariffs.

2. Most favoured nation treatment

Embedded in Article I:1 of GATT, Article II:2 of the General Agreement on Trade and Services (GATS) and Article 4 of the Agreement on Trade-Related Aspects of Intellectual Property Rights (TRIPs), the 'most favoured nation' principle precludes discrimination between one's trading partners. Any concessions or barriers enacted upon exchanges with one trading partner must be conferred to all other partners.

3. National treatment

This second non-discrimination principle is enshrined in Article III of GATT, Article XVII of GATS and Article 3 of TRIPs. National treatment requires extending treatment to foreign goods, service providers and rights holders that is identical to the treatment accorded to one's own nationals. Article III of GATT requires that imports be treated no less favourably than the same or similar domestically produced goods once they have passed customs.

4. Exceptions

The compendium of WTO agreements is not without exceptions clearly stated within the legal texts. The main two exceptions are Article XX of GATT, which allows

WTO members to violate WTO disciplines in tightly described circumstances, such as the protection of public health or national treasures. GATS and TRIPs contain similar provisions. The second, perhaps eventually even more important, exception is contained in Article XXIV: 5 of GATT and excludes customs unions or free-trade areas, under certain conditions, from compliance with WTO disciplines.

5. Reciprocity

Although not contained in the legal texts as such, this principle was traditionally a key element of the WTO legal order. In GATT it meant that the trade advantages granted by one party should be of equal weight with respect to the trading partners. This principle guided most trade liberalisation rounds in the first 50 years of the functioning of GATT. However, an important exception has been established more recently with regards to developing countries. It has now been recognised that reciprocity cannot be required from developing country members.

6. Special and differential treatment of developing countries

The principle of special and differential treatment was part of GATT 1947, in Article XXVIII *bis*, which requires that the special needs of developing countries be taken into account. In addition, Article XXXVI: 8 of GATT exempts developing countries from the application of reciprocity in trade negotiations. The principle is now contained in all WTO agreements which contain special provisions for developing countries and least developed countries. The Preamble of the WTO Agreement also recognises the special needs of developing countries.[1]

7. Trade liberalisation

There are some discussions as to whether trade liberalisation is a key concept of the world trading system. Some see trade regulation and the functioning of the trading system as a whole as the more important concepts. However, several key provisions aim to abolish barriers to trade (Articles II, VIII and XI:1 of GATT) and so liberalise trade. The dispute settlement system has recognised trade liberalisation as an important objective.[2]

8. Transparency

A key concept in the WTO is transparency. The legal order distinguishes between internal and external transparency. The former is mainly between states and involves ensuring that countries inform fellow WTO members about important trade policies and other trade rules. It is key to ensure effective negotiations and equal treatment between WTO members. All WTO agreements also contain provisions on transparency and establish national contacts or inquiry points. It has also been suggested that the WTO has similar obligations towards the public at large and non-governmental organisations (external transparency). The WTO Secretariat has

---

1 See Panel Report, *India – Quantitative Restrictions*, para 7.2.
2 See Panel Report, *Turkey – Textiles*, paras 9.161-9.163.

answered calls for increased external transparency through various measures such as:

- organising public symposia for dialogue and debate (including making provisions for observers/side events at ministerial conferences);
- analysing and disseminating WTO law and policy in publications; and
- greatly developing the WTO website as an important source of information.

9. Sustainable development

Sustainable development has recently been recognised as an objective of the WTO. It requires that economic, environmental and developmental priorities be reconciled – or at least accommodated jointly in a way that is 'mutually supportive' – in the interest of development that can last into the future. In the words of Director General Pascal Lamy, the objective of sustainable development mandates WTO members "to no longer compartmentalize [their] work; discussing environmental and developmental issues in isolation of the rest of what [they] do. These are issues that permeate all areas of the WTO."[3]

These concepts and principles are useful in understanding trade law in general and are among the key ideas upon which international trade treaties, the WTO and other trade institutions are founded.

10. Recommended resources

The WTO maintains a useful website with explanatory materials on many aspects of WTO negotiations, rules and disputes, as well as other resources. It is available at www.wto.org.

The North American Free Trade Agreement (NAFTA) Secretariat, which is responsible for the administration of the dispute settlement provisions of NAFTA, also maintains a useful website where copies of treaty texts, information on panel decisions and reports and links to further resources can be found. It is available at www.nafta-sec-alena.org.

The Directorate General for Trade of the European Commission, which is in charge of implementing the common trade policy of the European Union, maintains a useful website with information on European trade negotiations, rules and disputes, as well as many further resources. It is available at ec.europa.eu/trade.

For further information on these concepts, see the following:

- D van den Bossche, *The Law and Policy of the WTO: Text, Cases and Materials,* (Cambridge: Cambridge University Press, 2005).
- P C Mavroidis, *The General Agreement on Tariffs and Trade – A Commentary* (Oxford: Oxford University Press 2005).
- C Barnard, *The Substantive Law of the EU: The Four Freedoms* (Oxford: Oxford University Press, 2004).
- M Trebilcock and R Howse, *The Regulation of International Trade,* 3rd ed (New York: Routledge, 2005).

---

3 For more on sustainable development see the chapter entitled "Sustainable development concerns". See also M Gehring and MC Cordonier Segger, eds, *Sustainable Development in World Trade Law* (The Hague: Kluwer Law International, 2005).

Participation of private parties in trade policy and negotiations

1. Engaging in national trade debates

1.1 Who makes trade policy?

In most countries there is a ministry or department concerned with international trade, usually subsumed under the broader auspices of foreign or economic affairs. Decisions regarding international trade are usually centrally coordinated, but in federal political systems, regions may exert significant policy influence. As the international trade regime becomes increasingly interconnected with the environment, development and cultural affairs, other ministries may consult with the groups formally tasked with decision making. There is an emerging trend to conduct impact assessments (to evaluate environmental or sustainable development impacts) prior to signing trade agreements or solidifying multilateral negotiating positions. Throughout the process of information gathering and analysis, public input is encouraged and stakeholders are consulted. Most impact assessment frameworks stipulate that public concerns must be addressed when weighing alternative choices.

1.2 Are documents available online?

Many countries are committed to high levels of transparency. During trade negotiations and after, governments will post documents online to encourage public input and even send draft documents to relevant industry associations and groups. Some countries post all their public submissions to the World Trade Organisation (WTO) on their trade ministry websites, providing an up-to-date source of information even during ongoing negotiations. The WTO itself publishes official documents on its website, but sometimes with considerable delay due to translation and the opportunity for members to discuss proposals informally. In many cases, governments will draft white papers which allude to proposed courses of action for international trade issues. Some trade-related non-governmental organisations also collect information for dissemination purposes.

1.3 Industry associations and their role

Industry associations play an important role. They can register with the WTO and participate as non-governmental organisations in the ministerial conferences and other public WTO events. In order to register, associations must show proof of their legal existence and explain how their work relates to the WTO. Industry associations can also lobby government officials tasked with trade policy either informally or at formal governmental delegation meetings. Some countries will include several industry representatives in their delegation which grants them additional access to the otherwise restricted trade negotiations. Some industry associations fund expert reports on their sector-specific concerns which can have considerable influence on government trade policy.

2. Understanding world trade forums

2.1 Where do governments meet?

Governments meet at different levels and in different contexts when formulating trade policy. Ministerial conferences, including all WTO members represented by their trade ministers, take place every two years and are imperative in determining the direction of the WTO as a whole. The negotiation process itself tends to be 'government-only' and sometimes only the main trading partners of a particular product/service will meet in separate 'green room' negotiations. In some cases, especially during active trade negotiations, a smaller number of important WTO members will meet to prepare for the ministerial conference in 'mini-ministerials'. These smaller meetings provide an excellent opportunity to gain access to some of the key governments driving the negotiations. Information about these meetings tends to be scarce since governments want to avoid mass demonstrations (which now regularly occur during official ministerial conferences). The best way to learn about mini-ministerials is through the national trade ministries of important WTO members.

In between ministerials, the General Council, including all WTO members represented by their WTO ambassadors in Geneva, is the highest organ within the WTO. The General Council can take decisions with important policy implications. If a client has a particular pressing concern about a WTO issue (not just long-term interest), one of the most effective ways of informal participation is to approach trade diplomats in Geneva. Some countries are very transparent about their policies and will share their view about your client's interest and their public WTO mandate. However, given the proliferation of bilateral and regional trade agreements, trade policy is often discussed in a more intimate setting than the General Council.

2.2 Where do non-governmental organisations/business representatives meet?

Many non-governmental organisations concerned with the state of the international trade structure and future developments arrange meetings parallel to the ministerial conferences, often in the same cities. The WTO Secretariat now provides space for these non-governmental organisations at ministerial conferences, through workshops, side events, a non-governmental organisation (NGO) centre and other activities. These forums are extremely heterogeneous, ranging from academic discussions to groups zealously opposed to trade liberalisation. Special interest events are also organised, where private sector stakeholders can discuss developments and strategies in response to ongoing negotiations or implementation of trade law. In many countries, such meetings take place at a national level and at intervals between the ministerial conferences. Business, labour and other associations often have networks with counterparts in other countries, and many arrange regular meetings to discuss ways to influence domestic policy choices. The WTO Secretariat organises periodic informal symposia for NGOs dealing with civil society issues such as trade and the environment and trade facilitation.

2.3 How important are ministerial conferences?

As mentioned above, ministerial conferences take place every two years (independent of prior negotiation results) and present an opportunity for delegations to meet face to face. From a networking point of view, these meetings are paramount, because many trade diplomats and officials will be in attendance. In reality, the negotiations themselves will accommodate only a very small number of any WTO member's representatives. This means that important trade officials have comparatively more time to meet with NGOs including civil society and business representatives. Many industry associations have networks in several countries and will also organise informal meetings, some of which will also include high-ranking trade officials at times willing to discuss even informal policy choices.

2.4 'Government only' – what does this mean in practice?

The WTO is a state-centric organisation, but non-state actors (eg, NGOs, international organisations and international business consortia) can apply for observer status. As an accredited observer, these entities can submit reports if requested, but have no formal voting capacity. National delegations tend to include experts from the private sector or core national industries in an advisory role. Delegation members are entitled to enter the 'governmental' sector of the negotiations and consequently have a high degree of access to other governmental delegations (even though they will be restricted by their role as adviser for one of the WTO members and will often be bound by confidential negotiating instructions).

3. Mechanisms for participation

International trade policy, not unlike foreign policy, is the domain of the executive branch. Historically, even the influence from other parts of the constitutional order was limited. Now the results of trade negotiations are rendered in consultation with a member's parliament or legislative body. In some countries, legislators have an earlier avenue of influence and help formulate in detail national trade values and priorities. If that is the case in a particular country, normal methods of engagement with the domestic parliament or government might be the most effective route to pursue. Recently, several countries have formalised the process of interaction with civil society, an opening which might also be interesting for the trade law practitioner to investigate.

The 2001 Doha Development Agenda encourages WTO members to undertake national environmental impact assessments on a voluntary basis and to share their expertise and experience. In recent years, several legal mechanisms have been developed at the national, regional and (more nebulously) international levels to assess environmental and sustainable development impacts of trade negotiations.

The substance of these assessments is discussed in the chapter entitled "Sustainable development concerns", but the opportunities that these procedures can provide for participation in trade policy making is worthy of note.

3.1 US Environmental Review of Trade

In 1991 the United States conducted pilot assessments on an aspect of the North American Free Trade Agreement (NAFTA) negotiations. Several years later, on November 16 1999, President Bill Clinton signed Executive Order (EO) 13.141 codifying 'environmental reviews' as an internally binding assessment obligation for trade negotiations. The terminology was chosen to avoid confusion with environmental impact statements required for projects, but also to prevent litigants from using environmental review results in litigation against the government.

The environmental reviews were introduced as a formal participatory instrument in preparation for the upcoming 1999 Seattle WTO Ministerial Conference, because the administration sought to strengthen the inclusion of civil society in trade negotiations. EO 13.141 contains essentially the same process phases as a normal environmental impact assessment. As the terminology suggests, the environmental reviews are primarily an instrument to assess environmental impacts:

> *The United States is committed to a policy of careful assessment and consideration of the environmental impacts of trade agreements. The United States will factor environmental considerations into the development of its trade negotiating objectives. Responsible agencies will accomplish these goals through a process of ongoing assessment and evaluation, and, in certain instances, written environmental reviews.*

The level of disclosure and transparency is of particular interest for private companies in environmental reviews, because various aspects of ongoing trade negotiations are formally announced and explained in the publications and calls for public input. Environmentally related industries might also find the final environmental review reports interesting and might even detect business opportunities related to the trading partner or domestically.

3.2 Canada's environmental assessments of trade

In 1994 Canada carried out an environmental review of the WTO Uruguay Round agreements. Five years later, the government introduced the internally binding Strategic Environmental Assessment of Plans and Policies and included trade policy in its scope. At the beginning of 1999, the newly consolidated Department of Foreign Affairs and International Trade agreed to reassess the outcomes of the Uruguay Round agreements in their first four years of operation in order to prepare for the expected Millennium Round (the round of negotiations which was later postponed by the Seattle Ministerial Conference of 1999). This Retrospective Analysis of the 1994 Canadian Environmental Review of the Uruguay Round of Multilateral Trade Negotiations was published in November 1999. Building on these experiences, the Canadian government prepared for an analysis of the new WTO negotiations. Later, this framework was expanded to bilateral, regional and multilateral trade negotiations. All provinces and territories, representatives from the first nations and other civil society representatives were consulted. The Environmental Assessment of Trade Negotiations was adopted through a decision of Cabinet in February 2001. The framework of these assessments was also codified and implementation of the Cabinet Directive on the Strategic Environmental Assessment of Plans and Policies in the area of trade policy was allocated to the Department of Foreign Affairs and International Trade.

The Canadian environmental assessment consists of three primary phases; in each phase the current state of the negotiations is made public. All citizens, as well as businesses, are usually invited to comment. In an initial environmental assessment, the ministry analyses the scope of the negotiations and range of potential environmental effects. If these are found to be minimal, the formal assessment will stop at this stage. The second phase is the elaboration of a draft environmental assessment study and the third phase is a final environmental assessment. The draft environmental assessment is intended to assist Canadian trade negotiators. The final environmental assessment describes the result of the trade negotiations and speculates on the role environmental assessments played in reaching the conclusion. All stages contain extensive public participation requirements, including:

- information provision involving the publication of drafts;
- a website interface designed for interested stakeholders, including businesses, to comment on the assessment;
- interdepartmental and multilevel government consultation; and
- an explicit feedback loop in which concerns that have arisen are factored into the investigation.

Monitoring and assessment might be recommended after the final environmental assessment, but are not mandatory.

3.3 EU sustainability impact assessments on trade

The European Union has established a practice of conducting sustainability impact assessments of trade negotiations. These are mechanisms created to mainstream environmental and social concerns into policies with a view to promoting sustainable development. Sustainability impact assessments seek to identify potential social, economic and environmental impacts using indictors from all three 'pillars' of sustainable development. In the quest for a fully developed and rigorously defined sustainability impact assessment methodology, the indicators and measurements used have both quantitative and qualitative attributes. Today, sustainability impact assessment is at the vanguard of impact assessment tools, comprising all areas of sustainable development, showing evidence of being a fully integrated instrument and including recommendations for enhancement and mitigation where relevant.

In 1999 the EU Directorate General for Trade commissioned the first expert study conducted by a research team affiliated with the University of Manchester. This team was tasked with developing a methodology for a sustainability impact assessment.

After the methodology was formalised (with degrees of context-specific flexibility), the Directorate General for Trade inaugurated several studies using the framework to assess the impact of trade policy on sustainable development. After refining, the sustainability impact assessment consisted of four main phases:

- screening – to determine which measures require a sustainability impact assessment because they are likely to have significant impacts;
- scoping – to establish the appropriate coverage of each sustainability impact assessment;
- preliminary sustainability assessment – to identify potentially significant effects, positive and negative, on sustainable development; and
- mitigation and enhancement analysis – to suggest types of improvement which may enhance the overall impact on sustainable development of trade measures.

These phases, later duplicated in other sustainability impact assessments and contained in a Handbook on Sustainability Impact Assessment produced by the Directorate General for Trade, are infused with avenues of public participation and consultation with civil society organisations. A list-serve has been set up to consult with stakeholders, including business associations. Numerous workshops and consultations, both formal and informal, are held at each phase of the report derivation process. Intermittently, a website provides public access to reports and publications.

These mechanisms, although they are geared towards sustainable development, nevertheless tend to contain interesting business information. Clients ought to be kept up to date on trade policy reviews and impact assessments, even on specific negotiation proposals.

4. Recommended resources

For further information see the following:

- European Union, Directorate General for Trade, *Handbook on Sustainability Impact Assessment* (2006), available online at http://trade.ec.europa.eu/doclib/docs/2006/march/tradoc_127974.pdf.
- John S Odell, *Negotiating Trade,* (Cambridge: Cambridge University Press, 2006).
- M Halle, "Non Governmental Organisations and the WTO", *BRIDGES between Trade and Sustainable Development* Vol 1 No 1, 1997.
- International Center for Trade and Sustainable Development, "Accreditation Schemes and Other Arrangements for Public Participation in International Fora", *BRIDGES Series on Public Participation in the International Trading System* November 1999.

National enforcement of world trade law

Litigation involving the law of the World Trade Organisation (WTO) can occur in many circumstances. Some areas of national law are based on WTO rules and as such any interpretation of these laws could rely upon WTO law as an additional source of rules and principles. Cases related to the national tariff code for importation, IP rights litigation, cross-border services contracts, labelling requirements and health inspection at the border might all rely on points of world trade law for resolution. However, WTO rules are rarely the only source of law and are not always used in national courts or legislation. Indeed, WTO law does not generally have direct effect and private litigants (other than governmental entities) do not usually sue on the sole basis of WTO rules in national courts. The reason for this is relatively simple: many countries specifically exclude the direct applicability of WTO law in their ratification legislation (including the United States and Canada). For the European Union, the European Court of Justice has ruled that WTO law is directly applicable only where the relevant European legislation implements WTO agreements.[1] Even WTO rules which have been interpreted by the WTO Appellate Body do not have direct effect in European courts and therefore cannot be invoked by EU private litigants.[2]

This recognised, in certain specific areas of law such as subsidies, anti-dumping and other violations, national legislation essentially serves to implement procedures to ensure that the industries of other countries comply with WTO rules. Private litigants can bring complaints on the basis of these rules, within their countries. This chapter focuses on these areas of law, briefly explaining the mechanisms that exist and how they can be used, and recommending further resources.

1. Subsidies

1.1 The EU mechanisms guarding against subsidised imports

Entering into force on January 1 1995, the WTO Agreement on Subsidies and Countervailing Measures, negotiated as a component of the Uruguay Round package, is at the crux of international rules on subsidies. Concomitantly, the European Union adopted the WTO's precepts on this matter when devising its own

1 See ECJ, C-53/96, *Hermes International v FHT Marketing Choice BV* (judgment of June 16 1998).

2 See most recently CFI, T-19/01 *Chiquita Brands v Commission* (judgment of February 3 2005) and ECJ, C-377/02 *Van Parys* (judgment of March 1 2005).

regulation precluding subsidised imports, also enacted on January 1 1995. The EU regulation is externally oriented: it targets only particular goods produced outside EU borders. Countervailing duties on subsidised imports are imposed only on non-EU countries whose imports of a specific product either cause or threaten injury to EU producers of the identical product.

Three conditions must be satisfied before countervailing duties can gain legal traction:

- The rationale for pursuing action against a subsidised product must be precise, as should the classification of the economic harm invoked. Viable categories include:
  - an export subsidy or a subsidy limited to a company;
  - an industry or a group of companies or industries; or
  - a subsidy that is causally linked to the material injury of an EU industry.
- The import sales have jeopardised or already injured the vitality of a substantial part of the EU industry competing with the subsidised goods. For instance, loss of market share and lower prices for producers, which translate to downward pressure on production, sales and profits, could be demonstrated. Other indicators can also demonstrate the decline of an embattled industry.
- The interests of the European Union as a whole must be prejudiced. A rough calculus is formulated along the following lines: any costs incurred by the European Union in pursuing measures must not be disproportionate to the benefits obtained by doing so.

For countervailing duties, the European Commission is simultaneously responsible for performing the investigation and imposing the provisional measures deemed suitable. The Council of Ministers has the authority to enact definitive measures at the culmination of the process. The complaint and investigation procedures are very similar to the guidelines governing anti-dumping actions, which are discussed next in this chapter.

The EU legislation implementing the internationally agreed provisions for dealing with subsidised imports is set out in Council Regulation (EC) 2026/97 (the Basic Regulation). If a competitor is being subsidised, most often it is receiving a form of aid for production, export, sale or transport. This aid must be demonstrated before initiating an action under the European Anti-Subsidy Regulation. It should be possible to argue that the government of the exporting country has extended tangible pecuniary support (ie, tax concessions, direct grants or the public sponsorship of certain goods and services at subsidised levels). Further, this governmental assistance should be improving the financial situation of the recipient company (ie, loans below market value or debt forgiveness), and the subsidy must be specific. However, certain types of subsidy, although specific in composition, cannot prompt punitive countervailing measures. Regional fund redistribution for equalisation purposes, particular research initiatives and certain public funding allocated towards helping firms adopt more environmentally friendly operations are not actionable. Further details are explained in the chapter entitled "Subsidies".

To initiate a complaint, most begin by consulting informally with the European Commission and perhaps sending an informal letter detailing some of the underlying facts. At this stage, the European Commission might be willing to indicate an interest in pursuing the issue, or to the contrary express informally that on the basis of the facts provided, an investigation is unlikely to be successful. The next practical step is then to finalise and send the formal complaint. (See the flow chart overleaf for a step-by-step explanation of the procedure.)

In essence, a complaining party has to provide *prima facie* evidence that:

- an imported product has been subsidised (if possible, also the total amount of subsidy received);[3]
- an injury to the domestic/EC industry has been caused; and
- the import of the subsidised product caused the injury.

After the European Commission has received the formal complaint, it will examine the accuracy and adequacy of the evidence within 45 days and decide whether to engage in a proper anti-subsidies (or countervailing) investigation. The European Commission will also confirm whether the community industry as a whole supports the complaint. Before the investigation decision has been taken (which requires publication of the complaint), the European Commission will seek consultations with the country of origin of the subsidised product. If the evidence is deemed insufficient or the imports from the country in question fall below a 1% *de minimis* threshold, the European Commission may refuse to undertake a formal investigation.

A formal investigation commences with the *Official Journal* publication identifying the product and country of origin, providing a summary of the complaint and requesting that interested parties contact the European Commission. The European Commission also informs the country, exporters, importers and relevant European Community associations.

The European Commission then sends out questionnaires to exporters and importers in order to try to verify the evidence provided in the formal complaint. For this purpose, the complainants are asked to provide as many company details as possible, including fax numbers of exporting/producing companies from the country where the alleged subsidisation is occurring. The parties receiving a questionnaire then have 30 days to respond, with some adjustments for exporters overseas. The European Commission might also ask the member states to assist with the formal investigation by providing governmental information or on-site checks with the companies concerned. (This can also take place in third countries, but only if the company consents.) Interested parties that might be affected by the outcome of the investigation can request to have their point of view taken into consideration, mainly in written form, but the European Commission might also organise meetings where the complainants and their opponents can present their arguments and rebuttals. It is important to note that the European Commission has the right to impose provisional measures on the basis of a provisional determination that a subsidy exists.

3 For the substantive interpretation of these terms see the chapter entitled "Subsidies".

The formal investigation can end with the imposition of a formal countervailing duty by majority decision of the European Council (which has political discretion in these matters). It can also end when an undertaking is offered by the exporting country or companies, or when the investigation is terminated without the adoption of any measure. If the investigation is terminated, appeals are possible to the European Court of First Instance and then the European Court of Justice.

EU anti-dumping and countervailing duty programme investigation process

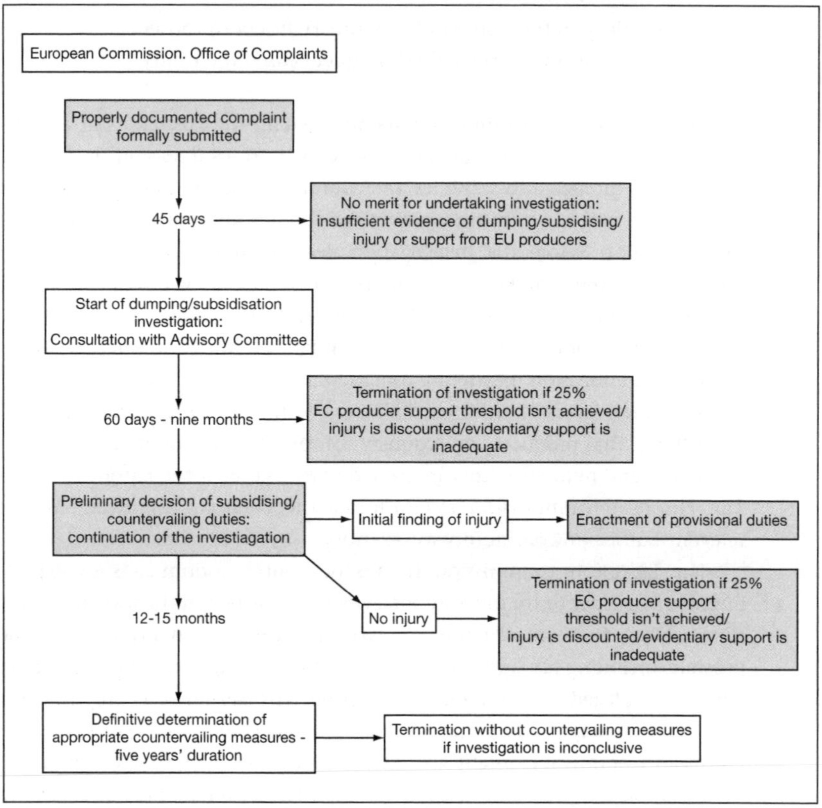

The Office of Complaints is a valuable resource, tasked with answering queries that arise during the countervailing complaint drafting process. Non-legally binding documentation published by the office is designed to support the filing of complaint and to respond to any uncertainties or complications. In particular, a useful guide can be found at http://trade.ec.europa.eu/doclib/docs/2004/january/tradoc_112233.pdf. This guide does not set out formal standards of acceptability in countervailing complaints and a complainant may follow different routes in outlining its concerns to the European Commission.

The contact information for the European Commission Services is:

European Commission
Office of Complaints, TDI Service
Rue de la Loi 200 (Office: J-79 06/33)
B-1049 Brussels
Belgium
Tel: +32 2 298 7873
Fax: +32 2 295 6505
http://ec.europa.eu/comm/trade/index_en.htm

1.2 The anti-subsidies legislation of the United States

Since the anti-subsidies and anti-dumping procedures are essentially the same in the United States, this process is discussed below.

2. Dumping and combined procedures

2.1 The EU regulations to protect against dumped imports

Regulations protecting the European Union against import dumping date back to its inception. Targeted at imports arriving in quantities that can cause significant injury to EU producers, the regulations aim to prevent third-country exporters from enjoying unfair competitive advantages which have obvious detrimental consequences for the European Union.

The original anti-dumping rules were revamped by a new anti-dumping regulation that came into force on January 1 1995. Subsequently, EC Regulation 384/96 modified the former regulation (March 6 1996) in order to take into account the European Union's obligations encapsulated in the Uruguay Round. One of the innovations of the new regulation involves stricter timelines for both the investigatory and decision-making processes, in order to seek greater efficiency in responding to complaints.

Dumping is often erroneously conceived as dealing with cheap or below-cost imports; the reality is much more complex. Three conditions from the 1996 Anti-dumping Regulation must be met in order to invoke the imposition of anti-dumping duties:

- Concrete evidence of dumping – complainants must show the discrepancy between the export price of the product being sold on the EU market versus the price at which it is sold in the producer's home market.
- Material injury to EU industry – put in concrete terms, the economic harm should be actually or potentially manifested in loss of market share, deterioration of a significant part of an industry within the European Union and/or reduced prices for producers galvanising downward pressure on production, sales, profits and productivity.
- Prejudice to the interests of the European Union as a whole – all issues considered, the costs borne by the European Union in taking measures to tackle the alleged dumping should be lower than the potential benefits that will accrue.

The duty to investigate complaints and consider applicable treatment falls on the European Commission. In certain cases – specifically coal and steel products – the

European Commission can invoke definitive measures, but in all other categories it is restricted to formulating provisional measures. The authority to impose definitive anti-dumping duties largely rests with the Council of Ministers.

Industries within the European Union that believe they have been materially harmed by the dumping of imports from non-EU countries may submit a complaint to the European Commission. The submission process can take place either through the national government or directly through the industry in question. Within a period of 45 days, the European Commission will assess the complaint, consult with member states (represented on an advisory committee) and resolve whether an investigation will be launched. Some preliminary information must be gathered and coalitions may need to be formed: the case will be abandoned outright if there is a lack of evidence or if the complainants do not represent at least 25% of the total EU production of the product in question.

Calculating the presence and severity of dumping is a complicated task. The European Commission will first establish whether dumping is actually occurring, followed by quantification of the material injury suffered by the EU industry. The analysis must be completed within a 15-month period and typically lasts a year. The European Commission can also take countervailing steps if the imports are stifling the development of a new industry or in the event that there is a clear and impending threat of material injury.

Anti-dumping measures will be imposed only if they are in harmony with EU interest as a whole. The 'EU interest' is broadly conceived and a diverse set of stakeholders (producers, importers, users and consumers) can convey their sentiments. After this consultation takes place, the member states provide their arguments and the commission may, within 60 days to nine months, endorse provisional duties. Any provisional action – lasting six to nine months while the investigation is ongoing – must not be in excess of the dumping margin (ie, the EU price of the product minus the price in the country of production). If the outcome of the investigation validates the complainant's case, definitive duties may begin after a decision has been taken by the Council of Ministers and member states. There is no guarantee that, even if a case has been shown, dues will be imposed, as the Council of Ministers has political and other discretion in this decision. Typically, definitive duties have a five-year lifespan, but further scrutiny is warranted if EU producers demonstrate that removal of duties is likely to lead to renewed dumping. Moreover, reopening the investigation and changing the duty levels is deemed reasonable if the original course of action fails to have the desired effect of eliminating the injury. A regulation imposing anti-dumping duties may be challenged in the European Court of First Instance and the WTO dispute settlement procedure may be employed to settle disputes between WTO signatories.

(i) *Initiating the complaint*

The EU anti-dumping legislation is founded on the WTO Anti-dumping Agreement. Aimed at forestalling dumping practices by third-country exporters, this agreement facilitates remedial action within a certain framework. In the event that an EU industry feels injured by dumped imports, the European Commission's Anti-dumping Service will process and investigate a complaint.

In anti-dumping cases, a 'complaint' is a document that includes information indicating a specific industry injury based on a certain product originating in a third country. Evidence of the product exported to the European Union at dumped prices (ie, invoices, price offers, publications in specialised press, official statistics) is mandatory to support the allegations.

To reiterate, dumping is a form of price discrimination that contravenes the edicts of free trade. Imported products are dumped when they are sold abroad at a cost below the domestic price in the exporting country, or when the exporter sells its goods at a loss.

'Injury' (aimed to cover deteriorations in competitiveness) can be shown by providing evidence that the competitor has suffered loss of market share, depreciating financial results or a precipitous drop in prices. The decline must be material, sustained and causally linked to the dumped imports in order for the complaint to progress.

In the terminology of anti-dumping complaints, 'EU industry' is regarded to be EU producers sustaining financial injury due to the dumping. Complaints can move forward only when corroborated by at least 25% of the total EU producers involved with the production of the product being dumped. In most cases, complainants take the initiative to garner support among colleagues situated in several member states prior to filing.

The dumped products may originate anywhere outside the European Union except Iceland, Liechtenstein and Norway (these three states are exempt from the application of the EU anti-dumping regulations).[4] In the event that several third countries are carrying out comparable alleged dumping practices, the grievances are usually amalgamated into one complaint. Any information submitted to the European Commission will remain confidential unless explicitly authorised for dissemination by the supplier.

(ii) *The investigation*

In order to determine whether remedial action is merited, the European Commission will launch an investigation into complaints found admissible 45 days after formal submission. In due course, the European Commission will explore the character of remedial steps in each particular context.

The maximum time allotted to the investigatory phase geared towards a provisional determination is nine months (during which provisional anti-dumping duties may come into force if justified). Subsequently, another six months may elapse while the European Commission formulates a definitive determination (if deemed suitable) that conventionally has a lifespan of five years.

If a practitioner's industry is being injured by dumping, the European Commission's Office of Anti-dumping Complaints can be contacted for further information at:

---

4 The exemption of Iceland, Liechtenstein and Norway is the result of their membership of the European Economic Area. Although not members of the European Union politically, their ratification of EU legislation in most areas qualifies them to be part of the single market.

European Commission
Office of Complaints, TDI Service (Office: J-79 06/33)
Rue de la Loi 200,
B-1049 Brussels, Belgium
Tel: +32 2 298 7873
Fax: +32 2 295 6505
http://ec.europa.eu/comm/trade/index_en.htm

The European Commission has published a useful brochure entitled *Guide on How to Draft an Anti-dumping Complaint*. The guide incorporates concise explanations about and commentary on the process of tendering anti-dumping complaints. The guide, available in all official EU languages, can be found at http://trade.ec.europa.eu/doclib/docs/2003/december/tradoc_112295.pdf.

2.2 US anti-dumping and countervailing duty investigations [5]

According to Title VII of the 1930 Tariff Act, within the US congressional system the US International Trade Commission (USITC) and the US Department of Commerce are responsible for conducting anti-dumping and countervailing duty investigations. The Tariff Act stipulates that there is a five-year sunset review for actions taken in this area. Analogous to the European procedures, US industries have legal recourse to petition the USITC and the Department of Commerce for support in coping with dumped and subsidised imports. The definition of 'dumping' applied by the US system is identical to that of the European Union: 'dumping' characterises a scenario where a foreign producer sells its goods abroad at prices lower than the market price established in its domestic market. Selling goods for prices lower than associated production costs is another version of dumping. Likewise, 'subsidising' is the act of a foreign government providing financial support that causes improvements in production processes, manufacture or exportation of a good. If a Department of Commerce investigation uncovers instances of dumping or unlawful subsidisation, an anti-dumping order or countervailing duty may be implemented. Similarly, the USITC may take parallel steps in the event that a US industry is being threatened or materially injured by third-party dumping or subsidisation.

The Bureau of Customs and Border Protection is tasked with enforcing and monitoring anti-dumping or countervailing duty orders, as well as facilitating the distribution of collected duties to injured producers. The USITC supplies the Customs Bureau with a list of affected domestic producers (ie, those producers that publicly endorsed the petition during the investigation) which are eligible for a share in the duties collected under anti-dumping and countervailing duty orders. However, several aspects of this system of re-allocation have been found to violate WTO rules (see the *US-Byrd Amendment Case*).

At five-year intervals, the Department of Commerce and the USITC must reassess each anti-dumping and countervailing duty order. Retraction of orders is based on

5 An explanation of the processes surrounding US trade remedies can be found at www.usitc.gov/trade_remedy/731_ad_701_cvd/handbook.pdf. Canada's perspective on the same topic is also available at www.dfait-maeci.gc.ca/tna-nac/disp/menu-en.asp.

the anticipated results of the withdrawal; orders are typically prolonged if a renewal of dumping or illegal subsidisation is predicted to ensue within a reasonable duration. However, there must be consensus between the two agencies for the orders to be extended.

Information about US anti-dumping and subsidisation regulations can be obtained from the USITC website.[6] There is an exhaustive schedule of key dates and events, staff contacts, Federal Register notices and news releases for each original anti-dumping and countervailing duty investigation and five-year (sunset) review. Also of great assistance is the provision of certain questionnaires (general ones and others prepared for specific cases), final USITC opinions and anti-dumping or countervailing duty orders.

US anti-dumping and countervailing duties investigatory process

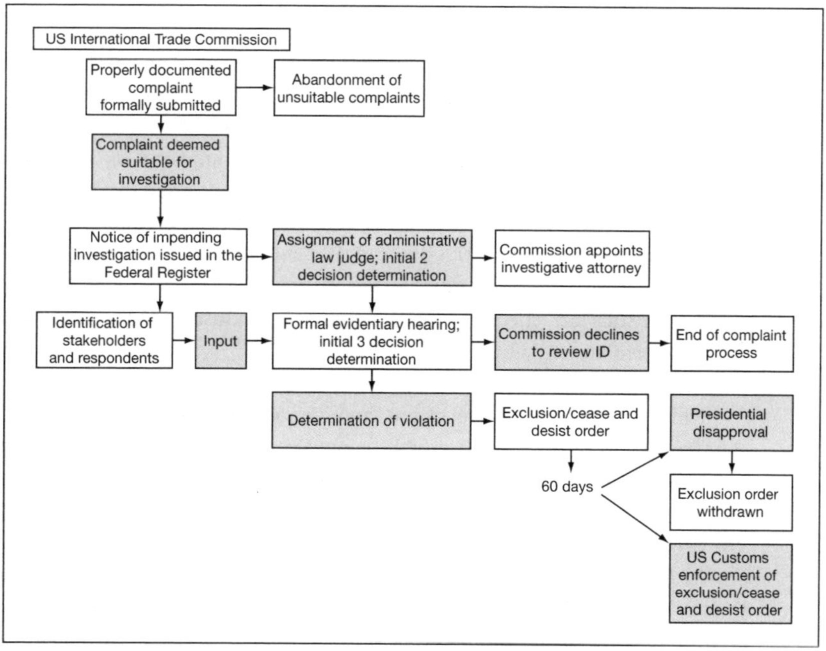

2.3 Canada's Special Import Measures Act

The Canadian Special Import Measures Act[7] is the legislation governing the imposition of anti-dumping and countervailing duties to protect Canadian producers. The Canada Border Services Agency (CBSA) provides an accessible overview of the act and clarifies definitions in the domain of anti-dumping, subsidies and countervailing measures. 'Dumping' occurs when goods are sold to importers in

6 See www.usitc.gov/trade_remedy/731_ad_701_cvd/handbook.pdf.

7 The text of the Special Import Measures Act can be found on the Finances Canada website at www.fin.gc.ca/gloss/gloss-l_f.html#loi.

Canada at prices that are lower than the sale price of comparable goods in the country of export. Likewise, dumping can be manifested in a situation where goods are sold to Canadian consumers at prices unprofitable to the producer. Consequently, 'anti-dumping duties' are designed to mitigate the injury caused to Canadian producers by the dumped products. The CBSA characterises 'subsidies' as a scenario where goods imported into Canada have accrued public financial assistance at their place of origin. Loans at preferential rates, debt forgiveness and extension of grants or tax incentives are apt examples of subsidising behaviour unlawful under the international trade regime. Countervailing duties are created to offset this financial aid and encourage true international competitiveness. For the imposition of countervailing duties to be viable, injury to Canadian industries (ie, reduced prices, lost market share, decreased profits) must be materially evident.

(a) *Initiating the complaint*

The CBSA and the Canadian International Trade Tribunal are jointly responsible for administering the Canadian Special Import Measures Act. The legislation empowers Canadian producers of products similar or identical to the competing imports to file a written complaint with the CBSA if they feel victimised by dumping or unlawful subsidisation. A single producer can prompt the complaint or, alternatively, an association of producers may file on behalf of the organisation's members. A written complaint must provide comprehensive information on the following:

- detailed accounts on the status of the Canadian produced goods as well as the competing imports; and
- statistics on the state of the domestic industry and conditions in the Canadian market.

Evidential support of the claims and causal linkages to the injury alleged is compulsory. On balance, in order for the complaint to progress, support (a 25% threshold is stipulated) must outweigh opposition to the initiative within the industry affected.

(b) *The investigation*

Provisional investigations into dumping and subsidy allegations are conducted by Revenue Canada; formal investigations include the collaboration of the CBSA. After an initial review of the complaint, if it finds some justification, the CBSA circulates a series of questionnaires addressed to exporters, importers and, in subsidy investigations, to the foreign government involved. The CBSA may also deal directly with the parties, requesting further information throughout the investigation.

Evaluations are made regarding the classification of the incident, the degree of injury wrought and appropriate remedial action, but the Canadian International Trade Tribunal has the final word on the execution of punitive measures.[8] Before the investigation can proceed to the final tribunal phase, the CBSA must determine the existence of dumping or a subsidy and the tribunal must determine the existence of

8 www.fin.gc.ca/gloss/gloss-s_e.html#sima.

an injury. In rendering a verdict, the tribunal will conduct an inquiry that includes public hearings where stakeholders (traditionally Canadian producers and importers, as well as foreign exporters) are allowed to present their arguments and question witnesses. During the seven-month timeline of the tribunal inquiry (public hearings are conducted at the later stages), the CBSA investigation takes place in parallel. Both processes render a preliminary and final decision.

(c) ***Canadian International Trade Tribunal***

The Canadian International Trade Tribunal is the primary quasi-judicial institution within Canada's trade remedy apparatus. It conducts all inquiries (eg, final, interim and preliminary).[9] It also hears appeals of decisions of the Canada Customs and Revenue Agency made under the Customs Act, the Excise Tax Act and the Special Import Measures Act. In some cases, the tribunal provides advice on economic, trade and tariffs issues solicited by the governor in council and the minister of finance. In addition, any supplier disagreements about federal government procurement under the auspices of the North American Free Trade Agreement, the Agreement on Internal Trade and/or the WTO Agreement on Government Procurement are subject to the tribunal's purview. The tribunal also has the jurisdiction to conduct safeguard inquiries in order to take pre-emptive action or allay fears of domestic producers concerned with increased imports. Finally, the tribunal explores the viability of requests from Canadian producers for tariff relief on imported textile inputs that they use in their production operations.

Following a positive preliminary decision to look into the matter further (by the tribunal and the CBSA), the CBSA is authorised to impose a temporary duty on imports of dumped or subsidised goods. Usually imposed within three months of the complaint submission, the temporary duty is designed to protect Canadian producers until the tribunal completes its analysis of the situation. In the event that the tribunal issues a final injury decision in favour of the Canadian industry, the CBSA imposes anti-dumping and countervailing duty orders on all applicable imports.

In order to avoid a pending imposition of a duty, exporters or foreign governments can propose 'undertakings' – that is, commitments to modify their pricing or subsidising practices, thereby eradicating the harm inflicted on Canadian industry. Undertakings are an optional route that avoids full investigations, tribunal inquiries and temporary duties, providing a faster and less costly solution to the dispute.

More information about Canadian anti-dumping and countervailing duty policy may be obtained from the CBSA as follows:

Anti-dumping and Countervailing Directorate
Canada Border Services Agency
The Urbandale Building
100 Metcalfe Street
11th Floor
Ottawa ON
K1A 0L8

9 www.citt-tcce.gc.ca/mandate/index_e.asp.

Anti-dumping and countervailing duty programme investigation process

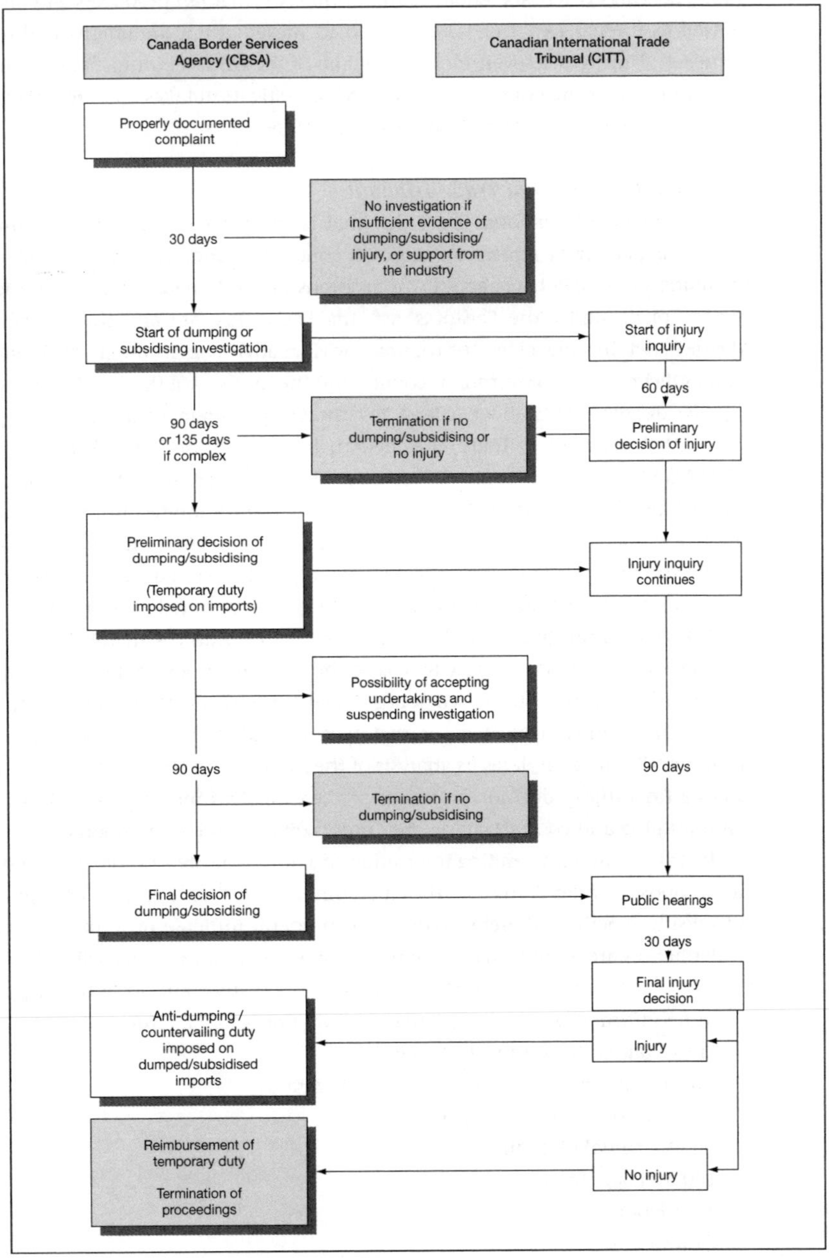

Source: Canadian Border Services[10]

10 See www.cbsa-asfc.gc.ca/sima/menu-e.html.

Canada
Tel: +1 613 954 7172
Fax: +1613 948 4844
Web: www.cbsa-asfc.gc.ca/sima/

3. Other violations and safeguards

3.1 The EU safeguards regulation

As the EU institutions govern the common import regime, individual member states are barred from adopting safeguard measures to protect their domestic industry from foreign imports. EC Regulations 3285/94 (for WTO members) and 519/94 (for non-WTO members) explain the conditions and procedures that are used by the EU in adopting a safeguard measure, in accordance with the WTO Agreement on Safeguards.

Safeguard measures, imposed in the EU interest, relate to imports escalating in potentially injurious trajectories. Member states may request investigations on a case-by-case basis, or alternatively the European Commission may commence its own analysis in conformity with the WTO Agreement on Safeguards. Unlike anti-dumping and countervailing duty cases, industry is precluded from requesting the application of safeguard measures.

The principles of the common import regime do not currently extend to certain imports (footwear, tableware and ceramics) from the People's Republic of China. Quotas on this merchandise are found in EC Regulation 519/94, but progressive retrenchment by 2005 (stemming from China's accession to the WTO) is indicated in Council Regulation 427/2003 (OJ L 65/1, March 8 2003) and European Commission Regulation 428/2003 (OJ L 65/12, March 8 2003).

'Surveillance' is a term describing a system of automatic import licensing; it is not an import constraining mechanism *per se*. Within the WTO framework, the Agreement on Import Licensing Procedures covers surveillance measures and ardently promotes free exportation. EEC Regulation 2603/69 provides the guidelines for the common export regime and clarifies exceptional cases where export restrictions may be viable.[11]

3.2 The US global and special safeguard regime

According to the Trade Act of 1974, responsibility for preparing global safeguard[12] ('escape clause') and market disruption investigations is delegated to the USITC. In the event that the USITC determines that imports in a particular industry are increasing at a potentially harmful rate, it formulates an offsetting remedy to balance out the competition and recommends it the president. The USITC does not need to find unfair trading behaviour to launch this sort of injunction. Relief of this sort is

11 A more detailed explanation of the applicable rules is available at http://europa.eu.int/comm/trade/issues/respectrules/safeguard/index_en.htm. The details of the global safeguard law are found in Section 201 of the 1974 Trade Act.

12 Applicable safeguard measures are found in Section 421 of the 1974 Trade Act.

finite (extended only while domestic industries adapt to the new market environment), and the president decides the contours of any measures enacted, such as increased tariffs or reduced quotas. For instance, when dealing with China,[13] the USITC explores whether comparable products are being imported into the United States at a market-disrupting rate. If the USITC makes an affirmative determination, it proposes a remedy. Thereafter, the USITC sends its report to the president and the US trade representative, and the president renders the final remedy decision.

In addition to assessing the market from an industry-specific lens, the USITC also conducts country or region-specific safeguard investigations. Any disturbing findings by the agency will be dealt with under the same procedure.

3.3 US IP rights violations

Section 337 of the 1930 Tariff Act[14] outlines the procedures involved in the USITC's investigations into allegations of certain unfair practices in import trade. Specifically, Section 337 asserts the contravention of statutory IP rights[15] and other forms of unfair competition in import trade to be unlawful practices.

In order for investigations to ensue, the USITC must receive an accurately completed complaint in full accord with procedural guidelines. If the complaint is suitable for examination, the USITC publishes a notice of the impending investigation in the Federal Register. For each inspection, an administrative judge chairs the USITC's proceedings and decides whether Section 337 has been violated. Additionally, the USITC appoints an investigative attorney (fully party to the proceedings) from its Office of Unfair Import Investigations. This attorney functions as an independent litigant representing the public interest in the investigation.

In the investigation notice the complainants and respondents that allegedly violated Section 337 are identified. The adversary procedure then follows usual procedural rules. Evidence is presented in front of the judge and parties may question, cross-examine and present counter-evidence. After the hearing, the initial determination will be issued and the USITC has then the opportunity to veto the judge's decision or approve it. If the USITC determines a violation, it can exclude products from being imported into the United States, which is enforced by US Customs. The president can veto orders on policy grounds and the decision can be reviewed in the District of Columbia Circuit Appellate Court.

(a) Initiating the complaint

The answers to many uncertainties surrounding the filing process can be found online. The USITC's website supplies the governing statute, relevant USITC rules (including crucial steps involved in filing the complaint) and reference materials at www.usitc.gov. The direct link to the Section 337 resources web page is

---

13 The majority of Section 337 enquiries relate to allegations of registered trademark or patent infringement. However, the substance of Section 337 authorises the USITC to scrutinise sundry forms of unfair competition, allegations of false advertising and breaches of antitrust laws.

14 19 USC § 1337.

15 The product list can be found online at www.ustr.gov/assets/Trade_Agreements/Monitoring_Enforcement/asset_upload_file985_6885.pdf.

www.usitc.gov/trade_remedy/int_prop/index.htm. All complaints are publicly available on the European Commission's main website at http://www.usitc.gov/secretary/edis.htm.

This chapter was co-authored by Kristen Price.

Private initiation of WTO disputes

This chapter focuses on the initiation of World Trade Organisation (WTO) disputes by private actors at the (supra) national level. Private actors cannot usually force a government to take a case to the WTO, as the decision to initiate an international trade dispute rests firmly with national authorities. However, certain countries have introduced legislation which provides for formal procedures that a private actor can use to bring a case forward, in order to force or request its country/region to initiate an international dispute in its interest. In addition to the formal procedures, there are many ways to ask informally the competent governmental department to investigate and later initiate an international trade dispute resolution process.[1]

1. US Section 301 procedure

Section 301 of the 1974 Trade Act was the first legislation of its kind and has a long history of bringing private trade disputes to the attention of the administration. In essence, the procedure helps private parties to initiate their country's engagement in a WTO dispute settlement process.

The enforcement of trade agreements, the settlement of trade disputes and ways to further market liberalisation are covered in Section 301 of the 1974 Trade Act. Trade sanctions against foreign countries deemed to be engaging in behaviour prejudicial to the economic interest of the United States are similarly governed by Section 301. The Office of the United States Trade Representative (USTR) deals with any alleged infringements of trade agreements and must abide by the consultation and dispute settlement procedures laid out by Section 301. In the event that an inspection uncovers practices which contravene the WTO agreements, the USTR seeks authority from the WTO's Dispute Settlement Body to suspend trade concessions (and increase import duties) previously granted to the foreign country.

1.2 Initiating the complaint

The Section 301 investigation can be initiated by any interested party with a petition to the USTR asking to begin investigation of a particular trade practice of a foreign country. The USTR can also start an investigation *ex officio*.

Within 45 days of the petition, the USTR determines whether to launch a formal investigation. The decision of the USTR is published in the Federal Register.

1 See the chapter entitled "Participation of private parties in trade policy and negotiations".

In Section 301 private party investigations, the USTR solicits public comments and, if requested, holds consultations. The USTR solicits public participation through a variety of avenues, including requests for written submissions or public hearings. Small and medium-sized enterprises are specifically encouraged to become active participants in the process.

For the next step in the formal Section 301 investigation, the USTR requests consultations with the foreign government in question. The USTR works towards a mutually acceptable settlement, usually informing and consulting with the private party. In the majority of cases, this consultation resolves the issue and restores compliance with the international obligations, thus avoiding formal legal action in the WTO or another international trade dispute settlement tribunal.

If the investigated practice appears to violate a trade agreement, the USTR will follow the procedures set out in the treaty. In the case of the WTO, this means that the WTO dispute settlement procedure will be followed. The formal investigation either ends 18 months after its initiation or is deemed complete one month after the formal dispute settlement process.

The USTR determines whether the practice is actionable under Section 301 and publishes the result in the Federal Register. If permitted by the trade dispute settlement decision, the USTR adopts Section 301 sanctions – that is, an increase of US import duties on a foreign country's products to respond to the trade damage. Once the violations have been found and determined, the final step is for an interagency Section 301 Committee (chaired by the USTR) to compile a list to determine which imported products from the offending state are legitimate targets for heightened duties.[2] The primary rationale of devising and publishing the list in the Federal Register is to enlighten the public (especially importers, consumers, workers and firms) and thereby minimise the adverse impact of raised import duties on US economic interests.

Taking public input into account, the Section 301 Committee creates a final list of products chosen from the exhaustive preliminary list. To counter the alleged trade violation, a final list of foreign target products is decided and, if the dispute settlement is successful, implemented.

More comprehensive information about Section 301 is available at www.ita.doc.gov/td/tradepolicy/section301.html and www.ita.doc.gov/td/industry/otea/301alert/index.html.

1.3 Trade Compliance Center

The Trade Compliance Center – the US government's focal point for monitoring compliance with foreign trade agreements – is situated within the US Department of Commerce's International Trade Administration. It administers a website (http://tcc.export.gov/) that is a valuable source of information regarding anti-dumping or countervailing duty cases.

2 A more detailed explanation can be found at http://ec.europa.eu/comm/trade/issues/respectrules/tbr/ov_whocan.htm.

2. EU Trade Barriers Regulation

The EU Trade Barriers Regulation, adopted in 1994 through Council Regulation (EC) 3286/94, is a tool to help EU producers overcome complications with exporting their wares, ensuring respect for patents abroad and dealing with discriminatory foreign trade policy. The regulation is also important in preventing harmful distortions in the EU internal market.

The regulation provides for direct access to the European Commission, and lays out a procedure for the acceptance and analysis of any complaints regarding trade-related malfeasance. There are two types of complaint from EU companies or EU industry associations that can be investigated: foreign trade obstacles and foreign harmful practices (eg, subsidies).[3] In drastic cases, obstacles to trade can have the effect of stopping trade. These obstacles are especially important under the Trade Barriers Regulation, and a complaint should be based on evidence that demonstrates the existence of such obstacles.[4] If remedial action suitable to both parties is not achieved, the regulation may forward the case to the WTO Dispute Settlement Body.

A useful synopsis of the regulation is available for download at http://trade.ec.europa.eu/doclib/docs/2005/april/tradoc_122567.pdf. In addition, a Powerpoint presentation on the utility of the regulation is available at http://trade-info.cec.eu.int/doclib/html/124292.htm. A step-by-step guide of how to file a complaint is also available at http://ec.europa.eu/comm/trade/issues/respectrules/tbr/ov_file.htm.

2.1 Initiating the complaint

Usually, the affected company will choose to contact the European Commission before complaining formally. This informal conversation can often determine whether a formal complaint is warranted and also provide important clarification on the procedure.

The complaining company must provide the following information:

- definition of the goods or services affected by the obstacle to trade and identification of the complainant;
- identification of the complainant;
- name, address, status and representation of the complainant;
- general presentation of the complainant's activities, including figures on turnover, production and number of employees;
- link with the product that is the subject of the obstacle to trade (producer, producer of a competing product, transformer, importer or exporter);
- data on trade flows in which the complainant is involved (as producer, transformer, importer or exporter);
- identification of the product or service which is the subject of the obstacle to trade;
- technical description and customs position;
- production, sales and imports and exports of the product or service; and
- *prima facie* evidence of the existence of the obstacle to trade.

---

3 For more information see http://ec.europa.eu/comm/trade/issues/respectrules/tbr/complaint/index_en.htm.

2.2 Trade obstruction and how to prove it

It is the complaining company's duty to provide the necessary evidence that a trade obstacle exists. This usually comprises:

- a description of the facts, including laws, regulations and decisions;
- other evidence of the trade practice, such as third-party correspondence;
- a description of the history of the trade practice;
- action taken by the aggrieved company; and
- a description of the relevant WTO provision(s) that the European Union can invoke.

2.3 Commercial injury and how to prove it

In order to move forward, the obstacles to trade should result in adverse trade effects and/or injury. Unlawful impediments to trade may suppress EU industry internally or, if affecting the market of a third country, may result in adverse trade effects for the EU enterprises. An injury can exist even if the trade practice in question has not yet been implemented.

The complaint must contain sufficient evidence to:

- demonstrate the injury or adverse trade effect; and
- demonstrate the causal link between obstacle and injury.

Normally this will be done by presenting:

- statistical data concerning the overall trade flows (EU-WTO member providing an obstacle);
- data on the impact – for example, profit margins, capacity, return on capital, investment, employment and prices; and
- prices of other EU companies.

The complaining company can also demonstrate that the alleged obstacle will create an injury in the immediate future.

The European Commission sees the Trade Barriers Regulation as an effective tool. As such, and after a Trade Barriers Regulation complaint, Colombia changed its tax law and treated European cars with high cubic capacity identically to lower-engine domestic vehicles. The European pharmaceutical industry used the regulation successfully to enter the Turkish market with imported products and achieved equal treatment with Turkish produced pharmaceutical products. A third example concerned compulsory import payments and minimum import prices of European textiles to Brazil. These were abolished in bilateral negotiations after Belgian textile producers filed a Trade Barriers Regulation complaint.

More extensive information on these and other Trade Barriers Regulation cases can be found at http://ec.europa.eu/comm/trade/issues/respectrules/tbr/cases/index_en.htm.

Participation of private parties in WTO disputes

Since the collapse of the world trade talks in Seattle in 1999, if not before, it has been clear that private parties are interested in and feel the effects of the activities of the World Trade Organisation (WTO). The unprecedented Seattle protests, at which at least 40,000 people demonstrated and blockaded the scheduled conferences of WTO ministers, were considered by many to be a reflection of the general public's concerns over a perceived lack of transparency and opportunity for participation in the affairs of the world trade body. The WTO, it was said, can no longer be a club of trade diplomats meeting in the bubble of Geneva, but must be a body that acknowledges its impact on civil society, individuals and their human rights. This chapter discusses recent developments in the participation of these private parties in the WTO generally, and in particular in its dispute settlement processes.

1. The WTO and participation, in theory

The WTO is an organisation composed of 149 member states.[1] Its key executive organ is the Ministerial Conference, a collection of trade ministers from each member. In a democratic country, the trade minister sent to represent that country in the WTO is an elected representative of the people, and any decisions and policies supported or rejected by that trade minister during WTO negotiations are representative of the views held by the citizens of the minister's country. The WTO agreements, for their part, impose obligations on and grant rights solely to members. It is the WTO members alone that have standing to attend negotiations, vote on decisions made and bring disputes to the Dispute Settlement Body.

The role of 'private' parties, on the other hand, is officially a limited one. The concept of private parties – meaning, for present purposes, those formally excluded from WTO participation – can include individuals, small or large corporations, industry associations, non-governmental organisations and research centres.[2] These players do not appear in WTO agreements and cannot appear directly before a panel or the Appellate Body. Panel proceedings and submissions to a panel or to the Appellate Body are confidential under the Dispute Settlement Understanding.[3]

1 As at December 2005.

2 States that are not WTO members are also formally excluded from any WTO participation; however, the focus of this chapter is on non-state private parties.

3 Articles 14 and 18.

Mavroidis and Zdouc describe the WTO as a "government contract with important repercussions on private parties' interests". They note that, in the absence of any formalised role for private party participation, "WTO members enjoy wide discretion when it comes to regulating the way in which private interests will be represented, the WTO contract itself imposing only an obligation to perform the WTO contract in good faith".[4] The 'monopoly of enforcement' granted to national governments by the WTO leaves private parties with little more than a hope that the enforcers will "make good use of their discretion".[5]

2. The WTO and participation, in practice

However, the practice of WTO law and policy is more complex. Private parties do participate extensively in WTO processes, in many "indirect, unofficial and largely ad hoc" ways.[6] The United States, the European Union and others have procedures for allowing private parties to initiate WTO disputes by making complaints to official government posts, which are then evaluated and, if necessary, taken further by the sanctioned WTO player – the government. It is thus possible to say that "[p]rivate firms depend on public actors for access to the WTO, while public actors rely on private parties for financial, political and informational support. Together these networked partners evaluate the costs and benefits of bringing a claim and litigating or settling the dispute."[7]

What is the ongoing role of these private parties once the dispute has been initiated by their government? How can private parties contribute to the process without formal recognition?

3. *Amicus curiae* briefs

One role in WTO disputes is a relatively recent development – the acceptance by panels and the Appellate Body of *amicus curiae* briefs. Under the traditional model of WTO dispute settlement, only the parties to the dispute may appear before a panel or the Appellate Body, and only the parties may give submissions and legal arguments to support their case. This would clearly exclude any role for private parties to make their opinion known to the panel or the Appellate Body. The only entry path for non-governmental organisations, including private parties, is to present their submissions to whichever side of the dispute they support and hope that their views are included in the member's official submission to the panel or Appellate Body.

However, there are suggestions in the constitutive documents of the WTO that it recognises the existence and interests of parties outside its own boundaries. Article V:1 of the Marrakesh Agreement requires the WTO General Council to cooperate with "other intergovernmental organizations concerned with matters related to those of

---

4 Mavroidis, PC and Zdouc, W, "Legal Means to Protect Private Parties' Interests in the WTO: The Case of the EC New Trade Barriers Regulation", 1 JIEL 407 (1998), 407.

5 *Ibid*, 409.

6 Dunoff, J, "The Misguided Debate over NGO Participation at the WTO", 1 JIEL 433 (1998), 433.

7 Shaffer, G, *Defending Interests: Public-Private Partnerships in WTO Litigation* (Brookings Institution Press: Washington DC, 2003), p 15.

the WTO", such as the United Nations and the International Monetary Fund. Article V:2 permits (although does not require) the WTO General Council to consult and cooperate with non-governmental organisations. Most importantly, Article 13 of the Dispute Settlement Understanding allows panels to "seek information and technical advice from any individual or body which it deems appropriate". The interpretation of this provision as allowing *amicus* briefs was discussed in the *Shrimp Turtle* dispute. While the panel rejected a submission made jointly by two non-governmental organisations – the Center for International Wildlife Law and the Center for Marine Conservation – on the grounds that Article 13 limited its authority, the Appellate Body in the same case reversed this finding and held that, despite the word 'seek' in Article 13, *amicus* submissions could be accepted even if unsolicited. In a later case, *US – Steel,* the Appellate Body clarified that both itself and panels could accept *amicus* briefs, including information and legal argument.[8]

In *EC – Asbestos*, the Appellate Body adopted an additional working procedure to govern the acceptance of *amicus* briefs for that case.[9] This procedure specified that "any person, whether natural or legal, other than a party or a third party to this dispute, wishing to file a written brief with the Appellate Body" was required to apply before a given deadline. The relatively detailed application was to:

- contain certain information about the applicant (including its special interest in the dispute);
- identify the specific issues of law to be addressed;
- state how the brief would contribute to resolution of the dispute beyond the parties' own submissions; and
- disclose any connections to or funding from the parties.

In a communication to the Dispute Settlement Body, the Appellate Body explained that it had instituted this working procedure in "the interests of fairness and orderly procedure".[10] Given the high public interest elements of the case, the Appellate Body had already received submissions from non-governmental organisations in 13 countries, including several developing countries (Swaziland, Sri Lanka, Thailand, Senegal, El Salvador and Colombia). These submissions were returned to the non-governmental organisations along with a letter informing them of the newly adopted procedure.[11] Perhaps because of the restrictive application requirements and short deadline (around one week), only one non-governmental organisation from a developing country – the Korea Asbestos Association – submitted an application for official permission to file its full *amicus* brief in time. Most of the

8 *United States–Imposition of Countervailing Duties on Certain Hot-Rolled Lead and Bismuth Carbon Steel Products Originating in the United Kingdom,* Report of the Appellate Body, November 8 2000, WT/DS138/AB/R.

9 This discussion is further developed in MC Cordonier Segger & M Gehring, "The Precautionary Principle in the WTO: The EU Asbestos Dispute" (2003) *Journal of Environmental Law,* Oxford University Press 15:3 289–321; and MC Cordonier Segger & M Gehring, "Precaution, Health and the World Trade Organisation: Moving Toward Sustainable Development" (2003) *Queen's Law Journal* 29:1 at 133

10 WT/DS135/9, November 8 2000.

11 This discussion relies on reports in ICTSD, "*Amicus* Brief Storm Highlights WTO's Unease with External Transparency", *Bridges Between Trade and Sustainable Development,* Year 4 No 9, Geneva, November-December 2000 and related articles.

other applications received in time were from non-governmental organisations in developed countries (including the United States, the United Kingdom, Australia, Switzerland, France, the Netherlands and Belgium). All of the applications made seeking leave to file a full *amicus* brief in the *EC – Asbestos Case* were "carefully reviewed and considered",[12] but ultimately rejected.

It can be convincingly argued that the Appellate Body was acting entirely within the scope of its powers in establishing the additional working procedure for *amicus* briefs. It has a general power to develop working procedures under Article 17(9) of the Dispute Settlement Understanding. Although the Appellate Body was careful to state that the particular *EC – Asbestos* additional working procedure was *not* an Article 17(9) generally applicable procedure, under Article 16(1) of the Working Procedures for Appellate Review,[13] the Appellate Body is actually empowered to establish procedures specific to a particular appeal where it is considered to be "in the interests of fairness and orderly procedure". Further, there are reasonable due process grounds for permitting *amicus curiae* briefs in WTO disputes. Due process has itself been recognised by the Appellate Body as applying to panel procedures and as implicit in the terms of the General Agreement on Tariffs and Trade (GATT).[14] An adherence to the principles of fairness and due process would require all arguments for each side in a dispute to be heard, and *amicus* briefs can clearly assist in this regard. Such briefs may also assist the panel or Appellate Body itself to determine the case, providing more information and hence better grounds of reasoning to accept or reject parties' arguments. Despite this, the additional working procedure and its wider consequences for the acceptance of *amicus* briefs remain controversial. Indeed, in the views of many at that time, opening up WTO debate to a wide range of private interests may allow it to be hijacked by powerful non-governmental organisations or firms.[15]

The creation of the WTO in 1995 ushered in new approaches to world trade dispute resolution, part of which was a rejection of the secrecy and opacity of former GATT dispute resolution when matters were resolved confidentially between diplomats, with little structure or legal reasoning. A legalisation of trade dispute resolution was effected by the WTO and Dispute Settlement Understanding, and public participation, including the right to submit *amicus* briefs, is a standard element of many domestic legal systems. Relying partly on the Appellate Body's actions, a North America Free Trade Agreement tribunal similarly declared itself favourable to *amicus* briefs, noting that its Chapter 11 arbitral process "could benefit

---

12 *European Communities–Measures Affecting Asbestos and Asbestos-Containing Products*, Report of the Appellate Body, March 12 2001, WT/DS135/AB/R, para 56.

13 January 4 2005, WT/AB/WP/5, drawn up pursuant to Article 17.9 of the Understanding on Rules and Procedures Governing the Settlement of Disputes.

14 *European Communities–Regime for the Importation, Sale and Distribution of Bananas*, Report of the Appellate Body adopted September 25 1997, WT/DS27/AB/R at para 144; *India–Patent Protection for Pharmaceutical and Agricultural Chemical Products*, Report of the Appellate Body adopted January 16 1998, WT/DS50/AB/R, at para 95; *Argentina–Certain Measures Affecting Imports of Footwear, Textiles, Apparel and Other Items*, Report of the Appellate Body adopted March 20 1997, WT/DS56/AB/R, at para 79; *Brazil–Measures Affecting Desiccated Coconut*, Report of the Appellate Body adopted March 20 1997, WT/DS22/AB/R at p 15. For measures implicit, see *United States–Restrictions on Imports of Cotton and Man-Made Fibre Underwear*, Report of the Appellate Body adopted February 251997, WT/DS24//AB/R, at p 10.

15 ICTSD, "*Amicus* Brief Storm Highlights WTO's Unease with External Transparency", *Bridges Between Trade and Sustainable Development*, Year 4 No 9, Geneva, November-December 2000.

from being perceived as more open or transparent; or conversely could be harmed if seen as unduly secretive".[16]

4. Other modes of private participation

Beyond participation by way of *amicus* briefs, private parties (especially corporations) often play significant roles in the course of WTO disputes through lobbying of the government officials running the case or submission of prepared written pleadings. In cases where a firm's business is at stake in a WTO dispute, the countries which are technically parties to the dispute may actually be mainly voices for the business interests involved. For example, the two disputes innocuously titled *European Communities – Measures Affecting Trade in Large Civil Aircraft*[17] and *United States – Measures Affecting Trade in Large Civil Aircraft*[18] essentially represent a cross-dispute between the firms of Airbus and Boeing over government subsidies provided to each company by its host government. Although the US trade representative (USTR) and the EU trade commissioner are the two authorities in charge of the dispute, it is almost certain that Airbus and Boeing are substantially involved in preparation of the arguments and conduct of the disputes, if only unofficially so. Indeed, under the US Section 301 procedure, the USTR is required to include applicants – such as Boeing – in every stage of WTO dispute resolution proceedings. Similarly, the case of *Japan – Measures Affecting Consumer Photographic Film and Paper* was in practice a battle between US firm Kodak and Japanese firm Fuji over market access.

Private parties have complete control of one dispute resolution forum within the WTO – the regime established by the Agreement on Pre-shipment Inspection. This agreement deals with the procedures and principles applicable to private entities that carry out inspection of goods on behalf of governments prior to shipment. Under the agreement, any disputes between pre-shipment inspection agencies and exporters are resolved by an independent body constituted jointly by organisations representing the interests of each party. As noted by Dunoff, this dispute settlement mechanism is "the first . . . formally open to private traders".[19]

Private players can also be involved in the post-dispute processes, centring on compliance issues. As Shaffer explains using the example of the Organization for International Investment (OFII), a non-governmental organisation that represents the foreign subsidiaries of US companies, during the foreign sales corporation tax dispute between the European Union and the United States,[20] OFII lobbied both the US government and the European Union, and then assisted with obtaining political support for compliance and ensuring that the US legislation proposed to implement the WTO ruling (against the United States) would meet EU demands.[21]

---

16 *Methanex Corporation v United States of America*, Decision of the Tribunal on Petitions from Third Persons to Intervene as *'Amicus Curiae'*, January 15 2001, at para 49, available at www.iisd.org/investment/methanex_background.asp.

17 WT/DS317.

18 WT/DS316.

19 Dunoff, J, "The Misguided Debate over NGO Participation at the WTO", 1 JIEL 433 (1998), 452.

20 *United States–Tax Treatment for "Foreign Sales Corporations"*, WT/DS108.

21 Shaffer, G, *Defending Interests: Public-Private Partnerships in WTO Litigation*, (Brookings Institution Press: Washington DC, 2003), p 78.

Although it is a national government (or regional grouping, in the case of the European Union) that officially appears before a WTO panel or the Appellate Body, there is nothing to prevent private counsel from representing those governments in a dispute. Developed countries will ordinarily have in-house government lawyers who are well equipped to make submissions and argue before a panel, but many developing countries may not have such capacity. In these situations, developing country governments seek assistance from private lawyers and advisers, whether from their own country or elsewhere. Even in cases where the government is able to represent itself before a WTO panel, a choice may still be made to enlist the assistance of private counsel with particular expertise in the field in question, or counsel whose ordinary clients have interests that match the government's own interests in the case at hand.[22]

Outside dispute settlement processes, the opportunities for inclusion of civil society in world trade debates are growing.[23] Non-governmental organisations, for instance, can assist in policy roles through relatively frequent WTO symposia on topics such as "Trade, Environment and Sustainable Development" or "Trade Facilitation". While the outcomes of these conferences cannot directly affect a dispute currently being heard in the WTO, the conferences present a chance for civil society to make its views known on current issues and disputes within the WTO, aiming towards future more direct influence. In the same vein, the WTO director general held a live online chat session in February 2006, responding to around 200 questions from the general public worldwide.[24]

Despite these discussions, and beyond the nascent recognition of *amicus curiae* briefs, the ability of private parties to participate in WTO dispute settlement processes remains relatively limited. The effects of these processes, on the other hand, are felt quite directly by private parties such as corporations and individuals. Alemanno takes the *Hormones* dispute as an example.[25] In 1998, the EU ban on hormone-fed beef was found to be inconsistent with the Agreement on the Application of Sanitary and Phytosanitary Measures; rather than remove the ban, however, the European Union chose to keep it and face retaliation from the complainant, the United States. The United States therefore currently maintains retaliatory measures against imports of EU products including German chocolate, Danish ham and French cheese as a means of compensation for the lost beef sales that its producers would otherwise have made in Europe but for the ban. This form of retaliation, authorised under the Dispute Settlement Understanding, certainly appears to be an effective incentive for countries to implement WTO rulings. Even so, the European Union claims that it prefers to pay rather than to lift its ban. However, the retaliation also has the effect of punishing private parties – French cheese producers, Danish ham producers and German chocolate producers – which

---

22 American Bar Association Section of International Law and Practice–Recommendation and Report, 2 JIEL 170 (1999).

23 See Chapter 3.

24 A transcript is available at www.wto.org/english/forums_e/chat_e/dg_chat_e.htm.

25 Alberto Alemanno, "Private Parties and WTO Dispute Settlement System", Cornell Law School LLM Papers Series, available online at http://lsr.nellco.org/cornell/lps/clacp/1/.

had nothing to do with the original dispute over beef hormones. Consumers in both Europe and the United States are also ultimately inconvenienced, through a restricted range of beef products available in Europe (potentially also at higher prices than would be available if US beef were permitted), and higher prices for European produce in US stores (due to the additional component of retaliatory measures on top of the ordinary prices). Alemanno takes this 'punishment' of innocent private parties as a reason to argue that those parties should be allowed to invoke a WTO ruling before domestic courts in the losing country, in order to claim damages for loss arising from the government's failure to implement the ruling. On this reasoning, as was argued in the European Court of Justice (ECJ) *Biret Case*,[26] a French meat trader (or perhaps a German chocolate maker) should be able to claim compensation from the European Union due to its inability to import and trade in US beef. Biret lost the case and thus far the ECJ has shown no inclination towards making damages actions available to private parties. As such, the focus remains on the involvement of private parties at the multilateral WTO level.

26 Case C-93/02, *Biret International v Council of the European Union*, [2003] ECR I-10497.

Tariffs and trade laws on import/export

1. A practical trade law problem

Smith Inc produces widgets in Country A and is considering exporting these widgets to Country B. Both countries are members of the World Trade Organisation (WTO). However, Country B maintains a 50% tariff on widgets and has bound this rate under its tariff schedule. It also has a free trade agreement with Country C under which it charges no tariff for widgets produced entirely in Country C. Further, Country B allows locally produced widgets to be sold without payment of its high value added tax (VAT), whereas foreign widgets can be sold only with the VAT. The government of Country B explains this latter measure as aimed at preserving the livelihoods of Country B-ans who work in the widget industry. Finally, Country B has imposed a ban on the sale of all widgets containing lead for human health reasons. Country B companies already comply with its ban, since no widgets produced in Country B contain lead, but a high proportion of the widgets produced by Smith Inc and others in Country A contain lead. Smith Inc is concerned about the Country B ban and also finds Country B's import rules far too costly. How could one provide Smith with legal advice about the trade rules?

2. Tariffs and GATT

Today's WTO and world trading system originated with the 1947 General Agreement on Tariffs and Trade (GATT). The central concept of GATT is that of tariffs: the percentage rates of customs duty charged at the border on imported goods.[1] Tariffs give a concrete measure of the barriers to trade imposed by a country and are therefore a useful tool in trade negotiations between countries. GATT also recognises non-tariff barriers to trade such as quotas or import licences. These kinds of trade barrier are usually more difficult to measure or quantify at a glance. They can also be subject to complex regulations, and may be vulnerable to unfair practices or corruption. GATT therefore institutes a process of 'tariffication' in order to convert these barriers into tariffs granting equivalent protection. Once all barriers to trade are in tariff form, the process established by GATT and the WTO aims to reduce gradually these tariffs to zero. In some cases zero tariffs have already been achieved, although the average tariff on industrial products imported into developed countries remains at around 4%.[2]

---

1 A great deal of helpful information on GATT and the WTO can be found at www.wto.org.

2 A list of all the original WTO members' commitments on tariffs, as well as a link to the schedules of members that joined after 1995, can be found at www.wto.org/english/tratop_e/schedules_e/goods_schedules_e.htm.

2.1 What is the structure of GATT?

(a) Schedules

Under GATT, each WTO member maintains a 'schedule of concessions', which is essentially a list of the tariff rates that it imposes on imported goods. A schedule is made up of four parts:

- maximum tariffs on goods from other WTO members (divided into Section I-A, for tariffs on agricultural goods; Section I-B, for tariff quotas on agricultural; and Section II, for other products);
- preferential tariff arrangements with particular countries;
- concessions granted to any countries on non-tariff measures; and
- commitments on agricultural export subsidies and domestic support subsidies.

The schedules contain details including the tariff item number (according to the World Customs Organisation's comprehensive classification system), a description of the product and the bound rate of duty.

(i) Binding

When members choose to 'bind' a certain tariff in their schedule, they are guaranteeing that their customs tariff on the product in question will not be higher than the bound rate. They may, of course, charge a tariff that is lower than their bound rate, but the treatment given to imported products must be "no less favourable" than what is inscribed in their schedule.

Members have no obligation under WTO law to lower their bound tariff rates, although they are obliged to continue negotiations to bind more product lines and to lower the tariffs on product lines already bound. Bound tariffs can be changed, but if this will result in higher tariffs then compensation may be payable to other affected members.

2.2 What obligations does GATT impose on WTO members?

(a) Tariffication

As referred to above, one principle of GATT is tariffication, which aims to convert all non-tariff barriers such as import quotas into tariffs. WTO members are therefore not permitted under GATT to maintain any "prohibitions or restrictions other than duties, taxes or other charges" on imports or exports. There are a limited number of exceptions to this principle; for example, export restrictions are allowed to prevent critical food shortages.

(b) Most favoured nation

The most favoured nation principle, a cornerstone of the world trading system, reflects the idea of non-discrimination in world trade. It requires that any advantage or favour granted by one country to another in respect of a particular product must be automatically granted to all other countries in respect of like products. In other words, one nation must treat others in the same manner as it treats its most favoured nation. This means that if Country A maintains a tariff on imported wooden chairs, for example, but then negotiates to allow wooden chairs made in Country B to enter without paying the tariff, the most favoured nation principle requires this favour granted to Country B to be extended to all other countries. It grants the benefit of the negotiations between Country A and Country B to all other countries, even without their involvement.

The phrase 'like products' is a key element of the most favoured nation principle. The principle will apply only to products that are considered 'like', or sufficiently similar. When Country A grants a favour to Country B regarding wooden chairs, the most favoured nation principle requires it to extend the favour to wooden chairs coming from other countries, but not to imported metal chairs, since metal and wood are not alike. However, is an oak chair 'like' a pine chair? How close must two products be before they are 'like' and the most favoured nation principle applies?

The phrase 'like product', in trade law, has been interpreted as relating to:

- the physical properties of the product;
- the end uses of the product;
- the tastes and habits of consumers in the territory (are the products usually considered as substitutes? Would a consumer buy a pine chair if no oak chairs were available?); and
- the international tariff classification of the product.[3]

All these factors must be considered in deciding whether the two products are like.

There are various exceptions to the most favoured nation principle which are discussed below.

(c) *National treatment*

The national treatment principle is the second reflection of non-discrimination in the world trading system. It requires essentially that foreign products be treated in the same way as domestic products. This means that no internal tax can be imposed on foreign products in a domestic market when the tax is not imposed on like domestic products. Internal taxes and laws affecting the internal sale of imported products must also not be applied so as to protect domestic production. Regarding non-fiscal measures, foreign products must be accorded treatment that is "no less favourable" than that accorded to like domestic products in respect of laws, regulations and requirements affecting their internal sale. The arguments above over which products are 'like' other products apply equally to the national treatment principle.

Internal taxes should be differentiated from import tariffs and taxes imposed at the border. Tariffs on imported goods are clearly still permitted under GATT (although the goal is to remove them) and do not violate the national treatment

3 *Japan–Taxes on Alcoholic Beverages*, WT/DS10/AB/R, Report of the Appellate Body, October 4 1996.

principle, since they are not internal taxes. National treatment applies only once the product has entered a domestic market - that is, once customs duties and border tariffs have been paid.

2.3 What exceptions to GATT principles are allowed?

(a) *General exceptions*

Several major exceptions to the GATT principles are contained in Article XX, which provides that members are still permitted to take measures:

- necessary to protect public morals;
- necessary to protect human, animal or plant life or health;
- relating to the importation or exportation of gold or silver;
- necessary to secure compliance with laws or regulations which are not inconsistent with the provisions of GATT;
- relating to the products of prison labour;
- imposed for the protection of national treasures of artistic, historic or archaeological value;
- relating to the conservation of exhaustible natural resources, if such measures are made effective in conjunction with restrictions on domestic production or consumption; and
- undertaken in pursuance of obligations under any intergovernmental commodity agreement.

Measures taken on any of these grounds must nevertheless not be applied in a manner which would constitute a disguised restriction on international trade, or a means of arbitrary or unjustifiable discrimination between countries where the same conditions prevail.

The two exceptions relating to health and natural resources allow countries to take environmental protection measures, for example, as long as the same environmental standards are imposed on both domestic and foreign producers. If a different standard were imposed on foreign producers, this would violate the national treatment principle, since the foreign producers would not enjoy treatment no less favourable than that given to domestic producers, and would also not be justified under the exception since it would constitute a disguised restriction on international trade. Unjustified discrimination has also been found to include failing to negotiate with other countries on alternative arrangements before imposing a ban on some product on environmental grounds.

(b) *Security exception*

Article XXI contains an exception on grounds of national security. It allows a WTO member to take any measures that it considers "necessary for the protection of its essential security interests . . . taken in time of war or other emergency international relations". As it stands, this is a largely self-judging exception, since it is left to individual members, using their own criteria, to decide what constitutes their essential security interests or an emergency in international relations. Some commentators suggest that the exception includes notions of good faith and reasonableness, so that a country attempting to rely on the exception to justify some trade-restrictive measure must show that its assessment of its security interests was done in good faith and is reasonable.[4]

Any measure purportedly taken under the general exceptions or the security exception above will, of course, stand until challenged by a complainant WTO member. The member taking the measure will then need to prove during consultations, negotiations and the WTO dispute settlement process, if the case proceeds, that the exception does indeed apply to cover the measure taken.

2.4 How do regional or bilateral trade agreements work?

Nearly all countries participate in bilateral or regional free trade arrangements (RTAs), of which the European Union is probably the most well known. These agreements are discriminatory by their very nature, as they are designed to grant certain trade preferences to the countries participating in the agreement. At first glance, therefore, they appear to be inconsistent with GATT principles such as most favoured nation, which establishes non-discrimination as a fundamental feature of the world trading system. However, in recognition of the fact that hundreds of free trade agreements exist, Article XXIV of GATT provides an exception for these arrangements.

For the exception to apply, two main conditions must be met:

- The tariff rates established under the RTA for products entering the new free trade area from outside must not be higher than the rates that existed for these products before the RTA was concluded; and
- Customs duties and regulations must be removed on "substantially all the trade" between the parties to the RTA.

If these conditions are not met, the RTA will not be considered valid and any preferences granted under it may be found to be in violation of GATT if they breach the most favoured nation principle or other obligations set out in GATT.

3. NAFTA and tariffs

The three parties to the North American Free Trade Agreement (NAFTA) - Canada, Mexico and the United States - have a general obligation to remove tariffs on goods traded between these countries and to meet NAFTA's rules of origin, following timelines established in the schedules to NAFTA. The national treatment principle also applies as it does under GATT. NAFTA incorporates the general exception in Article XX of GATT and a slightly amended version of the security exception in Article XXI of GATT.

4. The European Union and tariffs

The European Union is a single market, and one of its founding principles is that goods are traded and moved freely and without restrictions within the 25 EU

4 See, for example, Schloemann and Ohlhoff, "'Constitutionalization' and Dispute Settlement in the WTO: National Security as an Issue of Competence" (1999) 93 *American Journal of International Law* 242.

member states. There is no specific EU regime to cover trade in goods regarding parties outside the European Union. It is simply the European Union's WTO obligations that apply. However, the EU Trade Barriers Regulation does provide a mechanism for EU producers to complain about the trade practices of non-EU countries. It allows companies to request that the European Commission conduct an examination of a third country's trade practice where that practice is alleged to be prohibited by the WTO's rules on international trade - for example, because it is in breach of most favoured nation or national treatment obligations. The complainant must provide evidence of the obstacle to trade and the injury suffered due to the obstacle. Following the examination, the commission may decide to offset the obstacle to trade through suspension or withdrawal of some other concession made to the third country in question, or by appropriately modifying trade conditions with that country. Any action taken must be in accordance with the European Union's international obligations and the conclusions of any WTO dispute settlement on the issue. However, once a product has legally entered the European Union (ie, all applicable tariffs have been paid), it will be considered an EU product and also benefit from the broad free movement of goods provisions.

5. A world trade law solution to the practical problem

Smith Inc has four complaints to make about Country B's import rules:

- the high 50% tariff imposed on widgets imported into Country B;
- the fact that Country C can export its widgets to Country B without paying any tariffs;
- the tax imposed on the sale of foreign widgets in Country B; and
- the ban on widgets containing lead.

Some of these factors are potential violations of the General Agreement on Tariffs and Trade (GATT), by which Country B is bound as a WTO member.

Under GATT law, WTO members have no obligation to remove tariffs on imported goods or even to impose what are considered low tariffs. Each member is free to determine the level of tariffs it considers appropriate, although it is obliged to participate in ongoing negotiations to lower the tariff rates that its sets. Country B has bound its tariff on widgets in its goods schedule at 50%. In practice, this means that it can impose a tariff of anything up to (and including) 50%. The tariff is high, but Country B is not violating any GATT obligations in this regard and Smith Inc has no grounds for argument.

Country B's preferential arrangement with Country C, allowing widgets made in Country C to be imported into Country B at 0% tariff, appears to breach the most favoured nation principle. This principle would require Country B to extend the benefit it grants to Country C to all other countries, so that widgets from all other countries would be allowed into Country B with no tariff. However, since the preference is granted to Country C under a free trade agreement, it may be tolerated under Article XXIV of GATT. Country B would need to show that its agreement with Country C does not result in weighted average tariffs being raised after the agreement was completed, and also that substantially all goods trade between

Country C and Country B is both tariff and regulation-free. If it can show this, its Country C widgets preference will be considered acceptable under GATT; otherwise, Smith Inc can demonstrate a violation of the most favoured nation provision in Article I of GATT.

The VAT imposed on foreign widgets in Country B is a potential breach of the national treatment principle, which states that foreign goods must be treated no less favourably than domestic goods. In particular, no internal taxes may be applied to foreign goods that are not applied to domestic goods. Furthermore, internal taxes affecting the sale of imported goods must not be applied so as to protect domestic production. VAT is an internal tax imposed on goods once they have entered a market, and is not a tariff or border measure. Especially in light of Country B's statement that the tax is imposed in order to protect workers in domestic production, the fact that VAT is imposed only on foreign products seems a clear violation of Article III of GATT, the national treatment provision. Smith Inc therefore has a strong case that this measure is inconsistent with Country B's GATT obligations and must be removed.

The ban on the sale of widgets containing lead is a major problem for Smith Inc, given that a large proportion of its widgets contain lead. Under Article III:4 of GATT, as above, Country B must treat foreign widgets no less favourably than like domestic widgets. Since the domestic widgets do not contain lead, they are not affected by the ban, but the foreign widgets from Smith Inc in Country A do contain lead and hence are treated differently in Country B. In practice, this discrimination means that Country B is not permitted to maintain its ban under GATT unless it can show that its widgets are not like the Country A widgets. The products are both widgets and they perform the same function as each other. They also most likely would fall under the same tariff classification for trade purposes. However, if consumers consider the health risk in the lead-containing widgets as a differentiating factor from the lead-free widgets, the two products may not be considered substitutes in the marketplace. The health risk may thus be enough for Country B to demonstrate that its domestic widgets are not like foreign Country A's widgets. This would allow it to treat the two products differently and ban one but allow the sale of the other. Even if Country B cannot justify its ban on this ground, it may be able to show a general exception to GATT under Article XX, by characterising the ban as a measure necessary to protect human health.

The likely outcome for Smith Inc of consultations between the governments or trade representatives of Country A and Country B is that it will prove difficult to export widgets to Country B. The ban on lead-containing widgets will remain, meaning that Smith Inc can sell only its smaller proportion of lead-free widgets in Country B. The 50% tariff will remain, even on these lead-free widgets, although it acts as a major impediment to Smith Inc's market success in Country B. However, Smith Inc will likely benefit from being allowed to sell its widgets in Country B without having VAT added.

6. The *US-Venezuela Gasoline* dispute: a case study

The US Clean Air Act, passed in 1990, required gasoline producers to alter the chemical composition of their gasoline in order to cut pollution compared to a baseline. For domestic gasoline producers, the United States set the baseline as each producer's own 1990 level of pollution. For foreign producers, the United States claimed that it would be too difficult to determine each producer's own 1990 level due to a lack of data, and so the 1990 level established by the US Environmental Protection Agency was set as the foreign producers' baseline.

Venezuela complained about this regime to the WTO in 1995, three weeks after the WTO's commencement. It argued that the United States was discriminating against foreign gasoline producers, since some domestic producers may have had pollution levels higher than the EPA level and yet their gasoline could still have been sold in the United States, whereas foreign producers' gasoline at the same level of pollution could not have been sold under the Clean Air Act. Venezuela claimed that the US law was in violation of the national treatment provisions in GATT. In response, the United States argued that the law was justified by the general Article XX exception in GATT on environmental and natural resource conservation grounds.

In 1996, following earlier failed consultations on the dispute and a WTO panel hearing, the Appellate Body ruled in favour of Venezuela. It found that the Venezuelan gasoline was being treated less favourably than domestic gasoline in respect of laws affecting its sale, and hence that the US law breached GATT. It also found that the exception claimed by the United States did not apply. The Clean Air Act did relate to the conservation of resources, as required by the Article XX(g) exception, and was made effective with restrictions on domestic consumption as well. However, the act had been applied in a manner constituting unjustified discrimination and a disguised restriction on international trade, and so the exception could not apply.

At the end of the time given to comply with the Appellate Body ruling, the United States announced that it had adopted new regulations that were consistent with GATT.[5]

7. Recommended resources

The WTO maintains a useful website with explanatory materials on many aspects of WTO negotiations, rules and disputes, as well as other resources. It is available at www.wto.org.

The NAFTA Secretariat, which is responsible for the administration of the dispute settlement provisions of NAFTA, also maintains a useful website, where copies of treaty texts, information on panel decisions and reports and links to further resources can be found. It is available at www.nafta-sec-alena.org.

The Directorate General for Trade of the European Commission, which is in charge of implementing the common trade policy of the European Union, maintains a useful website on European trade negotiations, rules and disputes, as well as many further resources. It is available at ec.europa.eu/trade.

---

5 *United States–Standards for Reformulated and Conventional Gasoline*, WT/DS2.

For further information on tariffs and GATT, NAFTA or the European Union, see the following:

- D van den Bossche, *The Law and Policy of the WTO: Text, Cases and Materials*, (Cambridge: Cambridge University Press, 2005).
- P C Mavroidis, *The General Agreement on Tariffs and Trade - A Commentary* (Oxford: Oxford University Press 2005).
- L D'Arcy *et al*, *Schmitthoff's Export Trade: The Law and Practice of International Trade*, 10th ed (London: Sweet & Maxwell, 2000), especially Chapters 4, 5 and 7.
- C Barnard, *The Substantive Law of the EU: The Four Freedoms* (Oxford: Oxford University Press, 2004).
- M Trebilcock and R Howse, *The Regulation of International Trade* 3rd ed (New York: Routledge, 2005).

Technical and sanitary standards and labels

1. A practical trade law problem

Jones Inc produces telephones in Country A, a World Trade Organisation (WTO) member since 1995. The telephones for the domestic market have a specific set of components in order to conform to Telephone Producer Association standards of Country A. Jones Inc wants to export its telephones to neighbouring Country B, also a WTO member. The delivery of telephones is halted at the border by Country B Customs. The customs official explains that the components do not comply with the regulations for telephones developed by the Country B Institute for Standards. Further, labels from Consumers Rights Now, a Country B consumer awareness organisation, are not present as required on the telephones' packaging, nor is the exact plastic content of the telephones shown. Additionally, Jones Inc's telephones do not comply with Country B's laws on telephone recycling, which require manufacturers both to use certain process and production methods allowing the telephones to be recycled, and either to accept products back for recycling after use or to be represented by a domestic recycler.

For these reasons, the Country B customs official refuses to allow the shipment of Jones' phones to enter Country B. Jones Inc is amazed at this extensive level of bureaucracy: it had expected that its compliance with both International Organization for Standardization (ISO) standards for telephones and the Country A standards would be sufficient to allow entry to Country B. How can one advise Jones Inc?

2. Technical barriers to trade

The Agreement on Technical Barriers to Trade (TBT Agreement) was first concluded by the General Agreement on Tariffs and Trade (GATT) contracting parties in 1972, in recognition of concerns that technical regulations and standards can pose major problems for international trade in goods. During the Uruguay Round, the TBT Agreement was strengthened and clarified, and incorporated into the WTO's Single Undertaking of the Uruguay Round. It serves to ensure that technical regulations imposed by a country have some legitimate purpose and are not merely protectionist measures in disguise.

2.1 To what does the TBT Agreement apply?

The TBT Agreement applies to all products, including industrial and agricultural products. It covers technical regulations, although it does not cover health or plant-health related measures: these are covered by the Agreement on Sanitary and Phytosanitary Measures (SPS Agreement, further discussed below).

2.2 What are technical regulations?

One important concept in the TBT Agreement is that of a technical regulation. A technical regulation is a specification made by a government relating to the characteristics of a product. These characteristics may include the product's size, shape, design, functions or performance, or how the product is packaged or labelled. Technical regulations may also relate to a product's method or process of production, rather than the product itself. Importantly, technical regulations include only measures that are mandatory – in other words, measures which will prevent a product being sold in a country if they are not complied with.

In deciding whether a particular measure is a technical regulation, the WTO Appellate Body has said that the measure must be examined "as an integrated whole, taking into account . . . the prohibitive and the permissive elements that are part of it".[1]

2.3 What are standards?

Standards are similar to technical regulations, but the key difference is that compliance with standards is not mandatory. A measure taken by a country is considered as a standard under the TBT Agreement if it still allows a particular product to be sold despite not meeting the requirements of the measure. The product may not be as successful in the marketplace, however, depending on local consumers' preferences for products meeting standards.

2.4 What are members' obligations under the TBT Agreement?

The preamble to the TBT Agreement recognises a member's basic right to take measures "necessary to ensure the quality of its exports, or for the protection of human, animal, and plant life or health, of the environment, or for the prevention of deceptive practices, at the levels it considers appropriate". The major limitation that the TBT Agreement imposes on this right is that members' technical regulations must not be "prepared, adopted or applied with a view to or with the effect of creating unnecessary obstacles to international trade".

Unnecessary obstacles to trade arise in two ways: first, when a regulation is more restrictive than necessary to fulfil a legitimate objective, or second, when a regulation does not fulfil a legitimate objective at all.

Objectives considered legitimate by the TBT Agreement include:

- national security requirements;
- prevention of deceptive practices;
- protection of human health or safety;
- protection of animal or plant life or health; and
- protection of the environment.

This list is not exhaustive, however, and in appropriate circumstances members may be able to claim that a regulation was adopted to meet a different objective.

---

1 *EC–Measures Affecting Asbestos and Asbestos-Containing Products*, WT/DS135/AB/R (Appellate Body), para 64.

A regulation is considered more trade restrictive than necessary to fulfil one of these objectives if there is an alternative regulation or measure that would also fulfil the objective, but that is less trade restrictive in light of the risks that not meeting the objective would create. For example, specifying that a motorcycle helmet be made of plastic with a 1 centimetre thickness would likely be more trade restrictive than necessary to achieve an objective of human safety, when the same objective could be achieved by requiring only that the helmet not become damaged when struck with forces up to a certain minimum level. In this way, exporters in other countries are free to determine according to their own commercial and regulatory requirements how best to produce motorcycle helmets, as long as the helmets achieve the performance level prescribed by the importing country's regulation. This is a general principle included in the TBT Agreement: when regulations are specified in terms of a product's design or descriptive characteristics, rather than its performance, the regulations are more likely to be considered more trade restrictive than necessary.

(a) Conformity assessment procedures

The obligations above also apply to the procedures used by members in cases where testing is required to determine whether imported products conform to their technical regulations. Thus, such conformity assessment procedures must not be "adopted or applied with a view to or with the effect of creating unnecessary obstacles to trade". In this context, an unnecessary obstacle to trade may be created in various ways – for instance, when:

- the procedures are stricter than necessary to establish conformity;
- the procedures are not completed as quickly as possible by the inspection authorities; or
- the facilities used in establishing conformity are in a location that causes unnecessary inconvenience.

(b) Most favoured nation and national treatment

The most favoured nation and national treatment principles apply to technical regulations under the TBT Agreement. This means that a member must not discriminate between other members exporting like products to that member, or between its own products and like products exported from another member. For example, a member may not impose stricter technical regulations on imported products than it imposes on its own products, nor may it impose stricter regulations on imports from one member than on imports from another member.

These two principles also apply to conformity assessment procedures, so that these procedures must be carried out for imported products from one country in a manner that is no less favourable to those products than to "products of national origin or originating in any other country". This applies likewise to the fees charged for assessment, although some difference is permitted to account for "communication, transportation and other costs" that may be higher for foreign suppliers. The confidentiality of information given by foreign suppliers must also be respected as for domestic suppliers, in order to protect legitimate commercial interests.

2.5 What role do international standards play under the TBT Agreement?

WTO members are encouraged to base their technical regulations on international standards. When a member adopts a technical regulation that conforms to an international standard, the regulation is automatically presumed not to create an unnecessary obstacle to international trade. Another member could nevertheless still complain about the regulation, perhaps on most favoured nation or national treatment grounds.

Members are allowed to adopt regulations not based on international standards in one circumstance: if using the international standards would be an ineffective or inappropriate means to fulfil the legitimate policy objective desired. For instance, an international standard may fail to take into account particular geological or climatic conditions in a country such as excessive snowfalls or frequent earthquakes. In such situations, the technical regulations may be tailored to the country's requirements.

The same principles apply to conformity assessment procedures: if international standards exist for carrying out these procedures, members must use them unless they can show that the procedures are inappropriate in their particular circumstances.

2.6 How are labels relevant?

Countries often adopt technical regulations requiring particular labels to be displayed on products, usually for reasons of health and safety or to avoid deceiving consumers. For example, many countries require labels on cigarette packets explaining the product's risks to human health. Other products commonly require labels giving information such as their minimum fruit or meat content, to prevent consumer deception. These labels often affect whether an imported product will be purchased.

2.7 Can a country require labels on products?

Countries can require labelling of products along the same principles as any other regulation under the TBT Agreement – that is, countries can adopt regulations requiring labels as long as this does not create any unnecessary obstacles to international trade.

However, there is currently much debate over whether countries can require 'eco-labels'. These are labels that indicate that a product has been manufactured according to what are considered environmentally friendly processes and production methods. The characteristics of such a product are otherwise identical to a product manufactured according to traditional processes and production methods, and so consumers are unable to know that the product has been produced in any particular way without an eco-label to indicate this. However, several countries claim that they do not have the capacity to adjust their processes and production methods so as to be approved for eco-labels, or that requirements imposed by governments for eco-labels on products effectively risk pricing these products out of the market. The issue forms part of ongoing discussions within the WTO.

2.8 Are there any exclusions from the TBT Agreement?

(a) *Developing countries*

Some flexibility is permitted for developing countries in fulfilling their obligations under the TBT Agreement. In particular, developing countries may adopt technical regulations or conformity assessment procedures that aim to preserve indigenous technology, and production methods and processes "compatible with their development needs". Developing country members are also not expected to base their technical regulations on international standards where this would be inappropriate for their development, financial and trade needs.

(b) *Government procurement*

Specifications for goods required for government production or consumption are not subject to the TBT Agreement. They are covered in the Agreement on Government Procurement.

3. Sanitary and phytosanitary measures

The SPS Agreement deals with regulation for health-related purposes. Sanitary measures (relating to human and animal health) and phytosanitary measures (relating to plant health) are commonly adopted by governments to ensure food safety and to prevent the spread of pests and diseases within their territory. Usually these measures will involve a restriction on trade with other countries when their goods are considered to pose risks to human, animal or plant health. The SPS Agreement aims to define when such restrictions on trade are allowed and to prevent the restrictions acting merely as protectionist devices.[2]

Essentially, the SPS Agreement allows WTO members to adopt regulations intended to protect human, animal or plant life or health, as long as these regulations are "based on scientific principles and not maintained without sufficient scientific evidence".[3] A regulation that imposes more protection than would be imposed under the relevant international standard, if one exists, is allowed as long as there is a scientific justification, meaning that the regulation is based on a risk assessment taking scientific evidence into account as well as ecological and environmental conditions.

When not enough scientific evidence exists to justify a particular regulation, members may nevertheless take provisional measures, intended as short-term measures designed to protect the public while further scientific investigation is done.

---

2 For further information on technical and sanitary standards and the SPS and TBT Agreements, see: A Sykes, *Product Standards for Internationally Integrated Goods Markets*, (Washington: Brookings Institution Press, 1995); M Echols, *Food Safety and the WTO: The Interplay of Science, Culture and Technology* (The Hague: Kluwer Law International, 2001); C Button, *The Power to Protect: Trade, Health and Uncertainty in the WTO* (Oxford: Hart Publishing, 2004).

3 Under the SPS and TBT Agreements, each WTO member is required to maintain an enquiry point – that is, an office which serves to handle requests for information about that country's SPS measures or technical regulations, standards and conformity assessment procedures. Using the "Simple Search" on the WTO's DocumentsOnline database for document symbol G/SPS/ENQ or G/TBT/ENQ (as appropriate) will produce the latest list of enquiry points.

3.1 What is a sanitary or phytosanitary measure?

The SPS Agreement applies only to SPS measures adopted by members. These measures are defined as those applied:

- to protect human or animal life from the risks arising from additives, contaminants, toxins or disease-causing organisms in their food;
- to protect human life from pests or from diseases carried by animals or plants;
- to protect animal or plant life from pests or diseases; or
- to prevent or limit the damage caused in a country by pests.

Measures include laws, regulations, decrees, requirements and procedures relating to many different aspects of products. These include:

- testing, inspection, certification and approval procedures;
- processes and production methods; and
- packaging and labelling requirements directly related to food safety.

The measures need not necessarily be taken at the central government level; measures imposed by non-central governments such as state, provincial, regional or local governments are also covered.

The SPS Agreement also applies to any measures introduced before its entry into force in 1995. Since it may be difficult to prove that a measure taken by a member many years prior to 1995 was based on a scientific risk assessment, especially as the requirement to do so did not yet exist, the WTO Appellate Body has suggested that some flexibility be permitted in applying the requirement for earlier measures.

3.2 What kinds of sanitary or phytosanitary measures are valid under the SPS Agreement?

When a member takes an SPS measure, it must ensure that all of the following conditions are met for its measure to be valid under the SPS Agreement:

- The measure is applied only to the extent necessary to protect human, animal or plant life or health;
- The measure is based on scientific principles;
- The measure is not maintained without sufficient scientific evidence;
- It is not being applied in a manner which would constitute a disguised restriction on international trade; and
- It does not arbitrarily or unjustifiably discriminate between members where identical or similar conditions prevail.

If any one of these conditions is not met, the measure may be challenged by a complainant member as being in violation of the SPS Agreement.

The requirement of 'sufficient scientific evidence' has been interpreted as requiring a rational or objective relationship between the scientific evidence and the SPS measure taken in response. This relationship must be considered on a case-by-case basis, in light of the "characteristics of the measure at issue and the quality and quantity of the scientific evidence". In cases of risk of human casualties, the requirement may be relaxed somewhat, so that, even when there is only a small amount of scientific evidence suggesting a risk of death, a trade-restrictive SPS measure will be more likely tolerated under the SPS Agreement.

The fourth and fifth conditions listed above have been interpreted to contain three elements required to find a violation:

- The measure discriminates between the member imposing the measure and another member, or between two other members;
- The discrimination is arbitrary or unjustifiable; and
- Identical or similar conditions prevail in the territory of the two members compared.

Discrimination both between different products and between similar products is equally prohibited by the conditions. For example, SPS measures must not discriminate between one country's salmon and another's, but also must not discriminate between one country's salmon and another's tuna.

3.3 What role do international standards play?

WTO law requires members to harmonise their SPS standards, and for this purpose contains an obligation to base their SPS measures on international standards, guidelines or recommendations. Only certain international standards-setting bodies are recognised by the SPS Agreement:

- for food safety, the Codex Alimentarius Commission;[4]
- for animal health, the World Organisation for Animal Health;[5]
- for plant health, the International Plant Protection Convention;[6] and
- for other matters, any relevant international organisation identified by the SPS Committee.

When a member adopts an SPS measure that conforms to an international standard, guideline or recommendation, the conditions for the measure to be valid are automatically presumed to be satisfied. Another member could still complain about the measure, arguing perhaps that the measure is being applied in a manner that unjustifiably discriminates against it or more strictly than is necessary to protect human health, but this would be difficult to achieve given the deference shown to international standards by the SPS Agreement.

Members are allowed to adopt measures giving higher protection (ie, restricting more trade) than an international standard would require, but they must demonstrate that these measures have a scientific justification based on a risk assessment. The risk assessment must take into account:

- available scientific evidence;
- the prevalence of specific diseases or pests;
- the existence of disease or pest-free areas;
- relevant ecological and environmental conditions; and
- the possibility of quarantine or other treatment.

---

4 www.codexalimentarius.net.
5 www.oie.int.
6 www.ippc.int.

The assessment must also consider relevant economic factors, including:

- the potential financial damage if a disease or pest were to enter the country;
- the costs of control or eradication; and
- the relative cost effectiveness of alternative means to limit the risk.

The appropriate level of risk determined by a member following a risk assessment must be consistent with risk levels determined in other situations. Members must avoid arbitrary or unjustifiable distinctions if these distinctions result in discrimination or a disguised restriction on international trade.

3.4 What role do national standards play?

Each WTO member may have different health standards and inspection or testing techniques for goods coming into its territory. Goods might therefore meet the standards set in their country of origin but be rejected by a destination country due to non-compliance with that country's regulations: this is how most SPS disputes arise. However, if the exporting country can objectively show that its SPS measures are equivalent to those of the importing country – that is, the measures achieve the same level of protection, despite using different techniques or approaches – then the importing country is required to accept these measures. Goods entering a member's territory therefore cannot be blocked on grounds of non-compliance with health regulations, once equivalence is shown.

3.5 Are there any exceptions to these conditions?

(a) Provisional measures

Members can adopt provisional SPS measures in cases where there is not enough scientific information available to justify a ban under the normal conditions of the SPS Agreement. This allows members to adopt the precautionary principle to some extent, relying on a default position of a ban on suspected risky products until they can be proven safe. These provisional measures are intended to be only temporary, and members must seek further scientific information and review their provisional measures "within a reasonable time".

(b) Developing countries

The SPS Committee is authorised to grant time-limited exceptions to developing countries from obligations under the SPS Agreement, in light of their particular financial, trade and development needs. A search on the WTO's DocumentsOnline database (http://docsonline.wto.org) for document symbol G/SPS/GEN will produce all the documents of the SPS Committee, including documents relating to exceptions granted to developing countries.

4. NAFTA and technical/sanitary standards

The North American Free Trade Agreement (NAFTA) regime on SPS measures is substantially the same as the WTO regime under the SPS Agreement. Sanitary or phytosanitary measures based on scientific principles may be adopted if they are necessary to protect human, animal or plant life or health, provided that they do not arbitrarily or unjustifiably discriminate and are not disguised restrictions on trade. Measures based on international standards are automatically presumed to meet NAFTA obligations.

Chapter 9 of NAFTA affirms the TBT Agreement for technical standards, but extends the parties' obligations further by including land transportation services and telecommunications services in its scope (whereas the TBT Agreement deals only with technical standards for goods). NAFTA also covers provincial and state government measures.

5. The European Union and technical/sanitary standards

The European Union does not have any specific regime allowing its member states to adopt technical regulations or SPS measures. Any regulations or measures that the European Union or individual countries take must, of course, be consistent with domestic and EU law on, for example, food or product safety, and with the WTO SPS and TBT Agreements, but there are no further obligations imposed at the EU level. However, due to the *Cassis de Dijon* jurisprudence of the European Court of Justice, there is mutual recognition of product standards across the European Union unless a member state can invoke mandatory requirements to justify a particular national standard.

6. A world trade law solution to the practical problem

Country B appears to be imposing technical regulations on Jones Inc, preventing it from selling its telephones in Country B. As WTO members, both Country B and Country A are bound by the provisions of the TBT Agreement, which sets out the circumstances in which such technical regulations are allowed.

Jones Inc has encountered four problems at the Country B border:

- its non-compliance with Country B regulations on telephones;
- the missing Country B Consumers Rights Now labels on the packaging of its telephones;
- its failure to specify the exact plastic content of its telephones; and
- its non-compliance with Country B telephone recycling laws.

If Jones Inc can demonstrate that all these matters are violations of the TBT Agreement, it will have a strong case to present to the Country B government to remove the regulations and allow Jones Inc's telephones to be sold in Country B.

The first matter to address is whether these Country B customs requirements are in fact 'technical regulations' as defined by the TBT Agreement. Firstly, it appears that all the requirements are mandatory, since the shipment was denied entry by the customs official. This, of course, assumes that the customs official was correct in denying entry according to Country B law. If Jones Inc has reason to doubt that compliance with these requirements is actually mandatory, as the official claims, it should contact the Country B authorities for clarification.

Secondly, since the customs official claims that the telephones' components do not meet Country B regulations, it can be assumed that the Country B regulations require telephones to contain different components. Requirements on the permitted components in a product, as well as requirements on labelling, are considered technical regulations. This suggests that the first three problems are technical regulations for the purposes of the TBT Agreement.

Lastly, the definition of 'technical regulations' in Annex I of the TBT Agreement includes "related process and production methods", suggesting that the recycling laws are also technical regulations since they demand certain production methods. The requirement to take products back for recycling after use could arguably be considered part of the recycling technical regulation, as it may require certain labelling or notification to be given to consumers. It may also infringe the national treatment provisions of GATT.

Once it is established that Country B is applying technical regulations to Jones Inc's export of telephones, Jones Inc must then demonstrate that these technical regulations go beyond the TBT Agreement provisions on permitted regulations. The fact that Jones Inc's telephones meet the international ISO telephone standards is not strictly relevant; under the TBT Agreement, Country B is free to impose technical regulations that depart from international standards, but is not free to impose technical regulations that create unnecessary obstacles to international trade. This occurs when a technical regulation is more trade restrictive than necessary in meeting a legitimate objective.

Country B's legitimate objective in imposing the regulations on telephone components can be assumed to be the protection of human safety, and for the labelling requirement it can be assumed that the objective is the prevention of deceptive practices. The regulations on plastics content and recycling would most likely fall under the objective of protection of the environment. All these objectives are recognised as legitimate under Article 2.2 of the TBT Agreement. In any case, under the TBT Agreement's notification provisions, Country B would have had to notify WTO members of its regulations when adopted, along with the objectives that the regulations purport to fulfil.

To succeed in a challenge to these requirements, Jones Inc must therefore show that Country B's technical regulations are more trade restrictive than necessary in meeting these objectives, taking account of the risks that would be created by not meeting the objectives. Jones Inc could point to other means of fulfilling them. For instance, instead of specifying a telephone production method, the regulation could simply specify that telephones must be recyclable according to Country B's recycling processes; Jones Inc's telephones may well meet this requirement already.

Jones Inc can also present evidence on the trade-restrictive nature of the regulations, by detailing the difficulties it would have in meeting them. This might include, for instance, lengthy approval processes needed to be granted permission to use the Country B Consumers Rights Now labels or changes to its manufacturing processes that would be needed to measure accurately the plastic content of its telephones or to change their shape.

A finding of violation of the TBT Agreement, or at least a strong case presented by Country A to Country B, would push or force Country B to remove its technical regulations. One possible way forward is for Country B to harmonise its telephone regulations with those set by the ISO: this would bring Country B into a presumption of compliance with the TBT Agreement and would also allow Jones Inc to sell its telephones across the border.

7. The *EC – Hormones* dispute: a case study

In January 1989 the European Union passed a directive banning the import of US beef that had been treated with particular growth hormones. The United States challenged the ban, concerned about losing money on beef sales to the European market. The European Union claimed that the ban was necessary to protect human health, while the United States pointed to several tests showing no health risk and argued that the ban was in violation of the SPS Agreement, among other things. The United States eventually commenced dispute resolution proceedings in the WTO in 1996.

The WTO's Appellate Body ruled in 1998 in favour of the United States. It found that, although the EU ban imposed a higher level of protection than the relevant international standard would have required, this higher level had not been justified by a sufficient risk assessment. For five of the hormones being used, the Appellate Body found no relationship between the scientific evidence presented and the ban imposed, and for the sixth hormone the Appellate Body found that no risk assessment had been carried out.

The European Union, following arbitration on the length of time to be granted to implement the Appellate Body's ruling, was given until May 1999 to remove the ban. It failed to do so, and in July 1999 the WTO's Dispute Settlement Body authorised the United States to suspend $116 million per year in concessions granted to the European Union as compensation for the lost beef sales.

In 2003 the European Union claimed to have conducted new risk assessments and obtained new scientific evidence to justify its ongoing ban. The United States rejected this and refused to lift its retaliatory measures. As of 2006 the ban and the retaliation remain in place.[7]

8. Recommended resources

For further information on technical barriers to trade and sanitary and phytosanitary barriers in trade law, useful publications include the following:

- A O Sykes, *Product Standards for Internationally Integrated Goods Markets* (Washington: Brookings Institution Press 1995).
- G A Bermann and P C Mavroidis (eds), *Trade and Health in the World Trade Organization* (Cambridge: Cambridge University Press, 2006).
- G Marceau and J P Trachtman, "The TBT Agreement, the SPS Agreement and the GATT–A Map of the WTO Law of Domestic Regulation of Goods" *Journal of World Trade* 36 (2002) 811.

---

7 *European Communities – Measures Concerning Meat and Meat Products* (Hormones), WT/DS26.

Subsidies

---

1. A practical trade law problem

Country A supports its bicycle production with direct payments to two of the main producers, Smiling Cycles Inc and Roadrunner Ltd. Foreign-owned companies cannot receive such payments. The government of Country A also builds new roads and cycle paths for these companies. Country A's Private Bank, 25% of which is owned by the government, has granted the two companies a generous credit that did not take into account their normal credit rating and has much better conditions than are available on the market. Smiling Cycles Inc and Roadrunner Ltd were able to lower their prices significantly and have increased their market share not just in Country A, but also in neighbouring Country B. General Transport Inc, which produces bicycles in Country B, has noted that sales of its bicycles have sunk to an all-time low. It feels that it is not operating on a level playing field with Smiling Cycles Inc and Roadrunner Ltd. How could one advise General Transport Inc in trade law?

2. Subsidies

Governments are sometimes tempted to support domestic producers by granting them financial incentives in the form of subsidies on their production. These subsidies help to make the domestic producers more competitive by allowing them to sell their goods in local or foreign markets at cheaper prices. However, these subsidies can also hurt foreign producers and distort international trade. The World Trade Organisation (WTO) Agreement on Subsidies and Countervailing Measures sets out the situations in which subsidies are allowed and also when duties may be imposed to counter the effect of subsidies.

2.1 What are subsidies?

Under the Agreement on Subsidies and Countervailing Measures, a subsidy is a "financial contribution" made by a government or public body to industry within its territory. This can include various situations, such as:

- when a government practice involves a direct transfer of funds (eg, a grant, loan or equity infusion) or a potential transfer of funds (eg, a loan guarantee);
- when government revenue that would normally be due is not collected (eg, a tax credit);
- when a government purchases goods or provides goods or services apart from general infrastructure; or

- when a government directs a private body to undertake any of the activities above.

A direct cash grant to an enterprise is clearly a financial contribution, but giving an enterprise an exception for permitting procedures, for instance, is probably not a financial contribution, even though it may save the enterprise some money on compliance.

The financial contribution must also confer a benefit for it to be considered as a subsidy. This has been interpreted as requiring that the financial contribution be "provided on terms that are more advantageous than those that would be available to the recipient on the market". A loan provided to an enterprise on commercial terms - that is, at an interest rate no better than what is available generally in the marketplace - is a financial contribution to that enterprise, but it does not confer a benefit and so is not a subsidy.

2.2 To what kinds of subsidy does the Agreement on Subsidies and Countervailing Measures apply?

The Agreement on Subsidies and Countervailing Measures applies only to specific subsidies. Essentially, a subsidy is specific if it is available only to certain enterprises or industries. A subsidy is not considered specific if there are objective criteria for eligibility and the amount granted, as long as these criteria are neutral, non-discriminatory, economic in nature and horizontal in application. Eligibility must be automatic and the criteria must be strictly adhered to for the subsidy not to be considered specific.

A subsidy that appears to be non-specific may still be considered specific when other factors are taken into account. These factors include:

- predominant use of a subsidy programme by certain enterprises;
- disproportionately large grants to certain enterprises; and
- the granting body's use of discretion (eg, the reasons given for and the frequency of rejections and approvals).

Subsidies are also considered specific if they are limited to certain enterprises within a particular geographical region. Further, any subsidy in the 'red light' category of prohibited subsidies (further discussed below) is automatically considered to be specific.

Therefore, for the Agreement on Subsidies and Countervailing Measures to apply, a subsidy must:

- be found to exist; and
- be considered specific in light of the positive evidence available.

2.3 Which subsidies are permitted under the Agreement on Subsidies and Countervailing Measures? What is the 'traffic-light approach'?

The Agreement on Subsidies and Countervailing Measures implements a three-tier system for subsidies. Sometimes known as the 'traffic-light approach', the system permits certain subsidies ('green lights'), allows some subsidies to be challenged and establishes procedures for this ('amber lights'), and prohibits other subsidies outright ('red lights').

(a) ***Prohibited***

Part II of the Agreement on Subsidies and Countervailing Measures deals with the 'red light' category of prohibited subsidies. This category includes subsidies that are tied to export performance (eg, by requiring a certain level of export earnings before the subsidy is granted), and subsidies that are contingent on the use of domestic rather than imported goods. A particular complaints procedure is established, beginning with consultations between the complaining member and the member alleged to be granting a prohibited subsidy. If the consultations fail, the dispute is passed to the WTO's dispute resolution body as for the other WTO regimes, but is processed faster than usual, as the subsidies in question are almost certain to damage other countries' international trade. If the prohibited subsidy is not immediately removed following the dispute resolution procedure, the complaining WTO member is allowed to take countervailing measures (eg, by imposing a special duty on the goods being subsidised) in order to avoid the negative effects of the subsidy.

(b) ***Actionable***

The 'amber light' category of actionable subsidies is covered under Part III of the Agreement on Subsidies and Countervailing Measures. Actionable subsidies may or may not be permitted, depending on their effect on the interests of other WTO members. A subsidy maintained by one WTO member can be challenged if it causes:

- injury to another member's domestic industry;
- nullification or impairment of benefits accruing directly or indirectly to another member under the General Agreement on Tariffs and Trade (GATT), in particular the benefits of bound concessions; or
- serious prejudice to another member's interests.

Article 6 defines 'serious prejudice' in some detail. The term focuses on the effects of the subsidy, so that no serious prejudice will be found unless at least one of the following effects can be shown:

- Imports of a like product from the complaining country into the country granting the subsidy are displaced or impeded;
- Exports of a like product from the complaining country to a third country are displaced or impeded;
- There is significant price undercutting, price suppression, price depression or lost sales of another member's like product in the same market; or
- There is an increase in the world market share of the subsidising member in a particular primary product or commodity, compared to its average share in the previous three years.

The provisions in Article 6.1 of the Agreement on Subsidies and Countervailing Measures, setting out various specific types of subsidy causing serious prejudice, expired at the end of 1999. The types of subsidy in Article 6.1 must now meet the tests of their effects described above for them to cause serious prejudice.

Part III also establishes a complaints procedure similar to that used for prohibited subsidies. A member wishing to complain about an actionable subsidy first requests consultations with the member maintaining the subsidy, in order to "clarify the facts of the situation and to arrive at a mutually agreed solution". If no solution can be found, a panel is convened to resolve the dispute, with a possible appeal to the appellate body. If the subsidy is found to result in adverse effects to the complaining member, countervailing measures are authorised, "commensurate with the degree and nature of the adverse effects determined to exist".

(c) *Non-actionable*

The 'green light' category covers non-actionable subsidies – subsidies that members are permitted to maintain since they do not adversely affect international trade. The Agreement on Subsidies and Countervailing Measures deals only with subsidies that are specific. Therefore, any form of government assistance that is not classified as a subsidy is naturally not covered by the Agreement on Subsidies and Countervailing Measures and so is allowed, as is any subsidy that is not classified as specific.

The Agreement on Subsidies and Countervailing Measures defines other non-actionable subsidies in Article 8. However, these provisions expired in 1999, and so the types of subsidy defined there are now actionable and open to challenge if they cause an adverse effect on another member's international trade.

A WTO member is entitled to approach the Permanent Group of Experts – a panel of five independent experts established under the Agreement on Subsidies and Countervailing Measures – for a confidential advisory opinion on any subsidy that the member proposes or currently maintains. This opinion cannot be used in later proceedings against the member if the subsidy is challenged, but it can help members to ensure that any subsidies they maintain are in accordance with their WTO obligations.

2.4 What remedies are available against subsidies? What are countervailing measures?

The major remedies against prohibited and actionable subsidies are either the removal of the subsidy or, if removal is refused, the imposition of a countervailing duty. A countervailing duty is one imposed on imports to offset the benefit of the exporting country's subsidy on those goods. As a remedy, it is useful only against export subsidies; imposing a countervailing duty would not offset the benefits obtained from domestic subsidies (those granted to domestic industry to create an advantage over imported goods). Therefore, the criteria for imposing countervailing duties focus on injury to a domestic industry, as explained below, rather than the other grounds established in the Agreement on Subsidies and Countervailing Measures for challenging a subsidy (ie, nullification and impairment, and serious prejudice).

Article VI of GATT provides the basic authorisation for WTO members to impose countervailing duties in appropriate circumstances. Part V of the Agreement on

Subsidies and Countervailing Measures expands on Article VI and sets out the requirements for countervailing duties in more detail.

A member wishing to impose a countervailing duty as a remedy must first receive a request from domestic industry to commence a formal investigation into the subsidy. The investigation must show that:

- a subsidy exists;
- a domestic industry is being materially injured (or is threatened with material injury), or the establishment of a domestic industry is being impeded; and
- this situation was caused by the subsidy in question.

However, members are allowed to initiate investigations themselves when they have enough evidence of a subsidy, an injury and the causal link between the two. In addition, the first step in the investigation must be to hold consultations between interested members, and, if no solution is found, the opportunity to hold further consultations must continue to be offered as the formal investigation proceeds.

Article 15 of the Agreement on Subsidies and Countervailing Measures deals with the determination of injury and prescribes the factors to be considered in deciding, as part of a formal investigation, whether there is material injury to a domestic industry as required before countervailing duties can be imposed. Article 15 also covers the determination of the causal link between the subsidy and the injury. The Agreement on Subsidies and Countervailing Measures further defines strict procedures and timelines to be followed in conducting investigations, including a requirement that authorities give public notice of investigations and other determinations made that relate to countervailing duties. A standard time limit of five years is imposed on any countervailing measures taken.

The practicalities of imposing a countervailing duty are addressed in Article 19. This article specifies, for instance, that complainant members may decide for themselves whether any duty to be imposed will be the full amount of the subsidy or some smaller amount (although it must not be more than the subsidy). Article 19 also recommends that domestic parties which might be hurt by a countervailing duty be given a chance to voice their concerns before the duty is imposed.

(a) Agriculture subsidies

Subsidies on agricultural goods are treated under a different regime from other goods. Two main kinds of subsidy are covered – domestic support and export subsidies.

(i) Domestic support

The Agreement on Agriculture sets out two basic categories of domestic support: green box measures, which are considered not to distort trade, and amber box measures, which are trade distorting.

Green box measures under the Agreement on Agriculture are those that have "no, or at most minimal, trade-distorting effects". This means that the measure:

- must be provided through a publicly funded government programme not involving transfers from consumers; and
- must not have the effect of providing price support to producers.

Examples of these kinds of measures, given in Annex 2 to the Agreement on Agriculture, include research, pest and disease control, training services, inspection services, some forms of marketing services and infrastructural services not including on-farm facilities. Thus, a much wider range of domestic support is permitted for agricultural goods than for other kinds of goods – if the subsidising government can characterise its agricultural subsidy as one of the types listed in Annex 2, a complainant will have little success in challenging the subsidy.

Domestic support that does not fall into the green box is considered trade distorting and is part of the amber box. These are generally measures that support prices or are directly linked to production quantities. WTO members have agreed to reduce progressively the total value of their amber box measures, according to calculations expressed in Article 1 and Annexes 3 and 4 of the Agreement on Subsidies and Countervailing Measures. A small amount of domestic support (5% of agricultural production for developed countries or 10% for developing countries) is permitted to remain.

A third category, blue box measures, covers some kinds of domestic support that would otherwise be in the amber box. This support involves attaching conditions on limiting production to reduce its trade-distorting effect. There is no requirement to reduce the total value of blue box domestic support.

(ii) Export subsidies

The Agreement on Subsidies and Countervailing Measures also covers export subsidies, defined as "subsidies contingent on export performance". Article 9 lists the subsidies included in the definition, such as cost reduction measures, internal transport subsidies and subsidies on agricultural products to be included in other products made for export. WTO members have committed to reducing these export subsidies by amounts listed in schedules to the agreement. No export subsidies may be maintained that are not subject to these reduction commitments. The time period over which these reductions were to occur has now passed. However, negotiations are continuing on further reductions.

3. NAFTA and subsidies

The North American Free Trade Agreement contains some specific provisions on export subsidies for agricultural goods. Article 705(1) expresses the objective of elimination of agricultural export subsidies, while other provisions allow the use of these subsidies in certain circumstances with a requirement that the interests of other parties be considered before the subsidy is imposed.

4. The European Union and subsidies

The European Union incorporates the terms of the WTO's Agreement on Subsidies and Countervailing Measures into its own internal subsidies regime. An EU complainant company may apply to the European Commission, either directly or through its government, to have an investigation commenced into an alleged subsidy granted by a non-EU government to the non-EU country's industry. As under the Agreement on Subsidies and Countervailing Measures, the complainant must show that the non-EU government is granting a specific subsidy (a financial contribution conferring a benefit), and that this is causing material injury to EU industry. If these factors are shown and the benefits of taking action outweigh the costs, the European Commission can decide to impose countervailing duties. Commission Communication 98/C 394/04 sets out the commission's method of calculating subsidies, and hence the countervailing duties to be imposed, as well as its method of conducting investigations.[1] The non-EU country in question may challenge a subsidy determination in the European Court of First Instance, or may use the WTO dispute resolution process if it is a WTO member.

5. A world trade law solution to the practical problem

Country A is engaging in several practices that may constitute granting subsidies to its domestic bicycle producers. Specifically, Country A is:

- making direct payments to two of the major bicycle producers;
- building paths and roads for these producers; and
- providing credit on favourable terms to these producers.

As a WTO member, Country A is bound by the Agreement on Subsidies and Countervailing Measures, which defines the situations in which government subsidies to private industry are permitted. If General Transport Inc can show that Country A's practices are violations of the Agreement on Subsidies and Countervailing Measures, it will be able to take the case to its government in Country B to pursue a remedy, either by consultations with Country A or, if necessary, through a formal WTO dispute resolution procedure.

For each of Country A's government practices, General Transport Inc must consider several issues:

- whether there is a subsidy;
- whether the subsidy is prohibited or actionable;
- if actionable, whether the subsidy is specific; and
- if actionable, whether the subsidy causes one of the following:
    - injury to Country B's domestic bicycle industry;
    - nullification or impairment of Country B's benefits under GATT; or
    - serious prejudice to Country B's interests.

5.1 Direct payments

Country A's payments to Smiling Cycles Inc and Roadrunner Ltd would be considered financial contributions and clearly confer a benefit on those two companies. The payments are therefore subsidies under the Agreement on Subsidies and Countervailing Measures. Since they are paid only to two particular enterprises (Smiling Cycles Inc and Roadrunner Ltd), the payments are specific subsidies. They do not fall into the prohibited subsidies category, but they may be actionable subsidies. General Transport Inc will need to demonstrate that Country A's direct payments

1 The communication is available on europa.eu, the European Union's website.

cause injury to Country B's domestic bicycle industry by allowing Country A bicycle producers to export their bicycles cheaply to Country B, undercutting Country B producers (or at least one Country B producer – that is, General Transport Inc).

5.2 Construction of roads and bicycle paths

The provision of roads and paths as basic public infrastructure is an ordinary function of government, and it is possible that the paths and roads built by Country A's government fall under the 'general infrastructure' provision that is not considered a financial contribution. On the other hand, General Transport Inc should argue that, since the paths and roads were built specifically for Smiling Cycles Inc and Roadrunner Ltd (and would not otherwise have been built), the government of Country A is providing services to bicycle producers which would be classified as a financial contribution. The provision of the roads (depending on where they lead and who uses them) also clearly provides a benefit, since the two enterprises would have had to pay for this service in the marketplace, or perhaps could not have obtained the service at all, depending on Country A's regulations for new road construction. Therefore, the construction of the roads is arguably a subsidy.

If it is a subsidy, it is certainly specific, access to it being explicitly limited to only two specific enterprises in one particular industry. It is not a prohibited subsidy, as it is not contingent on either export performance or import substitution. Again, if General Transport Inc can show the injury to Country B's bicycle industry that Country A's road construction causes, the subsidy will be classified as actionable and may be challenged. However, General Transport Inc will have some factual hurdles to overcome in proving that Country A's provision of roads to its bicycle producers is the cause of General Transport Inc's economic woes in Country B. It will need to discount other possibilities, such as better-quality bicycles coming from the Country A producers or a failure of its domestic marketing campaign.

5.3 Credit provision

The issue around the credit provided by Country A's Private Bank to the two bicycle producers is whether the government is directing the bank to provide the credit on the favourable terms granted. This would most likely involve a factual inquiry into whether the government's 25% ownership of Country A's Private Bank is enough to provide it with any real control over the terms of credit granted by the bank. If it is, the government is providing a financial contribution and is also conferring a benefit, given the favourable terms.

The same arguments apply again regarding the rest of the case. The subsidy, if it is one, is clearly specific and is potentially actionable, depending on General Transport Inc's ability to show injury to Country B's bicycle industry.

Assuming that General Transport Inc can prove these violations of the Agreement on Subsidies and Countervailing Measures, it can seek either to remove the subsidies or to have Country B's government impose countervailing duties. In order to initiate an investigation into countervailing duties against Country A producers, General Transport Inc would ordinarily need the support of other Country B bicycle producers in two ways:

- so that the total bicycle output of those producers supporting an investigation is greater than the total bicycle output of those producers opposing one; and
- so that the total bicycle output of those producers supporting an investigation is at least 25% of Country B's total bicycle output.

In its application to initiate an investigation, General Transport Inc and its supporters must present evidence of the existence, amount and nature of the subsidy in question, as well as evidence of injury to the domestic bicycle industry and of the causal link between the subsidy and the injury. The authorities of Country B must then consider this evidence, conduct the investigation in accordance with the procedures in Part V of the Agreement on Subsidies and Countervailing Measures and make a determination as to whether to impose countervailing duties to offset the adverse effects of Country A's subsidies. This determination can be challenged in Country B's national courts, and also by Country A under the WTO dispute resolution process.

At all stages of the procedure, General Transport Inc would be advised to continue consultations and negotiations with the Country A authorities in order to achieve a mutually agreed solution without the need for countervailing duties or formal dispute resolution processes.

6. The *Canada – Autos* dispute: a case study

An agreement between Canada and the United States, known as the Auto Pact, allowed Canadian companies to import certain motor vehicles duty free. The companies' eligibility for the duty-free imports depended on companies meeting particular production-to-sales ratios. These ratios had the effect that, when the ratio was set at 100:100 or higher, an importing company could not sell in Canada any motor vehicles imported duty free unless it exported the same value of motor vehicles. When the ratio was set at less than 100:100, any exports of motor vehicles would allow a Canadian company to import (above its allowance already granted) an extra amount of vehicles duty free.

In July 1998 Japan requested consultations with Canada regarding these measures. A month later, the European Union also requested consultations. The consultations were not successful, and in February 1999 a single panel was established to hear both Japan's and the European Union's complaints against the Canadian measures. Together with various other arguments, Japan and the European Union claimed that the measures constituted a subsidy because the Canadian government was forgoing import duty revenue that it would otherwise have collected if the measures were not in place. They argued that the import duty exemption was therefore a financial contribution that conferred a benefit on the Canadian companies, under the terms of Article 1 of the Agreement on Subsidies and Countervailing Measures. Japan and the European Union also claimed that the subsidy was contingent upon export performance, since, whether the ratio was higher or lower than 100:100, the companies could not obtain the duty exemption without exporting.

The panel agreed with Japan and the European Union, finding that the import duty exemption was a subsidy and was contingent on export performance. The measure was thus held to be in violation of Article 3.1(a) of the Agreement on Subsidies and Countervailing Measures. Canada appealed this decision to the Appellate Body in March 2000. The Appellate Body supported Canada on several other aspects of the dispute, but on the subsidies issues referred to above, it upheld the panel's finding of violation. The Dispute Settlement Body then recommended that Canada remove the subsidy within 90 days of the Appellate Body's report (June 19 2000). This period was modified by arbitration to eight months, giving Canada until February 19 2001 to comply. Canada advised in March 2001 that it had complied with the recommendations and withdrawn the import duty exemption.[2]

7. Recommended resources

For further information on subsidies and the SCM Agreement, useful resources include the following:

- M Benitah, *The Law of Subsidies under the GATT/WTO System* (The Hague: Kluwer Law International, 2002).
- D van den Bossche, *The Law and Policy of the WTO: Text, Cases and Materials* (Cambridge: Cambridge University Press, 2005).
- M Matsushita *et al*, *The WTO: Law, Practice and Policy* (Oxford: Oxford University Press, 2003), especially Chapter 12.

2 *Canada – Certain Measures Affecting the Automotive Industry*, WT/DS139,142.

Dumping

---

1. A practical trade law problem

Country A, a large country with a planned non-market economy, produces laptop computers and sells them in Country B below the cost of production. Country B's Laptop Producers Association, whose members produce 40% of the total Country B production of laptops, is concerned about the actions of Country A's laptop producers. It fears that the cheap laptops from Country A, which are essentially identical to Country B's laptops, are reducing its share of the local laptop market. According to Country B's Laptop Producers Association, its members cannot compete on price with the laptops from Country A without losing money, as their profit margins are already quite small. Country A claims, in response, that it is in fact exporting laptops to Country B, at prices higher than available to consumers in Country A. Both countries are members of the World Trade Organisation (WTO). How could one advise Country B's Laptop Producers Association on what it can do to prevent injury to its members?

2. Dumping

When an exporting country sells its products in an importing country at a lower price than that at which the same products are sold in the exporting country's home market, the exporting country is said to be 'dumping'. Trade law prohibits this practice as a form of unfair price discrimination between nations and as contrary to the level playing field in international trade relations. If certain criteria are met, a claim of dumping can be successful and anti-dumping duties can be imposed to offset the damage done by the lower prices to the importing country's market. Anti-dumping measures are considered necessary because competition measures against predatory pricing are largely ineffective in a cross-border context. With growing international cooperation in the area of competition enforcement, there may eventually be less use for anti-dumping measures which have protectionist connotations.

Article VI of the General Agreement on Tariffs and Trade (GATT) provides the basic authorisation for anti-dumping duties to be imposed in certain cases. The Agreement on Implementation of Article VI of GATT 1994 (known as the Anti-dumping Agreement) adds more detail to the provisions, covering investigation, determination and application of anti-dumping duties.

2.1 What must be demonstrated in order to allow a government to impose anti-dumping duties?

The governments of WTO members can always decide for themselves whether to impose an extra duty on a particular imported product, but this decision will not always conform to their obligations under the WTO. If a duty is imposed and is challenged by another WTO member, the country imposing the duty must be able to justify it under WTO law or either remove it or face retaliation from the complainant.

To justify imposing anti-dumping duties, a WTO member must show three main factors:

- that dumping is occurring;
- that domestic industry producing a like product in the importing country is suffering material injury; and
- that there is a causal link between the two.

Proving that dumping is occurring is a relatively difficult task and very often involves more than a simple comparison of prices in the exporting and importing countries' markets. The Anti-dumping Agreement establishes various permitted methods for calculating the 'normal value' (the appropriate price of the product in the exporting country's market) and the 'export price' (the appropriate price of the product in the importing country's market). Once these two prices have been determined, a comparison can then be made to decide whether the exporter is dumping.

2.2 How is the normal value of a product calculated?

There are three permitted methods of calculating the normal value of a product. The basic case is determined by the price that consumers pay for the product "in the ordinary course of trade" in the exporting country. However, sales can sometimes be considered as not having been made in the ordinary course of trade, meaning that those sales are excluded from the calculation of normal value. This situation applies where the sales made in the exporting country market meet four criteria:

- the sales were made below cost;
- over an extended period of time;
- in substantial quantities; and
- at prices which do not allow for the recovery of costs within a reasonable time.

Article II of the Anti-dumping Agreement provides further definitions of these four criteria.

It is also possible that the product in question is not sold in the exporting country, or is sold in such small quantities as to prevent a proper comparison of prices in the exporting and importing countries' markets. The Anti-dumping Agreement provides that there are enough sales for comparison if the sales in the exporting country constitute at least 5% of the sales in the importing (or complainant) country, or if exporting country sales are less than 5% but are nevertheless 'of sufficient magnitude' to allow a fair comparison. If insufficient sales are found, the second and third permitted methods of calculating normal value may apply.

The second method involves calculating a 'constructed normal value'. This value is defined in the Anti-dumping Agreement as cost of production plus "a reasonable amount for administrative, selling and general costs and for profits". The Anti-dumping Agreement specifies the kinds of information on costs and expenses that can be used in the calculation, including, for example, start-up costs and non-recurring costs. Reasonable profits must be determined based on sales information from the particular exporter under investigation, or, where that is not possible, based on the profit "normally realized by other exporters . . . on sales of products of the same general category" in the exporting country market.

The third method calculates the normal value of a product by reference to its price when it (or a like product) is exported to an appropriate third country market, as long as that price is representative. For instance, if Country A claims that Country B is dumping laptops on its market, Country A could determine the normal value of the laptops by taking a representative price at which Country B exports the laptops to Country C. The Anti-dumping Agreement does not, however, define which third countries are considered 'appropriate' for the comparison.

Countries that operate under non-market economies, where domestic prices are substantially controlled by the government, are not always suitable for direct price comparisons. A relatively wide discretion is therefore allowed when calculating the normal value of products exported from such countries.

2.3 How is the export price of a product calculated?

As well as calculating the normal value of the product being exported, a party conducting an anti-dumping investigation must also calculate the product's export price. In general, the export price is simply the price at which the importer buys the product from the exporting country. However, this basic determination does not always apply; the export may be an internal company transfer, for instance, or the products may be bartered, or there may be a compensatory arrangement between exporter and importer. In these cases the 'constructed export price' is used. This is the price at which the imported goods are first resold to an independent buyer, or, if the goods are not resold or are resold in a different condition, any price determined on a reasonable basis.

2.4 What are the requirements for comparing the normal value and the export price?

Once the normal value and the export price of the product in question have been determined, the two prices must be fairly compared. This means that the comparison must be between prices at the same level of trade (normally the 'ex-factory level') and between prices of sales made at the same time. Differences in conditions and terms of sale, tax, quantities, physical characteristics and other differences must also be taken into account to adjust the normal value and/or export price for comparison. If currency conversion is required, the exchange rate to be used is the rate effective on the date of sale.

2.5 **How much anti-dumping duty may be imposed? What are dumping margins?**

Once the normal value and export price of the product in question have been determined, the margin of dumping must be determined. The margin of dumping essentially represents the advantage in monetary terms that the dumped product has over domestic like products, and is the basis for the amount of anti-dumping duty that may be imposed to counter this advantage. The dumping margin is usually calculated either by:

- a comparison of the weighted average normal value to the weighted average of all comparable export prices; or
- a comparison of normal value and export price on a 'transaction-to-transaction' basis.

A dumping margin must normally be calculated for each individual exporter in question, so that anti-dumping duties can be applied which are no higher than necessary to remove the injury to the domestic industry. However, in cases where there are a large number of exporters or producers, calculating individual dumping margins for each may not be practical, and so margins may be calculated for some statistically valid sample of a reasonable number of exporters or producers and then applied to all.

2.6 **How is material injury to a domestic industry shown?**

The first step in determining material injury to a domestic industry is to determine exactly which domestic industries are potentially concerned. This involves examination of which domestically produced products are like the exported product. The phrase 'like product' is defined in Article 2.6 as "a product which is identical, ie, alike in all respects", or if no such product exists, as a product which "has characteristics closely resembling those of the product under consideration". The domestic producers of the like product constitute the domestic industry allegedly being threatened by the dumping. A group of producers whose collective output constitutes a major proportion of the domestic production of the like product can also be considered itself as the domestic industry.

In exceptional circumstances, the requirement of injury may be satisfied when injury to only a particular part of the domestic industry can be shown, rather than to the whole. This is permitted when the importing country can be separated (perhaps geographically) into many individual markets (different geographic markets), with the producers in each market selling all (or almost all) of their production to consumers in the same geographic market, and consumer demand in each market being satisfied solely (or to a substantial degree) by producers in that market. If products are being dumped into one of these individual competitive markets and this is causing injury to the domestic producers in the individual market, the injury requirement is satisfied even though the dumping may injure only a small proportion of the importing country's domestic industry as a whole. Essentially, in these circumstances, each separate 'regional industry' is treated as a microcosm of the country's total domestic industry. When this situation arises and injury is found, duties must be imposed only on imported products destined for the area in question. If this is not constitutionally possible, the duties may be imposed without limitation unless the duties can be limited to specific producers which supply the area in question. The importing country must first give the exporting country an opportunity to cease the dumping or give a price undertaking, if the duties are to be imposed without limitation.

2.7 What is injury?

Three kinds of injury are accepted under the Anti-dumping Agreement:

- material injury to a domestic industry;
- threat of material injury to a domestic industry; or
- material retardation of the establishment of a domestic industry.

To establish material injury, a complainant country must examine the volume of dumped imports, their effect on prices of like products in the domestic market and the impact of the dumping on domestic producers of like products, taking into account all relevant economic factors such as actual or potential decline in sales, profits, output or market share. There is no definition of 'material', however. No single factor or combination of factors will necessarily determine the issue; each case must rather be taken as a whole in light of all the relevant circumstances.

To show a threat of material injury, relevant factors include the rate of increase of dumped imports, the capacities of the exporters and the likelihood of the lower-priced products increasing demand for more imports. The concept is not well defined beyond that, but the Anti-dumping Agreement does require claims of threat of material injury to be based on facts and not on allegation, conjecture or remote possibility. There is no explanation in the Anti-dumping Agreement on the scope of material retardation to the establishment of a domestic industry.

2.8 How is the causal link between the dumping and the injury proved?

A complainant country may have a strong case that dumping as defined under the Anti-dumping Agreement is occurring and that a domestic industry is suffering material injury. The last step in the argument is to prove that the dumping caused the injury being suffered. The Anti-dumping Agreement does not provide for any specific methods to do this, but allows the investigating authorities to establish their own analytical methods for an examination of "all relevant evidence". One element that must be examined, however, is "any known factors other than the dumped imports which at the same time are injuring the domestic industry". These might include:

- changes in demand or consumption patterns in the importing country market;
- any trade-restrictive or competitive practices in the exporting or importing countries' industries;
- technology development; and
- the productivity of the domestic industry.

The complaining country must aim to show that, after having examined all these other potential causes of the injury that their domestic industry is suffering, it is nevertheless the dumped imports from the exporting country that are the cause.

3. Procedural requirements

3.1 Who may commence an anti-dumping investigation?

The government of a WTO member state can carry out an anti-dumping investigation following a written request to do so, made "by or on behalf of the domestic industry". However, governments are authorised to commence an investigation only when there is evidence of enough support from domestic industry to warrant it. This means that, of the domestic producers that express an opinion to the authorities on commencing an investigation, the collective output of those in favour must be more than the collective output of those against. There is also a minimum threshold to reach, in that the collective output of those domestic producers supporting the initiation of an investigation must be more than 25% of the total production of the like product. (This threshold concerns the production of all domestic producers, whether or not they expressed an opinion on the investigation.)[1]

The written request must include evidence of the three factors necessary to justify imposing anti-dumping duties: dumping, injury and a causal link between the two. It must also include certain other "reasonably available" information relating to the claim, as follows:

- the identity of the applicant;
- the volume and value of domestic production of the like product in question
- a list of domestic producers of the like product and each one's share of the total domestic production;
- a description of the allegedly dumped product;
- the name of the exporting country in question;
- the identity of known exporters, foreign producers and domestic importers of the product;
- initial calculations of normal value and export price for the product in question, and any data used for these calculations;
- a history of changes in the volume of the allegedly dumped imports; and
- the effect of the imports on prices of domestic like products and on the domestic industry as a whole.[2]

A government can also commence an investigation on its own behalf, but only where it has sufficient evidence itself of dumping, injury and causal link.

If, after considering an application or during an investigation, the government authorities determine that there is not enough evidence, the application must be rejected or the investigation must be stopped. The Anti-dumping Agreement defines these situations as cases where:

- the margin of dumping is less than 2% of the export price; or
- the volume of allegedly dumped imports from the exporting country in question accounts for less than 3% of imports of the like product in the complaining country (unless dumped imports from several exporting

1 Article 5.4 of the Anti-dumping Agreement.
2 Article 5.2 of the Anti-dumping Agreement.

countries representing less than 3% each constitute together more than 7% of imports of the like product in the complaining country).[3]

3.2 How are investigations conducted?

The authorities must conduct anti-dumping investigations in accordance with procedures established by the Anti-dumping Agreement. All interested parties must be given an opportunity to present evidence and their views, and meetings between the parties must be arranged on request. Confidential and commercially sensitive information must be protected during the investigation. The investigating authorities must also provide the reasons and evidence on which the results of the investigation will be based to allow final opportunities for comment. Once an investigation has been initiated, the Anti-dumping Agreement requires that it last only 12 months or, in special circumstances, 18 months.

3.3 Provisional measures

After an investigation has proceeded for 60 days, the authorities are permitted to make a preliminary determination of dumping, injury and causation and impose provisional anti-dumping measures as a result. The Anti-dumping Agreement indicates that these provisional measures may be in the form of anti-dumping duties or, preferably, a security for the amount of the anti-dumping duty to be imposed. In general, the provisional measures are allowed to last only for a maximum of four months.

4. NAFTA and dumping

The North American Free Trade Agreement (NAFTA) does not contain its own anti-dumping regime, but allows each party to maintain its current laws. However, any modifications to a party's domestic anti-dumping regime must be notified to and discussed with the other parties. Chapter 19 of NAFTA also establishes a system of bi-national panels to hear appeals on anti-dumping matters under domestic law, as an alternative forum to the WTO for dumping dispute resolution.

5. European Union and dumping

The European Union's anti-dumping regime substantially mirrors the provisions of the WTO's Anti-dumping Agreement. An EU complainant company may apply, either directly or through its government, to the European Commission to have an investigation commenced into alleged dumping by a non-EU country. The same determinations of dumping, injury and causation apply under the EU regime as under the Anti-dumping Agreement. Before imposing anti-dumping duties, the commission must be satisfied that the costs of taking the measures are not disproportionate to the benefits to EU industry. The country against which the duties are imposed has the right to challenge the decision in the European Court of First Instance, or in the WTO's dispute settlement process if it is a WTO member. Council

3 Article 5.8 of the Anti-dumping Agreement.

Regulation (EC) 384/96 of December 22 1995, including amendments, establishes the EU anti-dumping regime.

6. A world trade law solution to the practical problem

Country B's Laptop Producers Association suspects that Country A's producers and exporters of laptop computers are engaging in dumping. Both Country B and Country A are members of the WTO, so the Anti-dumping Agreement applies to both countries. Country B's Laptop Producers Association and Country B may therefore be able to use the anti-dumping regime established by the Anti-dumping Agreement to push Country A to change the price at which it exports its laptop computers or legally to impose anti-dumping duties on Country A laptops to raise their price and avoid the injury to Country B's laptop industry.

Country B's Laptop Producers Association, as an industry association, is not a member of the WTO and cannot itself formally deal with Country A under the WTO system. However, since it represents the domestic laptop-producing industry, it should seek to have Country B government authorities commence an investigation into Country A's laptop computer export practices. The association will need to satisfy the Anti-dumping Agreement's procedural requirements in order to allow an investigation to be initiated. In particular, it must present to the Country B government a written application for an investigation. The application must set out the association's case with as much factual information as it can gather on the situation and the injury it is allegedly causing to Country B's laptop industry. The application must also be considered as being made "by or on behalf of the domestic industry". This means that, since the volume of laptop production of Country B's Laptop Producers Association members constitutes only 40% of Country B's total volume, the association's application will be rejected if other Country B laptop producers, representing 40% or more of the total volume of domestic laptop production, express their opposition to the investigation.

If the association's application is accepted, the Country B authorities will launch an investigation into Country A's laptop export trade to determine the extent of any dumping, any injury Country B's laptop industry is suffering and a causal link between these two circumstances. As mentioned above, the association must also present evidence on these matters in its application.

Country B's Laptop Producers Association and Country B must first show that dumping is in fact occurring, based on a comparison of the normal value and the export price of laptops. Despite Country A's claim that it is selling the laptops in Country B at a higher price than that at which they are sold in Country A, dumping may still be occurring if the normal value of the laptops can be shown to be higher than the export price. In Country A's case, given that it operates under a centrally planned, non-market economy, the price paid by consumers in Country A becomes less relevant in determining normal value. Further, the association may be able to show that the sales in Country A were not made "in the ordinary course of trade", depending on the evidence available. It appears that the laptops are sold in Country A below the cost of production, since the price there is even lower than the price in Country B and most likely does not allow for the recovery of costs within a reasonable time. If this price in Country A has persisted for an extended period of time in substantial quantities according to the Anti-dumping Agreement's definitions, sales made at that price in Country A may thus fit the criteria to be excluded from the normal value calculations, meaning that one of the other methods of calculation will have to be used.

Since there is no information on laptop exports to a third country, the constructed normal value approach will be the most useful. Country B's Laptop Producers Association must calculate the normal value of the laptops based on the cost of production plus a reasonable amount for administrative, sale and general costs, and for profits. The export price in this case should be straightforward to determine; it is simply the price at which Country A producers sell the laptops to Country B, as the sale appears to be an arm's-length market sale.

As long as a fair comparison is then made between the normal value and export price as determined, Country B's Laptop Producers Association can most likely mount a strong case that dumping is occurring since the export price is lower than the normal value of the laptops. The association and Country B can calculate a dumping margin, potentially to be imposed as an anti-dumping duty on laptops from Country A.

The association will also need to present evidence of injury or threatened injury to the domestic laptop industry, and of a causal link between the dumping and the injury. This complex analysis is highly dependent on the facts and evidence available to the investigating authorities and the specific situation of the country in question. If, after 60 days of the investigation, the Country B authorities have sufficient evidence of dumping, injury and causation to make a preliminary determination in the association's favour, they may impose provisional anti-dumping measures while the remainder of the investigation is more fully completed. On the other hand, if the dumping margin calculated by the Country B authorities is less than 2% of the export price, they must halt the investigation and the association will not be permitted to proceed any further with its claims of dumping. The investigation must also be halted if the volume of laptop imports from Country A represents less than 3% of Country B's laptop imports.

If the investigation results in Country B imposing anti-dumping duties, Country A may choose to initiate the WTO's formal dispute settlement procedure, beginning with consultations and leading to a panel or Appellate Body decision on the matter.

7. The *Argentina–Ceramic Tiles* dispute: a case study

In November 1999 Argentina imposed anti-dumping duties on imports of ceramic tiles from Italy, following an investigation by Argentina's trade authorities that had determined that dumping was occurring, Argentina's domestic industry was suffering material injury and there was a causal link between the two. As part of the investigation, Argentina had requested responses to a questionnaire from four Italian tile producers constituting around 70% of the tile trade between the two countries. The questionnaires sought information on the export price and normal value of the tiles, in order to allow a correct determination of the dumping margin that Argentina proposed to apply to each Italian exporter. However, Argentina then did not make use of the questionnaire responses, but applied a common margin to all four exporters based on information it had readily available.

The European Union (on Italy's behalf) requested consultations with Argentina on the matter in January 2000. The European Union claimed that the anti-dumping measures had been imposed in violation of the Anti-dumping Agreement – specifically, that Argentina had failed to:

- use information available to it;
- calculate individual margins for each exporter;
- consider physical differences between tiles exported to Argentina and tiles sold in Italy (which would affect the correct price of the tiles); and
- inform the exporters adequately of the reasons for its determination.

A panel was constituted to resolve the dispute and its report was released in September 2001. The panel agreed with all four of the European Union's claims. It found that the failure to use the questionnaire responses violated Article 6.8 of the Anti-dumping Agreement, which requires (in conjunction with Annex II, Article 6) that exporters be given an explanation and an opportunity to provide further details if information is rejected. The failure to calculate individual margins for each exporter violated Article 6.10 of the Anti-dumping Agreement, due essentially to Argentina's lack of explanation for doing so and its failure to request information required to make the calculations. The panel found further that Argentina violated Article 2.4 in that it should have considered the different tile colours and designs of exported tiles and those sold in Italy, which would have affected the normal value of the tiles and hence whether (or how much) dumping was occurring. Finally, Argentina violated Article 6.9 by not properly informing the exporters that their questionnaire responses would not be taken into account in the dumping determination.

The parties agreed that Argentina would have until April 5 2002 to comply with the panel's decision. Argentina eventually revoked the anti-dumping measures on April 24 2002.[4]

8. Recommended resources

For further information on dumping and the Anti-dumping Agreement, see the following:

- WTO Secretariat, *A Handbook of Anti-Dumping Investigations* (Geneva: WTO Press and Cambridge: Cambridge University Press, 2005).
- I Van Bael and J-F Bellis, *Anti-Dumping and Other Trade Protection Laws of the EC,* 4th ed (The Hague, Kluwer Law International, 2004).
- T Stewart and A Dwyer, *WTO Anti-Dumping and Subsidy Agreements: A Practitioner's Guide* (The Hague: Kluwer Law International, 2004).
- E Vermulst, *The WTO Anti-Dumping Agreement – A Commentary* (Oxford: Oxford University Press, 2006).

---

4 *Argentina–Definitive Anti-Dumping Measures on Imports of Ceramic Floor Tiles from Italy,* WT/DS189.

Services

1. A practical trade law problem

Prize-winning architectural firm Construct has created considerable worldwide interest through its buildings in its home country of Country A, a member of the World Trade Organisation (WTO). Construct was invited to submit drafts to an architectural competition in Country B and subsequently won the competition. However, before signing the contract, Country B's investor wants details from Construct on its submission of the plans and supervision of the building site.

Country B is a member of the WTO and has listed sector "CPC 8671 architectural services" in its schedule, with no limitations on market access. A border tax on temporary entry of professionals is listed under Country B's horizontal commitments as a limitation on national treatment under Mode 4, presence of natural persons. Country B's law requires architects to have local offices; only architects from neighbouring Country C, also a WTO member, are exempt from this requirement. However, all architects, whether domestic or foreign, are forbidden from sending plans to customers in Country B by email or post. In addition, Country B allows only 20 architectural firms to operate within its territory, as the government feels that it can better regulate the industry with a limited number.

Construct feels that these requirements are threatening its performance of the contract resulting from the architectural competition. How would one advise Construct in world trade law?

2. Services and GATS

During the Uruguay Round, services were included for the first time in the scope of the world trade negotiations. The General Agreement on Tariffs and Trade (GATT), concerned with international trade in goods, has existed since 1947, but it was only in January 1995, with the creation of the WTO, that the General Agreement on Trade in Services (GATS) was concluded. GATS is part of the WTO's Single Undertaking of the Uruguay Round, and all WTO members are therefore signatories to it and bound by the obligations it contains.

2.1 To what does GATS apply?

GATS applies to "measures by Members affecting trade in services". Measures include laws, regulations, rules, procedures, decisions and administrative action, and may be taken by any level of government as well as by non-governmental bodies exercising delegated powers. For a measure to affect trade in a service, it must have an effect on trade between two members in the service according to one of the four modes of supply. Governmental services "in the exercise of governmental authority" are excluded from the definition of 'services'.

2.2 What are services?

Services can be considered as intangible commodities satisfying human needs. Production and consumption of services generally occur simultaneously. Indeed, one classic definition of a service is "anything that you cannot drop on your foot"! In fact, services include many different categories and are traditionally separated into 12 core service sectors:[1]

- business services (including professional services and computer services);
- communication services;
- construction and related engineering services;
- distribution services;
- educational services;
- environmental services;
- financial services (including insurance and banking);
- health-related and social services;
- tourism and travel-related services;
- recreational, cultural and sporting services;
- transport services; and
- other services not included elsewhere.

These main sectors are then broken down into around 160 sub-sectors – some quite specific, such as 'maintenance and repair of vessels', and others relatively broad, such as 'entertainment services'.

2.3 What are modes of supply?

Goods are traded between countries in essentially one way: they are physically transported from one country to another. Services, on the other hand, can be traded in four different ways, called 'the four modes of supply':

- Cross-border supply – services supplied from the territory of one WTO member to the territory of another member. Examples include providing banking or legal services from one country to another via telephone or post;
- Consumption abroad – services consumed by a person in the territory of another member. Examples include tourism, education and healthcare services;
- Commercial presence – services provided by a company via a business presence (eg, an office) in another member's territory. Examples include domestic subsidiaries of foreign companies such as banks or hotel chains; and
- Presence of natural persons – services provided by persons temporarily entering another member's territory. Examples include the practices of professionals such as doctors, architects, accountants and teachers.

---

1 WTO doc MTN.GNS/W/120.

2.4 What is the structure of GATS? What are annexes and schedules?

GATS contains 29 articles that essentially set out the obligations of WTO members and the scope of those obligations, as well as some formalities and procedural issues. It also contains various annexes dealing with particular sectors and exemptions. Added to this is each member's schedule, which details the specific commitments the member makes in each sector.[2] The schedules use a positive list approach, meaning that a member assumes obligations for only those sectors inscribed into its schedule. This can be contrasted with a negative list approach, in which all service sectors would be automatically liberalised unless they were listed in a schedule. Once a sector is inscribed in a schedule, members can nevertheless place limitations on the obligations they wish to assume for that sector: these limitations are discussed below. There are also some obligations under GATS that are automatically imposed on members for all sectors, whether listed in their schedule or not: most favoured nation is one example.

Schedules are in fact composed of two sections: one for horizontal commitments and one for sector-specific commitments. Horizontal commitments set out limitations that apply across all sectors, while the sector-specific commitments contain limitations that apply only to the specified sector. Therefore, limitations might apply to a particular sector by virtue of a horizontal commitment in a member's schedule, even though no limitation is listed for that sector itself.

2.5 What are the basic obligations under GATS?

(a) ***Most favoured nation***

The most favoured nation principle, a longstanding element of international trade in goods, is also a key principle in trade in services under GATS. It provides that any privileges in services trade granted by one member to another must be automatically extended to all other members. Under GATS, the obligation is unconditional, meaning that it applies to all members, to all sectors – whether listed in the member's schedule or not – and for all modes of supply. Therefore, if Country A negotiates bilaterally to grant Country B preferential access in accounting services, this preferential access must immediately be granted to all other countries as well, even though Country A may not have listed accounting services in its GATS schedule. Other countries will be able to challenge Country A under GATS if it does not grant access to them.

At the time of signing GATS, members were allowed to submit exemptions from the most favoured nation principle in an annex on Article II. These were intended to last only 10 years (and thus should now have expired), but may be extended in time if members desire. The most favoured nation principle will not apply to any exemption listed in this annex, allowing members to maintain specific measures that favour one country over others. Countries' existing most favoured nation exemptions can be found in the WTO Services Database at http://tsdb.wto.org/wto/WTOHomepublic.htm.

---

2 The schedules are searchable online in the WTO Services Database at http://tsdb.wto.org/wto/WTOHomepublic.htm (June 2006).

(b) *National treatment*

The national treatment principle requires countries to treat both foreign and domestic service providers equally. Strictly speaking, foreign providers must be given treatment that is "no less favourable" than that given to domestic providers. This obligation implies the absence of all discriminatory measures that may modify the conditions of competition to the detriment of foreign services or service providers. It does not matter whether the treatment provided to foreign and domestic services and service providers is formally different or formally identical – what counts is the practical result of the treatment.

National treatment under GATS is a conditional obligation, meaning that it applies only to sectors specifically listed by a member in its GATS schedule. In addition, members may list limitations on how far they will guarantee national treatment. For instance, a member might impose certain conditions on foreign banks (but not domestic banks) wishing to operate in their territory. If these conditions were not inscribed as limitations on national treatment in the banking services sector in the member's schedule, they would be violations of the principle and liable to challenge. On the other hand, if banking services were not inscribed in the member's schedule at all, no challenge to the discriminatory conditions could be brought by other members.

Note that no new limitations on national treatment should be inscribed into a member's schedule; this opportunity passed after a member initially signed GATS. Since the goal of GATS is to produce ever-higher levels of service liberalisation, limitations inscribed by members can be added to or modified only if compensation is paid to adversely affected members. Article XXI sets out the procedures for modification of schedules.

(c) *Market access*

Once a specific sector is inscribed in a WTO member's schedule, there are certain restrictions on market access that the member is not permitted to impose. These include restrictions on:

- the number of service suppliers in the sector;
- the value of service transactions in the sector;
- the number of service operations or quantity of output in the sector;
- the number of persons employed in the sector;
- the type of legal entity or joint venture that may supply services in the sector; and
- the participation of foreign capital (eg, a maximum percentage limit on foreign shareholding).

As with national treatment, the market access obligation is conditional since it applies only once a sector is listed in a member's schedule. Members are similarly permitted to inscribe limitations to market access in their schedules. For example, a member might impose a limitation on market access by restricting the number of workers employed in the tourist guide services sector, with a view to reducing the human impact of tourism on an environmentally significant site.

Provided that this limitation is inscribed in the tourist guide services sector in the member's schedule, or if the sector as a whole is not contained at all in the schedule, then no challenge can be brought by other members against the limitation.

While new sectors may be added to a WTO member's schedule at any time, since this serves to open up the market of that particular member to further services liberalisation, removing a sector or modifying or adding to limitations imposed in a sector may result in compensation being paid to other adversely affected members. This also explains why the current Doha Round negotiations focus only on liberalisation of services.

2.6 What are the major exceptions allowed under GATS?

(a) General exceptions

GATS includes Article XIV, which was drafted based on the language of Article XX of GATT. It allows members to take any measures necessary to protect human, animal or plant life or health, as long as these measures do not result in arbitrary or unjustifiable discrimination, or operate as a disguised restriction on trade in services. Measures necessary to protect public morals or to maintain public order are also permitted, as well as other measures relating to safety, privacy, fraud, tax collection and double taxation.

Measures taken under these exceptions are not required to be listed anywhere in a member's schedule or in a GATS annex. Essentially, a member may take such measures unilaterally and would then rely on an exception if challenged by another member. The burden of proof falls on the member seeking to rely on the exception to show that:

- the measure is necessary to achieve the public goal sought (public order, human health, etc); and
- the measure does not result in arbitrary or unjustifiable discrimination or operate as a disguised restriction on trade.

For a measure to be necessary, it ordinarily must be the least trade-restrictive or least GATS-inconsistent measure available to the member (although the member does not have to demonstrate that every other possible measure is more trade restrictive than that taken).

Under Article XIV*bis*, members are allowed take measures that they consider "necessary for the protection of [their] essential security interests . . . in time of war or other emergency in international relations". As with the analogous exception in GATT, this is a largely self-judging exception, since it is again left to individual members to decide for themselves what constitutes their essential security interests or an emergency in international relations.

In this case, members must keep the GATS Council of Trade in Services informed of any measures taken under Article XIV*bis*. If challenged, the burden of proof still rests with the member taking the measures to demonstrate that they conform to the requirements of the exception.

(b) *Governmental services*

Any services provided "in the exercise of governmental authority" are excluded entirely from GATS, meaning that members make no commitments at all to other members regarding such services. This relates to services "supplied neither on a commercial basis, nor in competition with one or more service suppliers" and would include services such as police, fire brigade and tax collection.

In light of recent trends towards privatisation of many traditionally public services such as water, electricity and even prisons, there are suggestions that the governmental authority exception is much smaller than it appears. Where a fee is charged for these services above their cost, for instance, this may indicate that the service is being provided on a commercial basis (regardless of the margin involved) and would thus be included in the scope of GATS. Also, in cases where a private provider supplies a service alongside a governmental provider (eg, public and private schools operating in the same environment), it is possible that the government will then be 'in competition' with the private service provider, with the result that the sector is not covered by the governmental authority exception and must comply with all general GATS obligations. The scope of this exception is therefore somewhat unclear.

(c) *Bilateral or regional trade agreements*

In certain circumstances, members are exempted from the most favoured nation principle where they have concluded bilateral or multilateral/regional agreements on services trade liberalisation. The agreement must have "substantial sectoral coverage" and must remove "substantially all discrimination" between the parties. The history and context of trade liberalisation and economic integration between the parties may be considered in determining whether these conditions have been met. These requirements are also relaxed slightly where the parties are developing countries.

This means in practical terms that if, for instance, Member A has concluded a treaty with Member B granting certain services trade privileges to Member B, and that treaty meets the conditions on sectoral coverage and discrimination, then the most favoured nation principle will not apply to Member A. No other member could challenge Member A claiming that it has breached its most favoured nation obligations under GATS by not extending the privilege granted to Member B to all other members.

(d) *Other specific exceptions*

The maritime transport sector is excluded entirely from GATS, unless members decide to make specific commitments in the sector themselves. Measures affecting air traffic rights and directly related services are also excluded, as they are considered to be covered already under the Chicago Convention. Three other services in the air transport industry – aircraft repair and maintenance, the selling and marketing of air transport services and computer reservation systems – are nevertheless included.

Trade in services may also be restricted in cases of "serious balance-of-payments and external financial difficulties". This allows a member to restrict services trade in appropriate cases in order to maintain domestic financial reserves. The restrictions must not discriminate among members, must be only those necessary to deal with the circumstances and must avoid unnecessary damage to other members' interests.

2.7 Why are financial services, transport and telecommunications services different?

Services such as banks, train companies and telecommunications operators are commonly required to perform other services: for example, to allow service providers to travel to or contact their customers, and to transport goods necessary to perform services. These services have gained special recognition in several annexes to GATS covering financial services, transport services and telecommunications services.

3. NAFTA and services

Chapter 12 of the North American Free Trade Agreement (NAFTA) imposes obligations on its three parties in the field of services broadly similar to those imposed under GATS. The major difference is that NAFTA takes a negative list approach, meaning that all service sectors are automatically covered, except for financial services, air transportation services and government procurement. However, NAFTA parties can choose to opt out of coverage for other services by listing them in the annexes to NAFTA. When considering a case under NAFTA, complainants must therefore check that the service sector in question is not one of the generally excluded sectors and, further, has not been specifically excluded by the party against which the complaint is made. Otherwise, NAFTA cannot apply.

Whereas GATS applies in covered sectors to measures affecting trade in services, NAFTA applies to five measures, affecting:

- the production, marketing, distribution, sale and delivery of a service;
- the purchase or use of a service;
- the access to and use of distribution or transportation systems in connection with the provision of a service;
- the presence of a foreign service provider in a party's territory; and
- the provision of financial security as a condition for providing a service.

For NAFTA to apply, the measures must relate to three of GATS's four modes of supply: consumption abroad, presence of natural persons and cross-border supply. The fourth mode of supply, commercial presence, is covered by a NAFTA provision that prevents a party from requiring that foreign service providers establish a domestic office or residence before they may provide their service in that party's territory.

The basic two obligations of national treatment and most favoured nation apply under NAFTA as under GATS. NAFTA requires parties to provide whichever treatment is better, flowing from these two obligations. NAFTA does not grant any rights of entry or employment to one party's citizens in respect of other parties. It also does not prevent each party's government from providing public services in a manner "not inconsistent" with NAFTA.

There are specific provisions in NAFTA relating to telecommunications services and financial services. Chapter 13 sets out obligations allowing for reasonable and non-discriminatory conditions of access to telecommunications in order to provide cross-border services, while Chapter 14 grants certain rights (including national treatment and most favoured nation) to financial institutions to operate in the territory of foreign NAFTA parties.

4. The European Union and services

The freedom to provide cross-border services within the European Union is one of the fundamental freedoms contained in the EC Treaty and is "central to the effective functioning of the EU Internal Market".[3] The scope of the freedom has been comprehensively examined by the European Court of Justice in its jurisprudence, a guide to which is available from the EU website.[4] A new attempt was recently undertaken to liberalise services with the Services Directive. One of the key elements – to legislate a country of origin principle according to which service providers would have to comply only with their own domestic services legislation – was rejected. New initiatives focus on making provisions more transparent and facilitating compliance through online information and applications.

As regards non-EU service providers wishing to operate within the European Union, there is no particular European regime. EU law has implemented the obligations established under GATS by which each EU member state is bound.

5. A world trade law solution to the practical problem

Four particular circumstances are threatening Construct:

- the border tax on temporary professional entry into Country B;
- the requirement for architects (except those from Country C) to maintain a local office;
- the prohibition on sending architectural plans by email or post; and
- the restriction on the number of architects operating in Country B.

Construct would like to remove all of these problems, and GATS is potentially the tool to allow it to do that.

5.1 Does GATS apply?

GATS applies to "measures affecting trade in services". The four problems are all laws of Country B, which is enough to define them as 'measures'. The laws all affect the supply of architectural services from one country to another according to one or more modes of supply:

- The first problem relates to Mode 4, presence of natural persons;
- The second problem relates to Mode 3, commercial presence;
- The third problem relates to Mode 1, cross-border supply; and
- The fourth problem relates to Modes 1 and 3.

Therefore, the problems are all "measures affecting trade in services" and GATS will apply.

---

3 http://europa.eu.int/comm/internal_market/services/principles_en.htm.
4 http://ec.europa.eu/internal_market/services/index_en.htm.

5.2 What are Country B's GATS commitments?

Country B is a WTO member and is therefore bound by all the general obligations in GATS, including the most favoured nation principle across all sectors. It has not listed any exemptions to the most favoured nation principle in an Article II annex, so any benefits that it grants to one member must be automatically extended to all other members. It also has no bilateral or regional services trade arrangements in place under Article V that might lessen its most favoured nation commitments.

Country B has listed "CPC 8671 architectural services" in its GATS schedule, with the result that the sector is bound by the conditional obligations of GATS, including national treatment and market access. These obligations are decreased by one factor: the limitation on national treatment that Country B has listed as a horizontal commitment. The limitation thus applies across all sectors, to allow Country B to impose a border tax on any professionals, including architects, entering its territory temporarily in order to provide a service.

5.3 Do any of Country B's measures violate its GATS commitments?

There are several likely violations of GATS commitments arising from Country B's measures.

As noted above, Country B is under a most favoured nation obligation to extend any benefits granted in favour of one country to all other countries. The exemption for Country C architects from the local office requirement must therefore be extended so that all other members, including Country A, are exempt from the local office requirement. In other words, the requirement must be removed entirely, as it violates the most favoured nation obligation under GATS.

The prohibition on sending architectural plans by email or post applies to both domestic and foreign architects, and so appears to be non-discriminatory and permissible, since all providers are being treated equally. However, on closer inspection, the prohibition serves to modify the conditions of competition between foreign and domestic providers. The only method of delivery permitted by the law is physical delivery by the architect to the client, which is clearly easier for a Country B-an architect to achieve than a foreign one in light of problems such as geographical location, transport costs and immigration and customs issues. The result is that foreign architects are left less competitive than domestic architects, a situation not permitted under GATS. The prohibition is not listed as a limitation on national treatment in Country B's GATS schedule, and so it violates Country B's national treatment commitments.

Under the market access provisions of GATS, members are not permitted to maintain restrictions on the number of service suppliers in any sector inscribed in their schedule. Since the architectural services sector is inscribed in Country B's schedule, the restriction on the number of architects operating in Country B is not permitted by GATS. To be allowed to maintain this measure, Country B would need to list it as a limitation on market access for this sector.

The border tax on temporary professional entry would ordinarily violate the principle of national treatment, since it discriminates between domestic and foreign service providers by imposing an additional cost on foreign providers and making them less competitive than domestic providers. Country B has not listed any limitations on national treatment specifically for the architectural services sector. However, because the limitation is listed as a horizontal commitment in Country B's schedule, it applies across all sectors in the schedule (including "CPC 8671 architectural services"). Hence this violation is permitted and cannot be challenged by Construct.

5.4 What is the likely outcome for Construct?

Given that private companies or firms cannot bring claims against WTO member governments, Construct should first contact the trade department in the Country A government and explain the situation. Following the WTO dispute resolution process, Country A would then request consultations with Country B on the matter. If no mutually acceptable solution can be found, Country A may choose to request the establishment of a WTO panel to hear the case. However, although dispute resolution in the WTO operates according to relatively strict timelines, Construct may prefer not to wait for the panel process, finding alternative solutions such as opening an office in Country B, delivering the plans in person, paying the tax imposed as an additional cost to its business or partnering with an architectural firm from Country B to avoid the numerical restriction.

If the dispute were to proceed to a panel then, based on the discussion above, the panel would likely find that the local office requirement, the email/post prohibition and the numerical restriction are all violations of GATS and must be repealed by Country B. The border tax would be allowed to stand, but Construct may accept this and choose not to send representatives to Country B in person to supervise the building site, perhaps hiring Country B's workers instead.

6. The *US – Gambling* dispute: a case study

The United States maintained a collection of laws at federal, state and local levels of government that addressed online gambling. In March 2003 Antigua and Barbuda requested consultations with the United States regarding these laws, claiming that they amounted to a prohibition on the cross-border supply (ie, via the Internet) of gambling and betting services contrary to the GATS commitments made in the sector by the United States. Specifically, Antigua and Barbuda argued (among other things) that the US prohibitions amounted to a limitation on the number of service suppliers using the cross-border mode of supply by effectively imposing a quota of zero. The United States claimed in response that the measures were justified by the general exceptions to GATS in Article XIV, as being measures necessary for the protection of public morals.

A panel was established to hear the case in July 2003. The panel's report was delivered in November 2004, following an extension of time and a suspension of proceedings (later resumed) while the parties again attempted negotiations for a mutually acceptable solution. The panel largely agreed with Antigua and Barbuda, finding that the United States had breached its market access commitments. The panel also held that the laws in question did relate to public morals, but were not necessary to protect public morals; the United States therefore could not rely on the general exception.

Both parties appealed various aspects of the decision to the Appellate Body, which gave its judgment in April 2005. The Appellate Body agreed with the panel that the United States had breached its market access commitments, but found that the measures were to be considered necessary to protect public morals. However, the Appellate Body also found that the United States had not shown on the evidence that the measures were applied to domestic as well as foreign gambling service suppliers. This meant that the measures were being applied in a manner constituting arbitrary or unjustified discrimination between countries. Therefore, the Appellate Body decided that the general exception did not apply and that the United States was in violation of its GATS obligations.

Following arbitration, it was determined that the United States would have until April 3 2006 to implement the Appellate Body's decision by amending its laws as necessary. In May 2006 Antigua and Barbuda prepared to challenge the steps towards implementation taken by the United States and the disagreement continued.[5]

7. Recommended resources

For further information on services and GATS, certain publications are particularly useful, including the following:

- WTO Secretariat, *Guide to GATS, An Overview of Issues for Further Liberalization* (The Hague: Kluwer Law International, 2000).
- International Trade Centre, *Business Guide to the General Agreement on Trade in Services* (Geneva: ITC, 2001).
- M Krajewski, *National Regulation and Trade Liberalization in Services* (The Hague: Kluwer Law International, 2003).

5 *United States – Measures Affecting the Cross-Border Supply of Gambling and Betting Services*, WT/DS285

IP rights

1. A practical trade law problem

The logo of Mucci, a famous fashion house based in Country A, is well known worldwide due to a long history of marketing and promotion. Mucci's logo is protected by trademark law in Country A and in other countries where it sells its products (which include handbags, clothes and shoes). Mucci has recently discovered that a company in Country B is producing a range of handbags bearing the Mucci logo without authorisation. Mucci investigates the situation with the Country B's judicial authorities, but finds that the company has registered the logo as a trademark in Country B, and that using another's trademark without authorisation is in fact not prohibited according to Country B's law.

Mucci also holds a patent on a machine that produces handbags more quickly and of a higher quality than most of Mucci's international competitors. The patent is registered in various countries including Country A and Country C. Mucci discovers that a company in Country C has constructed an identical machine to produce handbags, infringing Mucci's patent. However, it finds that, as a foreign company, it does not have the right to bring a patent infringement case in Country C's judicial system.

Country A, Country B and Country C are all members of the World Trade Organisation (WTO). Mucci wishes to stop Country B's company from using the Mucci logo on its handbags. It also wants to prevent Country C's company from making handbags with the infringing machine. Advise Mucci.

2. IP rights

The Agreement on Trade-Related Aspects of Intellectual Property Rights (TRIPs) was included as Annex 1C of the Marrakesh Agreement signed in 1994 that established the WTO. TRIPs covers IP rights including copyrights, patents, trademarks, geographical indications, circuit layouts, industrial designs and trade secrets, and it brings these rights into the multilateral trading system for the first time. TRIPs was intended to combat the barrier to international trade that existed in inadequate protection of IP rights in some countries. Goods with a significant proportion of their value contained in their design or brand name, for instance, could be imported and then copied to produce counterfeits with relative impunity. This acted as a strong disincentive for the producers of these goods to export them into countries with weak IP rights protection. The goal of TRIPs was therefore to establish harmonised international rules on intellectual property and effective enforcement mechanisms and dispute settlement to ensure the removal of this barrier to trade.

2.1 What are the basic principles underlying the TRIPs Agreement?

TRIPs adopts two of the major principles that underpin many of the WTO's agreements – most favoured nation and national treatment. In the context of TRIPs, these principles have two consequences:

- Any advantage in IP rights protection that one country grants to another country must be extended unconditionally to all other countries – that is, all nations must be treated in the same manner as the most favoured nation; and
- Countries must treat foreigners no less favourably than they treat their own citizens in terms of IP rights protection.

2.2 What kinds of IP laws must countries have under TRIPs?

Part II of TRIPs implements the harmonisation of IP laws in WTO member states by setting out the required laws on each of the branches of intellectual property covered by TRIPs. In some cases, the level of protection required is that established under earlier conventions of the World Intellectual Property Organisation (WIPO). TRIPs therefore incorporates by reference the provisions of the Berne Convention (on copyright) and the Paris Convention (on patents and industrial designs).[1] In other areas, TRIPs adds new levels of protection or requires higher levels than under the two conventions.

(a) Copyright

The basic requirements for protection of copyright under TRIPs are those set out in Articles 1 to 21 of, and the appendix to, the Berne Convention as amended in 1971. The convention defines:

- the material that is to be protected (including books, other writings, musical compositions, drawings, paintings and other works);
- the rights that are granted to authors of protected materials (reproduction, translation, public performance, broadcasting, adaptation and other rights); and
- the term for which these rights must be granted (generally, for a period of the life of the author plus 50 years, after which time the work enters the public domain and may be freely copied, translated, performed etc).

The convention also defines certain allowed limitations to the rights granted, including:

- reproduction of political speeches or speeches made during legal proceedings;
- reproduction for teaching purposes; and
- reproduction in the course of presenting news and current affairs.

Moral rights (the right to be identified as the author of a work and to object to any derogatory action in relation to the work which would prejudice the author's honour or reputation) are excluded entirely from TRIPs's incorporation of the convention.

1 The Berne and Paris Conventions are available on the WIPO website at http://www.wipo.int/treaties/en/.

TRIPs contains several other specific provisions. Article 9.2 restates the copyright principle that protection extends only to expressions and not to ideas, procedures, methods of operation or mathematical concepts. Computer programs are protected as literary works under Article 10.1, regardless of whether the programs are in the form of source or object code. Databases are protected by reason of the particular selection or arrangement of the data held in them (although the information stored may itself not be copyright protected). Article 11 grants authors of computer programs and cinematographic works the right to authorise or prohibit the commercial rental of their works, although for cinematographic works this applies only where rental has led to widespread copying which is materially impairing the author's exclusive right of reproduction.

As mentioned above, the general term of protection under the convention and TRIPs is the life of the work's author plus 50 years. In some cases, the convention allows for different term lengths:

- For cinematographic works, countries are permitted to grant terms lasting until 50 years after the work has been publicly released with the author's consent. If such a release does not occur within 50 years after the work was made, countries may also grant a term lasting until 50 years after the making of the work.
- For anonymous or pseudonymous works, the term lasts until 50 years after the work was lawfully released to the public, unless the name used is clear enough to identify the author or the author chooses to reveal his identity, in which case the general term applies.
- For photographic works and works of applied art, a minimum term of 25 years from the work's making must be granted.

TRIPs adds the requirement that, whenever a protection term is calculated on a basis other than the life of a person (eg, for cinematographic works or anonymous works), a minimum term of 50 years from the end of the calendar year of authorised publication must be granted. If the work was not published within 50 years of its making, a minimum of 50 years from the end of the calendar year of making must be granted. This additional requirement does not apply to photographic works and works of applied art.

Any limitations or exceptions to exclusive rights granted by WTO members must, under Article 13 of TRIPs, still allow for a normal exploitation of the work and must be applied in a manner that does not unreasonably prejudice the legitimate interests of the right holder.

TRIPs grants performers the right to prevent recordings of live performances and unauthorised wireless broadcasting and communication to the public of live performances. Producers of sound recordings are granted exclusive reproduction and rental rights, although where a system of commercial rental of sound recordings that fairly compensates right holders exists as at April 15 1994, the system may remain as long as it does not materially impair the exclusive reproduction rights of right holders. These rights must last for at least 50 years from the end of the calendar year in which the recording was made or the performance took place.

(b) Trademarks

Article 15 of TRIPs sets out the kinds of sign that must be protected as trademarks in WTO members and the minimum protection that these signs must be given.

Essentially, signs that are capable of distinguishing one company's goods or services from those of another must be registrable as trademarks. Signs can include words, personal names, letters, numerals, figurative elements and combinations of colours, or any combination of these. TRIPs allows members to require that signs be visually perceptible (therefore excluding, for example, sounds and smells), although members can permit registration of such signs as trademarks if they wish.

Enterprises within WTO members must be permitted to apply for registration of a sign as a trademark despite not having actually used the sign, although members are permitted under TRIPs to refuse registration on grounds of non-use. Enterprises must, however, be given three years from the date of application in which to use the trademark applied for; only after this period has expired can members refuse a trademark application on grounds of non-use.

Once a trademark is registered in respect of particular goods or services, its owner must be granted the exclusive right to prevent others from using an identical or similar sign in respect of identical or similar goods or services, where the use would result in a likelihood of confusion. Confusion is to be presumed if an identical sign is used in respect of identical goods.

If a trademark is well known in a particular country, the Paris Convention (incorporated into TRIPs by Article 2.1) requires members to refuse or cancel registration of, and to prohibit the use of, a mark used in respect of identical or similar goods that is liable to create confusion with the well-known mark. Article 16.2 of TRIPs also extends that protection to services, while Article 16.3 extends it to goods or services that are not similar to those in respect of which the well-known mark was registered. This latter protection means that a party may not use another party's well-known mark in respect of goods or services not similar to those which the well-known mark covers, if this use would suggest a connection between the goods or services and the owner of the mark, and if the interests of the owner are likely to be damaged by the use.

The term of trademark protection must be no less than seven years, but must also be indefinitely renewable. Exceptions may be made to trademark protection (eg, the fair use of a descriptive term in a trademark), as long as these exceptions take account of the legitimate interests of the trademark owner and other parties.

Trademarks must not be cancelled on grounds of non-use unless there has been an uninterrupted period of at least three years of non-use. If the trademark owner can nevertheless show valid reasons based on the existence of obstacles to use, the trademark must not be cancelled. Valid reasons include import or other government restrictions on goods or services covered by the trademark. Use of a trademark by a party under the control of the trademark owner must be recognised as use for the purposes of preventing cancellation.

(c) Geographical indications

Geographical indications identify goods as originating in the territory of a WTO member, or a region or locality of the member, such as Champagne, Roquefort or

Tequila. In cases where a particular quality, reputation or other characteristic of the goods can be attributed to their geographical origin, such geographical indications must be protected under TRIPs. Legal means must exist for interested parties to prevent the use of indications which mislead the public as to a good's geographical origin, or which constitute unfair competition as defined in Article 10*bis* of the Paris Convention.

Under Article 22.3 of TRIPs, trademarks that use geographical indications in a way that misleads the public as to the real place of origin of the goods or services covered by the trademark must be refused or cancelled upon the request of an interested party.

Wines and spirits are protected under additional measures in Article 23. Members' legal systems must provide means to prevent geographical indications being used for wines or spirits not originating in the place referred to by the indication. This obligation applies even if the public is not misled, there is no unfair competition, the true origin of the wines or spirits is shown, or words such as 'imitation', 'style', 'kind' or 'type' are used together with the geographical indication.

Exceptions to these requirements are set out in Article 24. The main exceptions recognised are:

- when a geographical indication has become the generic term for describing a product (eg, 'cheddar' now refers to a particular kind of cheese rather than a specific cheese originating from the British town of Cheddar);
- when an indication has previously been registered in good faith as a trademark; and
- when an indication is not protected, ceases to be protected or falls into disuse in its country of origin.

In general, rights acquired before TRIPs was signed (April 15 1994) will also not be prejudiced by any of its provisions.

(d) Patents

TRIPs states that WTO members must allow patents to be registered for any invention in all fields of technology, whether products or processes, without discrimination as to place of invention and whether products are locally produced or imported. The rules of novelty, inventive step (non-obviousness) and commercial application (usefulness) must be satisfied before a patent is obliged to be granted. Three exceptions apply:

- Members do not have to grant patents over inventions, the prevention of the commercial exploitation of which is necessary to protect public morality – for example, inventions dangerous to human health or seriously prejudicial to the environment.
- Members may refuse patents over diagnostic, therapeutic and surgical methods for the treatment of humans or animals.
- Plants, animals and biological processes for their production are not required to be patentable. This does not include micro-organisms or non-biological or micro-biological processes for producing plants or animals, all of which may

be patentable. Plant varieties must also be protected either by patents or by some other specialised system.

The exclusive rights conferred on an owner by a patent must include:

- for products, the right to make, use, offer for sale, sell and import the product;
- for processes, the right to use, offer for sale, sell and import the product obtained directly by the process, as well as the right to prevent others from using the process; and
- the right to assign or transfer the patent, and to conclude licensing contracts.

Under TRIPs, members must grant patent protection for at least 20 years from the patent filing date. Members must also require patent applicants to disclose their invention in sufficiently clear terms so as to allow it to be carried out by a person skilled in the art. Article 32 further specifies that members must provide an opportunity for judicial review of any decision to revoke or forfeit a patent.

For process patents, courts in WTO members are required to have the power to order an alleged infringer to prove that, despite an identical product being obtained, the process used to obtain it is different from the process patented by the complainant.

Compulsory licensing of patented material is permitted under TRIPs. However, certain conditions set out in Article 31 must be met for the licensing to be valid:

- The party seeking to use the patented material must have tried (but failed) to obtain a licence from the patent holder on reasonable terms and within a reasonable time;
- The patent holder must be paid adequately, in light of the economic value of the licence; and
- Decisions to grant compulsory licences must be subject to judicial or other independent review by a distinct higher authority.

Especially with regards to essential medicines, this provision was controversial and is currently being amended, incorporating the right for developing countries to grant compulsory licences for endemic diseases.

2.3 How must countries enforce IP rights protection under TRIPs?

Apart from setting out the minimum standards of protection that WTO members must have for IP rights, Part III of TRIPs also establishes a minimum regime required to enforce these rights.[2]

Article 41 defines some basic features of the required IP rights enforcement regime:

- Members' laws must permit effective action against infringement of IP rights;
- There must be expeditious remedies in order to prevent infringement;

2 Note that some also claim it increasingly establishes a maximum regime above which countries are not allowed to grant IP rights protection.

- Remedies available must act as a deterrent to further infringement; and
- Due process must be accorded, meaning that procedures must be fair and equitable, not unnecessarily complicated or costly nor unreasonably slow, with decisions based only on evidence in respect of which parties were given an opportunity to be heard, and judicial review being available.

There is no requirement that any separate system of IP rights protection be set up outside members' general legal systems, nor that any resources be diverted from general law enforcement to enforcement of IP rights in particular.

Further due process requirements on notice, appearances, representation, evidence and confidential information are given in Article 42. Courts must, for instance, be able to order the production from one party of evidence they hold that is beneficial to the other party.

2.4 What remedies and provisional measures must WTO members be able to grant for infringement of IP rights?

Articles 44 to 46 deal with the remedies that must be available for IP rights infringement. Members must be empowered to grant injunctions to prevent infringement, as well as compensation for injury suffered from deliberate or reckless infringement, and expenses including attorneys' fees. Members may also choose to grant recovery of profits and/or payment of pre-established damages, even in cases where the infringer did not act in bad faith. In order to create effective deterrents to infringement, judicial authorities must further have the power either to dispose of infringing goods outside the channels of commerce or, where legally possible, to destroy them. The same requirement applies to materials and implements used in the infringement. The remedies ordered must always be proportional to the seriousness of the infringement, also taking into account third parties' interests. For trademark infringements, simply removing the unlawfully affixed trademark is not considered enough to allow the goods to be sold.

To avoid ongoing infringement while a court determines the availability of the remedies discussed above, or to preserve evidence relating to an alleged infringement, members must also be able to grant provisional measures. Complainants can be required to produce certain information, such as proof that they are in fact the rights holder, evidence that their right is being infringed and information necessary to identify the goods concerned. In cases where delay is likely to cause irreparable harm to the IP rights holder, or where there is a demonstrable risk of destruction of evidence, provisional measures can be adopted without notifying the alleged infringer. Notification must be nevertheless given as early as possible, and at the latest once the measures have been adopted.

Complainants can be required to give a security or equivalent assurance to judicial authorities, in order to guard against abusive allegations of infringement. The provisional measures must also be reviewed upon request by the alleged infringer and may be modified, revoked or confirmed. If the complainant does not commence proceedings leading to a decision on the merits within a reasonable time as determined by the authorities (or the longer of 20 working days and 31 calendar days, if no determination is made), the provisional measures must be revoked on request by the alleged infringer. Members must also have the power to grant compensation to the alleged infringer for injury from provisional measures in cases where the measures are revoked or lapse due to any act or omission by the complainant, or if no infringement is subsequently found.

The remedies outlined above are minimum standards that TRIPs imposes on WTO members. Parties complaining of IP infringement claim not under TRIPs, therefore, but under the infringing country's domestic law, with the procedures established and remedies offered by that country's domestic legal system. The use of TRIPs lies in cases where complainants encounter obstacles to the protection of their IP rights in other countries; in such cases, complainants can mount arguments based on TRIPs obligations that the infringing country's laws on intellectual property are not sufficient or that its enforcement mechanisms are inadequate to meet TRIPs standards.

3. NAFTA and IP rights

The substantive rights on IP protection found in Chapter 17 of the North American Free Trade Agreement (NATFA) are essentially the same as those in TRIPs, with the same obligations also on enforcement systems and availability of domestic legal measures for complaints and review. The national treatment principle applies, requiring each NAFTA party to provide to foreigners IP protection no less favourable than is provided to its own nationals.

4. The European Union and IP rights

IP rights within the European Union are protected under each country's national laws, with TRIPs obligations as a minimum. Directive 2004/48/EC introduces certain EU-wide enforcement provisions, including:

- the availability of interlocutory injunctions (granted pending the final determination of a case);
- seizure of infringers' bank accounts to ensure payment of damages;
- recall of infringing goods; and
- a choice of lump-sum damages or compensation for lost profits.[3]

5. A world trade law solution to the practical problem

Mucci has encountered two problems: the inadequate trademark laws of Country B and its inability to access the Country C courts to enforce its patent rights. Under TRIPs, Country B and Country C are bound to provide certain levels of IP protection, and the trade authorities of Mucci's home government in Country A may therefore be able to initiate a WTO dispute procedure to force Country B and Country C to change their IP regimes.

---

3 Further information on the EU regime is available from the Europa website at http://ec.europa.eu/internal_market/copyright/index_en.htm (copyright) and http://ec.europa.eu/internal_market/indprop/index_en.htm (patents, designs and trademarks).

Country B has allowed a company to register Mucci's internationally known logo as a trademark without Mucci's authorisation. Mucci is able to sue the company in Country B's courts, but has found that the company's actions are legal under the law of Country B, meaning that Mucci would simply lose its case. However, the Paris Convention, incorporated into TRIPs, requires countries to refuse or cancel the registration of well-known trademarks, under its special provisions on such marks. TRIPs recognises that such marks may become well known due to years of promotion, whether or not the trademark has been used or the products have been available for purchase in a particular country. Article 16(1) of TRIPs also requires that the owner of a registered trademark in respect of certain goods be able to prevent others from using the trademark on identical goods, where the use would be likely to confuse. Here, the company's use of Mucci's logo would not be illegal in Country B even if Mucci were registered as the trademark owner.

Mucci can therefore demonstrate violations of TRIPs, and a successful WTO case against Country B would result in a WTO recommendation that Country B change its IP laws so that well-known marks may not be used or registered except by their owner, and so that trademark owners may prevent others from using their mark without authorisation. This would then allow Mucci to register its logo as a trademark in Country B and to use Country B's courts (if necessary) to prevent the company from producing handbags bearing its logo.

In Country C, the patent laws themselves pose no problem to Mucci, but it has found itself unable to enforce its rights through Country C's domestic courts. Part III of TRIPs sets out certain minimum legal standards that members must provide to allow IP rights to be enforced. Article 41(1) requires members to ensure that enforcement procedures are available under their law, in order to permit effective action against acts of infringement. Article 42(1) further specifies that civil judicial proceedings must be available to rights holders (in this case, including Mucci) concerning the enforcement of IP rights covered by TRIPs. By preventing Mucci from bringing an action, Country C is in breach of these TRIPs provisions.

While a successful case in the WTO would not immediately stop the company's use of its infringing handbag machine, it would force Country C to change its rules on access to its courts by foreigners. Mucci could then use Country C's existing (TRIPs-compliant) patent law regime to take action against the rival company.

6. The *Canada – Pharmaceutical Patents* dispute: a case study

New products are sometimes required to pass lengthy approval processes before they are allowed to be sold on the market. This is particularly the case for pharmaceutical companies. For manufacturers wishing to take advantage of the expiry of a competitor's patent to begin producing generic copies of the patented product (patented drug, in the case of pharmaceutical companies), these approval periods can pose a significant barrier to their successful competition. In Canada, Section 55.2 of the Patent Act contained two particular exceptions designed to get around this issue for generic manufacturers. Section 55.2(1), known as the 'regulatory review' exception, allowed competing manufacturers to use a patented invention for purposes related to obtaining government approvals, so that the competitors would have the necessary permission to sell their copies as soon as the patent expires. Section 55.2(2), known as the 'stockpiling exception', allowed competitors to produce and stockpile the copies for six months before patent expiry, so that sales of the copies could actually begin on patent expiry.

The European Union requested consultations with Canada in December 1997 on this issue, claiming that the two exceptions meant that Canada was providing a lower level of patent protection than was required under Article 27.1 (patentable subject matter), Article 28 (rights conferred) and Article 33 (term of protection) of TRIPs. Canada claimed in response that its Patent Act provisions were justified based on Article 30 of TRIPs, which allows for "limited exceptions to the exclusive rights conferred by a patent", as long as the exceptions do not unreasonably conflict with the normal exploitation of the patent nor prejudice the legitimate interests of the patent owner.

The consultations failed and in February 1999 a WTO panel was established to hear the case. Eleven other countries reserved their rights to intervene in the dispute. The panel's report was released in March 2000. The panel found that Article 30 covered the regulatory review exception in Section 55.2(1) but not the stockpiling exception in Section 55.2(2), since stockpiling was considered as a "substantial curtailment of the exclusionary rights required to be granted to patent owners" under Article 28.1 of TRIPs and therefore not a 'limited' exception. Section 55.2(2) was therefore found to be in violation of TRIPs.

Canada requested a reasonable time period in which to implement the panel's findings. It could not agree with the European Union, however, on how long a reasonable period was. Following arbitration in June 2000, an implementation date of October 7 2000 was set. Canada then amended the Patent Act by repealing Section 55.2(2) and reported its compliance back to the WTO Dispute Settlement Body on October 23 2000.[4]

7. Recommended resources

For further information on IP rights and TRIPs, several publications can be recommended, including the following:

- K Maskus (ed), *The WTO, Intellectual Property Rights and the Knowledge Economy* (Cheltenham: Edward Elgar Publishing, 2004).
- C Bellmann, G Dutfield and R Melendez-Ortiz, *Trading in Knowledge: Development Perspectives on TRIPS, Trade and Sustainability* (London: Earthscan, 2003).
- C Correa, *Trade Related Aspects of Intellectual Property Rights – A Commentary on the TRIPs Agreement* (Oxford: Oxford University Press, 2006).
- C Correa, *Intellectual Property Rights, the WTO and Developing Countries: The TRIPs Agreement and Policy Options* (London: Zed Books, 2000).

4 *Canada – Patent Protection of Pharmaceutical Products*, WT/DS114.

Sustainable development concerns

1. Introduction

For much of its history, trade law has been viewed as a largely self-contained set of principles and diplomatic arrangements relating to economics and commerce between countries. Agreements on trade were concluded for the economic benefits that they would bring to each party, with little regard for any broader effects. However, in recent decades, observers have begun to identify linkages and relationships between international trade and other concerns such as environmental protection, human health and social development. There is growing recognition that trade law cannot (and does not) exist in a vacuum. It is connected to other policy priorities of national governments. And the connection of trade law to environmental law, human rights law, public health policy and social development policies must not merely be a begrudging accommodation of these objectives. The elaboration of international law, the proliferation of instruments making commitments to human rights and growing awareness of environmental and development issues show that these are entirely legitimate public objectives that stand alongside trade and economic development. Viewed in this way, there is no reason for trade law to attempt to override these priorities. Rather, accommodation and mutual support are needed.

The World Trade Organisation (WTO), as the major arbiter of world trade rules, has begun to change its rules and procedures to accommodate the concerns of its members in these areas. Developments within the WTO in recent years demonstrate a willingness to expand on its potential to be an instrument of sustainable development. The WTO Committees on Environment and Development both have mandates to examine such issues, while the Doha Round launched various relevant negotiations and discussions. The jurisprudence of WTO panels and the Appellate Body has also referred to sustainable development as one of the objectives of world trade in the *Shrimp/Turtle Case*, while the *Gasoline* and *Asbestos Cases* among others, have recognised national governments' rights (and duties) to protect the environment and human health, finding no inconsistency between these objectives and the WTO rules.

There is a less well-developed aspect of this trend. Companies and business associations that focus on sustainability products and services are increasingly realising the scope they have to employ international trade law and the WTO in their favour. Using the WTO's fundamental principle of non-discrimination, these companies and associations can challenge governments that impose protectionist measures. The resulting outcomes can benefit all interests: the sustainability companies benefit economically, consumers worldwide benefit from cleaner products and technologies at the lowest price available, and the environment, health and development interests also benefit.

This chapter first presents three case studies of hypothetical (although increasingly likely) situations in which companies and business associations with a sustainable development focus might take advantage of the rules of world trade law. The second part of the chapter provides an overview of the growing links between trade law and sustainable development.

2. Market access for renewable resources

2.1 A practical problem in world trade law

Country A maintains strict standards for the production of renewable energy equipment such as solar power panels, and these standards specify exactly how the solar panels need to be produced. In particular, the standards require that solar panel producers must use only Country A's technologies and pass Country A's inspections twice per year. An international association of manufacturers of solar products (including solar panel producers from Country B) is concerned that the standards do not allow them to market their solar panels in Country A. How would one advise the association, in world trade law?

2.2 A world trade law solution to the practical problem

The WTO has no role in setting the international standards for sustainable resource development or environmental protection. International bodies such as the United Nations Environment Programme or the International Organization for Standardization (ISO) assume part of this role, as do the many bilateral and multilateral agreements concluded between sovereign domestic governments, such as the United Nations Framework Convention on Climate Change and the United Nations Convention on Biological Diversity. Further, the WTO has no ability to dictate domestic governments' environmental laws, policies, regulations or standards. National governments and environmental agencies retain these powers. However, the WTO can assist in cases where national environmental laws or standards appear to be merely covers for the protection of domestic interests. Such protection can be harmful not only to foreign countries and producers, but also to the global environment. For instance, in some situations such laws could support existing domestic producers that meet certain types of environmental standards while locking out other producers worldwide that operate under potentially higher, or 'cleaner', standards.

In the situation above, Country A has passed environmental standards which purport to encourage solar power. Seeking to ensure that solar panels are produced under controlled and regulated conditions so as to maintain quality, the standards require producers to use only technologies that have been developed in Country A. Producers must also submit to inspections of their production facilities twice a year by A's authorities.

These standards might make sense in a domestic context, but for foreign businesses seeking to gain access to a large market they represent an enormous obstacle. The international association of manufacturers of solar products may rely on technological advantages embodied in processes developed by its members which are outside Country A; under the solar panel standards, however, they are unable to use these processes in the production of solar panels destined for A's market. Licensing A's technologies for use in order to meet the standards of A may well destroy the companies' competitive advantage and affect the long-term viability of the industry. In addition, the requirement for twice-yearly inspections by A's authorities could, in practice, entail the establishment of production facilities within Country A. Without local production facilities, the authorities are likely to claim that inspection is not practically possible, and therefore that the foreign manufacturers do not meet the solar panel standards. However, meeting this requirement would involve the unnecessary high costs of establishing a local presence, which again may threaten the companies' profitability or even survival.

At this point, the role of trade law becomes apparent. Under Article III(4) of the General Agreement on Tariffs and Trade (GATT), products imported into a country must be given treatment no less favourable than that given to domestic products in respect of laws, regulations and requirements affecting their sale in that country. The solar panel standards imposed by Country A constitute requirements affecting the sale of solar power products in A, and by virtue of Article III(4) these standards must therefore treat imported products no less favourably than domestic ones. Given that the standards represent a significant obstacle for the foreign producers wishing to market their energy in Country A, the standards arguably discriminate in favour of domestic producers and thus violate Article III(4).

The standards may also breach Country A's obligations under the Technical Barriers to Trade Agreement. As a measure intended to protect the environment, the standards are permitted unless they pose an unnecessary obstacle to international trade. Imposing a requirement for Country A technologies and inspection does not in itself further any objective to promote solar power. If it does so, it is arguably more trade restrictive than necessary. If Country A could point to an internationally agreed standard recommending the use of A's technology and inspection practices (eg, one developed by ISO), it could perhaps counter this argument; otherwise, the energy standards are likely to constitute a violation of the Technical Barriers to Trade Agreement.

Armed with this legal position as support, the international association can petition Country A either to:

- remove the standards; or
- modify them to remove the discrimination that they entail.

For instance, the standards could require that the products marketed comply with a certain power production level, leaving producers free to use any available technology or process that achieves the specified level. The standards might also recognise the capabilities of foreign inspectors by providing that holding regular inspections of facilities by authorities in the country of production is enough to satisfy the authorities in Country A. These modifications would achieve the regulatory purpose sought without discrimination against foreign producers and without unnecessarily restricting international trade.

If Country A refuses to remove or modify the standards, formal consultations under the WTO's dispute settlement regime can be invoked. Neither the complaining manufacturers nor the international association that represents them can directly call on the WTO's dispute settlement regime themselves, so the request for consultations must be sponsored by one or more of the manufacturers' governments.[1] If the consultations fail, the dispute can be escalated to a panel hearing and (if necessary) an Appellate Body ruling. A result in favour of the manufacturers' governments would then require Country A either to modify the standards or to face retaliatory trade sanctions from the complainant countries.

There is, of course, a need to ensure that trade laws are not used to weaken laws and standards to promote solar power, or to constrain the adoption of new rules making solar power products more accessible. However, the strength of entrenched interests could also lead a domestic government to pass regulations or standards which actually operate to favour only those interests. In such situations, the WTO rules have the potential to break down trade barriers imposed by such regulations or standards, allowing more solar panel manufacturers to flourish and grow, and to compete more effectively with, for example, fossil fuel companies in more domestic markets worldwide.

2.3 Recommended resources

- ISO – www.iso.org (Life Cycle Assessment Standards and Environmental Management Standards).
- United Nations Framework Convention on Climate Change – http://unfccc.int (Library).
- Renewable Energy and Energy Efficiency Partnership – www.reeep.org/ (Renewable Energy and International Law Project).

3. Globalisation of health, human rights and labour standards

3.1 A practical problem in world trade law

A fair trade cooperative produces sports equipment, ensuring that its footballs are not produced with child labour and its shirts are made with fibres from pesticide-free organic cotton. An independent, open, voluntary labelling scheme has been developed and the cooperative meets its criteria. Due to non-governmental organisation activism and consumer awareness, all major sports associations are now adopting the cooperative's labelled balls and shirts, even though these are twice as expensive as those of its main competitors. The international competitors join forces to challenge the label itself, arguing that it violates Article III of GATT, as well as the Agreement on Technical Barriers to Trade and the Agreement on the Application of

1 See Chapters 3, 5 and 6.

Sanitary and Phytosanitary Measures. How would one advise the sports cooperative, in order to have its label found legitimate in world trade law?

3.2 A world trade law solution to the practical problem

As awareness of human rights, labour and environmental health has increased over recent years, there has been growing recognition that consumers are concerned not only with the quality and cost of the products that they purchase, but also with the way in which the products were made. Consumers are now more willing to pay a higher price for goods that are identical in performance, appearance and use to cheaper alternatives if they know that these have been produced according to processes and production methods that consumers consider to be more ethical or environmentally friendly than the alternatives' processes and production methods. In cases where prices are equal, consumers are more likely to prefer such goods with processes and production methods that minimise negative social and environmental impacts.

Producers that use more sustainable processes and production methods therefore perceive a market advantage in labelling their products to publicise this fact. In some cases, as in the situation described above, independent labelling schemes have been developed that permit producers to use a certain label or designation (eg, 'Fairtrade' or 'Forest Stewardship Council-certified') if the producers meet the schemes' criteria on environmental management, labour standards, use of chemical products and other things. Producers that meet the criteria are entirely free to choose whether they wish to use the fair trade label or eco-label. In other cases, a government may aim to support environmental and labour standards objectives (or at least consumer protection objectives) by specifically requiring that products be labelled to indicate, for instance, their energy efficiency or the source of materials used to make them. Such labels are mandatory, in that producers must display them if they wish to sell their products in that government's territory.

Whether the use of a label is voluntary or mandatory has important consequences for the label's legitimacy under world trade law. In the hypothetical situation above, the international competitors of the fair trade cooperative will likely lose business due to the cooperative's use of the label on its sporting equipment and the general public's recognition of and support for the label. For commercial reasons, the competitors are thus seeking to prevent the label's use, arguing that it violates world trade law.

One of the WTO's foundational principles is non-discrimination. It appears in two major forms in the WTO agreements: non-discrimination between countries (the most favoured nation principle) and non-discrimination between domestic and foreign trade (the national treatment principle). The principle operates, however, with several limitations. One is that it applies only to acts of governments, expressed in GATT as "laws, regulations, and requirements" affecting the internal sale of products and "customs duties . . . rules and formalities" on the importation of products. The label being challenged here is voluntary, meaning that governments have no laws or requirements regulating its use and producers that meet its criteria are free to choose whether to use it. The label is therefore not a law, regulation or requirement affecting the sale of sports equipment in any country, as would be required for Article III:4 of GATT to apply. It is also not a customs duty or a rule or formality in connection with importation, as would be required for Article I:1 to apply. Therefore, the cooperative's international competitors will not be able to claim that the voluntary label discriminates against their products and violates GATT.

The competitors have also claimed that the label violates the Agreement on Technical Barriers to Trade. This agreement prevents countries from establishing barriers to trade in the disguised form of technical regulations that products must meet before they are allowed onto domestic markets. It requires countries imposing technical regulations to base those regulations on agreed international standards where possible, or otherwise to ensure that regulations are no more trade restrictive than necessary to meet a legitimate objective (eg, protection of the environment). Importantly, the agreement applies only to mandatory technical regulations – that is, ones that must be complied with to allow a product to be sold in a domestic market. Since the label here is a voluntary one that the cooperative has chosen to affix (rather than one that a government required it to affix), it cannot be classified as a technical regulation under the agreement and the competitors cannot successfully argue that it breaches the agreement.

The competitors' third claim is that the label is in breach of the Agreement on Sanitary and Phytosanitary Measures. This agreement permits countries to take measures to protect human, animal or plant life or health, as long as these regulations are "based on scientific principles and not maintained without sufficient scientific evidence". Once again, since the label is voluntary, it cannot be considered as a 'measure' taken by a government (ie, a mandatory requirement that producers must meet). Even if the label were mandatory, it would be difficult to argue that requiring producers of sporting equipment to provide information on their processes and production methods is intended to fulfil an objective of protecting human, animal or plant life or health. Any claim that the label is covered by, and then breaches, the Agreement on Sanitary and Phytosanitary Measures will therefore not succeed.

In light of this, the international competitors will fail in their efforts to challenge the eco-label. It is relatively clear that such voluntary fair trade or eco-labels, as used here by the fair trade cooperative, are permitted under world trade law.

The cooperative should note, on the other hand, that if governments (due perhaps to non-governmental lobbying or changing consumer attitudes) later decree that particular sporting equipment must bear the label – to indicate that the equipment has been produced according to the approved processes and production methods – then the label's legality under world trade law would become far less clear. A mandatory label is considered a regulation affecting the internal sale of the labelled product (since the product cannot be sold without the label affixed), and so the label would come under the non-discrimination provisions of Articles I:1 and III:4 of GATT. But another limitation of the non-discrimination principle in the WTO agreements is that it is enforced only as between like products. Different products are, understandably, allowed to have different laws and regulations applied to them.

The question then arises as to whether the cooperative's 'sustainable' products are to be considered like their competitors' identical but 'unsustainable' counterparts. In other words, does world trade law allow countries to discriminate based on processes and production methods? Even though the footballs and shirts produced by the fair trade cooperative are identical in themselves to those of its international competitors, the cooperative's concerns to avoid child labour and pesticides in its processes and production methods create a perception in the marketplace that its products are less socially and environmentally adverse. The cooperative therefore would consider them not to be like its competitors' products. The Appellate Body has considered the question of likeness in various cases, but no definitive answer has yet been provided on the processes and production methods issue.

A mandatory label may also be caught under the Agreement on Technical Barriers to Trade. If made mandatory, the label would qualify as a 'technical regulation' under the agreement and any government requiring it could then be challenged in the WTO to show that it does not create an unnecessary obstacle to international trade. To avoid this charge, the label requirement must be found to be no more restrictive than necessary to fulfil the legitimate objective of protection of human rights and environmental standards. Eco-labels and fair trade labels can, in fact, create significant obstacles to trade where the costs of certification to obtain the label would be prohibitively high for some producers, or where the practical difficulties in altering the manufacturing process would be too great. In this case, the sports associations and general public appear quite willing to pay more for labelled products, so the cooperative could argue that their competitors would easily recoup the extra costs of label certification. The competitors might respond that there are less trade-restrictive ways of making the public aware of the processes and production methods used for their products, and that the labelling requirement is overly burdensome and hence illegal. The relationship between labelling and the WTO Agreements is the subject of continuing debate within the WTO.

3.3 Recommended resources

- WTO, Committee on Trade and Environment, Information Relevant to the Consideration of the Market Access Effects of Eco-Labelling Schemes, WT/CTE/W/150, June 29 2000.
- Fairtrade Labelling Organizations International – www.fairtrade.net/.
- International Institute for Environment and Development – www.iied.org (sustainable markets).

4. The promotion of trade in environmental goods and services

4.1 A practical problem in world trade law

Countries from Region A have recently made new liberalisation commitments under the General Agreement on Trade in Services (GATS). Assess Eco Assets, a firm from Country B which provides environmental and health impact assessment services, wishes to take advantage of these new commitments, in order to compete in bids for tenders to assess the impacts of new shrimp aquaculture projects in the region. However, Assess Eco Assets is not sure that its work falls under the WTO definition of environmental services. How could one advise the firm in world trade law?

4.2 A world trade law solution to the practical problem

Under GATS, countries can make liberalisation and access commitments in several service sectors, such as engineering, financial, tourism and transport. Each of these service sectors is defined in a sectoral classification system devised by the United Nations and adopted by the WTO for GATS. The system is intended to be exhaustive, covering the entire range of services that can be provided. Countries are free to adopt their own classification systems and make commitments according to them as they wish, but for the most part they use the standard system, meaning that commitments are made according to the 12 defined service sectors.

The GATS classification system defines environmental services to include sewage services, refuse disposal services, sanitation and similar services, cleaning of exhaust gases, noise abatement services, and nature and landscape protection services. This is a relatively limited definition that reflects several factors:

- the difficulty in defining exactly what is meant by environmental services (and goods);
- the traditionally restricted role of the private sector in the provision of public utilities such as water and sanitation; and
- a focus in the past on 'end-of-pipe' services that deal with remediation and treatment of pollution rather than prevention and provision of cleaner technology.

In recent times, however, trends towards privatisation mean that, even where natural monopolies exist, certain formerly public utilities are being provided by private companies. A desire to bring about environmentally beneficial outcomes without sacrificing economic efficiency has led to recognition of the scope for competition in the provision of various environmental services. The worldwide market for environmentally friendly technologies and services is also growing, pushed by increasing government regulation in the area and increasing public awareness of environmental issues. Therefore, environmental service providers worldwide are recognising the potential of their businesses in foreign countries, aiming for a triple-win situation where:

- the service providers benefit commercially;
- the service recipients benefit from an expansion in the quality and range of services and generally lower prices; and
- the environment benefits from the environmental services themselves.

In this context, environmental service providers are keen to use GATS commitments to allow this access to foreign markets. The narrow definitions in GATS, however, place obstacles in their path. Contemporary environmental services may cut across several GATS service sectors, such as engineering, construction and management. The service to be provided may not fall neatly under any of the categories within environmental services and the target countries' commitments in other related sectors may not be uniform or complete, potentially meaning that only a part of the environmental service could be provided – clearly an unworkable situation for the service provider.

There is therefore much support for broadening the definition of environmental services to take into account the reality of the environmental industry worldwide. The European Union, for instance, considers that an expanded definition would encourage more commitments in the sector from countries "concerned at safeguarding their environment in the most effective manner".[2] While the difficulty in defining environmental goods and services remains, negotiations are now underway within the WTO on a new definition and several proposals have been put forward.

The Country B firm in the situation above would find itself supporting a new definition of environmental services. The Region A countries' commitments (most probably) follow the standard GATS service sectors, meaning that the commitments extend only to the narrow categories of environmental services outlined above. The environmental and health impact assessment services offered by the Country B firm would not be covered by the existing environmental services sector, and so the firm cannot take advantage of the Country B liberalisation commitments to begin providing its services in those countries.

One proposed new definition of environmental services is the Organisation for Economic Cooperation and Development (OECD)/Eurostat definition, which includes services provided to "measure, prevent, limit, minimise or correct environmental damage to water, air and soil, as well as problems related to waste, noise and ecosystems".[3] Three categories are included: pollution management, cleaner technologies and products, and resource management. The latter group refers to activities that prevent environmental damage to air, water or soil, and services for sustainable agriculture and fisheries. This would probably cover the Country B firm's consultancy services, meaning that the firm could take advantage of any liberalisation commitments made by countries in this category. The United States, the European Union, Canada and Japan have expressed support for the OECD/Eurostat definition.

The United Nations Conference on Trade and Development proposes another definition. It identifies certain core, traditional environmental services, including drinking water infrastructure services, waste water treatment and waste management. To this it adds 'next-generation' environmental services in four segments: environmental infrastructure services, air pollution control services, remediation services and support services.[4] The last segment includes consulting services, which would cover environmental impact assessment services.

As it stands, the Country B firm gains no benefit from the Region A countries' new commitments under GATS. Its best course of action is to participate in national trade policy debates on environmental services, and to encourage the Country B government to support (ideally in conjunction with its neighbours, to add weight to its cause) a revised and expanded definition in the WTO/GATS. Given that Country

2 EU Submission (1999), Section III [FIELD paper p 11].

3 *Environmental Goods and Services Industry Manual for the Collection and Analysis of Data*, OECD/Eurostat, 1999.

4 *A Primer on Environmental Goods and Services: Definitional Challenges to the Negotiation of Further Liberalisation*, Foundation for International Environmental Law and Development.

B has already made fully liberal commitments on three of the four modes of supply in the existing environmental services sector, its government might be expected to support further liberalisation, which is encouraging for the consultancy firm.

Assuming that the definition were revised and the Region A countries' commitments now included environmental and health impact assessment services, the firm could then rely on these commitments to expand its business outside Country B. The most relevant modes of supply under GATS will be commercial presence (ie, the firm setting up an office in the Region A countries, in order to provide its services), and presence of natural persons (eg, firm personnel examining an aquaculture project in the target country, or conducting tests on water in the vicinity). The full obligations of GATS will apply, so that:

- local firms must not be favoured over the Country B firm (the national treatment principle);
- any favour granted to environmental consultancies providing like services from other countries must also be granted to the Country B firm (the most favoured nation principle); and
- the firm must be guaranteed certain levels of market access.

4.3 Recommended resources

- OECD – www.oecd.org (environment and trade, environmental goods and services).
- United Nations Environment Programme – www.unep.ch/etb/.
- International Centre for Trade and Sustainable Development – www.ictsd.org (services).

5. Sustainable development in world trade law

As world trade rules continue to be debated and negotiated, the potential grows for win-win-win solutions for the environment, social development and economic growth. These developments, as suggested in the practical problems discussed above, are being closely followed by companies and associations with environmental, development or sustainability orientations. Such developments are part of a wider trend in sustainability policy discussions and law making. The remainder of this chapter therefore sets out an overview of these recent trends, primarily for legal practitioners who may wish to brief clients in the field, to help them to identify triple-win situations or to participate more generally in the negotiation and interpretation of new rules and policy directions.

It is useful to start with a note about the concept of 'sustainable development' itself. The idea has existed for thousands of years, as a guiding principle of many ancient cultures and traditions.[5] Its modern definition is usually taken to be that set out in the Brundtland Report of 1987, where it is considered as "development that meets the needs of the present without compromising the ability of future

5 *Case Concerning the Gabcikovo-Nagymaros Dam* (Hungary/Slovakia) (September 25 1997) ICJ Rep 7, Judge Weeramantry (Separate Opinion).

generations to meet their own needs".[6] To fulfil this objective, trade and economic growth priorities must be balanced with social and environmental priorities in the interest of development that can last over the long term. Sustainable development can therefore be viewed as a concept lying at the intersection of economic, environmental and social interests. References to sustainable development are now almost routinely included within world trade instruments. The preamble to the Marrakesh Agreement Establishing the World Trade Organisation presents sustainable development as an objective of world trade, and a commitment to promote sustainable development appears in many regional and bilateral trade treaties, including the North American Free Trade Agreement, the Canada-Costa Rica Free Trade Agreement, the US-Chile Free Trade Agreement, the US-Australia Free Trade Agreement, the EU-Egypt Free Trade Agreement, the EU-Africa Caribbean Pacific Cotonou Agreement, the EU-Chile Economic Association Agreement and the Panama-Taiwan Free Trade Agreement, all of which commit in various ways to promote sustainable development.

Within the WTO, trends in sustainable development have proceeded in a number of directions. The Committee on Trade and Environment[7] (CTE) was established along with the WTO in 1995 in order to study the relationship between the WTO agreements and environmental protection, and recommend changes where considered necessary. It examines 10 particular areas, including eco-labelling, transparency, intellectual property and where to handle disputes, as well as a general examination of the WTO agreements and their effect on the environment and governments' ability to regulate for environmental purposes. The Committee on Trade and Development[8] (CTD) is intended as a forum for discussion of all cross-cutting issues relevant to developing countries, including technical assistance, special and differential treatment and problems facing small economies.

The Doha Round of negotiations in the WTO, launched in 2001, was billed as a 'development round', placing issues around the relations between trade and development at the forefront of global trade discussions. The Doha Development Agenda calls on the CTE and CTD to ensure that sustainable development is appropriately reflected in negotiations. In the ministerial declaration issuing from the Doha Round, WTO members "strongly reaffirm[ed their] commitment to the objective of sustainable development" and confirmed that the multilateral trading system, environmental protection and sustainable development must be mutually supportive.[9] The declaration also launched three sets of negotiations on the environment:

- on the relationship between trade and environmental protection as set out in multilateral environmental agreements;
- on procedures for information exchange between multilateral environmental agreement secretariats and WTO committees; and

6 World Commission on Environment and Development, *Our Common Future* (Oxford: Oxford University Press, 1987) at p 43.
7 www.wto.org/english/tratop_e/envir_e/envir_e.htm.
8 www.wto.org/english/tratop_e/devel_e/devel_e.htm.
9 Para 6.

- on the reduction of tariff and non-tariff barriers to trade in environmental goods and services.[10]

A wide-ranging decision on implementation was also agreed in Doha, focusing on the interests and needs of developing countries. In spite of the encouraging language of the WTO, however, the Doha Development Agenda has achieved far less than was initially hoped. The Doha Round's continued faltering progress represents a challenge to the further integration of sustainable development into world trade.

The jurisprudence of WTO panels and the Appellate Body, on the other hand, has begun to clarify the WTO's approach to sustainable development. Several important cases have highlighted the potential for a rules-based trade body such as the WTO to balance competing priorities in trade liberalisation, environmental protection and social development. One such case is the *Shrimp/Turtle* Appellate Body decision. This case concerned measures taken by the United States under the 1973 Endangered Species Act intended to protect certain species of sea turtle. The measures required shrimp trawlers to use 'turtle-excluding' nets so as not to catch turtles along with shrimp, and also prohibited shrimp imports from waters where the nets were not used. India, Malaysia, Pakistan and Thailand complained about the measure, claiming a violation of GATT. The Appellate Body found in favour of the complainants, holding that the US provisions could not be justified by the exceptions to trade rules contained in Article XX of GATT.

In doing so, the Appellate Body referred to the incorporation of sustainable development into the preamble of the WTO's founding Marrakesh Agreement, and noted that the concept involves integration of "economic and social development and environmental protection".[11] In the Appellate Body's view, the concept of sustainable development informed the intention of members expressed in all of the WTO agreements. The *Shrimp/Turtle* decision also referred to the Rio Declaration on Environment and Development and Agenda 21 (the UN plan of action on sustainable development), and pointed to the creation of the CTE as further evidence of WTO members' concern both to "[uphold] and [safeguard] an open, non-discriminatory and equitable multilateral trading system" and also to "[act] for the protection of the environment, and the promotion of sustainable development".[12] This notwithstanding, the result of the case was that the US measures aimed at environmental protection were found to be in contravention of GATT, a major world trade agreement.

The *EC – Hormones Case* dealt with WTO members' rights under the Agreement on the Application of Sanitary and Phytosanitary Measures to set their own standards to protect the health of their citizens. The case involved an EU ban on the use of growth hormones in beef production. The United States and Canada sought to challenge this ban, arguing that the EU ban was not sufficiently scientifically justified as required by the Agreement on the Application of Sanitary and

10 Para 31(i) and (ii).
11 FN 107 in AB Report.
12 Para 154 in AB Report.

Phytosanitary Measures. The European Union claimed that the precautionary principle, one aspect of sustainable development,[13] should operate to allow it to impose the ban pending further scientific analysis. Although the Appellate Body accepted that "responsible, representative governments commonly act from perspectives of prudence and precaution where risks of irreversible, for example, life-terminating, damage to human health are concerned",[14] it considered that the precautionary principle did not operate in this context outside of Article 5.7 of the agreement, which covers provisional measures. As the European Union had not fulfilled the requirements of Article 5.7 in relation to its hormones ban, the ban violated the agreement.

The later *EC – Asbestos Case* raised similar issues of scientific uncertainty. The case centred on a French ban on asbestos products due to human health concerns. Canada complained, arguing that its asbestos products were suffering discrimination in the French market compared with French substitutes. While the scientific evidence on the health risks of asbestos was clear, the evidence was far less clear on whether the substitutes were actually any less harmful than careful use of asbestos. The Appellate Body held that there was no requirement to quantify a risk to human health, but that a qualitative assessment was sufficient. It also held that countries were entitled to base health and environmental protection measures on scientific opinions held by only a minority of scientists. On Canada's claim that the ban violated the GATT requirement of non-discrimination between like products, the Appellate Body considered that carcinogenic asbestos products were not 'like' the French domestic substitutes due to their different health implications, and so the inconsistent treatment (ie, one product allowed and the other banned) was permitted. The decision confirmed members' undisputed rights to determine the level of health protection they deem appropriate.

Outside of the WTO, at the bilateral and regional level, countries have sought to develop other innovative approaches to sustainable development as an objective of a trade agreement. The North American Agreement for Environmental Cooperation (NAAEC) and North American Agreement on Labor Cooperation (NAALC)[15] are two side agreements adopted by Canada, the United States and Mexico together with the North American Free Trade Agreement (NAFTA). As part of its mandate to examine the ongoing environmental effects of NAFTA, the Commission on Environmental Cooperation[16] established by NAAEC adopted an analytic framework in 2000.[17] The framework sets out six main areas to focus its review of NAFTA, including:

- consideration of the connections between NAFTA's liberalised trade rules and an increased use of environmentally friendly products; and
- consideration of the potential for upward convergence of environmental practice and regulation in the public and private sectors.

13 See New Delhi Principles etc.
14 Para 124.
15 www.naalc.org.
16 www.cec.org.
17 CEC, *Analytic Framework for Assessing the Environmental Effects of the North American Free Trade Agreement* (Montreal: CEC 1999), at www.cec.org/files/pdf/ECONOMY/Frmwrk-e_EN.pdf (August 2005).

One innovative element of NAAEC is the process allowing for civil society groups to complain to the commission of a member country's non-compliance with environmental laws and regulations. Although such complaints cannot lead to any binding determination, they have been both a source of embarrassment and an important way of maintaining public support for NAAEC and NAFTA. NAALC, for its part, takes as its focus labour standards in the three NAFTA countries, aiming to promote compliance with and enforcement of national labour laws and to foster continual improvement of working conditions and living standards.

A highly practical example of the integration of economic, social and environmental concerns (as envisaged by sustainable development) is found in the increasing use of impact assessment tools in the international arena. These tools come in various forms, ranging in scope from environmental impact assessments and human rights impact assessments to the broadest tool, sustainability impact assessments. Impact assessments operate as a formalised consideration of the wider effects of particular policies (usually trade policies or development projects), and aim to ensure that trade and development decisions result from processes that promote sustainability and public participation. Although it remains unusual for any national development decision or regional or bilateral trade agreement to require some form of impact assessment, the European Union, the United States and Canada have all adopted the tool to some degree, to be used either before or after the decision or agreement has been concluded.

The 1992 Rio Declaration recognised the potential of impact assessment in Principle 17: "Environmental impact assessment, as a national instrument, shall be undertaken for proposed activities that are likely to have a significant adverse impact on the environment and are subject to a decision of a competent national authority." At the international level, certain environmental treaties contain obligations to perform environmental impact assessments in situations where one country's activity may flow across a border or when areas of common concern, such as the high seas[18] or the Antarctic,[19] are involved. The application of such instruments to trade agreements is relatively new, but developing rapidly, and in some instances the assessments include a regulatory dimension.

In Canada, the Framework for Conducting Environmental Assessments of Trade Negotiations[20] has been used since 2001 to conduct environmental assessments of new bilateral and regional trade negotiations, and since 2005 this has also been applied to investment agreements. The assessments seek to assist Canadian negotiators in integrating environmental considerations into the negotiating process (as envisaged by the Doha Development Agenda), and to address public concerns. The framework includes provisions for actively seeking public input into assessments from non-governmental organisations, businesses, indigenous peoples and the general public. Similarly, the Office of the US Trade Representative has conducted

---

18 *UN Convention on the Law of the Sea*, December 10 1982, UN Doc A/CONF.62/122, 21 ILM 1245 (entered into force November 16 1994), preamble, Articles 192 and 194.

19 *Antarctic Environmental Protocol*, 30 ILM 1461 (1991), Article 23(1).

20 Available at www.dfait-maeci.gc.ca/tna-nac/Environment-en.asp.

environmental reviews of all bilateral and regional trade agreements signed by the United States since 1999, in which regulatory impacts, public advice and potential impacts in the territory of the proposed new trading partner are taken seriously and addressed.[21] Developing countries have, in some cases, also found such assessments useful for economic policy making. For instance, as discussed by the International Institute for Sustainable Development, Senegal recently found that stocks of certain species of fish with high market values were being seriously depleted through the use of trade impact assessment.[22]

Sustainability impact assessments are more complex, innovative studies which take economic, environmental and social impacts into account to provide a complete picture of the expected effects of a trade policy or project. They include target-related indicators, which attempt to measure sustainability against a set of defined goals, and process-related indicators, which are based on the principle that the process itself by which policies and decisions are adopted plays a substantial role in achieving sustainable development goals. Indicators of sustainability used in the assessments fall into three categories:

- economic indicators, including average real income, fixed capital formation and employment rates;
- social indicators, including poverty rates, health and education levels and equity; and
- environmental indicators, including air and water quality indicators, biological diversity and natural resources.[23]

Sustainability impact assessments are mostly in use within the European Union, which developed a framework for analysis in 1999 and has since applied it to the WTO Doha Round negotiations and EU bilateral and regional trade agreements with Chile, Mercosur, the African-Caribbean-Pacific nations and the Gulf Cooperation Council nations. EU sustainability impact assessments place much emphasis on consultation both within EU member states and in the third country trade partners. The assessments themselves are conducted by independent experts commissioned by the European Union, which then receives a response paper from the European Commission. All results are made public.

This survey provides only a brief overview of recent trends and developments in this area: it is a vibrant and rapidly emerging field of study and practice.

6. Recommended resources

Useful online resources include the following:

- Impact Assessment Research Centre, University of Manchester – www.sed.manchester.ac.uk/idpm/research/iarc/.
- International Centre for Trade and Sustainable Development – www.ictsd.org.

21 Available online at www.ustr.gov/Trade_Sectors/Environment/Environmental_Reviews/Section_Index.html.
22 IISD, *Environment and Trade – A Handbook*, p 112.
23 EUROPA, *Sustainability Impact Assessment*, http://ec.europa.eu/comm/trade/issues/global/sia/index_en.htm.

- Centre for International Sustainable Development Law – www.cisdl.org (trade, investment and competition law).
- International Institute for Sustainable Development – www.iisd.ca (trade knowledge network).

Other helpful sources of knowledge on these issues include the following:

- MC Cordonier Segger & A Khalfan, *Sustainable Development Law: Principles, Practice and Prospects* (Oxford: Oxford University Press, 2004).
- M Gehring & MC Cordonier Segger, eds, *Sustainable Development in World Trade Law* (The Hague: Kluwer Law International, 2005).
- G Sampson, *The WTO and Sustainable Development* (Tokyo: United Nations University, 2005).
- International Institute for Sustainable Development, *Environment and Trade – A Handbook*, 2nd ed, (Winnipeg: IISD / UNEP, 2005) – http://www.iisd.org/trade/handbook/.
- T Cottier, J Pauwelyn & E Burgi (eds), *Human Rights and International Trade* (Oxford: Oxford University Press, 2005).

Other emerging issues in world trade law

1. Trade facilitation

The World Trade Organisation (WTO) began during a period of tariffication – that is, converting formal trade barriers (eg, quotas, import licences and others) into pure tariffs. The WTO would then seek progressively to negotiate these tariffs down to zero, on a reciprocal basis. Even in cases where this has occurred, however, other barriers continue to impede the import and export of goods and services. Exporters may be unaware of, or may lack access to, the right forms to be used so that their products are classified correctly. Where tariffs do apply, companies may not know what they are, how to pay them or how they might be reduced. These bureaucratic procedures have real effects in the marketplace, and especially affect small and medium-sized firms that do not regularly deal with such procedures. Due to such barriers, many enterprises may even find that the education and compliance costs of international trade actually outweigh any benefits from increased sales. Producers in developing countries can suffer from inefficient customs processes and poor transportation infrastructure, to the point that even trade in goods with their closest neighbours becomes difficult. Corruption can also be an issue, with each customs post or checkpoint providing another opportunity for bribery to speed up clearance approval for the goods.

The WTO agreements contain numerous provisions to address the different aspects of trade facilitation. For example, Article V of the General Agreement on Tariffs and Trade (GATT) deals with freedom of transit of goods across WTO members' territories, while Article VIII covers fees and formalities connected with import and export, and Article X requires prompt publication of trade regulations.

In 1996, the Singapore Ministerial Conference gave a mandate to the WTO Goods Council to study "the simplification of trade procedures in order to assess the scope for WTO rules in this area". The Doha Conference in 2001 extended the Goods Council's work, requesting it to identify the trade facilitation needs and priorities of WTO members, especially developing country members. The Doha Conference also called for a review of GATT Articles V, VIII and X, but suspended actual negotiations on the matter until after the 2003 Cancun conference.

After the Singapore Ministerial Conference, and several years of exploratory work and analysis, in August 2004 WTO members agreed to commence negotiations on new binding rules for trade facilitation. The negotiations "aim at enhancing technical assistance and support for capacity building in this area", and at "provisions for effective cooperation between customs or any other appropriate authorities on trade facilitation and customs compliance issues".[1] They also include an aim to "clarify and improve" the relevant GATT articles. The negotiations are managed by the Negotiating Group on Trade Facilitation, established in October 2004. Input is sought from other international organisations such as the International Monetary Fund, the Organisation for Economic Cooperation and Development (OECD), the Asia-Pacific Economic Cooperation (APEC), the United Nations Conference on Trade and Development, the World Customs Organisation and the World Bank. APEC has provided a list of principles that form part of the discussions around trade facilitation, including transparency, simplification, practicability, non-discrimination, consistency, harmonisation, use of technology, due process and cooperation.

Developing countries have expressed some concerns over broadened requirements on trade facilitation, fearing that they may be exposed to dispute resolution mechanisms if they fail to meet new obligations. Some are also sceptical that improving trade facilitation will bring much benefit to them, suggesting instead that it will be mostly to the advantage of the developed world where businesses rely much more on fast turnaround times throughout their global supply chains.

Developing countries face a special situation with regard to trade facilitation measures. Beyond the usual extension of time for compliance granted to developing and least-developed countries, WTO members have acknowledged that these countries will "not be obliged to undertake investments in infrastructure projects beyond their means" and will be required only to make commitments consistent with their needs and capabilities. Members have committed to provide technical assistance and support for capacity building during the negotiations. Another special interest group is landlocked countries, which at the first meeting of the negotiating group expressed concerns over the higher transportation costs that they face compared to other members and their particular interest in practical outcomes from the negotiations.

Trade facilitation measures have the potential to enhance development to the extent that it provides the certainty needed to encourage investment in developing countries and assists developing country producers in bringing goods to world markets. Many governments stipulate that these measures should not, however, jeopardise the ability of states to implement specific customs processes on quarantine, environmental or human health protection (rather than harmonised, universal 'lowest-common-denominator' systems), or to detect illegal activity at the border. Any binding agreement on trade facilitation will likely recognise these concerns.

Further information on the status of the trade facilitation negotiations is available on the WTO website at www.wto.org/english/tratop_e/tradfa_e/tradfa_negoti_docs_e.htm, or via a search on DocsOnline (http://docsonline.wto.org/gen_home.asp?language=1&_=1) for document code TN/TF/*. A compilation of members' submissions on clarification and improvement of GATT, Articles V, VIII and X is available under document code TN/TF/W/43.

---

1 WT/L/579, page D-1.

2. Competition

Trade has obvious links to competition policy. Where monopolies exist or exclusive service supplier arrangements are in place, trade by other companies in the same field is nearly impossible, or all gains from trade are immediately captured by the cartel rather than reaching consumers. While the WTO agreements aim to prevent discrimination in world markets and provide an ever-higher level of access to them, national competition policy can potentially limit this through restrictive requirements on market access or even through a lack of regulation, for instance to prevent abuses of market power. For this reason, GATT and the General Agreement on Trade in Services (GATS) both contain provisions on monopolies and exclusive service suppliers, and the Agreement on Trade-Related Aspects of Intellectual Property Rights (TRIPs) contains provisions allowing governments to act against anti-competitive behaviour.

Competition policy can become relevant when multinational firms merge with or acquire domestic businesses and competitors. A multinational may wish to expand its operations into a particular country and can do so by buying out an existing domestic company in the same field. This may, however, have the result of lessening consumer choice in that country or provide scope for improper use of the new actor's newly acquired market power through, for example, price fixing or restrictive distribution arrangements.

Competition also has links to development, in that "practices that impede or negate the realization of benefits from international trade . . . thereby [inhibit] economic and social development, particularly of developing countries".[2] Effective competition policy, together with trade liberalisation, can provide "a basis for sustained growth and development, including employment growth, poverty alleviation and the narrowing of income inequalities".[3] Nevertheless, such a view is not universally held in the WTO. Many developing countries are concerned about the effects of instituting more competitive markets, particularly those with long histories of state-run enterprises and more highly regulated economic environments.[4] Many countries have also expressed the view that new commitments in the area of competition would overburden their institutional capacity.

After the Singapore Ministerial Conference, a multilateral Working Group on the Interaction between Trade and Competition Policy was established. This working group was to:

- clarify the core principles of competition policy (eg, transparency and non-discrimination);
- examine provisions on hardcore cartels (ie, cartels formally created);
- determine methods for voluntary cooperation between national competition authorities; and
- provide support for the continuing reinforcement of competition authorities' capacity in developing countries.

---

2 WT/WGTCP/W/127, para 14.

3 UNCTAD/DITC/CLP/2006/1, COMPAL Global Annual Report 2005, p 6.

4 WT/WGTCP/W/80, *Synthesis Paper on the Relationship of Trade and Competition Policy to Development and Economic Growth*, p 20.

The work of the group was suspended as a result of the WTO General Council's August 2004 decision, when negotiations effectively ceased on this issue. However, during its operation the group produced several analyses of WTO members' competition policy, including a Background Note on the Fundamental Principles of Competition Policy.[5] The background note highlights three broad categories of competition principles:

- the overriding goals of competition policy (eg, the promotion of economic efficiency and development, or the promotion of consumer welfare);
- operational principles of policy design and application (eg, the distinction between 'horizontal' and 'vertical' arrangements in markets); and
- the institutions and processes through which competition policy is applied (eg, adherence to due process).

The International Competition Network (ICN), launched in 2001, is an informal association of national and regional competition authorities. It is essentially a forum for discussion of competition policy, aimed at increasing convergence on competition law and enforcement processes worldwide. The ICN plays no formal role in setting out national competition policy or law, but its members are free to consider its recommendations and implement them where desired. It operates under three substantive working groups (Competition Policy Implementation, Cartels and Mergers), and three support working groups (Funding, Memberships and Operational Framework).

One pilot programme currently running in the ICN's Competition Policy Implementation Working Group is a partnership arrangement between countries with experienced competition agencies and countries with less well-developed agencies. Common issues, such as definition of markets, barriers to entry and efficiencies, are identified, and the agencies, working in pairs, share information and experience as a means to increase the capacity of the lesser-developed agencies. Under this scheme, for instance, Japan's Fair Trade Commission is partnered with Indonesia's *Komisi Pengawas Persaingan Usaha*, and Germany's *Bundeskartellamt* is working with the Mongolian Unfair Competition Monitoring Agency. Such initiatives are highly practical examples of the technical assistance and capacity building adopted as a key principle of the Doha Development Agenda and expressed in the Doha Declaration.

The Cartels Working Group focuses on the problems posed by the increasing possibilities for the formation of worldwide cartels that come with increasing globalisation and integration of world markets. To counter activities such as price fixing, bid rigging and market sharing, the working group examines recommended legal frameworks as well as enforcement techniques (including searches, raids and inspections). The Mergers Working Group considers regimes for reviewing proposed corporate mergers in order to ensure that domestic and international competition is not threatened. The working group's goals are to:

- enhance the effectiveness of merger review mechanisms;

5 WT/WGTCP/W/127.

- facilitate procedural and substantive convergence in review processes; and
- reduce the time and cost associated with merger reviews.

As a governmental network, the ICN provides a wealth of information for the practitioner on its website. Although some have commented on the lack of effective non-governmental scrutiny, it may provide an alternative to multilateral competition law negotiations.

Documents from the operation before 2004 of the Working Group on the Interaction between Trade and Competition Policy are available on DocsOnline under the document code WT/WGTCP/*, or on the WTO website at www.wto.org/english/tratop_e/comp_e/comp_e.htm#documents. The ICN can be found at www.internationalcompetitionnetwork.org.

3. Investment

Foreign direct investment is an important aspect of world trade.[6] Much trade between countries occurs via companies' manufacturing facilities located in foreign countries, and the establishment of such facilities constitutes foreign investment. The WTO further notes that about one-third of world trade in goods and services is trade *within* companies, "for example between subsidiaries in different companies or between a subsidiary and its headquarters", which indicates the strong links between trade and investment.[7] Investment, whether foreign or domestic, also plays a key role in economic development, since it is the path to more productive (and often more environmentally friendly) technologies. It can moreover, bring better working practices and established processes into countries with little prior experience of or exposure to them, thereby raising worldwide standards.

However, investment, and especially foreign direct investment, is also the cause of some controversy in developing countries. These countries often depend on the inflow of financial capital from abroad to bolster their own small economies, and with this dependence comes a danger of exploitation or unwarranted dominance of the target country by the investors. Some countries offer financial incentives (eg, tax breaks) for the establishment of export processing zones and the like in their territories; these incentives, though, can end up nullifying most of the benefit that the foreign investment might have entailed. There are suggestions, too, that countries may lower social/labour or environmental standards, or at least see little value in attempting to raise them, in order to attract foreign currency inflows. Investment in the natural resources sector, a common form of investment in developing countries, can have unintended consequences for the environment and local communities (eg, by encouraging further, unplanned development along a mine access road), even if large financial benefits are thereby obtained.

There are three areas of work on investment within the WTO. First, the Working Group on the Relationship between Trade and Investment studies the implications of the relationship between trade and investment for development and economic

---

6 As opposed to foreign portfolio investment, which is an important aspect of the global financial system.
7 http://www.wto.org/english/thewto_e/whatis_e/tif_e/bey3_e.htm.

growth, and analyses existing international instruments and agreements. Second, the Agreement on Trade-Related Aspects of Investment Measures (known as TRIMs) forms part of the WTO agreements, binding on all members. TRIMs prevents members from maintaining investment measures that restrict and distort trade, such as requirements that foreign enterprises purchase certain percentages of local goods or import a level of goods related to the amount they export. The agreement is monitored by the TRIMs Committee. Third, GATS includes provisions on foreign investment in services through its modes of supply, particularly the commercial presence mode. Note, however, that work in the WTO Doha Round on the relationship between trade and investment has been suspended following the General Council's August 2004 declaration and negotiations have effectively ceased in this area.

Much foreign investment is governed not by a multilateral system such as the WTO, but by bilateral investment treaties. From their origins in the late 1950s, there are now more than 2,000 such treaties in force, a large proportion of which are between developed and developing countries.[8] Bilateral investment treaties aim to establish standards of treatment for investors in host countries, as well as some guarantee of protection against nationalisation of investors' property and dispute settlement mechanisms for both state-state and investor-state disputes. The focus of these instruments is generally on protection of investors' rights, and they rarely contain any provisions either explicitly addressing the development (economic or otherwise) of the host country or implicitly permitting development-based measures via exceptions or 'special and differential treatment' provisions.[9] The dispute settlement mechanisms that they establish also suffer from problems of transparency and a lack of adherence to precedent, leading to uncertainty for host countries over the scope of the obligations that they have accepted.

In any case, at a practical level (and even assuming that foreign direct investment does benefit a host country's development), the World Bank has concluded that the proliferation of bilateral investment treaties does "not seem to have increased flows of investment to signatory developing countries",[10] and the World Wildlife Fund points to evidence suggesting that the link between strong investment rules and increased foreign direct investment is not necessarily supported. It comments that China, for instance, receives much of the developed world's foreign direct investment despite its highly regulated business environment, "restrictions on foreign ownership, performance requirements and an unreliable legal system".[11]

The International Institute for Sustainable Development (IISD) Model International Agreement on Investment for Sustainable Development was developed in 2005 in response to a perceived failure of bilateral investment treaties over the preceding 50 years to establish a coherent framework for foreign investment, as well

---

8 International Institute for Sustainable Development (IISD), Bilateral Investment Treaties and Development Policy-Making, p 3.

9 *Ibid.*, p. 5.

10 World Bank, *2003 Global Economic Prospects*, p 118.

11 World Wildlife Fund-UK, "A Framework for Regulating International Investment", www.wwf.org.uk/filelibrary/pdf/csd.pdf.

as the failure of the three attempts (in the United Nations, the OECD and the WTO) at a multilateral agreement on investment. Rather than focusing on investors' rights, this non-governmental organisation proposal seeks to balance investors' rights with "a novel mix of voluntary and binding investor responsibilities, and with both host and home state rights and obligations".[12] It takes sustainable development and the aspirations of developing countries as the starting point of foreign direct investment and sets these in an overarching context of good governance which it describes as fundamental to any investment agreement. The IISD Model Agreement also proposes reforms to the investor-state arbitration process, including more use of mediation as a precursor to arbitration, greater transparency in decision-making and acceptance of *amicus curiae* briefs.

Documents of the Working Group on the Relationship between Trade and Investment are available on DocsOnline under the document code WT/WGTI/*. TRIMs Committee documents are found under the document code G/TRIMS/*. For the practitioner, this is an important area of international law because private parties are directly impacted by national and bilateral investment rules.

4. Government procurement

The purchase of goods and services by governments has traditionally been left out of WTO agreements. The national treatment principle in GATT and GATS, for instance, does not apply to "the procurement by governmental agencies of [products or services] purchased for governmental purposes".[13] Governments have generally felt that they needed more flexibility than private industry in procurement, mostly for reasons of effective administration, politics and sovereignty. However, government is often the largest consumer in any country, purchasing from private companies a wide range of goods and services typically worth around 15% of gross domestic product,[14] and any world trading system that excludes such a significant proportion of world trade would struggle to be effective. Thus in 1981, during the Tokyo Round, an Agreement on Government Procurement (GPA) was negotiated to establish a transparent, non-discriminatory and non-protectionist procurement regime. The creation of the WTO in 1995 saw the agreement expanded to include services, sub-central government procurement and public utilities. It incorporates the principles of most favoured nation and national treatment, largely addressing procedures for tendering and providing rights of complaint to unsuccessful bidders. The GPA works on a positive list approach, requiring members to list the commitments they wish to make rather than catching everything automatically.

Unlike most of the other WTO agreements, the GPA is a plurilateral agreement, meaning that WTO members can choose whether to be bound by it. There are currently 38 members (including the European Union itself and its 25 states) and nine members negotiating accession. The relatively low accession rate perhaps reflects the internal conflicts that governments face when dealing with procurement

---

12 IISD Model Agreement, p vi.
13 GATT, Article III:8(a); GATS, Article XIII:1.
14 www.wto.org/english/tratop_e/gproc_e/over_e.htm.

negotiations in the WTO; they have a mandate from their citizens to act in the best interests of domestic producers and providers (pushing them to reject the GPA), but they also wish to seek the best price internationally for goods and services (encouraging acceptance of the GPA). Further, in such a situation, governments are both setting the rules and bound to follow them, which has raised certain concerns.

It has been suggested that one effect of the GPA is potentially to include more criteria in governmental procurement decisions, as a disguised way of protecting or encouraging domestic producers and providers which may have some advantage in meeting certification criteria. Even if it is no more than disguised protection, however, and as long as the GPA's requirements are followed so that the tendering process is fair, such a development should be encouraged. In cases where governments already impose environmental, labour or other standards on bidders, further liberalisation and transparency in government procurement should not necessarily lead to an abandonment of these standards. The existing GPA allows for discrimination by way of exceptions to protect human, animal or plant life or health, along the same lines as GATT and GATS. As with many aspects of the world trade negotiations, whether environmental and social criteria constitute valid grounds for discrimination is the subject of ongoing debate.

Apart from the GPA, there were to be two other areas of work within the WTO on government procurement. The Working Group on Transparency in Government Procurement Practices was a multilateral committee set up to examine the extent to which governments make information about their purchasing practices freely available. The Working Group had a mandate (arising from the 1996 Singapore Ministerial Conference) to develop an agreement on transparency out of the results of its studies. The second area of work, the Working Party on GATS Rules, was intended to continue negotiations on government procurement of services. Following the failed Cancun conference in 2004 and the General Council's decision of August 2004,[15] however, both bodies' work has been suspended.

Some critics of further liberalisation in government procurement consider that competition for government contracts would harm emerging industries in developing countries, faced with cheaper or more sophisticated foreign providers. If developing country governments are tempted to accept foreign providers' tenders, the critics claim, balance-of-payments issues would also arise. The current GPA recognises this to some degree, allowing for certain negotiated exceptions for developing countries "in their need to safeguard their balance-of-payments position . . . promote the establishment or development of domestic industries . . . and encourage their economic development".[16] Some commentators call for much greater support from developed countries in capacity building before developing countries should consider signing any binding agreement that may be developed.[17] One way forward, in the short term at least, may lie in restricting the scope of negotiations on

15 WT/L/579.
16 Article V:1.
17 ActionAid, *Government Procurement: ActionAid's concerns and recommendations.*

procurement to transparency obligations, without discussing any limitations on governments' rights to give preference to domestic suppliers.

Documents of the Working Group on Transparency in Government Procurement Practices and the Working Party on GATS Rules are available on DocsOnline under document codes WT/WGTGP/* and S/WPGR/* respectively. Further discussion of the GPA can be found on the WTO website at www.wto.org/english/tratop_e/gproc_e/gproc_e.htm#plurilateral. See also Arrowsmith and Trybus (eds), *Public Procurement: The Continuing Revolution* (Kluwer Law International, 2003).

Conclusion

World trade law has become a key part of legal practice. Over many decades, since the beginning of the modern era of world trade in the 1940s, the international law and legal regimes governing trade have developed and expanded at pace with an increasingly global commercial system. Today it is difficult to find a commercial transaction that is not in some way affected by world trade law. The practice of world trade law has correspondingly grown, not only within governments, but also in private commercial firms where deals are frequently framed by trade issues. Many global law firms now specialise in trade law and even more have trade law divisions, with clients from governments to industry bodies, firms and private investors.

The agreement in 1994 to create the World Trade Organisation (WTO) was a major milestone in the history of world trade law. It brought about a new emphasis on the rule of law in international economic affairs and a new commitment to certainty, impartiality and effective dispute resolution between trading partners. For both its supporters and its critics, the WTO has played a significant role in broadening the scope of world trade negotiations and debate on the rules governing economic exchanges. Besides continuing liberalisation of trade in goods and services, it has fostered discussion on a raft of legal, commercial and political issues affecting world trade, including IP rights, competition, government procurement and trade facilitation. It is beginning to discuss sustainable development concerns relating to protection of the environment, social development and poverty eradication. The WTO's pervasiveness has led some commentators to talk of global economic integration, as countries come closer to harmonising certain laws and trade structures governed as a whole by the WTO agreements.

Outside of the WTO, there are continual major developments in bilateral and regional trade agreements. These agreements provide a fertile ground for cross-pollination – concepts introduced in one region or agreement, such as sustainability impact assessments, can become incorporated in others, leading to their increased acceptance and further widespread use. In practice, bilateral and regional agreements often contain useful mechanisms for dispute resolution or more specific obligations on the parties that can, for example, provide for lower tariffs than would be available under the WTO's General Agreement on Tariffs and Trade. When assessing any client's position, it is essential to consider such relevant agreements before identifying any wider principles of WTO law.

Sections 1 and 2 of this book examined ways in which interested parties can participate in trade policy-making and negotiations. The key to effective participation in this regard is innovation. In a rapidly changing legal and policy environment, with the creation of new legal instruments and new interpretations of old instruments, innovative arguments can gain policy and legal relevance. There are also often as many informal means of participation as formal ones, and practitioners aim to open as many avenues of debate as possible in order to advance their client's case. To participate effectively in these debates, though, legal practitioners need a solid basic understanding of the relevant legal principles and the particular rules which provide the foundations for this system, set out in Section 3. At the boundaries of trade law, and becoming progressively more central to the debates through advocacy and innovation, are the developments surveyed in Section 4. These developments represent the future of the discipline and are important knowledge for any serious practitioner in the field.

Trade law is one of the most dynamic areas of international law today. Academics, practitioners and others are constantly pushing its boundaries and breaking new ground with the mutual goal of a rules-based world trading system that brings benefits – economic, environmental, social and other benefits – to all. *World Trade Law in Practice* is intended as a contribution to that goal and as basic guidance for students and legal professionals whose practice is affected by, and might affect, this rapidly developing field.

Recommended resources

1. General background information

The first section of the following list encompasses resources that provide a broad overview of the historical progression of international economic law and the configuration of pertinent institutions therein. Tariffs, subsidies and import/export practices are topics also explored in these texts. Descriptions are edited versions of their promotional material.

- L Glick & W Ince, *Manual for the Practice of US International Trade Law* (Boston, MA: Kluwer Law International, 2002). This guide is focused on an explication of the legal procedures that control US imports.
- M Benitah, *The Law of Subsidies Under GATT/WTO System*, (The Hague/ London/New York: Kluwer Law International, 2002). This text explains World Trade Organisation (WTO) subsidies rules.
- WTO Secretariat, *WTO Basic Instruments and Selected Documents* (Geneva: WTO Press, 2004). This work is the official collection of legal documents, protocols and reports adopted by the WTO. It contains the protocols for accession for new WTO members along with other legal instruments pertaining to each year, and is the successor of the General Agreement on Tariffs and Trade's (GATT) basic instruments and selected documents.
- WTO Secretariat, *WTO Analytical Index – Guide to WTO Law and Practice* (Co-published by the WTO and Bernan Press). This is the authoritative guide to the interpretation and application of findings and decisions of WTO panels, the WTO Appellate Body and other ancillary WTO bodies.
- D Van den Bossche, *The Law and Policy of the WTO: Text, Cases and Materials* (Cambridge: Cambridge University Press, 2005). This book is a great reference for WTO policy and practice. Included is commentary on the organisation itself, as well as the foundational principles of the international trade regime.
- H van Houtte, *The Law of International Trade*, 2nd ed (London: Sweet & Maxwell, 2002).
- M Bronckers and G Horlick (eds), *WTO Jurisprudence and Policy – Practitioner's Perspectives* (London: Cameron May International Law Publishers, 2005).
- J Jackson, *The World Trading System: Law and Policy of International Economic Relations*, 2nd ed (London: MIT Press, 1997). This leading book is the WTO successor of the first law book about the world trading system.
- M Matsushita *et al*, *The WTO: Law, Practice and Policy – The Oxford International Law Library* (Oxford: Oxford University Press, 2003).

- W Goode, *Dictionary of Trade Policy Terms*, 4th ed (Cambridge: Cambridge University Press, 2004). This text contains helpful definitions to terms associated with international trade law, economic theory, international economic treaties, WTO institutions and mechanisms, and international organisations associated with international trade.
- S Schnitzer, *Understanding International Trade Law* (Exeter: Law Matter Publishing, 2006).
- L D'Arcy *et al*, *Schmitthoff's Export Trade: The Law and Practice of International Trade*, 10th ed (London: Sweet & Maxwell, 2000). This provides coverage of developments across the whole field of the law and practice of international trade.
- R Folsom *et al*, *International Trade and Economic Relations in a Nutshell* (United States: West Publishing Company, 2004).
- R Bhala, *International Trade Law Handbook* 2nd ed (LexisNexis: Mathew Bender Publishers, 1998).
- P Gallagher, *The First Ten Years of the WTO: 1995–2005* (Cambridge: Cambridge University Press, 2005). A useful reference guide for policy makers and all requiring a detailed understanding of the WTO.
- P Gallagher, P Low & A Stoler (eds), *Managing the Challenges of WTO Participation*, (Cambridge: Cambridge University Press, 2005). Consisting of 45 case studies, this book reflects on the disparate experiences in addressing the challenges of participating in the WTO.
- L Glick, *Guide to Customs and Trade Law: After the Customs Modernization* (The Hague: Aspen Publishers, 1997). This book is a guide to US customs and trade laws.

2. Technical and sanitary standards and labels

- A Sykes, *Product Standards for Internationally Integrated Goods Markets* (Washington: Brookings Institution Press, 1995). This book provides economic and legal analysis of international efforts to police technical barriers in the WTO/GATT system, the European Union, the US federal system and the North American Free Trade Agreement (NAFTA).
- M Echols, *Food Safety and the WTO: The Interplay of Science, Culture and Technology* (The Hague: Kluwer Law International, 2001). This book delves into the relationship between the Agreement on the Application of Sanitary and Phytosanitary Measures, food traditions, science and technology.
- YS Lee, *Safeguard Measures in World Trade: The Legal Analysis*, 2nd ed (The Hague: Kluwer Law International, 2003). This provides comprehensive coverage on safeguards supplemented by legal analysis of the important issues in the interpretation and application of the current rules on safeguards.

3. Trade negotiations in the WTO

- A Hoda, *Tariff Negotiations and Renegotiations Under the GATT and the WTO: Procedures and Practices* (Cambridge: Cambridge University Press, 2002). This book reviews the evolution of tariff negotiations as well as the procedures adopted and practices followed by the contracting parties to GATT 1947 and the members of the WTO.

- G Schaffer, *Defending Interests: Public-Private Partnerships in WTO Litigation* (Washington: Brookings Institution Press, 2003). This book examines the growing interaction between private enterprises and public officials to challenge foreign trade barriers. It calls attention to the ways in which well-organised private parties are using the WTO legal system to advance their own commercial ambitions, and how public officials increasingly are dependent on their assistance.

4. Dispute settlement information

- R Yerxa and B Wilson (eds), *Key Issues in WTO Dispute Settlement – The First Ten Years* (Cambridge: Cambridge University Press, 2005). Co-published with the WTO. This explains the operation and evolution of the WTO dispute settlement system by WTO Secretariat professionals and outside experts, covering the first 10 years of the WTO.
- WTO Secretariat, *WTO Appellate Body Repertory of Reports and Awards 1995–2004* (Cambridge: Cambridge University Press and Geneva: WTO Press, 2005).
- WTO Secretariat, *Dispute Settlement Procedures*, 2nd ed (Cambridge: Cambridge University Press and Geneva: WTO Press, 2004). This new edition takes into account legal decisions and other legal instruments adopted since 1995 including Working Procedures for Appellate Review and the Rules of Conduct for the Dispute Settlement Understanding (DSU).
- WTO Secretariat, *Guide to Dispute Settlement* (Geneva: WTO Press and Kluwer Law International Press, 2004). An accessible guide to 'bringing a case' before the WTO or responding to a case already in progress for lawyers, businesspeople or government officials confronted with a disputable trade issue.
- WTO Secretariat, *A Handbook on the WTO Dispute Settlement System* (Cambridge: Cambridge University Press, 2004). This book is a guide to the dispute settlements processes within the WTO.
- E-U Petersmann & M Pollack, *Transaltantic Economic Disputes: The EU, the US and the WTO (International Economic Law Series)* (United States: Oxford University Press, 2004). Surveying a variety of transatlantic governance and dispute settlement problems, this book is replete with instructive case studies of economic and regulatory disputes written by leading EU and US trade experts.
- D Palmeter, *Dispute Settlement in the WTO: Practise and Procedure* (Cambridge: Cambridge University Press, 2004). A procedural guide which, among many other topics, includes sections on jurisdiction; sources of law; function, form and responsibility of panels; and developing country-related provisions of the DSU.

5. Information on the General Agreement on Trade in Services (GATS)

- WTO Secretariat, *Handbook on the GATS Agreement* (Cambridge: Cambridge University Press and Geneva: WTO Press, 2005). The handbook contains an explication of the basic purposes and concepts of GATS as well as pertinent primary documents.

- WTO Secretariat, *Guide to GATS, An Overview of Issues for Further Liberalization* (The Hague: Kluwer Law International, 2000). This book examines the prospects and impediments surrounding service liberalisation in myriad sectors.
- M Krajweski, *National Regulation and Trade Liberalization in Services* (The Hague: Kluwer Law International, 2003). This investigates topics such as the political and ideological dynamics of GATS negotiations; services trade liberalisation in regional integration systems (particularly in EU law); policies common to diverse national regulatory systems; the notions of deregulation and privatisation; and GATS transparency obligations.

6. Regional trade agreements

- J Crawford and R Fiorentino, Discussion Paper No 8: Analysis and Special Reports, *The Changing Landscape of Regional Trade Agreements* (Geneva: WTO Press, 2005). This paper looks at main trends and characteristics of regional trade agreements both in force and under negotiation. It also examines their effects on third parties and on the multilateral trading system.
- JH Mathis, *Regional Trade Agreements in the GATT/WTO, Article XX and the Internal Trade Requirement* (The Hague: TMC Asser Press, 2002). Divided into two parts, this book analyses the interaction between regional trade agreements and the WTO. Part 1 of the book contains explanations on pre-GATT preference and the most favoured nation response. Part 2 discusses regionalism in the GATT, regional practice in the WTO and its response.

7. Dumping

- WTO Secretariat, *A Handbook of Anti-Dumping Investigations* (Geneva: WTO Press and Cambridge: Cambridge University Press, 2005). This handbook, prepared by specialists in the WTO Secretariat, covers the primary mechanisms and frameworks regulating anti-dumping investigations as embodied in the relevant WTO provisions.
- Van Bael & Bellis, *Anti-dumping and Other Trade Protection Laws of the EC*, 4th ed (The Hague, Kluwer Law International, 2004). Focused on anti-dumping measures as well as international economic law in more general terms, this book would be useful for practitioners dealing with the European Union.
- T Stewart & A Dwyer, *A Practitioner's Guide to WTO Anti-Dumping and Subsidies Agreements* (The Hague: Kluwer Law International, 1998).
- E Vermulst and F Graafsma, *WTO Disputes, Subsidies and Safeguards* (London: Cameron May International Law Publishing, 2002). This book analyses WTO panel and Appellate Body reports with respect to four commercial defence agreements: the Anti-dumping Agreement, the Agreement on Subsidies and Countervailing Measures, the Safeguards Agreement and the Agreement on Textiles and Clothing.
- United Nations Conference on Trade and Development (UNCTAD), "Anti-Dumping and Countervailing Procedures: Use or Abuse? Implications for

Developing Countries" (Geneva, United Nations Conference on Trade and Development, 2001).

8. IP rights

- Maskus, Keith E (ed) *The WTO, Intellectual Property Rights and the Knowledge Economy* (Cheltenham: Edward Elgar Publishing, 2004). A guide to a nuanced understanding of the issues, regulations and processes governing the IP rights regime.
- Miller & M Davis, *Intellectual Property: Patents, Trademarks, and Copyright (Nutshell Series)* 3rd ed (United States: West Group Publishing, 2000). This text includes a discussion of the legal issues surrounding patents, trademarks and copyrights.
- R Schechter and J Thomas, *Principles of Patent Law: Hornback Series* (United States: West Group Publishing, 2004). This book – written primarily from a US point of view – is a concise guide to patent law and includes a part on patent law from an international perspective.
- UNCTAD-International Centre for Trade and Sustainable Development (ICTSD), *Resource Book on TRIPS and Development* (Cambridge: Cambridge University Press, 2005). A valuable guide to the WTO's Agreement on Trade-Related Aspects of Intellectual Property Rights.
- J Radcliffe, *Patents World Law and Practice* (London: Sweet & Maxwell, 2005).
- J Masterton, *International Trademarks and Copyrights: Enforcement and Management*, (American Bar Association, 2004).
- A Ilardi & M Blakeney (eds), *International Encyclopedia of Intellectual Property Treaties* (Oxford: Oxford University Press, 2004).

9. Trade and sustainable development

- C Button, *The Power to Protect: Trade, Health and the World Trade Organization* (Oxford: Hart Publishing, 2004).
- P Könz, C Bellmann, L Assuncao and R Melendez-Otiz (eds), *Trade, Environment, and Sustainable Development* (Geneva: UNU/IAS & ICTSD, 2000). This reference document gathers a unique collection of analytical, research, commentary and case study articles from sub-Saharan African and Latin American authors on the hard issues in the current debate on trade, environment and sustainable development.
- G Sampson, *The World Trade Organisation and Sustainable Development* (Tokyo: UNU Press, 2006). This book argues that the WTO has evolved into a World Trade and Sustainable Development Organization. Many of the issues that are on the WTO agenda – endangered species, public health, genetic modification, the patenting of life forms – are far from what could be considered traditional trade policy matters.
- MC Cordonier Segger and A Khalfan, *Sustainable Development Law: Principles, Practices, and Prospects* (Oxford: Oxford University Press, 2004). This textbook analyses recent developments in international sustainable development law, a field emerging at the intersection between international economic, environmental and social law.

- M Gehring and MC Cordonier Segger, *Sustainable Development in World Trade Law* (The Hague: Kluwer Law International, 2005). This collection of papers, sponsored by the Centre for International Sustainable Development Law, demonstrates that sustainable development serves as a unifying concept with the potential to facilitate much-needed respect for international law and timely implementation of diverse and overlapping international commitments between trade and other areas of international law.
- MC Cordonier Segger and M Reynal, *Beyond the Barricades – The Americas Trade and Sustainable Development Agenda* (New York: Ashgate Publishers, 2005). Beyond the barricades surrounding recent economic meetings, a constructive agenda is being developed on trade and sustainability issues in the Americas. This book brings together a diversity of perspectives and expertise on environment and development issues from governments, civil society and businesses in the Western Hemisphere. The book reviews specific areas where trade, environment and social policies intersect in the Americas, proposing that more integrated laws and policies could strengthen hemispheric progress towards sustainable development.
- D French, *International Law and Policy of Sustainable Development* (Manchester: Manchester University Press, 2005).
- B Hoekman *et al* (eds), *Development, Trade and the WTO: A Handbook (World Bank Trade and Development Series)* (Washington: IBRD/World Bank, 2002). This book – a compilation of articles from scholars in trade law – takes a substantive look at the intersection between trade and development.

10. International finance

- M Sornarajah, *The International Law on Foreign Investment,* 2nd ed (Cambridge: Cambridge University Press, 2004). Focusing on the protection of foreign investment and its associated problems, this book explores treaty-based methods and examines several bilateral and regional investment treaties, as well as relevant literature in economics, political science and other associated disciplines.
- G Walker, *International Banking Regulation: Law Policy and Practise* (The Hague: Kluwer Law International, 2001). This work offers a comprehensive examination of the development and structure of the current provisions for the control of international financial markets.

11. Investment international arbitration

- N Horn & S Kroll, *Arbitrating Foreign Investment Disputes: Procedural and Substantive Legal Aspects (Studies in Transnational Economic Law)* (The Hague: Kluwer Law International, 2004).
- R Bishop (ed), *The Art of Advocacy in International Arbitration* (Berne: Stämpfli Verlag, 2004).
- T Weiler, *NAFTA Investment Law and Arbitration: Past Issues, Current Practice, Future Prospects* (Transnational Publishers, 2004). This book, written by prominent scholars within the field of trade and investment law, covers both

the substantive laws, which govern how NAFTA governments must treat investors and their investments, and the procedural ground rules by which disputes are settled.

- H Alvarez *et al, Model Law Decision Cases, Applying the UNCITRAL Model Law on International Commercial Arbitration (1985–2001)* (The Hague: Kluwer Law International, 2002). This book includes several case studies from Canada, Singapore, Hong Kong, the United States, Bermuda and India, among others.
- A & K Tweedale, *Arbitration of Commercial Disputes; International and English Law and Practise* (Oxford: Oxford University Press, 2005). This text will be helpful for those dealing with the arbitration of commercial disputes within the English legal framework.

12. International competition law

- H Tzong-Leh *et al, The Future Development Of Competition Framework (International Competition Law)* (The Hague: Kluwer Law International, 2004).
- YC Chao *et al, International and Comparative Competition Laws and Policies (International Law Series Vol 3)* (The Hague: Kluwer Law International, 2001). This book explores the prospects for competition policy, its likely development and its ever-more-central role in the world trade regime.
- M Holmes *et al* (eds), *A Practical Guide To National Competition Rules Across Europe (International Competition Law Series)* (The Hague: Kluwer Law International, 2004).

13. Journals and newsletters

- *Arbitration Law Monthly*, Informa Legal Publishing UK.
- *Business Law International*, Sweet & Maxwell.
- *International and Comparative Law Quarterly*, Oxford University Press on behalf of the British Institute for International and Comparative Law.
- *International Arbitration Law Review*, Sweet & Maxwell.
- *Journal of Business Law*, Sweet & Maxwell.
- *International Trade Law and Regulation*, Sweet & Maxwell.
- *Journal of International Banking Law*, Sweet & Maxwell.
- *International Maritime Law*, Lawtext Publishing.
- *Lloyd's Law Reports*, Informa Legal Publishing UK.
- *Lloyd's List Law Reports*, Informa Legal Publishing UK.
- *Lloyd's Maritime and Commerical Law Quarterly*, Informa Legal Publishing UK.
- *Lloyd's Maritime Newsletter*, Informa Legal Publishing UK.
- *P&I International*, Informa Legal Publishing UK.
- *Shipping and Trade Law*, Informa Legal Publishing UK.
- *Journal of World Trade*, Kluwer Law International.
- *Legal Issues of Economic Integration*, Kluwer Law International.
- *World Trade and Arbitration Materials*, Kluwer Law International.
- *World Trade Review*, WTO Secretariat and Cambridge University Press.
- *Journal of International Economic Law*, Oxford University Press.

- *Journal of Competition Law and Economics*, Oxford University Press.
- *GAD – The Global Anti-Dumping Handbook*, Cameron May International Law Publishers.
- *WTO Decisions – A Comprehensive Topic Index*, Cameron May International Law Publishers.
- *ITLR – The International Trade Law Reports*, Cameron May International Law Publishers.
- *WTG – The Weekly Trade Globe*, Cameron May International Law Publishers.
- *NAFTA – The NAFTA Arbitration Reports*, Cameron May International Law Publishers.
- *Yale Journal of International Law*, Yale Law School.
- *European Journal of International Law*, Cambridge University Press.

14. Online sources

- UNCTAD: www.unctad.org.
- American Society of International Law, Guide to Electronic Resources for International Law (private international law; international commercial arbitration; international sale of goods and IOs): www.eisil.org/index.php?cat=19&t=sub_pages.
- WTO: www.wto.org.
- Europa (official information server of the European Union): www.europa.eu.int.
- Georgetown University's Institute of International Economic Law: www.ll.georgetown.edu/intl/iiel/home.htm.
- Office of the US Trade Representative: www.ustr.gov/index.html.
- US International Trade Commission: www.usitc.gov/.
- New York University Law School – WTO and GATT Research: www.law.nyu.edu/library/wtoguide.html.
- HierosGamos – Worldwide Legal Directories: www.hg.org/trade.html.
- WorldTradeLaw.net: www.worldtradelaw.net/.
- ICTSD: www.ictsd.org/.
- Revised Guide to International Trade Law Sources on the Internet: www.llrx.com/features/trade3.htm.
- Northwestern Law School – International Trade, Business and Economic Law: www.law.northwestern.edu/lawlibrary/research/foreign/inttrade.htm.
- Centre for International Sustainable Development Law: www.cisdl.org/programmes001.html.
- Trade Law Centre for Southern Africa: www.tralac.org/.

About the authors

Marie-Claire Cordonier Segger
Director, Centre for International Sustainable Development Law
Fellow, Lauterpacht Centre for International Law, Faculty of Law, University of Cambridge
mccs2@cam.ac.uk

Marie-Claire Cordonier Segger, DPhil (Oxon) (tbc), MEM (Yale), BCL & LLB (McGill), BA Hons, is director of the Centre for International Sustainable Development Law (CISDL), based at McGill University. She also serves as head of international affairs at the Canadian Ministry of Natural Resources, and as a fellow of the Lauterpacht Centre for International Law at the University of Cambridge. She is author/editor of 10 books and over 60 other publications on international law and policy in the field of sustainable development, including *Sustainable Development Law: Principles, Practices and Prospects* (Oxford University Press, 2004) with A Khalfan, and *Sustainable Justice* (Martinus Nijhoff, 2004) with Judge CG Weeramantry.

She advises on the implementation of international sustainable development treaties to the United Nations and member governments in Africa, Asia and Latin America. She is an instructor for the International Development Law Organisation, chairs the International Law on Sustainable Development Partnership under the auspices of the United Nations Commission on Sustainable Development, and lectures for several law faculties in the United Kingdom, Canada, Chile, Kenya and other countries.

Markus W Gehring
Lead Counsel, Centre for International Sustainable Development Law
Lecturer in Law, Robinson College, Cambridge
Director of European Studies MPhil, CIS, University of Cambridge
mwg24@cam.ac.uk

Markus W Gehring, LLM (Yale), Dr jur (Hamburg), *Rechtsanwalt* (Frankfurt), is a lecturer in international and European law at the Centre of International Studies and a fellow in law at Robinson College, University of Cambridge. He serves as lead counsel for sustainable international trade, investment and competition law with the Centre of International Sustainable Development Law (CISDL), based at McGill University, Canada. He represented the CISDL at WTO ministerials in Doha, Cancun and Hong Kong. Prior to joining Cambridge, Dr Gehring practised European and international trade law at the Brussels office of Cleary Gottlieb. He tutored in international law at the University of Oxford and worked as a legal researcher with Professor Vaughan Lowe. He also taught and researched at the Faculty of Law, Hamburg University, and was a legal fellow at the International Centre for Trade and Sustainable Development in Geneva. Dr Gehring has published on various aspects of trade law, including *Sustainable Development in World Trade Law* with Marie-Claire Cordonier Segger (Kluwer Law International, 2005).

Jarrod Hepburn
Legal Research Fellow, Centre for International Sustainable Development Law
jhepburn@cisdl.org

Jarrod Hepburn, LLB (Hons), BE (SoftEng) (Hons), LMusA, is a legal research fellow with the CISDL in the Trade, Investment and Competition Law Research Programme. He authored several working papers as part of the CISDL "Recent Developments in International Law Related to Sustainable Development" series, produced with a contribution from Foreign Affairs Canada. His research interests lie in the relations between trade and development, balancing wealth creation through trade and traditional ways of life, and the role of sustainable development law in poverty eradication.

Mr Hepburn has served on the editorial board of the *Melbourne University Law Review* and spent time in France studying the French, European and global systems for protection of human rights and freedoms. He also has experience in the IP department of Australian corporate law firm Mallesons Stephen Jaques.

Mr Hepburn has travelled in Europe, Africa and North America. He speaks English, French and basic German.

John H Jackson
Director, Institute of International Economic Law, Georgetown University
jacksojh@law.georgetown.edu

John H Jackson is university professor of law at the Georgetown University Law Center and director of the Law Center's Institute of International Economic Law. He joined the Georgetown faculty after a distinguished career as Hessel E Yntema professor of law at the University of Michigan. He has advised the US and other governments and international organisations on international trade law, and from 1973 to 1974 was general counsel of the Office of the United States Trade Representative. In June 2003, Professor Jackson was awarded the honorary degree of doctor *iuris honoris causa* by Hamburg University Faculty of Law and was also appointed to the WTO Consultative Board. The board released a report entitled "The Future of the WTO: Addressing Institutional Challenges in the New Millennium" in January 2005. He has published widely in the area of international trade law, including *The Jurisprudence of GATT and the WTO: Insights on Treaty Law and Economic Relations* (Cambridge University Press, 2000).

Kristin Price
Researcher, Centre for International Sustainable Development Law
kristin_price89@hotmail.com

Kristin Price is a researcher with the CISDL, focused primarily on international law and international relations aspects of sustainable international trade and sustainable development law. Based out of Cambridge, United Kingdom, Ms Price originally hails from Calgary, Alberta, Canada. She received her BA in political science from Brown University (Providence, RI, United States) in May 2005. Ms Price is pursuing an MPhil degree in international relations at the University of Cambridge.

Agreement Establishing the World Trade Organization

The *Parties* to this Agreement,

Recognizing that their relations in the field of trade and economic endeavour should be conducted with a view to raising standards of living, ensuring full employment and a large and steadily growing volume of real income and effective demand, and expanding the production of and trade in goods and services, while allowing for the optimal use of the world's resources in accordance with the objective of sustainable development, seeking both to protect and preserve the environment and to enhance the means for doing so in a manner consistent with their respective needs and concerns at different levels of economic development,

Recognizing further that there is need for positive efforts designed to ensure that developing countries, and especially the least developed among them, secure a share in the growth in international trade commensurate with the needs of their economic development,

Being desirous of contributing to these objectives by entering into reciprocal and mutually advantageous arrangements directed to the substantial reduction of tariffs and other barriers to trade and to the elimination of discriminatory treatment in international trade relations,

Resolved, therefore, to develop an integrated, more viable and durable multilateral trading system encompassing the General Agreement on Tariffs and Trade, the results of past trade liberalization efforts, and all of the results of the Uruguay Round of Multilateral Trade Negotiations,

Determined to preserve the basic principles and to further the objectives underlying this multilateral trading system,

Agree as follows:

Article I

Establishment of the Organization

The World Trade Organization (hereinafter referred to as "the WTO") is hereby established.

Article II

Scope of the WTO

1. The WTO shall provide the common institutional framework for the conduct of trade relations among its Members in matters related to the agreements and associated legal instruments included in the Annexes to this Agreement.

2. The agreements and associated legal instruments included in Annexes 1, 2 and 3 (hereinafter referred to as "Multilateral Trade Agreements") are integral parts of this Agreement, binding on all Members.

3. The agreements and associated legal instruments included in Annex 4 (hereinafter referred to as "Plurilateral Trade Agreements") are also part of this Agreement for those Members that have accepted them, and are binding on those Members. The Plurilateral Trade Agreements do not create either obligations or rights for Members that have not accepted them.

4. The General Agreement on Tariffs and Trade 1994 as specified in Annex 1A (hereinafter referred to as "GATT 1994") is legally distinct from the General Agreement on Tariffs and Trade, dated 30 October 1947, annexed to the Final Act Adopted at the Conclusion of the Second Session of the Preparatory Committee of the United Nations Conference on Trade and Employment, as subsequently rectified, amended or modified (hereinafter referred to as "GATT 1947").

Article III

Functions of the WTO

1. The WTO shall facilitate the implementation, administration and operation, and further the objectives, of this Agreement and of the Multilateral Trade Agreements, and shall also provide the framework for the implementation, administration and operation of the Plurilateral Trade Agreements.

2. The WTO shall provide the forum for negotiations among its Members concerning their multilateral trade relations in matters dealt with under the agreements in the Annexes to this Agreement. The WTO may also provide a forum for further negotiations among its Members concerning their multilateral trade relations, and a framework for the implementation of the results of such negotiations, as may be decided by the Ministerial Conference.

3. The WTO shall administer the Understanding on Rules and Procedures Governing the Settlement of Disputes (hereinafter referred to as the "Dispute Settlement Understanding" or "DSU") in Annex 2 to this Agreement.

4. The WTO shall administer the Trade Policy Review Mechanism (hereinafter referred to as the "TPRM") provided for in Annex 3 to this Agreement.

5. With a view to achieving greater coherence in global economic policy-making, the WTO shall cooperate, as appropriate, with the International Monetary Fund and with the International Bank for Reconstruction and Development and its affiliated agencies.

Article IV

Structure of the WTO

1. There shall be a Ministerial Conference composed of representatives of all the Members, which shall meet at least once every two years. The Ministerial Conference shall carry out the functions of the WTO and take actions necessary to this effect. The Ministerial Conference shall have the authority to take decisions on all matters under any of the Multilateral Trade Agreements, if so requested by a Member, in accordance with the specific requirements for decision-making in this Agreement and in the relevant Multilateral Trade Agreement.

2. There shall be a General Council composed of representatives of all the Members, which shall meet as appropriate. In the intervals between meetings of the Ministerial Conference, its

functions shall be conducted by the General Council. The General Council shall also carry out the functions assigned to it by this Agreement. The General Council shall establish its rules of procedure and approve the rules of procedure for the Committees provided for in paragraph 7.

3. The General Council shall convene as appropriate to discharge the responsibilities of the Dispute Settlement Body provided for in the Dispute Settlement Understanding. The Dispute Settlement Body may have its own chairman and shall establish such rules of procedure as it deems necessary for the fulfilment of those responsibilities.

4. The General Council shall convene as appropriate to discharge the responsibilities of the Trade Policy Review Body provided for in the TPRM. The Trade Policy Review Body may have its own chairman and shall establish such rules of procedure as it deems necessary for the fulfilment of those responsibilities.

5. There shall be a Council for Trade in Goods, a Council for Trade in Services and a Council for Trade-Related Aspects of Intellectual Property Rights (hereinafter referred to as the "Council for TRIPS"), which shall operate under the general guidance of the General Council. The Council for Trade in Goods shall oversee the functioning of the Multilateral Trade Agreements in Annex 1A. The Council for Trade in Services shall oversee the functioning of the General Agreement on Trade in Services (hereinafter referred to as "GATS"). The Council for TRIPS shall oversee the functioning of the Agreement on Trade-Related Aspects of Intellectual Property Rights (hereinafter referred to as the "Agreement on TRIPS"). These Councils shall carry out the functions assigned to them by their respective agreements and by the General Council. They shall establish their respective rules of procedure subject to the approval of the General Council. Membership in these Councils shall be open to representatives of all Members. These Councils shall meet as necessary to carry out their functions.

6. The Council for Trade in Goods, the Council for Trade in Services and the Council for TRIPS shall establish subsidiary bodies as required. These subsidiary bodies shall establish their respective rules of procedure subject to the approval of their respective Councils.

7. The Ministerial Conference shall establish a Committee on Trade and Development, a Committee on Balance-of-Payments Restrictions and a Committee on Budget, Finance and Administration, which shall carry out the functions assigned to them by this Agreement and by the Multilateral Trade Agreements, and any additional functions assigned to them by the General Council, and may establish such additional Committees with such functions as it may deem appropriate. As part of its functions, the Committee on Trade and Development shall periodically review the special provisions in the Multilateral Trade Agreements in favour of the least-developed country Members and report to the General Council for appropriate action. Membership in these Committees shall be open to representatives of all Members.

8. The bodies provided for under the Plurilateral Trade Agreements shall carry out the functions assigned to them under those Agreements and shall operate within the institutional framework of the WTO. These bodies shall keep the General Council informed of their activities on a regular basis.

Article V

Relations with Other Organizations

1. The General Council shall make appropriate arrangements for effective cooperation with other intergovernmental organizations that have responsibilities related to those of the WTO.

2. The General Council may make appropriate arrangements for consultation and cooperation with non-governmental organizations concerned with matters related to those of the WTO.

Article VI

The Secretariat

1. There shall be a Secretariat of the WTO (hereinafter referred to as "the Secretariat") headed by a Director-General.

2. The Ministerial Conference shall appoint the Director-General and adopt regulations setting out the powers, duties, conditions of service and term of office of the Director-General.

3. The Director-General shall appoint the members of the staff of the Secretariat and determine their duties and conditions of service in accordance with regulations adopted by the Ministerial Conference.

4. The responsibilities of the Director-General and of the staff of the Secretariat shall be exclusively international in character. In the discharge of their duties, the Director-General and the staff of the Secretariat shall not seek or accept instructions from any government or any other authority external to the WTO. They shall refrain from any action which might adversely reflect on their position as international officials. The Members of the WTO shall respect the international character of the responsibilities of the Director-General and of the staff of the Secretariat and shall not seek to influence them in the discharge of their duties.

Article VII

Budget and Contributions

1. The Director-General shall present to the Committee on Budget, Finance and Administration the annual budget estimate and financial statement of the WTO. The Committee on Budget, Finance and Administration shall review the annual budget estimate and the financial statement presented by the Director-General and make recommendations thereon to the General Council. The annual budget estimate shall be subject to approval by the General Council.

2. The Committee on Budget, Finance and Administration shall propose to the General Council financial regulations which shall include provisions setting out:

(a) the scale of contributions apportioning the expenses of the WTO among its Members; and

(b) the measures to be taken in respect of Members in arrears.

The financial regulations shall be based, as far as practicable, on the regulations and practices of GATT 1947.

3. The General Council shall adopt the financial regulations and the annual budget estimate by a two-thirds majority comprising more than half of the Members of the WTO.

4. Each Member shall promptly contribute to the WTO its share in the expenses of the WTO in accordance with the financial regulations adopted by the General Council.

Article VIII

Status of the WTO

1. The WTO shall have legal personality, and shall be accorded by each of its Members such legal capacity as may be necessary for the exercise of its functions.

2. The WTO shall be accorded by each of its Members such privileges and immunities as are necessary for the exercise of its functions.

3. The officials of the WTO and the representatives of the Members shall similarly be accorded by each of its Members such privileges and immunities as are necessary for the independent exercise of their functions in connection with the WTO.

4. The privileges and immunities to be accorded by a Member to the WTO, its officials, and the representatives of its Members shall be similar to the privileges and immunities stipulated in the Convention on the Privileges and Immunities of the Specialized Agencies, approved by the General Assembly of the United Nations on 21 November 1947.

5. The WTO may conclude a headquarters agreement.

Article IX

Decision-Making

1. The WTO shall continue the practice of decision-making by consensus followed under GATT 1947.[1] Except as otherwise provided, where a decision cannot be arrived at by consensus, the matter at issue shall be decided by voting. At meetings of the Ministerial Conference and the General Council, each Member of the WTO shall have one vote. Where the European Communities exercise their right to vote, they shall have a number of votes equal to the number of their member States[2] which are Members of the WTO. Decisions of the Ministerial Conference and the General Council shall be taken by a majority of the votes cast, unless otherwise provided in this Agreement or in the relevant Multilateral Trade Agreement.[3]

2. The Ministerial Conference and the General Council shall have the exclusive authority to adopt interpretations of this Agreement and of the Multilateral Trade Agreements. In the case of an interpretation of a Multilateral Trade Agreement in Annex 1, they shall exercise their authority on the basis of a recommendation by the Council overseeing the functioning of that Agreement. The decision to adopt an interpretation shall be taken by a three-fourths majority of the Members. This paragraph shall not be used in a manner that would undermine the amendment provisions in Article X.

3. In exceptional circumstances, the Ministerial Conference may decide to waive an obligation imposed on a Member by this Agreement or any of the Multilateral Trade Agreements, provided that any such decision shall be taken by three fourths[4] of the Members unless otherwise provided for in this paragraph.

(a) A request for a waiver concerning this Agreement shall be submitted to the Ministerial Conference for consideration pursuant to the practice of decision-making by consensus. The Ministerial Conference shall establish a time-period, which shall not exceed 90 days, to consider the request. If consensus is not reached during the time-period, any decision to grant a waiver shall be taken by three fourths4 of the Members.

---

1 The body concerned shall be deemed to have decided by consensus on a matter submitted for its consideration, if no Member, present at the meeting when the decision is taken, formally objects to the proposed decision.

2 The number of votes of the European Communities and their member States shall in no case exceed the number of the member States of the European Communities.

3 Decisions by the General Council when convened as the Dispute Settlement Body shall be taken only in accordance with the provisions of paragraph 4 of Article 2 of the Dispute Settlement Understanding.

4 A decision to grant a waiver in respect of any obligation subject to a transition period or a period for staged implementation that the requesting Member has not performed by the end of the relevant period shall be taken only by consensus.

(b) A request for a waiver concerning the Multilateral Trade Agreements in Annexes 1A or 1B or 1C and their annexes shall be submitted initially to the Council for Trade in Goods, the Council for Trade in Services or the Council for TRIPS, respectively, for consideration during a time-period which shall not exceed 90 days. At the end of the time-period, the relevant Council shall submit a report to the Ministerial Conference.

4. A decision by the Ministerial Conference granting a waiver shall state the exceptional circumstances justifying the decision, the terms and conditions governing the application of the waiver, and the date on which the waiver shall terminate. Any waiver granted for a period of more than one year shall be reviewed by the Ministerial Conference not later than one year after it is granted, and thereafter annually until the waiver terminates. In each review, the Ministerial Conference shall examine whether the exceptional circumstances justifying the waiver still exist and whether the terms and conditions attached to the waiver have been met. The Ministerial Conference, on the basis of the annual review, may extend, modify or terminate the waiver.

5. Decisions under a Plurilateral Trade Agreement, including any decisions on interpretations and waivers, shall be governed by the provisions of that Agreement.

Article X

Amendments

1. Any Member of the WTO may initiate a proposal to amend the provisions of this Agreement or the Multilateral Trade Agreements in Annex 1 by submitting such proposal to the Ministerial Conference. The Councils listed in paragraph 5 of Article IV may also submit to the Ministerial Conference proposals to amend the provisions of the corresponding Multilateral Trade Agreements in Annex 1 the functioning of which they oversee. Unless the Ministerial Conference decides on a longer period, for a period of 90 days after the proposal has been tabled formally at the Ministerial Conference any decision by the Ministerial Conference to submit the proposed amendment to the Members for acceptance shall be taken by consensus. Unless the provisions of paragraphs 2, 5 or 6 apply, that decision shall specify whether the provisions of paragraphs 3 or 4 shall apply. If consensus is reached, the Ministerial Conference shall forthwith submit the proposed amendment to the Members for acceptance. If consensus is not reached at a meeting of the Ministerial Conference within the established period, the Ministerial Conference shall decide by a two-thirds majority of the Members whether to submit the proposed amendment to the Members for acceptance. Except as provided in paragraphs 2, 5 and 6, the provisions of paragraph 3 shall apply to the proposed amendment, unless the Ministerial Conference decides by a three-fourths majority of the Members that the provisions of paragraph 4 shall apply.

2. Amendments to the provisions of this Article and to the provisions of the following Articles shall take effect only upon acceptance by all Members:

Article IX of this Agreement;
Articles I and II of GATT 1994;
Article II:1 of GATS;
Article 4 of the Agreement on TRIPS.

3. Amendments to provisions of this Agreement, or of the Multilateral Trade Agreements in Annexes 1A and 1C, other than those listed in paragraphs 2 and 6, of a nature that would alter the rights and obligations of the Members, shall take effect for the Members that have accepted them upon acceptance by two thirds of the Members and thereafter for each other Member upon

acceptance by it. The Ministerial Conference may decide by a three-fourths majority of the Members that any amendment made effective under this paragraph is of such a nature that any Member which has not accepted it within a period specified by the Ministerial Conference in each case shall be free to withdraw from the WTO or to remain a Member with the consent of the Ministerial Conference.

4. Amendments to provisions of this Agreement or of the Multilateral Trade Agreements in Annexes 1A and 1C, other than those listed in paragraphs 2 and 6, of a nature that would not alter the rights and obligations of the Members, shall take effect for all Members upon acceptance by two thirds of the Members.

5. Except as provided in paragraph 2 above, amendments to Parts I, II and III of GATS and the respective annexes shall take effect for the Members that have accepted them upon acceptance by two thirds of the Members and thereafter for each Member upon acceptance by it. The Ministerial Conference may decide by a three-fourths majority of the Members that any amendment made effective under the preceding provision is of such a nature that any Member which has not accepted it within a period specified by the Ministerial Conference in each case shall be free to withdraw from the WTO or to remain a Member with the consent of the Ministerial Conference. Amendments to Parts IV, V and VI of GATS and the respective annexes shall take effect for all Members upon acceptance by two thirds of the Members.

6. Notwithstanding the other provisions of this Article, amendments to the Agreement on TRIPS meeting the requirements of paragraph 2 of Article 71 thereof may be adopted by the Ministerial Conference without further formal acceptance process.

7. Any Member accepting an amendment to this Agreement or to a Multilateral Trade Agreement in Annex 1 shall deposit an instrument of acceptance with the Director-General of the WTO within the period of acceptance specified by the Ministerial Conference.

8. Any Member of the WTO may initiate a proposal to amend the provisions of the Multilateral Trade Agreements in Annexes 2 and 3 by submitting such proposal to the Ministerial Conference. The decision to approve amendments to the Multilateral Trade Agreement in Annex 2 shall be made by consensus and these amendments shall take effect for all Members upon approval by the Ministerial Conference. Decisions to approve amendments to the Multilateral Trade Agreement in Annex 3 shall take effect for all Members upon approval by the Ministerial Conference.

9. The Ministerial Conference, upon the request of the Members parties to a trade agreement, may decide exclusively by consensus to add that agreement to Annex 4. The Ministerial Conference, upon the request of the Members parties to a Plurilateral Trade Agreement, may decide to delete that Agreement from Annex 4.

10. Amendments to a Plurilateral Trade Agreement shall be governed by the provisions of that Agreement.

Article XI

Original Membership

1. The contracting parties to GATT 1947 as of the date of entry into force of this Agreement, and the European Communities, which accept this Agreement and the Multilateral Trade Agreements and for which Schedules of Concessions and Commitments are annexed to GATT 1994 and for which Schedules of Specific Commitments are annexed to GATS shall become original Members of the WTO.

2. The least-developed countries recognized as such by the United Nations will only be required to undertake commitments and concessions to the extent consistent with their individual development, financial and trade needs or their administrative and institutional capabilities.

Article XII

Accession

1. Any State or separate customs territory possessing full autonomy in the conduct of its external commercial relations and of the other matters provided for in this Agreement and the Multilateral Trade Agreements may accede to this Agreement, on terms to be agreed between it and the WTO. Such accession shall apply to this Agreement and the Multilateral Trade Agreements annexed thereto.

2. Decisions on accession shall be taken by the Ministerial Conference. The Ministerial Conference shall approve the agreement on the terms of accession by a two-thirds majority of the Members of the WTO.

3. Accession to a Plurilateral Trade Agreement shall be governed by the provisions of that Agreement.

Article XIII

Non-Application of Multilateral Trade Agreements between Particular Members

1. This Agreement and the Multilateral Trade Agreements in Annexes 1 and 2 shall not apply as between any Member and any other Member if either of the Members, at the time either becomes a Member, does not consent to such application.

2. Paragraph 1 may be invoked between original Members of the WTO which were contracting parties to GATT 1947 only where Article XXXV of that Agreement had been invoked earlier and was effective as between those contracting parties at the time of entry into force for them of this Agreement.

3. Paragraph 1 shall apply between a Member and another Member which has acceded under Article XII only if the Member not consenting to the application has so notified the Ministerial Conference before the approval of the agreement on the terms of accession by the Ministerial Conference.

4. The Ministerial Conference may review the operation of this Article in particular cases at the request of any Member and make appropriate recommendations.

5. Non-application of a Plurilateral Trade Agreement between parties to that Agreement shall be governed by the provisions of that Agreement.

Article XIV

Acceptance, Entry into Force and Deposit

1. This Agreement shall be open for acceptance, by signature or otherwise, by contracting parties to GATT 1947, and the European Communities, which are eligible to become original Members of the WTO in accordance with Article XI of this Agreement. Such acceptance shall apply to this Agreement and the Multilateral Trade Agreements annexed hereto. This Agreement and the Multilateral Trade Agreements annexed hereto shall enter into force on the date

determined by Ministers in accordance with paragraph 3 of the Final Act Embodying the Results of the Uruguay Round of Multilateral Trade Negotiations and shall remain open for acceptance for a period of two years following that date unless the Ministers decide otherwise. An acceptance following the entry into force of this Agreement shall enter into force on the 30th day following the date of such acceptance.

2. A Member which accepts this Agreement after its entry into force shall implement those concessions and obligations in the Multilateral Trade Agreements that are to be implemented over a period of time starting with the entry into force of this Agreement as if it had accepted this Agreement on the date of its entry into force.

3. Until the entry into force of this Agreement, the text of this Agreement and the Multilateral Trade Agreements shall be deposited with the Director-General to the CONTRACTING PARTIES to GATT 1947. The Director-General shall promptly furnish a certified true copy of this Agreement and the Multilateral Trade Agreements, and a notification of each acceptance thereof, to each government and the European Communities having accepted this Agreement. This Agreement and the Multilateral Trade Agreements, and any amendments thereto, shall, upon the entry into force of this Agreement, be deposited with the Director-General of the WTO.

4. The acceptance and entry into force of a Plurilateral Trade Agreement shall be governed by the provisions of that Agreement. Such Agreements shall be deposited with the Director-General to the CONTRACTING PARTIES to GATT 1947. Upon the entry into force of this Agreement, such Agreements shall be deposited with the Director-General of the WTO.

Article XV

Withdrawal

1. Any Member may withdraw from this Agreement. Such withdrawal shall apply both to this Agreement and the Multilateral Trade Agreements and shall take effect upon the expiration of six months from the date on which written notice of withdrawal is received by the Director-General of the WTO.

2. Withdrawal from a Plurilateral Trade Agreement shall be governed by the provisions of that Agreement.

Article XVI

Miscellaneous Provisions

1. Except as otherwise provided under this Agreement or the Multilateral Trade Agreements, the WTO shall be guided by the decisions, procedures and customary practices followed by the CONTRACTING PARTIES to GATT 1947 and the bodies established in the framework of GATT 1947.

2. To the extent practicable, the Secretariat of GATT 1947 shall become the Secretariat of the WTO, and the Director-General to the CONTRACTING PARTIES to GATT 1947, until such time as the Ministerial Conference has appointed a Director-General in accordance with paragraph 2 of Article VI of this Agreement, shall serve as Director-General of the WTO.

3. In the event of a conflict between a provision of this Agreement and a provision of any of the Multilateral Trade Agreements, the provision of this Agreement shall prevail to the extent of the conflict.

4. Each Member shall ensure the conformity of its laws, regulations and administrative procedures with its obligations as provided in the annexed Agreements.

5. No reservations may be made in respect of any provision of this Agreement. Reservations in respect of any of the provisions of the Multilateral Trade Agreements may only be made to the extent provided for in those Agreements. Reservations in respect of a provision of a Plurilateral Trade Agreement shall be governed by the provisions of that Agreement.

6. This Agreement shall be registered in accordance with the provisions of Article 102 of the Charter of the United Nations.

DONE at Marrakesh this fifteenth day of April one thousand nine hundred and ninety-four, in a single copy, in the English, French and Spanish languages, each text being authentic.

Explanatory Notes:

The terms "country" or "countries" as used in this Agreement and the Multilateral Trade Agreements are to be understood to include any separate customs territory Member of the WTO.

In the case of a separate customs territory Member of the WTO, where an expression in this Agreement and the Multilateral Trade Agreements is qualified by the term "national", such expression shall be read as pertaining to that customs territory, unless otherwise specified.

General Agreement on Tariffs and Trade 1994

1. The General Agreement on Tariffs and Trade 1994 ("GATT 1994") shall consist of:

(a) the provisions in the General Agreement on Tariffs and Trade, dated 30 October 1947, annexed to the Final Act Adopted at the Conclusion of the Second Session of the Preparatory Committee of the United Nations Conference on Trade and Employment (excluding the Protocol of Provisional Application), as rectified, amended or modified by the terms of legal instruments which have entered into force before the date of entry into force of the WTO Agreement;

(b) the provisions of the legal instruments set forth below that have entered into force under the GATT 1947 before the date of entry into force of the WTO Agreement:

(i) protocols and certifications relating to tariff concessions;

(ii) protocols of accession (excluding the provisions (*a*) concerning provisional application and withdrawal of provisional application and (*b*) providing that Part II of GATT 1947 shall be applied provisionally to the fullest extent not inconsistent with legislation existing on the date of the Protocol);

(iii) decisions on waivers granted under Article XXV of GATT 1947 and still in force on the date of entry into force of the WTO Agreement[1];

(iv) other decisions of the CONTRACTING PARTIES to GATT 1947;

(c) the Understandings set forth below:

(i) Understanding on the Interpretation of Article II:1(b) of the General Agreement on Tariffs and Trade 1994;

(ii) Understanding on the Interpretation of Article XVII of the General Agreement on Tariffs and Trade 1994;

(iii) Understanding on Balance-of-Payments Provisions of the General Agreement on Tariffs and Trade 1994;

1 The waivers covered by this provision are listed in footnote 7 on pages 11 and 12 in Part II of document MTN/FA of 15 December 1993 and in MTN/FA/Corr.6 of 21 March 1994. The Ministerial Conference shall establish at its first session a revised list of waivers covered by this provision that adds any waivers granted under GATT 1947 after 15 December 1993 and before the date of entry into force of the WTO Agreement, and deletes the waivers which will have expired by that time.

(iv) Understanding on the Interpretation of Article XXIV of the General Agreement on Tariffs and Trade 1994;

(v) Understanding in Respect of Waivers of Obligations under the General Agreement on Tariffs and Trade 1994;

(vi) Understanding on the Interpretation of Article XXVIII of the General Agreement on Tariffs and Trade 1994; and

(d) the Marrakesh Protocol to GATT 1994.

2. *Explanatory Notes*

(a) The references to "contracting party" in the provisions of GATT 1994 shall be deemed to read "Member". The references to "less-developed contracting party" and "developed contracting party" shall be deemed to read "developing country Member" and "developed country Member". The references to "Executive Secretary" shall be deemed to read "Director-General of the WTO".

(b) The references to the CONTRACTING PARTIES acting jointly in Articles XV:1, XV:2, XV:8, XXXVIII and the Notes *Ad* Article XII and XVIII; and in the provisions on special exchange agreements in Articles XV:2, XV:3, XV:6, XV:7 and XV:9 of GATT 1994 shall be deemed to be references to the WTO. The other functions that the provisions of GATT 1994 assign to the CONTRACTING PARTIES acting jointly shall be allocated by the Ministerial Conference.

(c) (i) The text of GATT 1994 shall be authentic in English, French and Spanish.

(ii) The text of GATT 1994 in the French language shall be subject to the rectifications of terms indicated in Annex A to document MTN.TNC/41.

(iii) The authentic text of GATT 1994 in the Spanish language shall be the text in Volume IV of the Basic Instruments and Selected Documents series, subject to the rectifications of terms indicated in Annex B to document MTN.TNC/41.

3. (a) The provisions of Part II of GATT 1994 shall not apply to measures taken by a Member under specific mandatory legislation, enacted by that Member before it became a contracting party to GATT 1947, that prohibits the use, sale or lease of foreign-built or foreign-reconstructed vessels in commercial applications between points in national waters or the waters of an exclusive economic zone. This exemption applies to: (*a*) the continuation or prompt renewal of a non-conforming provision of such legislation; and (*b*) the amendment to a non-conforming provision of such legislation to the extent that the amendment does not decrease the conformity of the provision with Part II of GATT 1947. This exemption is limited to measures taken under legislation described above that is notified and specified prior to the date of entry into force of the WTO Agreement. If such legislation is subsequently modified to decrease its conformity with Part II of GATT 1994, it will no longer qualify for coverage under this paragraph.

(b) The Ministerial Conference shall review this exemption not later than five years after the date of entry into force of the WTO Agreement and thereafter every two years for as long as the exemption is in force for the purpose of examining whether the conditions which created the need for the exemption still prevail.

(c) A Member whose measures are covered by this exemption shall annually submit a detailed statistical notification consisting of a five-year moving average of actual and expected deliveries of relevant vessels as well as additional information on the use, sale, lease or repair of relevant vessels covered by this exemption.

(d) A Member that considers that this exemption operates in such a manner as to justify a reciprocal and proportionate limitation on the use, sale, lease or repair of vessels constructed in the territory of the Member invoking the exemption shall be free to introduce such a limitation subject to prior notification to the Ministerial Conference.

(e) This exemption is without prejudice to solutions concerning specific aspects of the legislation covered by this exemption negotiated in sectoral agreements or in other fora.

General Agreement on Tariffs and Trade 1947

This Appendix contains the complete text of the General Agreement together with all the amendments which became effective since its entry into force. For the convenience of the reader, asterisks mark the portions of the text which should be read in conjunction with notes and supplementary provisions in Annex I of the Agreement.

THE GENERAL AGREEMENT ON TARIFFS AND TRADE

The Governments of the Commonwealth of Australia, the Kingdom of Belgium, the United States of Brazil, Burma, Canada, Ceylon, the Republic of Chile, the Republic of China, the Republic of Cuba, the Czechoslovak Republic, the French Republic, India, Lebanon, the Grand-Duchy of Luxemburg, the Kingdom of the Netherlands, New Zealand, the Kingdom of Norway, Pakistan, Southern Rhodesia, Syria, the Union of South Africa, the United Kingdom of Great Britain and Northern Ireland, and the United States of America:

Recognizing that their relations in the field of trade and economic endeavour should be conducted with a view to raising standards of living, ensuring full employment and a large and steadily growing volume of real income and effective demand, developing the full use of the resources of the world and expanding the production and exchange of goods,

Being desirous of contributing to these objectives by entering into reciprocal and mutually advantageous arrangements directed to the substantial reduction of tariffs and other barriers to trade and to the elimination of discriminatory treatment in international commerce,

Have through their Representatives agreed as follows:

PART I

Article I

General Most-Favoured-Nation Treatment

1. With respect to customs duties and charges of any kind imposed on or in connection with importation or exportation or imposed on the international transfer of payments for imports or exports, and with respect to the method of levying such duties and charges, and with respect to all rules and formalities in connection with importation and exportation, and with respect to all matters referred to in paragraphs 2 and 4 of Article III,* any advantage, favour, privilege or immunity granted by any contracting party to any product originating in or destined for any other country shall be accorded immediately and unconditionally to the like product originating in or destined for the territories of all other contracting parties.

2. The provisions of paragraph 1 of this Article shall not require the elimination of any preferences in respect of import duties or charges which do not exceed the levels provided for in paragraph 4 of this Article and which fall within the following descriptions:

(*a*) Preferences in force exclusively between two or more of the territories listed in Annex A, subject to the conditions set forth therein;

(*b*) Preferences in force exclusively between two or more territories which on July 1, 1939, were connected by common sovereignty or relations of protection or suzerainty and which are listed in Annexes B, C and D, subject to the conditions set forth therein;

(*c*) Preferences in force exclusively between the United States of America and the Republic of Cuba;

(*d*) Preferences in force exclusively between neighbouring countries listed in Annexes E and F.

3. The provisions of paragraph 1 shall not apply to preferences between the countries formerly a part of the Ottoman Empire and detached from it on July 24, 1923, provided such preferences are approved under paragraph 5[1], of Article XXV which shall be applied in this respect in the light of paragraph 1 of Article XXIX.

4. The margin of preference* on any product in respect of which a preference is permitted under paragraph 2 of this Article but is not specifically set forth as a maximum margin of preference in the appropriate Schedule annexed to this Agreement shall not exceed:

(*a*) in respect of duties or charges on any product described in such Schedule, the difference between the most-favoured-nation and preferential rates provided for therein; if no preferential rate is provided for, the preferential rate shall for the purposes of this paragraph be taken to be that in force on April 10, 1947, and, if no most-favoured-nation rate is provided for, the margin shall not exceed the difference between the most-favoured-nation and preferential rates existing on April 10, 1947;

(*b*) in respect of duties or charges on any product not described in the appropriate Schedule, the difference between the most-favoured-nation and preferential rates existing on April 10, 1947.

In the case of the contracting parties named in Annex G, the date of April 10, 1947, referred to in subparagraph (*a*) and (*b*) of this paragraph shall be replaced by the respective dates set forth in that Annex.

Article II

Schedules of Concessions

1. (*a*) Each contracting party shall accord to the commerce of the other contracting parties treatment no less favourable than that provided for in the appropriate Part of the appropriate Schedule annexed to this Agreement.

(*b*) The products described in Part I of the Schedule relating to any contracting party, which are the products of territories of other contracting parties, shall, on their importation into the

---

1 The authentic text erroneously reads "subparagraph 5 (a)".

territory to which the Schedule relates, and subject to the terms, conditions or qualifications set forth in that Schedule, be exempt from ordinary customs duties in excess of those set forth and provided therein. Such products shall also be exempt from all other duties or charges of any kind imposed on or in connection with the importation in excess of those imposed on the date of this Agreement or those directly and mandatorily required to be imposed thereafter by legislation in force in the importing territory on that date.

(*c*) The products described in Part II of the Schedule relating to any contracting party which are the products of territories entitled under Article I to receive preferential treatment upon importation into the territory to which the Schedule relates shall, on their importation into such territory, and subject to the terms, conditions or qualifications set forth in that Schedule, be exempt from ordinary customs duties in excess of those set forth and provided for in Part II of that Schedule. Such products shall also be exempt from all other duties or charges of any kind imposed on or in connection with importation in excess of those imposed on the date of this Agreement or those directly or mandatorily required to be imposed thereafter by legislation in force in the importing territory on that date. Nothing in this Article shall prevent any contracting party from maintaining its requirements existing on the date of this Agreement as to the eligibility of goods for entry at preferential rates of duty.

2. Nothing in this Article shall prevent any contracting party from imposing at any time on the importation of any product:

(*a*) a charge equivalent to an internal tax imposed consistently with the provisions of paragraph 2 of Article III* in respect of the like domestic product or in respect of an article from which the imported product has been manufactured or produced in whole or in part;

(*b*) any anti-dumping or countervailing duty applied consistently with the provisions of Article VI;*

(*c*) fees or other charges commensurate with the cost of services rendered.

3. No contracting party shall alter its method of determining dutiable value or of converting currencies so as to impair the value of any of the concessions provided for in the appropriate Schedule annexed to this Agreement.

4. If any contracting party establishes, maintains or authorizes, formally or in effect, a monopoly of the importation of any product described in the appropriate Schedule annexed to this Agreement, such monopoly shall not, except as provided for in that Schedule or as otherwise agreed between the parties which initially negotiated the concession, operate so as to afford protection on the average in excess of the amount of protection provided for in that Schedule. The provisions of this paragraph shall not limit the use by contracting parties of any form of assistance to domestic producers permitted by other provisions of this Agreement.*

5. If any contracting party considers that a product is not receiving from another contracting party the treatment which the first contracting party believes to have been contemplated by a concession provided for in the appropriate Schedule annexed to this Agreement, it shall bring the matter directly to the attention of the other contracting party. If the latter agrees that the treatment contemplated was that claimed by the first contracting party, but declares that such treatment cannot be accorded because a court or other proper authority has ruled to the effect that the product involved cannot be classified under the tariff laws of such contracting party so as to permit the treatment contemplated in this Agreement, the two contracting parties, together with any other contracting parties substantially interested, shall enter promptly into further negotiations with a view to a compensatory adjustment of the matter.

6. (*a*) The specific duties and charges included in the Schedules relating to contracting parties members of the International Monetary Fund, and margins of preference in specific duties and charges maintained by such contracting parties, are expressed in the appropriate currency at the par value accepted or provisionally recognized by the Fund at the date of this Agreement. Accordingly, in case this par value is reduced consistently with the Articles of Agreement of the International Monetary Fund by more than twenty per centum, such specific duties and charges and margins of preference may be adjusted to take account of such reduction; *provided* that the CONTRACTING PARTIES (*i.e.*, the contracting parties acting jointly as provided for in Article XXV) concur that such adjustments will not impair the value of the concessions provided for in the appropriate Schedule or elsewhere in this Agreement, due account being taken of all factors which may influence the need for, or urgency of, such adjustments.

(*b*) Similar provisions shall apply to any contracting party not a member of the Fund, as from the date on which such contracting party becomes a member of the Fund or enters into a special exchange agreement in pursuance of Article XV.

7. The Schedules annexed to this Agreement are hereby made an integral part of Part I of this Agreement.

PART II

*Article III**

National Treatment on Internal Taxation and Regulation

1. The contracting parties recognize that internal taxes and other internal charges, and laws, regulations and requirements affecting the internal sale, offering for sale, purchase, transportation, distribution or use of products, and internal quantitative regulations requiring the mixture, processing or use of products in specified amounts or proportions, should not be applied to imported or domestic products so as to afford protection to domestic production.*

2. The products of the territory of any contracting party imported into the territory of any other contracting party shall not be subject, directly or indirectly, to internal taxes or other internal charges of any kind in excess of those applied, directly or indirectly, to like domestic products. Moreover, no contracting party shall otherwise apply internal taxes or other internal charges to imported or domestic products in a manner contrary to the principles set forth in paragraph 1.*

3. With respect to any existing internal tax which is inconsistent with the provisions of paragraph 2, but which is specifically authorized under a trade agreement, in force on April 10, 1947, in which the import duty on the taxed product is bound against increase, the contracting party imposing the tax shall be free to postpone the application of the provisions of paragraph 2 to such tax until such time as it can obtain release from the obligations of such trade agreement in order to permit the increase of such duty to the extent necessary to compensate for the elimination of the protective element of the tax.

4. The products of the territory of any contracting party imported into the territory of any other contracting party shall be accorded treatment no less favourable than that accorded to like products of national origin in respect of all laws, regulations and requirements affecting their internal sale, offering for sale, purchase, transportation, distribution or use. The provisions of this paragraph shall not prevent the application of differential internal transportation charges which are based exclusively on the economic operation of the means of transport and not on the nationality of the product.

5. No contracting party shall establish or maintain any internal quantitative regulation relating to the mixture, processing or use of products in specified amounts or proportions which requires, directly or indirectly, that any specified amount or proportion of any product which is the subject of the regulation must be supplied from domestic sources. Moreover, no contracting party shall otherwise apply internal quantitative regulations in a manner contrary to the principles set forth in paragraph 1.*

6. The provisions of paragraph 5 shall not apply to any internal quantitative regulation in force in the territory of any contracting party on July 1, 1939, April 10, 1947, or March 24, 1948, at the option of that contracting party; *Provided* that any such regulation which is contrary to the provisions of paragraph 5 shall not be modified to the detriment of imports and shall be treated as a customs duty for the purpose of negotiation.

7. No internal quantitative regulation relating to the mixture, processing or use of products in specified amounts or proportions shall be applied in such a manner as to allocate any such amount or proportion among external sources of supply.

8. (*a*) The provisions of this Article shall not apply to laws, regulations or requirements governing the procurement by governmental agencies of products purchased for governmental purposes and not with a view to commercial resale or with a view to use in the production of goods for commercial sale.

(*b*) The provisions of this Article shall not prevent the payment of subsidies exclusively to domestic producers, including payments to domestic producers derived from the proceeds of internal taxes or charges applied consistently with the provisions of this Article and subsidies effected through governmental purchases of domestic products.

9. The contracting parties recognize that internal maximum price control measures, even though conforming to the other provisions of this Article, can have effects prejudicial to the interests of contracting parties supplying imported products. Accordingly, contracting parties applying such measures shall take account of the interests of exporting contracting parties with a view to avoiding to the fullest practicable extent such prejudicial effects.

10. The provisions of this Article shall not prevent any contracting party from establishing or maintaining internal quantitative regulations relating to exposed cinematograph films and meeting the requirements of Article IV.

Article IV

Special Provisions relating to Cinematograph Films

If any contracting party establishes or maintains internal quantitative regulations relating to exposed cinematograph films, such regulations shall take the form of screen quotas which shall conform to the following requirements:

(*a*) Screen quotas may require the exhibition of cinematograph films of national origin during a specified minimum proportion of the total screen time actually utilized, over a specified period of not less than one year, in the commercial exhibition of all films of whatever origin, and shall be computed on the basis of screen time per theatre per year or the equivalent thereof;

(*b*) With the exception of screen time reserved for films of national origin under a screen quota, screen time including that released by administrative action from screen time reserved for films of national origin, shall not be allocated formally or in effect among sources of supply;

(*c*) Notwithstanding the provisions of subparagraph (*b*) of this Article, any contracting party may maintain screen quotas conforming to the requirements of subparagraph (*a*) of this Article which reserve a minimum proportion of screen time for films of a specified origin other than that of the contracting party imposing such screen quotas; *Provided* that no such minimum proportion of screen time shall be increased above the level in effect on April 10, 1947;

(*d*) Screen quotas shall be subject to negotiation for their limitation, liberalization or elimination.

Article V

Freedom of Transit

1. Goods (including baggage), and also vessels and other means of transport, shall be deemed to be in transit across the territory of a contracting party when the passage across such territory, with or without trans-shipment, warehousing, breaking bulk, or change in the mode of transport, is only a portion of a complete journey beginning and terminating beyond the frontier of the contracting party across whose territory the traffic passes. Traffic of this nature is termed in this article "traffic in transit".

2. There shall be freedom of transit through the territory of each contracting party, via the routes most convenient for international transit, for traffic in transit to or from the territory of other contracting parties. No distinction shall be made which is based on the flag of vessels, the place of origin, departure, entry, exit or destination, or on any circumstances relating to the ownership of goods, of vessels or of other means of transport.

3. Any contracting party may require that traffic in transit through its territory be entered at the proper custom house, but, except in cases of failure to comply with applicable customs laws and regulations, such traffic coming from or going to the territory of other contracting parties shall not be subject to any unnecessary delays or restrictions and shall be exempt from customs duties and from all transit duties or other charges imposed in respect of transit, except charges for transportation or those commensurate with administrative expenses entailed by transit or with the cost of services rendered.

4. All charges and regulations imposed by contracting parties on traffic in transit to or from the territories of other contracting parties shall be reasonable, having regard to the conditions of the traffic.

5. With respect to all charges, regulations and formalities in connection with transit, each contracting party shall accord to traffic in transit to or from the territory of any other contracting party treatment no less favourable than the treatment accorded to traffic in transit to or from any third country.*

6. Each contracting party shall accord to products which have been in transit through the territory of any other contracting party treatment no less favourable than that which would have been accorded to such products had they been transported from their place of origin to their destination without going through the territory of such other contracting party. Any contracting party shall, however, be free to maintain its requirements of direct consignment existing on the date of this Agreement, in respect of any goods in regard to which such direct consignment is a requisite condition of eligibility for entry of the goods at preferential rates of duty or has relation to the contracting party's prescribed method of valuation for duty purposes.

7. The provisions of this Article shall not apply to the operation of aircraft in transit, but shall apply to air transit of goods (including baggage).

Article VI

Anti-dumping and Countervailing Duties

1. The contracting parties recognize that dumping, by which products of one country are introduced into the commerce of another country at less than the normal value of the products, is to be condemned if it causes or threatens material injury to an established industry in the territory of a contracting party or materially retards the establishment of a domestic industry. For the purposes of this Article, a product is to be considered as being introduced into the commerce of an importing country at less than its normal value, if the price of the product exported from one country to another

(*a*) is less than the comparable price, in the ordinary course of trade, for the like product when destined for consumption in the exporting country, or,

(*b*) in the absence of such domestic price, is less than either

(i) the highest comparable price for the like product for export to any third country in the ordinary course of trade, or

(ii) the cost of production of the product in the country of origin plus a reasonable addition for selling cost and profit.

Due allowance shall be made in each case for differences in conditions and terms of sale, for differences in taxation, and for other differences affecting price comparability.*

2. In order to offset or prevent dumping, a contracting party may levy on any dumped product an anti-dumping duty not greater in amount than the margin of dumping in respect of such product. For the purposes of this Article, the margin of dumping is the price difference determined in accordance with the provisions of paragraph 1.*

3. No countervailing duty shall be levied on any product of the territory of any contracting party imported into the territory of another contracting party in excess of an amount equal to the estimated bounty or subsidy determined to have been granted, directly or indirectly, on the manufacture, production or export of such product in the country of origin or exportation, including any special subsidy to the transportation of a particular product. The term "countervailing duty" shall be understood to mean a special duty levied for the purpose of offsetting any bounty or subsidy bestowed, directly, or indirectly, upon the manufacture, production or export of any merchandise.*

4. No product of the territory of any contracting party imported into the territory of any other contracting party shall be subject to anti-dumping or countervailing duty by reason of the exemption of such product from duties or taxes borne by the like product when destined for consumption in the country of origin or exportation, or by reason of the refund of such duties or taxes.

5. No product of the territory of any contracting party imported into the territory of any other contracting party shall be subject to both anti-dumping and countervailing duties to compensate for the same situation of dumping or export subsidization.

6. (*a*) No contracting party shall levy any anti-dumping or countervailing duty on the importation of any product of the territory of another contracting party unless it determines that the effect of the dumping or subsidization, as the case may be, is such as to cause or threaten material injury to an established domestic industry, or is such as to retard materially the establishment of a domestic industry.

(*b*) The CONTRACTING PARTIES may waive the requirement of subparagraph (*a*) of this paragraph so as to permit a contracting party to levy an anti-dumping or countervailing duty on the importation of any product for the purpose of offsetting dumping or subsidization which causes or threatens material injury to an industry in the territory of another contracting party exporting the product concerned to the territory of the importing contracting party. The CONTRACTING PARTIES shall waive the requirements of subparagraph (*a*) of this paragraph, so as to permit the levying of a countervailing duty, in cases in which they find that a subsidy is causing or threatening material injury to an industry in the territory of another contracting party exporting the product concerned to the territory of the importing contracting party.*

(*c*) In exceptional circumstances, however, where delay might cause damage which would be difficult to repair, a contracting party may levy a countervailing duty for the purpose referred to in subparagraph (*b*) of this paragraph without the prior approval of the CONTRACTING PARTIES; *Provided* that such action shall be reported immediately to the CONTRACTING PARTIES and that the countervailing duty shall be withdrawn promptly if the CONTRACTING PARTIES disapprove.

7. A system for the stabilization of the domestic price or of the return to domestic producers of a primary commodity, independently of the movements of export prices, which results at times in the sale of the commodity for export at a price lower than the comparable price charged for the like commodity to buyers in the domestic market, shall be presumed not to result in material injury within the meaning of paragraph 6 if it is determined by consultation among the contracting parties substantially interested in the commodity concerned that:

(*a*) the system has also resulted in the sale of the commodity for export at a price higher than the comparable price charged for the like commodity to buyers in the domestic market, and

(*b*) the system is so operated, either because of the effective regulation of production, or otherwise, as not to stimulate exports unduly or otherwise seriously prejudice the interests of other contracting parties.

Article VII

Valuation for Customs Purposes

1. The contracting parties recognize the validity of the general principles of valuation set forth in the following paragraphs of this Article, and they undertake to give effect to such principles, in respect of all products subject to duties or other charges* or restrictions on importation and exportation based upon or regulated in any manner by value. Moreover, they shall, upon a request by another contracting party review the operation of any of their laws or regulations relating to value for customs purposes in the light of these principles. The CONTRACTING PARTIES may request from contracting parties reports on steps taken by them in pursuance of the provisions of this Article.

2. (*a*) The value for customs purposes of imported merchandise should be based on the actual value of the imported merchandise on which duty is assessed, or of like merchandise, and should not be based on the value of merchandise of national origin or on arbitrary or fictitious values.*

(*b*) "Actual value" should be the price at which, at a time and place determined by the legislation of the country of importation, such or like merchandise is sold or offered for sale in the ordinary course of trade under fully competitive conditions. To the extent to which the price of such or like merchandise is governed by the quantity in a particular transaction, the price to be considered should uniformly be related to either (i) comparable quantities, or (ii) quantities not less favourable to importers than those in which the greater volume of the merchandise is sold in the trade between the countries of exportation and importation.*

(*c*) When the actual value is not ascertainable in accordance with subparagraph (*b*) of this paragraph, the value for customs purposes should be based on the nearest ascertainable equivalent of such value.*

3. The value for customs purposes of any imported product should not include the amount of any internal tax, applicable within the country of origin or export, from which the imported product has been exempted or has been or will be relieved by means of refund.

4. (*a*) Except as otherwise provided for in this paragraph, where it is necessary for the purposes of paragraph 2 of this Article for a contracting party to convert into its own currency a price expressed in the currency of another country, the conversion rate of exchange to be used shall be based, for each currency involved, on the par value as established pursuant to the Articles of Agreement of the International Monetary Fund or on the rate of exchange recognized by the Fund, or on the par value established in accordance with a special exchange agreement entered into pursuant to Article XV of this Agreement.

(*b*) Where no such established par value and no such recognized rate of exchange exist, the conversion rate shall reflect effectively the current value of such currency in commercial transactions.

(*c*) The CONTRACTING PARTIES, in agreement with the International Monetary Fund, shall formulate rules governing the conversion by contracting parties of any foreign currency in respect of which multiple rates of exchange are maintained consistently with the Articles of Agreement of the International Monetary Fund. Any contracting party may apply such rules in respect of such foreign currencies for the purposes of paragraph 2 of this Article as an alternative to the use of par values. Until such rules are adopted by the Contracting Parties, any contracting party may employ, in respect of any such foreign currency, rules of conversion for the purposes of paragraph 2 of this Article which are designed to reflect effectively the value of such foreign currency in commercial transactions.

(*d*) Nothing in this paragraph shall be construed to require any contracting party to alter the method of converting currencies for customs purposes which is applicable in its territory on the date of this Agreement, if such alteration would have the effect of increasing generally the amounts of duty payable.

5. The bases and methods for determining the value of products subject to duties or other charges or restrictions based upon or regulated in any manner by value should be stable and should be given sufficient publicity to enable traders to estimate, with a reasonable degree of certainty, the value for customs purposes.

Article VIII

*Fees and Formalities connected with Importation and Exportation**

1. (*a*) All fees and charges of whatever character (other than import and export duties and other than taxes within the purview of Article III) imposed by contracting parties on or in connection with importation or exportation shall be limited in amount to the approximate cost of services rendered and shall not represent an indirect protection to domestic products or a taxation of imports or exports for fiscal purposes.

(*b*) The contracting parties recognize the need for reducing the number and diversity of fees and charges referred to in subparagraph (*a*).

(*c*) The contracting parties also recognize the need for minimizing the incidence and complexity of import and export formalities and for decreasing and simplifying import and export documentation requirements.*

2. A contracting party shall, upon request by another contracting party or by the CONTRACTING PARTIES, review the operation of its laws and regulations in the light of the provisions of this Article.

3. No contracting party shall impose substantial penalties for minor breaches of customs regulations or procedural requirements. In particular, no penalty in respect of any omission or mistake in customs documentation which is easily rectifiable and obviously made without fraudulent intent or gross negligence shall be greater than necessary to serve merely as a warning.

4. The provisions of this Article shall extend to fees, charges, formalities and requirements imposed by governmental authorities in connection with importation and exportation, including those relating to:

(*a*) consular transactions, such as consular invoices and certificates;

(*b*) quantitative restrictions;

(*c*) licensing;

(*d*) exchange control;

(*e*) statistical services;

(*f*) documents, documentation and certification;

(*g*) analysis and inspection; and

(*h*) quarantine, sanitation and fumigation.

Article IX

Marks of Origin

1. Each contracting party shall accord to the products of the territories of other contracting parties treatment with regard to marking requirements no less favourable than the treatment accorded to like products of any third country.

2. The contracting parties recognize that, in adopting and enforcing laws and regulations relating to marks of origin, the difficulties and inconveniences which such measures may cause to the commerce and industry of exporting countries should be reduced to a minimum, due regard being had to the necessity of protecting consumers against fraudulent or misleading indications.

3. Whenever it is administratively practicable to do so, contracting parties should permit required marks of origin to be affixed at the time of importation.

4. The laws and regulations of contracting parties relating to the marking of imported products shall be such as to permit compliance without seriously damaging the products, or materially reducing their value, or unreasonably increasing their cost.

5. As a general rule, no special duty or penalty should be imposed by any contracting party for failure to comply with marking requirements prior to importation unless corrective marking is unreasonably delayed or deceptive marks have been affixed or the required marking has been intentionally omitted.

6. The contracting parties shall co-operate with each other with a view to preventing the use of trade names in such manner as to misrepresent the true origin of a product, to the detriment of such distinctive regional or geographical names of products of the territory of a contracting party as are protected by its legislation. Each contracting party shall accord full and sympathetic consideration to such requests or representations as may be made by any other contracting party regarding the application of the undertaking set forth in the preceding sentence to names of products which have been communicated to it by the other contracting party.

Article X

Publication and Administration of Trade Regulations

1. Laws, regulations, judicial decisions and administrative rulings of general application, made effective by any contracting party, pertaining to the classification or the valuation of products for customs purposes, or to rates of duty, taxes or other charges, or to requirements, restrictions or prohibitions on imports or exports or on the transfer of payments therefor, or affecting their sale, distribution, transportation, insurance, warehousing inspection, exhibition, processing, mixing or other use, shall be published promptly in such a manner as to enable governments and traders to become acquainted with them. Agreements affecting international trade policy which are in force between the government or a governmental agency of any contracting party and the government or governmental agency of any other contracting party shall also be published. The provisions of this paragraph shall not require any contracting party to disclose confidential information which would impede law enforcement or otherwise be contrary to the public interest or would prejudice the legitimate commercial interests of particular enterprises, public or private.

2. No measure of general application taken by any contracting party effecting an advance in a rate of duty or other charge on imports under an established and uniform practice, or imposing a new or more burdensome requirement, restriction or prohibition on imports, or on the transfer of payments therefor, shall be enforced before such measure has been officially published.

3. (*a*) Each contracting party shall administer in a uniform, impartial and reasonable manner all its laws, regulations, decisions and rulings of the kind described in paragraph 1 of this Article.

(*b*) Each contracting party shall maintain, or institute as soon as practicable, judicial, arbitral or administrative tribunals or procedures for the purpose, *inter alia*, of the prompt review and correction of administrative action relating to customs matters. Such tribunals or procedures shall be independent of the agencies entrusted with administrative enforcement and their decisions shall be implemented by, and shall govern the practice of, such agencies unless an appeal is lodged with a court or tribunal of superior jurisdiction within the time prescribed for appeals to be lodged by importers; *Provided* that the central administration of such agency may take steps to obtain a review of the matter in another proceeding if there is good cause to believe that the decision is inconsistent with established principles of law or the actual facts.

(*c*) The provisions of subparagraph (*b*) of this paragraph shall not require the elimination or substitution of procedures in force in the territory of a contracting party on the date of this Agreement which in fact provide for an objective and impartial review of administrative action even though such procedures are not fully or formally independent of the agencies entrusted with administrative enforcement. Any contracting party employing such procedures shall, upon request, furnish the CONTRACTING PARTIES with full information thereon in order that they may determine whether such procedures conform to the requirements of this subparagraph.

*Article XI**

General Elimination of Quantitative Restrictions

1. No prohibitions or restrictions other than duties, taxes or other charges, whether made effective through quotas, import or export licences or other measures, shall be instituted or maintained by any contracting party on the importation of any product of the territory of any other contracting party or on the exportation or sale for export of any product destined for the territory of any other contracting party.

2. The provisions of paragraph 1 of this Article shall not extend to the following:

(*a*) Export prohibitions or restrictions temporarily applied to prevent or relieve critical shortages of foodstuffs or other products essential to the exporting contracting party;

(*b*) Import and export prohibitions or restrictions necessary to the application of standards or regulations for the classification, grading or marketing of commodities in international trade;

(*c*) Import restrictions on any agricultural or fisheries product, imported in any form,* necessary to the enforcement of governmental measures which operate:

(i) to restrict the quantities of the like domestic product permitted to be marketed or produced, or, if there is no substantial domestic production of the like product, of a domestic product for which the imported product can be directly substituted; or

(ii) to remove a temporary surplus of the like domestic product, or, if there is no substantial domestic production of the like product, of a domestic product for which the imported product can be directly substituted, by making the surplus available to certain groups of domestic consumers free of charge or at prices below the current market level; or

(iii) to restrict the quantities permitted to be produced of any animal product the production of which is directly dependent, wholly or mainly, on the imported commodity, if the domestic production of that commodity is relatively negligible.

Any contracting party applying restrictions on the importation of any product pursuant to subparagraph (*c*) of this paragraph shall give public notice of the total quantity or value of the product permitted to be imported during a specified future period and of any change in such quantity or value. Moreover, any restrictions applied under (i) above shall not be such as will reduce the total of imports relative to the total of domestic production, as compared with the proportion which might reasonably be expected to rule between the two in the absence of restrictions. In determining this proportion, the contracting party shall pay due regard to the proportion prevailing during a previous representative period and to any special factors* which may have affected or may be affecting the trade in the product concerned.

*Article XII**

Restrictions to Safeguard the Balance of Payments

1. Notwithstanding the provisions of paragraph 1 of Article XI, any contracting party, in order to safeguard its external financial position and its balance of payments, may restrict the quantity

or value of merchandise permitted to be imported, subject to the provisions of the following paragraphs of this Article.

2. (*a*) Import restrictions instituted, maintained or intensified by a contracting party under this Article shall not exceed those necessary:

   (i) to forestall the imminent threat of, or to stop, a serious decline in its monetary reserves; or

   (ii) in the case of a contracting party with very low monetary reserves, to achieve a reasonable rate of increase in its reserves.

Due regard shall be paid in either case to any special factors which may be affecting the reserves of such contracting party or its need for reserves, including, where special external credits or other resources are available to it, the need to provide for the appropriate use of such credits or resources.

(*b*) Contracting parties applying restrictions under sub-paragraph (*a*) of this paragraph shall progressively relax them as such conditions improve, maintaining them only to the extent that the conditions specified in that sub-paragraph still justify their application. They shall eliminate the restrictions when conditions would no longer justify their institution or maintenance under that subparagraph.

3. (*a*) Contracting parties undertake, in carrying out their domestic policies, to pay due regard to the need for maintaining or restoring equilibrium in their balance of payments on a sound and lasting basis and to the desirability of avoiding an uneconomic employment of productive resources. They recognize that, in order to achieve these ends, it is desirable so far as possible to adopt measures which expand rather than contract international trade.

(*b*) Contracting parties applying restrictions under this Article may determine the incidence of the restrictions on imports of different products or classes of products in such a way as to give priority to the importation of those products which are more essential.

(*c*) Contracting parties applying restrictions under this Article undertake:

   (i) to avoid unnecessary damage to the commercial or economic interests of any other contracting party;*

   (ii) not to apply restrictions so as to prevent unreasonably the importation of any description of goods in minimum commercial quantities the exclusion of which would impair regular channels of trade; and

   (iii) not to apply restrictions which would prevent the importations of commercial samples or prevent compliance with patent, trade mark, copyright, or similar procedures.

(*d*) The contracting parties recognize that, as a result of domestic policies directed towards the achievement and maintenance of full and productive employment or towards the development of economic resources, a contracting party may experience a high level of demand for imports involving a threat to its monetary reserves of the sort referred to in paragraph 2 (*a*) of this Article. Accordingly, a contracting party otherwise complying with the provisions of this Article shall not be required to withdraw or modify restrictions on the ground that a change in those policies would render unnecessary restrictions which it is applying under this Article.

4. (*a*) Any contracting party applying new restrictions or raising the general level of its existing restrictions by a substantial intensification of the measures applied under this Article shall immediately after instituting or intensifying such restrictions (or, in circumstances in which prior consultation is practicable, before doing so) consult with the CONTRACTING PARTIES as to the nature of its balance of payments difficulties, alternative corrective measures which may be available, and the possible effect of the restrictions on the economies of other contracting parties.

(*b*) On a date to be determined by them,* the CONTRACTING PARTIES shall review all restrictions still applied under this Article on that date. Beginning one year after that date, contracting parties applying import restrictions under this Article shall enter into consultations of the type provided for in subparagraph (*a*) of this paragraph with the CONTRACTING PARTIES annually.

(*c*) (i) If, in the course of consultations with a contracting party under subparagraph (*a*) or (*b*) above, the CONTRACTING PARTIES find that the restrictions are not consistent with provisions of this Article or with those of Article XIII (subject to the provisions of Article XIV), they shall indicate the nature of the inconsistency and may advise that the restrictions be suitably modified.

(ii) If, however, as a result of the consultations, the CONTRACTING PARTIES determine that the restrictions are being applied in a manner involving an inconsistency of a serious nature with the provisions of this Article or with those of Article XIII (subject to the provisions of Article XIV) and that damage to the trade of any contracting party is caused or threatened thereby, they shall so inform the contracting party applying the restrictions and shall make appropriate recommendations for securing conformity with such provisions within the specified period of time. If such contracting party does not comply with these recommendations within the specified period, the CONTRACTING PARTIES may release any contracting party the trade of which is adversely affected by the restrictions from such obligations under this Agreement towards the contracting party applying the restrictions as they determine to be appropriate in the circumstances.

(*d*) The CONTRACTING PARTIES shall invite any contracting party which is applying restrictions under this Article to enter into consultations with them at the request of any contracting party which can establish a *prima facie* case that the restrictions are inconsistent with the provisions of this Article or with those of Article XIII (subject to the provisions of Article XIV) and that its trade is adversely affected thereby. However, no such invitation shall be issued unless the CONTRACTING PARTIES have ascertained that direct discussions between the contracting parties concerned have not been successful. If, as a result of the consultations with the CONTRACTING PARTIES, no agreement is reached and they determine that the restrictions are being applied inconsistently with such provisions, and that damage to the trade of the contracting party initiating the procedure is caused or threatened thereby, they shall recommend the withdrawal or modification of the restrictions. If the restrictions are not withdrawn or modified within such time as the CONTRACTING PARTIES may prescribe, they may release the contracting party initiating the procedure from such obligations under this Agreement towards the contracting party applying the restrictions as they determine to be appropriate in the circumstances.

(*e*) In proceeding under this paragraph, the CONTRACTING PARTIES shall have due regard to any special external factors adversely affecting the export trade of the contracting party applying the restrictions.*

(*f*) Determinations under this paragraph shall be rendered expeditiously and, if possible, within sixty days of the initiation of the consultations.

5. If there is a persistent and widespread application of import restrictions under this Article, indicating the existence of a general disequilibrium which is restricting international trade, the CONTRACTING PARTIES shall initiate discussions to consider whether other measures might be taken, either by those contracting parties the balance of payments of which are under pressure or by those the balance of payments of which are tending to be exceptionally favourable, or by any appropriate intergovernmental organization, to remove the underlying causes of the disequilibrium. On the invitation of the CONTRACTING PARTIES, contracting parties shall participate in such discussions.

*Article XIII**

Non-discriminatory Administration of Quantitative Restrictions

1. No prohibition or restriction shall be applied by any contracting party on the importation of any product of the territory of any other contracting party or on the exportation of any product destined for the territory of any other contracting party, unless the importation of the like product of all third countries or the exportation of the like product to all third countries is similarly prohibited or restricted.

2. In applying import restrictions to any product, contracting parties shall aim at a distribution of trade in such product approaching as closely as possible the shares which the various contracting parties might be expected to obtain in the absence of such restrictions and to this end shall observe the following provisions:

(*a*) Wherever practicable, quotas representing the total amount of permitted imports (whether allocated among supplying countries or not) shall be fixed, and notice given of their amount in accordance with paragraph 3 (*b*) of this Article;

(*b*) In cases in which quotas are not practicable, the restrictions may be applied by means of import licences or permits without a quota;

(*c*) Contracting parties shall not, except for purposes of operating quotas allocated in accordance with subparagraph (*d*) of this paragraph, require that import licences or permits be utilized for the importation of the product concerned from a particular country or source;

(*d*) In cases in which a quota is allocated among supplying countries the contracting party applying the restrictions may seek agreement with respect to the allocation of shares in the quota with all other contracting parties having a substantial interest in supplying the product concerned. In cases in which this method is not reasonably practicable, the contracting party concerned shall allot to contracting parties having a substantial interest in supplying the product shares based upon the proportions, supplied by such contracting parties during a previous representative period, of the total quantity or value of imports of the product, due account being taken of any special factors which may have affected or may be affecting the trade in the product. No conditions or formalities shall be imposed which would prevent any contracting party from utilizing fully the share of any such total quantity or value which has been allotted to it, subject to importation being made within any prescribed period to which the quota may relate.*

3. (*a*) In cases in which import licences are issued in connection with import restrictions, the contracting party applying the restrictions shall provide, upon the request of any contracting party having an interest in the trade in the product concerned, all relevant information concerning the administration of the restrictions, the import licences granted over a recent period and the distribution of such licences among supplying countries; *Provided*

that there shall be no obligation to supply information as to the names of importing or supplying enterprises.

(*b*) In the case of import restrictions involving the fixing of quotas, the contracting party applying the restrictions shall give public notice of the total quantity or value of the product or products which will be permitted to be imported during a specified future period and of any change in such quantity or value. Any supplies of the product in question which were *en route* at the time at which public notice was given shall not be excluded from entry; *Provided* that they may be counted so far as practicable, against the quantity permitted to be imported in the period in question, and also, where necessary, against the quantities permitted to be imported in the next following period or periods; and *Provided* further that if any contracting party customarily exempts from such restrictions products entered for consumption or withdrawn from warehouse for consumption during a period of thirty days after the day of such public notice, such practice shall be considered full compliance with this subparagraph.

(*c*) In the case of quotas allocated among supplying countries, the contracting party applying the restrictions shall promptly inform all other contracting parties having an interest in supplying the product concerned of the shares in the quota currently allocated, by quantity or value, to the various supplying countries and shall give public notice thereof.

4. With regard to restrictions applied in accordance with paragraph 2 (*d*) of this Article or under paragraph 2 (*c*) of Article XI, the selection of a representative period for any product and the appraisal of any special factors* affecting the trade in the product shall be made initially by the contracting party applying the restriction; *Provided* that such contracting party shall, upon the request of any other contracting party having a substantial interest in supplying that product or upon the request of the CONTRACTING PARTIES, consult promptly with the other contracting party or the CONTRACTING PARTIES regarding the need for an adjustment of the proportion determined or of the base period selected, or for the reappraisal of the special factors involved, or for the elimination of conditions, formalities or any other provisions established unilaterally relating to the allocation of an adequate quota or its unrestricted utilization.

5. The provisions of this Article shall apply to any tariff quota instituted or maintained by any contracting party, and, in so far as applicable, the principles of this Article shall also extend to export restrictions.

*Article XIV**

Exceptions to the Rule of Non-discrimination

1. A contracting party which applies restrictions under Article XII or under Section B of Article XVIII may, in the application of such restrictions, deviate from the provisions of Article XIII in a manner having equivalent effect to restrictions on payments and transfers for current international transactions which that contracting party may at that time apply under Article VIII or XIV of the Articles of Agreement of the International Monetary Fund, or under analogous provisions of a special exchange agreement entered into pursuant to paragraph 6 of Article XV.*

2. A contracting party which is applying import restrictions under Article XII or under Section B of Article XVIII may, with the consent of the CONTRACTING PARTIES, temporarily deviate from the provisions of Article XIII in respect of a small part of its external trade where the benefits to the contracting party or contracting parties concerned substantially outweigh any injury which may result to the trade of other contracting parties.*

3. The provisions of Article XIII shall not preclude a group of territories having a common quota in the International Monetary Fund from applying against imports from other countries,

but not among themselves, restrictions in accordance with the provisions of Article XII or of Section B of Article XVIII on condition that such restrictions are in all other respects consistent with the provisions of Article XIII.

4. A contracting party applying import restrictions under Article XII or under Section B of Article XVIII shall not be precluded by Articles XI to XV or Section B of Article XVIII of this Agreement from applying measures to direct its exports in such a manner as to increase its earnings of currencies which it can use without deviation from the provisions of Article XIII.

5. A contracting party shall not be precluded by Articles XI to XV, inclusive, or by Section B of Article XVIII, of this Agreement from applying quantitative restrictions:

(*a*) having equivalent effect to exchange restrictions authorized under Section 3 (*b*) of Article VII of the Articles of Agreement of the International Monetary Fund, or

(*b*) under the preferential arrangements provided for in Annex A of this Agreement, pending the outcome of the negotiations referred to therein.

Article XV

Exchange Arrangements

1. The CONTRACTING PARTIES shall seek co-operation with the International Monetary Fund to the end that the CONTRACTING PARTIES and the Fund may pursue a co-ordinated policy with regard to exchange questions within the jurisdiction of the Fund and questions of quantitative restrictions and other trade measures within the jurisdiction of the CONTRACTING PARTIES.

2. In all cases in which the CONTRACTING PARTIES are called upon to consider or deal with problems concerning monetary reserves, balances of payments or foreign exchange arrangements, they shall consult fully with the International Monetary Fund. In such consultations, the CONTRACTING PARTIES shall accept all findings of statistical and other facts presented by the Fund relating to foreign exchange, monetary reserves and balances of payments, and shall accept the determination of the Fund as to whether action by a contracting party in exchange matters is in accordance with the Articles of Agreement of the International Monetary Fund, or with the terms of a special exchange agreement between that contracting party and the CONTRACTING PARTIES. The CONTRACTING PARTIES in reaching their final decision in cases involving the criteria set forth in paragraph 2 (*a*) of Article XII or in paragraph 9 of Article XVIII, shall accept the determination of the Fund as to what constitutes a serious decline in the contracting party's monetary reserves, a very low level of its monetary reserves or a reasonable rate of increase in its monetary reserves, and as to the financial aspects of other matters covered in consultation in such cases.

3. The CONTRACTING PARTIES shall seek agreement with the Fund regarding procedures for consultation under paragraph 2 of this Article.

4. Contracting parties shall not, by exchange action, frustrate* the intent of the provisions of this Agreement, nor, by trade action, the intent of the provisions of the Articles of Agreement of the International Monetary Fund.

5. If the CONTRACTING PARTIES consider, at any time, that exchange restrictions on payments and transfers in connection with imports are being applied by a contracting party in a manner inconsistent with the exceptions provided for in this Agreement for quantitative restrictions, they shall report thereon to the Fund.

6. Any contracting party which is not a member of the Fund shall, within a time to be determined by the CONTRACTING PARTIES after consultation with the Fund, become a member of the Fund, or, failing that, enter into a special exchange agreement with the CONTRACTING PARTIES. A contracting party which ceases to be a member of the Fund shall forthwith enter into a special exchange agreement with the CONTRACTING PARTIES. Any special exchange agreement entered into by a contracting party under this paragraph shall thereupon become part of its obligations under this Agreement.

7. (*a*) A special exchange agreement between a contracting party and the CONTRACTING PARTIES under paragraph 6 of this Article shall provide to the satisfaction of the CONTRACTING PARTIES that the objectives of this Agreement will not be frustrated as a result of action in exchange matters by the contracting party in question.

(*b*) The terms of any such agreement shall not impose obligations on the contracting party in exchange matters generally more restrictive than those imposed by the Articles of Agreement of the International Monetary Fund on members of the Fund.

8. A contracting party which is not a member of the Fund shall furnish such information within the general scope of section 5 of Article VIII of the Articles of Agreement of the International Monetary Fund as the CONTRACTING PARTIES may require in order to carry out their functions under this Agreement.

9. Nothing in this Agreement shall preclude:

(*a*) the use by a contracting party of exchange controls or exchange restrictions in accordance with the Articles of Agreement of the International Monetary Fund or with that contracting party's special exchange agreement with the CONTRACTING PARTIES, or

(*b*) the use by a contracting party of restrictions or controls in imports or exports, the sole effect of which, additional to the effects permitted under Articles XI, XII, XIII and XIV, is to make effective such exchange controls or exchange restrictions.

*Article XVI**

Subsidies

Section A - Subsidies in General

1. If any contracting party grants or maintains any subsidy, including any form of income or price support, which operates directly or indirectly to increase exports of any product from, or to reduce imports of any product into, its territory, it shall notify the CONTRACTING PARTIES in writing of the extent and nature of the subsidization, of the estimated effect of the subsidization on the quantity of the affected product or products imported into or exported from its territory and of the circumstances making the subsidization necessary. In any case in which it is determined that serious prejudice to the interests of any other contracting party is caused or threatened by any such subsidization, the contracting party granting the subsidy shall, upon request, discuss with the other contracting party or parties concerned, or with the CONTRACTING PARTIES, the possibility of limiting the subsidization.

Section B - Additional Provisions on Export Subsidies*

2. The contracting parties recognize that the granting by a contracting party of a subsidy on the export of any product may have harmful effects for other contracting parties, both importing and exporting, may cause undue disturbance to their normal commercial interests, and may hinder the achievement of the objectives of this Agreement.

3. Accordingly, contracting parties should seek to avoid the use of subsidies on the export of primary products. If, however, a contracting party grants directly or indirectly any form of subsidy which operates to increase the export of any primary product from its territory, such subsidy shall not be applied in a manner which results in that contracting party having more than an equitable share of world export trade in that product, account being taken of the shares of the contracting parties in such trade in the product during a previous representative period, and any special factors which may have affected or may be affecting such trade in the product.*

4. Further, as from 1 January 1958 or the earliest practicable date thereafter, contracting parties shall cease to grant either directly or indirectly any form of subsidy on the export of any product other than a primary product which subsidy results in the sale of such product for export at a price lower than the comparable price charged for the like product to buyers in the domestic market. Until 31 December 1957 no contracting party shall extend the scope of any such subsidization beyond that existing on 1 January 1955 by the introduction of new, or the extension of existing, subsidies.*

5. The CONTRACTING PARTIES shall review the operation of the provisions of this Article from time to time with a view to examining its effectiveness, in the light of actual experience, in promoting the objectives of this Agreement and avoiding subsidization seriously prejudicial to the trade or interests of contracting parties.

Article XVII

State Trading Enterprises

1.* (*a*) Each contracting party undertakes that if it establishes or maintains a State enterprise, wherever located, or grants to any enterprise, formally or in effect, exclusive or special privileges,* such enterprise shall, in its purchases or sales involving either imports or exports, act in a manner consistent with the general principles of non-discriminatory treatment prescribed in this Agreement for governmental measures affecting imports or exports by private traders.

(*b*) The provisions of subparagraph (*a*) of this paragraph shall be understood to require that such enterprises shall, having due regard to the other provisions of this Agreement, make any such purchases or sales solely in accordance with commercial considerations,* including price, quality, availability, marketability, transportation and other conditions of purchase or sale, and shall afford the enterprises of the other contracting parties adequate opportunity, in accordance with customary business practice, to compete for participation in such purchases or sales.

(*c*) No contracting party shall prevent any enterprise (whether or not an enterprise described in subparagraph (*a*) of this paragraph) under its jurisdiction from acting in accordance with the principles of subparagraphs (*a*) and (*b*) of this paragraph.

2. The provisions of paragraph 1 of this Article shall not apply to imports of products for immediate or ultimate consumption in governmental use and not otherwise for resale or use in the production of goods* for sale. With respect to such imports, each contracting party shall accord to the trade of the other contracting parties fair and equitable treatment.

3. The contracting parties recognize that enterprises of the kind described in paragraph 1 (*a*) of this Article might be operated so as to create serious obstacles to trade; thus negotiations on a reciprocal and mutually advantageous basis designed to limit or reduce such obstacles are of importance to the expansion of international trade.*

4. (*a*) Contracting parties shall notify the CONTRACTING PARTIES of the products which are imported into or exported from their territories by enterprises of the kind described in paragraph 1 (*a*) of this Article.

(*b*) A contracting party establishing, maintaining or authorizing an import monopoly of a product, which is not the subject of a concession under Article II, shall, on the request of another contracting party having a substantial trade in the product concerned, inform the CONTRACTING PARTIES of the import mark-up* on the product during a recent representative period, or, when it is not possible to do so, of the price charged on the resale of the product.

(*c*) The CONTRACTING PARTIES may, at the request of a contracting party which has reason to believe that its interest under this Agreement are being adversely affected by the operations of an enterprise of the kind described in paragraph 1 (*a*), request the contracting party establishing, maintaining or authorizing such enterprise to supply information about its operations related to the carrying out of the provisions of this Agreement.

(*d*) The provisions of this paragraph shall not require any contracting party to disclose confidential information which would impede law enforcement or otherwise be contrary to the public interest or would prejudice the legitimate commercial interests of particular enterprises.

*Article XVIII**

Governmental Assistance to Economic Development

1. The contracting parties recognize that the attainment of the objectives of this Agreement will be facilitated by the progressive development of their economies, particularly of those contracting parties the economies of which can only support low standards of living* and are in the early stages of development.*

2. The contracting parties recognize further that it may be necessary for those contracting parties, in order to implement programmes and policies of economic development designed to raise the general standard of living of their people, to take protective or other measures affecting imports, and that such measures are justified in so far as they facilitate the attainment of the objectives of this Agreement. They agree, therefore, that those contracting parties should enjoy additional facilities to enable them (*a*) to maintain sufficient flexibility in their tariff structure to be able to grant the tariff protection required for the establishment of a particular industry* and (*b*) to apply quantitative restrictions for balance of payments purposes in a manner which takes full account of the continued high level of demand for imports likely to be generated by their programmes of economic development.

3. The contracting parties recognize finally that, with those additional facilities which are provided for in Sections A and B of this Article, the provisions of this Agreement would normally be sufficient to enable contracting parties to meet the requirements of their economic development. They agree, however, that there may be circumstances where no measure consistent with those provisions is practicable to permit a contracting party in the process of economic development to grant the governmental assistance required to promote the establishment of particular industries* with a view to raising the general standard of living of its people. Special procedures are laid down in Sections C and D of this Article to deal with those cases.

4. (*a*) Consequently, a contracting party, the economy of which can only support low standards of living* and is in the early stages of development,* shall be free to deviate temporarily from the provisions of the other Articles of this Agreement, as provided in Sections A, B and C of this Article.

(*b*) A contracting party, the economy of which is in the process of development, but which does not come within the scope of subparagraph (*a*) above, may submit applications to the CONTRACTING PARTIES under Section D of this Article.

5. The contracting parties recognize that the export earnings of contracting parties, the economies of which are of the type described in paragraph 4 (*a*) and (*b*) above and which depend on exports of a small number of primary commodities, may be seriously reduced by a decline in the sale of such commodities. Accordingly, when the exports of primary commodities by such a contracting party are seriously affected by measures taken by another contracting party, it may have resort to the consultation provisions of Article XXII of this Agreement.

6. The CONTRACTING PARTIES shall review annually all measures applied pursuant to the provisions of Sections C and D of this Article.

Section A

7. (*a*) If a contracting party coming within the scope of paragraph 4 (*a*) of this Article considers it desirable, in order to promote the establishment of a particular industry* with a view to raising the general standard of living of its people, to modify or withdraw a concession included in the appropriate Schedule annexed to this Agreement, it shall notify the CONTRACTING PARTIES to this effect and enter into negotiations with any contracting party with which such concession was initially negotiated, and with any other contracting party determined by the CONTRACTING PARTIES to have a substantial interest therein. If agreement is reached between such contracting parties concerned, they shall be free to modify or withdraw concessions under the appropriate Schedules to this Agreement in order to give effect to such agreement, including any compensatory adjustments involved.

(*b*) If agreement is not reached within sixty days after the notification provided for in subparagraph (*a*) above, the contracting party which proposes to modify or withdraw the concession may refer the matter to the CONTRACTING PARTIES which shall promptly examine it. If they find that the contracting party which proposes to modify or withdraw the concession has made every effort to reach an agreement and that the compensatory adjustment offered by it is adequate, that contracting party shall be free to modify or withdraw the concession if, at the same time, it gives effect to the compensatory adjustment. If the CONTRACTING PARTIES do not find that the compensation offered by a contracting party proposing to modify or withdraw the concession is adequate, but find that it has made every reasonable effort to offer adequate compensation, that contracting party shall be free to proceed with such modification or withdrawal. If such action is taken, any other contracting party referred to in subparagraph (*a*) above shall be free to modify or withdraw substantially equivalent concessions initially negotiated with the contracting party which has taken the action.*

Section B

8. The contracting parties recognize that contracting parties coming within the scope of paragraph 4 (*a*) of this Article tend, when they are in rapid process of development, to experience balance of payments difficulties arising mainly from efforts to expand their internal markets as well as from the instability in their terms of trade.

9. In order to safeguard its external financial position and to ensure a level of reserves adequate for the implementation of its programme of economic development, a contracting party coming within the scope of paragraph 4 (*a*) of this Article may, subject to the provisions of paragraphs 10 to 12, control the general level of its imports by restricting the quantity or value of merchandise permitted to be imported; *Provided* that the import restrictions instituted, maintained or intensified shall not exceed those necessary:

(*a*) to forestall the threat of, or to stop, a serious decline in its monetary reserves, or

(*b*) in the case of a contracting party with inadequate monetary reserves, to achieve a reasonable rate of increase in its reserves.

Due regard shall be paid in either case to any special factors which may be affecting the reserves of the contracting party or its need for reserves, including, where special external credits or other resources are available to it, the need to provide for the appropriate use of such credits or resources.

10. In applying these restrictions, the contracting party may determine their incidence on imports of different products or classes of products in such a way as to give priority to the importation of those products which are more essential in the light of its policy of economic development; *Provided* that the restrictions are so applied as to avoid unnecessary damage to the commercial or economic interests of any other contracting party and not to prevent unreasonably the importation of any description of goods in minimum commercial quantities the exclusion of which would impair regular channels of trade; and *Provided* further that the restrictions are not so applied as to prevent the importation of commercial samples or to prevent compliance with patent, trade mark, copyright or similar procedures.

11. In carrying out its domestic policies, the contracting party concerned shall pay due regard to the need for restoring equilibrium in its balance of payments on a sound and lasting basis and to the desirability of assuring an economic employment of productive resources. It shall progressively relax any restrictions applied under this Section as conditions improve, maintaining them only to the extent necessary under the terms of paragraph 9 of this Article and shall eliminate them when conditions no longer justify such maintenance; *Provided* that no contracting party shall be required to withdraw or modify restrictions on the ground that a change in its development policy would render unnecessary the restrictions which it is applying under this Section.*

12. (*a*) Any contracting party applying new restrictions or raising the general level of its existing restrictions by a substantial intensification of the measures applied under this Section, shall immediately after instituting or intensifying such restrictions (or, in circumstances in which prior consultation is practicable, before doing so) consult with the CONTRACTING PARTIES as to the nature of its balance of payments difficulties, alternative corrective measures which may be available, and the possible effect of the restrictions on the economies of other contracting parties.

(*b*) On a date to be determined by them* the CONTRACTING PARTIES shall review all restrictions still applied under this Section on that date. Beginning two years after that date, contracting parties applying restrictions under this Section shall enter into consultations of the type provided for in subparagraph (*a*) above with the CONTRACTING PARTIES at intervals of approximately, but not less than, two years according to a programme to be drawn up each year by the CONTRACTING PARTIES; *Provided* that no consultation under this subparagraph shall take place within two years after the conclusion of a consultation of a general nature under any other provision of this paragraph.

(*c*) (i) If, in the course of consultations with a contracting party under subparagraph (*a*) or (*b*) of this paragraph, the CONTRACTING PARTIES find that the restrictions are not consistent with the provisions of this Section or with those of Article XIII (subject to the provisions of Article XIV), they shall indicate the nature of the inconsistency and may advise that the restrictions be suitably modified.

(ii) If, however, as a result of the consultations, the CONTRACTING PARTIES determine that the restrictions are being applied in a manner involving an inconsistency of a serious nature with the provisions of this Section or with those of Article XIII (subject to the provisions of Article XIV) and that damage to the trade of any contracting party is caused or threatened thereby, they shall so inform the contracting party applying the restrictions and shall make appropriate recommendations for securing conformity with such provisions within a specified period. If such contracting party does not comply with these recommendations within the specified period, the CONTRACTING PARTIES may release any contracting party the trade of which is adversely affected by the restrictions from such obligations under this Agreement towards the contracting party applying the restrictions as they determine to be appropriate in the circumstances.

(*d*) The CONTRACTING PARTIES shall invite any contracting party which is applying restrictions under this Section to enter into consultations with them at the request of any contracting party which can establish a *prima facie* case that the restrictions are inconsistent with the provisions of this Section or with those of Article XIII (subject to the provisions of Article XIV) and that its trade is adversely affected thereby. However, no such invitation shall be issued unless the CONTRACTING PARTIES have ascertained that direct discussions between the contracting parties concerned have not been successful. If, as a result of the consultations with the CONTRACTING PARTIES no agreement is reached and they determine that the restrictions are being applied inconsistently with such provisions, and that damage to the trade of the contracting party initiating the procedure is caused or threatened thereby, they shall recommend the withdrawal or modification of the restrictions. If the restrictions are not withdrawn or modified within such time as the CONTRACTING PARTIES may prescribe, they may release the contracting party initiating the procedure from such obligations under this Agreement towards the contracting party applying the restrictions as they determine to be appropriate in the circumstances.

(*e*) If a contracting party against which action has been taken in accordance with the last sentence of subparagraph (*c*) (ii) or (*d*) of this paragraph, finds that the release of obligations authorized by the CONTRACTING PARTIES adversely affects the operation of its programme and policy of economic development, it shall be free, not later than sixty days after such action is taken, to give written notice to the Executive Secretary[2] to the Contracting Parties of its intention to withdraw from this Agreement and such withdrawal shall take effect on the sixtieth day following the day on which the notice is received by him.

(*f*) In proceeding under this paragraph, the CONTRACTING PARTIES shall have due regard to the factors referred to in paragraph 2 of this Article. Determinations under this paragraph shall be rendered expeditiously and, if possible, within sixty days of the initiation of the consultations.

Section C

13. If a contracting party coming within the scope of paragraph 4 (*a*) of this Article finds that governmental assistance is required to promote the establishment of a particular industry* with a view to raising the general standard of living of its people, but that no measure consistent with the other provisions of this Agreement is practicable to achieve that objective, it may have recourse to the provisions and procedures set out in this Section.*

14. The contracting party concerned shall notify the CONTRACTING PARTIES of the special difficulties which it meets in the achievement of the objective outlined in paragraph 13 of this Article and shall indicate the specific measure affecting imports which it proposes to introduce in order to remedy these difficulties. It shall not introduce that measure before the expiration of the

---

2 By the Decision of 23 March 1965, the CONTRACTING PARTIES changed the title of the head of the GATT secretariat from "Executive Secretary" to "Director-General".

time-limit laid down in paragraph 15 or 17, as the case may be, or if the measure affects imports of a product which is the subject of a concession included in the appropriate Schedule annexed to this Agreement, unless it has secured the concurrence of the CONTRACTING PARTIES in accordance with provisions of paragraph 18; *Provided* that, if the industry receiving assistance has already started production, the contracting party may, after informing the CONTRACTING PARTIES, take such measures as may be necessary to prevent, during that period, imports of the product or products concerned from increasing substantially above a normal level.*

15. If, within thirty days of the notification of the measure, the CONTRACTING PARTIES do not request the contracting party concerned to consult with them,* that contracting party shall be free to deviate from the relevant provisions of the other Articles of this Agreement to the extent necessary to apply the proposed measure.

16. If it is requested by the CONTRACTING PARTIES to do so, *the contracting party concerned shall consult with them as to the purpose of the proposed measure, as to alternative measures which may be available under this Agreement, and as to the possible effect of the measure proposed on the commercial and economic interests of other contracting parties. If, as a result of such consultation, the CONTRACTING PARTIES agree that there is no measure consistent with the other provisions of this Agreement which is practicable in order to achieve the objective outlined in paragraph 13 of this Article, and concur* in the proposed measure, the contracting party concerned shall be released from its obligations under the relevant provisions of the other Articles of this Agreement to the extent necessary to apply that measure.

17. If, within ninety days after the date of the notification of the proposed measure under paragraph 14 of this Article, the CONTRACTING PARTIES have not concurred in such measure, the contracting party concerned may introduce the measure proposed after informing the CONTRACTING PARTIES.

18. If the proposed measure affects a product which is the subject of a concession included in the appropriate Schedule annexed to this Agreement, the contracting party concerned shall enter into consultations with any other contracting party with which the concession was initially negotiated, and with any other contracting party determined by the CONTRACTING PARTIES to have a substantial interest therein. The CONTRACTING PARTIES shall concur* in the measure if they agree that there is no measure consistent with the other provisions of this Agreement which is practicable in order to achieve the objective set forth in paragraph 13 of this Article, and if they are satisfied:

(*a*) that agreement has been reached with such other contracting parties as a result of the consultations referred to above, or

(*b*) if no such agreement has been reached within sixty days after the notification provided for in paragraph 14 has been received by the CONTRACTING PARTIES, that the contracting party having recourse to this Section has made all reasonable efforts to reach an agreement and that the interests of other contracting parties are adequately safeguarded.*

The contracting party having recourse to this Section shall thereupon be released from its obligations under the relevant provisions of the other Articles of this Agreement to the extent necessary to permit it to apply the measure.

19. If a proposed measure of the type described in paragraph 13 of this Article concerns an industry the establishment of which has in the initial period been facilitated by incidental protection afforded by restrictions imposed by the contracting party concerned for balance of payments purposes under the relevant provisions of this Agreement, that contracting party may

resort to the provisions and procedures of this Section; *Provided* that it shall not apply the proposed measure without the concurrence* of the CONTRACTING PARTIES.*

20. Nothing in the preceding paragraphs of this Section shall authorize any deviation from the provisions of Articles I, II and XIII of this Agreement. The provisos to paragraph 10 of this Article shall also be applicable to any restriction under this Section.

21. At any time while a measure is being applied under paragraph 17 of this Article any contracting party substantially affected by it may suspend the application to the trade of the contracting party having recourse to this Section of such substantially equivalent concessions or other obligations under this Agreement the suspension of which the CONTRACTING PARTIES do not disapprove;* *Provided* that sixty days' notice of such suspension is given to the CONTRACTING PARTIES not later than six months after the measure has been introduced or changed substantially to the detriment of the contracting party affected. Any such contracting party shall afford adequate opportunity for consultation in accordance with the provisions of Article XXII of this Agreement.

Section D

22. A contracting party coming within the scope of subparagraph 4 (*b*) of this Article desiring, in the interest of the development of its economy, to introduce a measure of the type described in paragraph 13 of this Article in respect of the establishment of a particular industry* may apply to the CONTRACTING PARTIES for approval of such measure. The CONTRACTING PARTIES shall promptly consult with such contracting party and shall, in making their decision, be guided by the considerations set out in paragraph 16. If the CONTRACTING PARTIES concur* in the proposed measure the contracting party concerned shall be released from its obligations under the relevant provisions of the other Articles of this Agreement to the extent necessary to permit it to apply the measure. If the proposed measure affects a product which is the subject of a concession included in the appropriate Schedule annexed to this Agreement, the provisions of paragraph 18 shall apply.*

23. Any measure applied under this Section shall comply with the provisions of paragraph 20 of this Article.

Article XIX

Emergency Action on Imports of Particular Products

1. (*a*) If, as a result of unforeseen developments and of the effect of the obligations incurred by a contracting party under this Agreement, including tariff concessions, any product is being imported into the territory of that contracting party in such increased quantities and under such conditions as to cause or threaten serious injury to domestic producers in that territory of like or directly competitive products, the contracting party shall be free, in respect of such product, and to the extent and for such time as may be necessary to prevent or remedy such injury, to suspend the obligation in whole or in part or to withdraw or modify the concession.

(*b*) If any product, which is the subject of a concession with respect to a preference, is being imported into the territory of a contracting party in the circumstances set forth in subparagraph (*a*) of this paragraph, so as to cause or threaten serious injury to domestic producers of like or directly competitive products in the territory of a contracting party which receives or received such preference, the importing contracting party shall be free, if that other contracting party so requests, to suspend the relevant obligation in whole or in part or to withdraw or modify the concession in respect of the product, to the extent and for such time as may be necessary to prevent or remedy such injury.

2. Before any contracting party shall take action pursuant to the provisions of paragraph 1 of this Article, it shall give notice in writing to the CONTRACTING PARTIES as far in advance as may be practicable and shall afford the CONTRACTING PARTIES and those contracting parties having a substantial interest as exporters of the product concerned an opportunity to consult with it in respect of the proposed action. When such notice is given in relation to a concession with respect to a preference, the notice shall name the contracting party which has requested the action. In critical circumstances, where delay would cause damage which it would be difficult to repair, action under paragraph 1 of this Article may be taken provisionally without prior consultation, on the condition that consultation shall be effected immediately after taking such action.

3. (*a*) If agreement among the interested contracting parties with respect to the action is not reached, the contracting party which proposes to take or continue the action shall, nevertheless, be free to do so, and if such action is taken or continued, the affected contracting parties shall then be free, not later than ninety days after such action is taken, to suspend, upon the expiration of thirty days from the day on which written notice of such suspension is received by the CONTRACTING PARTIES, the application to the trade of the contracting party taking such action, or, in the case envisaged in paragraph 1 (*b*) of this Article, to the trade of the contracting party requesting such action, of such substantially equivalent concessions or other obligations under this Agreement the suspension of which the CONTRACTING PARTIES do not disapprove.

(*b*) Notwithstanding the provisions of subparagraph (*a*) of this paragraph, where action is taken under paragraph 2 of this Article without prior consultation and causes or threatens serious injury in the territory of a contracting party to the domestic producers of products affected by the action, that contracting party shall, where delay would cause damage difficult to repair, be free to suspend, upon the taking of the action and throughout the period of consultation, such concessions or other obligations as may be necessary to prevent or remedy the injury.

Article XX

General Exceptions

Subject to the requirement that such measures are not applied in a manner which would constitute a means of arbitrary or unjustifiable discrimination between countries where the same conditions prevail, or a disguised restriction on international trade, nothing in this Agreement shall be construed to prevent the adoption or enforcement by any contracting party of measures:

(*a*) necessary to protect public morals;

(*b*) necessary to protect human, animal or plant life or health;

(*c*) relating to the importations or exportations of gold or silver;

(*d*) necessary to secure compliance with laws or regulations which are not inconsistent with the provisions of this Agreement, including those relating to customs enforcement, the enforcement of monopolies operated under paragraph 4 of Article II and Article XVII, the protection of patents, trade marks and copyrights, and the prevention of deceptive practices;

(*e*) relating to the products of prison labour;

(*f*) imposed for the protection of national treasures of artistic, historic or archaeological value;

(*g*) relating to the conservation of exhaustible natural resources if such measures are made effective in conjunction with restrictions on domestic production or consumption;

(*h*) undertaken in pursuance of obligations under any intergovernmental commodity agreement which conforms to criteria submitted to the CONTRACTING PARTIES and not disapproved by them or which is itself so submitted and not so disapproved;*

(*i*) involving restrictions on exports of domestic materials necessary to ensure essential quantities of such materials to a domestic processing industry during periods when the domestic price of such materials is held below the world price as part of a governmental stabilization plan; *Provided* that such restrictions shall not operate to increase the exports of or the protection afforded to such domestic industry, and shall not depart from the provisions of this Agreement relating to non-discrimination;

(*j*) essential to the acquisition or distribution of products in general or local short supply; *Provided* that any such measures shall be consistent with the principle that all contracting parties are entitled to an equitable share of the international supply of such products, and that any such measures, which are inconsistent with the other provisions of the Agreement shall be discontinued as soon as the conditions giving rise to them have ceased to exist. The CONTRACTING PARTIES shall review the need for this sub-paragraph not later than 30 June 1960.

Article XXI

Security Exceptions

Nothing in this Agreement shall be construed

(*a*) to require any contracting party to furnish any information the disclosure of which it considers contrary to its essential security interests; or

(*b*) to prevent any contracting party from taking any action which it considers necessary for the protection of its essential security interests

(i) relating to fissionable materials or the materials from which they are derived;

(ii) relating to the traffic in arms, ammunition and implements of war and to such traffic in other goods and materials as is carried on directly or indirectly for the purpose of supplying a military establishment;

(iii) taken in time of war or other emergency in international relations; or

(*c*) to prevent any contracting party from taking any action in pursuance of its obligations under the United Nations Charter for the maintenance of international peace and security.

Article XXII

Consultation

1. Each contracting party shall accord sympathetic consideration to, and shall afford adequate opportunity for consultation regarding, such representations as may be made by another contracting party with respect to any matter affecting the operation of this Agreement.

2. The CONTRACTING PARTIES may, at the request of a contracting party, consult with any contracting party or parties in respect of any matter for which it has not been possible to find a satisfactory solution through consultation under paragraph 1.

Article XXIII

Nullification or Impairment

1. If any contracting party should consider that any benefit accruing to it directly or indirectly under this Agreement is being nullified or impaired or that the attainment of any objective of the Agreement is being impeded as the result of

(*a*) the failure of another contracting party to carry out its obligations under this Agreement, or

(*b*) the application by another contracting party of any measure, whether or not it conflicts with the provisions of this Agreement, or

(*c*) the existence of any other situation,

the contracting party may, with a view to the satisfactory adjustment of the matter, make written representations or proposals to the other contracting party or parties which it considers to be concerned. Any contracting party thus approached shall give sympathetic consideration to the representations or proposals made to it.

2. If no satisfactory adjustment is effected between the contracting parties concerned within a reasonable time, or if the difficulty is of the type described in paragraph 1 (*c*) of this Article, the matter may be referred to the CONTRACTING PARTIES. The CONTRACTING PARTIES shall promptly investigate any matter so referred to them and shall make appropriate recommendations to the contracting parties which they consider to be concerned, or give a ruling on the matter, as appropriate. The CONTRACTING PARTIES may consult with contracting parties, with the Economic and Social Council of the United Nations and with any appropriate inter-governmental organization in cases where they consider such consultation necessary. If the CONTRACTING PARTIES consider that the circumstances are serious enough to justify such action, they may authorize a contracting party or parties to suspend the application to any other contracting party or parties of such concessions or other obligations under this Agreement as they determine to be appropriate in the circumstances. If the application to any contracting party of any concession or other obligation is in fact suspended, that contracting party shall then be free, not later than sixty days after such action is taken, to give written notice to the Executive Secretary[3] to the Contracting Parties of its intention to withdraw from this Agreement and such withdrawal shall take effect upon the sixtieth day following the day on which such notice is received by him.

PART III

Article XXIV

Territorial Application - Frontier Traffic - Customs Unions and Free-trade Areas

1. The provisions of this Agreement shall apply to the metropolitan customs territories of the contracting parties and to any other customs territories in respect of which this Agreement has been accepted under Article XXVI or is being applied under Article XXXIII or pursuant to the Protocol of Provisional Application. Each such customs territory shall, exclusively for the purposes of the territorial application of this Agreement, be treated as though it were a

3 By the Decision of 23 March 1965, the CONTRACTING PARTIES changed the title of the head of the GATT secretariat from "Executive Secretary" to "Director-General".

contracting party; *Provided* that the provisions of this paragraph shall not be construed to create any rights or obligations as between two or more customs territories in respect of which this Agreement has been accepted under Article XXVI or is being applied under Article XXXIII or pursuant to the Protocol of Provisional Application by a single contracting party.

2. For the purposes of this Agreement a customs territory shall be understood to mean any territory with respect to which separate tariffs or other regulations of commerce are maintained for a substantial part of the trade of such territory with other territories.

3. The provisions of this Agreement shall not be construed to prevent:

(*a*) Advantages accorded by any contracting party to adjacent countries in order to facilitate frontier traffic;

(*b*) Advantages accorded to the trade with the Free Territory of Trieste by countries contiguous to that territory, provided that such advantages are not in conflict with the Treaties of Peace arising out of the Second World War.

4. The contracting parties recognize the desirability of increasing freedom of trade by the development, through voluntary agreements, of closer integration between the economies of the countries parties to such agreements. They also recognize that the purpose of a customs union or of a free-trade area should be to facilitate trade between the constituent territories and not to raise barriers to the trade of other contracting parties with such territories.

5. Accordingly, the provisions of this Agreement shall not prevent, as between the territories of contracting parties, the formation of a customs union or of a free-trade area or the adoption of an interim agreement necessary for the formation of a customs union or of a free-trade area; *Provided* that:

(*a*) with respect to a customs union, or an interim agreement leading to a formation of a customs union, the duties and other regulations of commerce imposed at the institution of any such union or interim agreement in respect of trade with contracting parties not parties to such union or agreement shall not on the whole be higher or more restrictive than the general incidence of the duties and regulations of commerce applicable in the constituent territories prior to the formation of such union or the adoption of such interim agreement, as the case may be;

(*b*) with respect to a free-trade area, or an interim agreement leading to the formation of a free-trade area, the duties and other regulations of commerce maintained in each of the constituent territories and applicable at the formation of such free-trade area or the adoption of such interim agreement to the trade of contracting parties not included in such area or not parties to such agreement shall not be higher or more restrictive than the corresponding duties and other regulations of commerce existing in the same constituent territories prior to the formation of the free-trade area, or interim agreement as the case may be; and

(*c*) any interim agreement referred to in subparagraphs (*a*) and (*b*) shall include a plan and schedule for the formation of such a customs union or of such a free-trade area within a reasonable length of time.

6. If, in fulfilling the requirements of subparagraph 5 (*a*), a contracting party proposes to increase any rate of duty inconsistently with the provisions of Article II, the procedure set forth in Article XXVIII shall apply. In providing for compensatory adjustment, due account shall be taken of the compensation already afforded by the reduction brought about in the corresponding duty of the other constituents of the union.

7. (*a*) Any contracting party deciding to enter into a customs union or free-trade area, or an interim agreement leading to the formation of such a union or area, shall promptly notify the CONTRACTING PARTIES and shall make available to them such information regarding the proposed union or area as will enable them to make such reports and recommendations to contracting parties as they may deem appropriate.

(*b*) If, after having studied the plan and schedule included in an interim agreement referred to in paragraph 5 in consultation with the parties to that agreement and taking due account of the information made available in accordance with the provisions of subparagraph (*a*), the CONTRACTING PARTIES find that such agreement is not likely to result in the formation of a customs union or of a free-trade area within the period contemplated by the parties to the agreement or that such period is not a reasonable one, the CONTRACTING PARTIES shall make recommendations to the parties to the agreement. The parties shall not maintain or put into force, as the case may be, such agreement if they are not prepared to modify it in accordance with these recommendations.

(*c*) Any substantial change in the plan or schedule referred to in paragraph 5 (*c*) shall be communicated to the CONTRACTING PARTIES, which may request the contracting parties concerned to consult with them if the change seems likely to jeopardize or delay unduly the formation of the customs union or of the free-trade area.

8. For the purposes of this Agreement:

(*a*) A customs union shall be understood to mean the substitution of a single customs territory for two or more customs territories, so that

(i) duties and other restrictive regulations of commerce (except, where necessary, those permitted under Articles XI, XII, XIII, XIV, XV and XX) are eliminated with respect to substantially all the trade between the constituent territories of the union or at least with respect to substantially all the trade in products originating in such territories, and,

(ii) subject to the provisions of paragraph 9, substantially the same duties and other regulations of commerce are applied by each of the members of the union to the trade of territories not included in the union;

(*b*) A free-trade area shall be understood to mean a group of two or more customs territories in which the duties and other restrictive regulations of commerce (except, where necessary, those permitted under Articles XI, XII, XIII, XIV, XV and XX) are eliminated on substantially all the trade between the constituent territories in products originating in such territories.

9. The preferences referred to in paragraph 2 of Article I shall not be affected by the formation of a customs union or of a free-trade area but may be eliminated or adjusted by means of negotiations with contracting parties affected.* This procedure of negotiations with affected contracting parties shall, in particular, apply to the elimination of preferences required to conform with the provisions of paragraph 8 (*a*)(i) and paragraph 8 (*b*).

10. The CONTRACTING PARTIES may by a two-thirds majority approve proposals which do not fully comply with the requirements of paragraphs 5 to 9 inclusive, provided that such proposals lead to the formation of a customs union or a free-trade area in the sense of this Article.

11. Taking into account the exceptional circumstances arising out of the establishment of India and Pakistan as independent States and recognizing the fact that they have long constituted an

economic unit, the contracting parties agree that the provisions of this Agreement shall not prevent the two countries from entering into special arrangements with respect to the trade between them, pending the establishment of their mutual trade relations on a definitive basis.*

12. Each contracting party shall take such reasonable measures as may be available to it to ensure observance of the provisions of this Agreement by the regional and local governments and authorities within its territories.

Article XXV

Joint Action by the Contracting Parties

1. Representatives of the contracting parties shall meet from time to time for the purpose of giving effect to those provisions of this Agreement which involve joint action and, generally, with a view to facilitating the operation and furthering the objectives of this Agreement. Wherever reference is made in this Agreement to the contracting parties acting jointly they are designated as the CONTRACTING PARTIES.

2. The Secretary-General of the United Nations is requested to convene the first meeting of the CONTRACTING PARTIES, which shall take place not later than March 1, 1948.

3. Each contracting party shall be entitled to have one vote at all meetings of the CONTRACTING PARTIES.

4. Except as otherwise provided for in this Agreement, decisions of the CONTRACTING PARTIES shall be taken by a majority of the votes cast.

5. In exceptional circumstances not elsewhere provided for in this Agreement, the CONTRACTING PARTIES may waive an obligation imposed upon a contracting party by this Agreement; *Provided* that any such decision shall be approved by a two-thirds majority of the votes cast and that such majority shall comprise more than half of the contracting parties. The CONTRACTING PARTIES may also by such a vote

(i) define certain categories of exceptional circumstances to which other voting requirements shall apply for the waiver of obligations, and

(ii) prescribe such criteria as may be necessary for the application of this paragraph[4].

Article XXVI

Acceptance, Entry into Force and Registration

1. The date of this Agreement shall be 30 October 1947.

2. This Agreement shall be open for acceptance by any contracting party which, on 1 March 1955, was a contracting party or was negotiating with a view to accession to this Agreement.

3. This Agreement, done in a single English original and a single French original, both texts authentic, shall be deposited with the Secretary-General of the United Nations, who shall furnish certified copies thereof to all interested governments.

---

4 The authentic text erroneously reads "sub-paragraph".

4. Each government accepting this Agreement shall deposit an instrument of acceptance with the Executive Secretary[5] to the Contracting Parties, who will inform all interested governments of the date of deposit of each instrument of acceptance and of the day on which this Agreement enters into force under paragraph 6 of this Article.

5. (*a*) Each government accepting this Agreement does so in respect of its metropolitan territory and of the other territories for which it has international responsibility, except such separate customs territories as it shall notify to the Executive Secretary[5] to the CONTRACTING PARTIES at the time of its own acceptance.

(*b*) Any government, which has so notified the Executive Secretary[5] under the exceptions in subparagraph (*a*) of this paragraph, may at any time give notice to the Executive Secretary[5] that its acceptance shall be effective in respect of any separate customs territory or territories so excepted and such notice shall take effect on the thirtieth day following the day on which it is received by the Executive Secretary.[5]

(*c*) If any of the customs territories, in respect of which a contracting party has accepted this Agreement, possesses or acquires full autonomy in the conduct of its external commercial relations and of the other matters provided for in this Agreement, such territory shall, upon sponsorship through a declaration by the responsible contracting party establishing the above-mentioned fact, be deemed to be a contracting party.

6. This Agreement shall enter into force, as among the governments which have accepted it, on the thirtieth day following the day on which instruments of acceptance have been deposited with Executive Secretary[6] to the Contracting Parties on behalf of governments named in Annex H, the territories of which account for 85 per centum of the total external trade of the territories of such governments, computed in accordance with the applicable column of percentages set forth therein. The instrument of acceptance of each other government shall take effect on the thirtieth day following the day on which such instrument has been deposited.

7. The United Nations is authorized to effect registration of this Agreement as soon as it enters into force.

Article XXVII

Withholding or Withdrawal of Concessions

Any contracting party shall at any time be free to withhold or to withdraw in whole or in part any concession, provided for in the appropriate Schedule annexed to this Agreement, in respect of which such contracting party determines that it was initially negotiated with a government which has not become, or has ceased to be, a contracting party. A contracting party taking such action shall notify the CONTRACTING PARTIES and, upon request, consult with contracting parties which have a substantial interest in the product concerned.

---

5 By the Decision of 23 March 1965, the CONTRACTING PARTIES changed the title of the head of the GATT secretariat from "Executive Secretary" to "Director-General".

6 By the Decision of 23 March 1965, the CONTRACTING PARTIES changed the title of the head of the GATT secretariat from "Executive Secretary" to "Director-General".

*Article XXVIII**

Modification of Schedules

1. On the first day of each three-year period, the first period beginning on 1 January 1958 (or on the first day of any other period* that may be specified by the CONTRACTING PARTIES by two-thirds of the votes cast) a contracting party (hereafter in this Article referred to as the "applicant contracting party") may, by negotiation and agreement with any contracting party with which such concession was initially negotiated and with any other contracting party determined by the CONTRACTING PARTIES to have a principal supplying interest* (which two preceding categories of contracting parties, together with the applicant contracting party, are in this Article hereinafter referred to as the "contracting parties primarily concerned"), and subject to consultation with any other contracting party determined by the CONTRACTING PARTIES to have a substantial interest* in such concession, modify or withdraw a concession* included in the appropriate schedule annexed to this Agreement.

2. In such negotiations and agreement, which may include provision for compensatory adjustment with respect to other products, the contracting parties concerned shall endeavour to maintain a general level of reciprocal and mutually advantageous concessions not less favourable to trade than that provided for in this Agreement prior to such negotiations.

3. (*a*) If agreement between the contracting parties primarily concerned cannot be reached before 1 January 1958 or before the expiration of a period envisaged in paragraph 1 of this Article, the contracting party which proposes to modify or withdraw the concession shall, nevertheless, be free to do so and if such action is taken any contracting party with which such concession was initially negotiated, any contracting party determined under paragraph 1 to have a principal supplying interest and any contracting party determined under paragraph 1 to have a substantial interest shall then be free not later than six months after such action is taken, to withdraw, upon the expiration of thirty days from the day on which written notice of such withdrawal is received by the CONTRACTING PARTIES, substantially equivalent concessions initially negotiated with the applicant contracting party.

(*b*) If agreement between the contracting parties primarily concerned is reached but any other contracting party determined under paragraph 1 of this Article to have a substantial interest is not satisfied, such other contracting party shall be free, not later than six months after action under such agreement is taken, to withdraw, upon the expiration of thirty days from the day on which written notice of such withdrawal is received by the CONTRACTING PARTIES, substantially equivalent concessions initially negotiated with the applicant contracting party.

4. The CONTRACTING PARTIES may, at any time, in special circumstances, authorize* a contracting party to enter into negotiations for modification or withdrawal of a concession included in the appropriate Schedule annexed to this Agreement subject to the following procedures and conditions:

(*a*) Such negotiations* and any related consultations shall be conducted in accordance with the provisions of paragraph 1 and 2 of this Article.

(*b*) If agreement between the contracting parties primarily concerned is reached in the negotiations, the provisions of paragraph 3 (*b*) of this Article shall apply.

(*c*) If agreement between the contracting parties primarily concerned is not reached within a period of sixty days* after negotiations have been authorized, or within such longer period as the CONTRACTING PARTIES may have prescribed, the applicant contracting party may refer the matter to the CONTRACTING PARTIES.

(*d*) Upon such reference, the CONTRACTING PARTIES shall promptly examine the matter and submit their views to the contracting parties primarily concerned with the aim of achieving a settlement. If a settlement is reached, the provisions of paragraph 3 (*b*) shall apply as if agreement between the contracting parties primarily concerned had been reached. If no settlement is reached between the contracting parties primarily concerned, the applicant contracting party shall be free to modify or withdraw the concession, unless the CONTRACTING PARTIES determine that the applicant contracting party has unreasonably failed to offer adequate compensation.* If such action is taken, any contracting party with which the concession was initially negotiated, any contracting party determined under paragraph 4 (*a*) to have a principal supplying interest and any contracting party determined under paragraph 4 (*a*) to have a substantial interest, shall be free, not later than six months after such action is taken, to modify or withdraw, upon the expiration of thirty days from the day on which written notice of such withdrawal is received by the CONTRACTING PARTIES, substantially equivalent concessions initially negotiated with applicant contracting party.

5. Before 1 January 1958 and before the end of any period envisaged in paragraph 1 a contracting party may elect by notifying the CONTRACTING PARTIES to reserve the right, for the duration of the next period, to modify the appropriate Schedule in accordance with the procedures of paragraph 1 to 3. If a contracting party so elects, other contracting parties shall have the right, during the same period, to modify or withdraw, in accordance with the same procedures, concessions initially negotiated with that contracting party.

Article XXVIII bis

Tariff Negotiations

1. The contracting parties recognize that customs duties often constitute serious obstacles to trade; thus negotiations on a reciprocal and mutually advantageous basis, directed to the substantial reduction of the general level of tariffs and other charges on imports and exports and in particular to the reduction of such high tariffs as discourage the importation even of minimum quantities, and conducted with due regard to the objectives of this Agreement and the varying needs of individual contracting parties, are of great importance to the expansion of international trade. The CONTRACTING PARTIES may therefore sponsor such negotiations from time to time.

2. (*a*) Negotiations under this Article may be carried out on a selective product-by-product basis or by the application of such multilateral procedures as may be accepted by the contracting parties concerned. Such negotiations may be directed towards the reduction of duties, the binding of duties at then existing levels or undertakings that individual duties or the average duties on specified categories of products shall not exceed specified levels. The binding against increase of low duties or of duty-free treatment shall, in principle, be recognized as a concession equivalent in value to the reduction of high duties.

(*b*) The contracting parties recognize that in general the success of multilateral negotiations would depend on the participation of all contracting parties which conduct a substantial proportion of their external trade with one another.

3. Negotiations shall be conducted on a basis which affords adequate opportunity to take into account:

(*a*) the needs of individual contracting parties and individual industries;

(*b*) the needs of less-developed countries for a more flexible use of tariff protection to assist their economic development and the special needs of these countries to maintain tariffs for revenue purposes; and

(*c*) all other relevant circumstances, including the fiscal,* developmental, strategic and other needs of the contracting parties concerned.

Article XXIX

The Relation of this Agreement to the Havana Charter

1. The contracting parties undertake to observe to the fullest extent of their executive authority the general principles of Chapters I to VI inclusive and of Chapter IX of the Havana Charter pending their acceptance of it in accordance with their constitutional procedures.*

2. Part II of this Agreement shall be suspended on the day on which the Havana Charter enters into force.

3. If by September 30, 1949, the Havana Charter has not entered into force, the contracting parties shall meet before December 31, 1949, to agree whether this Agreement shall be amended, supplemented or maintained.

4. If at any time the Havana Charter should cease to be in force, the CONTRACTING PARTIES shall meet as soon as practicable thereafter to agree whether this Agreement shall be supplemented, amended or maintained. Pending such agreement, Part II of this Agreement shall again enter into force; *Provided* that the provisions of Part II other than Article XXIII shall be replaced, *mutatis mutandis,* in the form in which they then appeared in the Havana Charter; and *Provided* further that no contracting party shall be bound by any provisions which did not bind it at the time when the Havana Charter ceased to be in force.

5. If any contracting party has not accepted the Havana Charter by the date upon which it enters into force, the CONTRACTING PARTIES shall confer to agree whether, and if so in what way, this Agreement in so far as it affects relations between such contracting party and other contracting parties, shall be supplemented or amended. Pending such agreement the provisions of Part II of this Agreement shall, notwithstanding the provisions of paragraph 2 of this Article, continue to apply as between such contracting party and other contracting parties.

6. Contracting parties which are Members of the International Trade Organization shall not invoke the provisions of this Agreement so as to prevent the operation of any provision of the Havana Charter. The application of the principle underlying this paragraph to any contracting party which is not a Member of the International Trade Organization shall be the subject of an agreement pursuant to paragraph 5 of this Article.

Article XXX

Amendments

1. Except where provision for modification is made elsewhere in this Agreement, amendments to the provisions of Part I of this Agreement or the provisions of Article XXIX or of this Article shall become effective upon acceptance by all the contracting parties, and other amendments to this Agreement shall become effective, in respect of those contracting parties which accept them, upon acceptance by two-thirds of the contracting parties and thereafter for each other contracting party upon acceptance by it.

2. Any contracting party accepting an amendment to this Agreement shall deposit an instrument of acceptance with the Secretary-General of the United Nations within such period as the CONTRACTING PARTIES may specify. The CONTRACTING PARTIES may decide that any amendment made effective under this Article is of such a nature that any contracting party which has not accepted it within a period specified by the CONTRACTING PARTIES shall be free to withdraw from this Agreement, or to remain a contracting party with the consent of the CONTRACTING PARTIES.

Article XXXI

Withdrawal

Without prejudice to the provisions of paragraph 12 of Article XVIII, of Article XXIII or of paragraph 2 of Article XXX, any contracting party may withdraw from this Agreement, or may separately withdraw on behalf of any of the separate customs territories for which it has international responsibility and which at the time possesses full autonomy in the conduct of its external commercial relations and of the other matters provided for in this Agreement. The withdrawal shall take effect upon the expiration of six months from the day on which written notice of withdrawal is received by the Secretary-General of the United Nations.

Article XXXII

Contracting Parties

1. The contracting parties to this Agreement shall be understood to mean those governments which are applying the provisions of this Agreement under Articles XXVI or XXXIII or pursuant to the Protocol of Provisional Application.

2. At any time after the entry into force of this Agreement pursuant to paragraph 6 of Article XXVI, those contracting parties which have accepted this Agreement pursuant to paragraph 4 of Article XXVI may decide that any contracting party which has not so accepted it shall cease to be a contracting party.

Article XXXIII

Accession

A government not party to this Agreement, or a government acting on behalf of a separate customs territory possessing full autonomy in the conduct of its external commercial relations and of the other matters provided for in this Agreement, may accede to this Agreement, on its own behalf or on behalf of that territory, on terms to be agreed between such government and the CONTRACTING PARTIES. Decisions of the CONTRACTING PARTIES under this paragraph shall be taken by a two-thirds majority.

Article XXXIV

Annexes

The annexes to this Agreement are hereby made an integral part of this Agreement.

Article XXXV

Non-application of the Agreement between Particular Contracting Parties

1. This Agreement, or alternatively Article II of this Agreement, shall not apply as between any contracting party and any other contracting party if:

(*a*) the two contracting parties have not entered into tariff negotiations with each other, and

(*b*) either of the contracting parties, at the time either becomes a contracting party, does not consent to such application.

2. The CONTRACTING PARTIES may review the operation of this Article in particular cases at the request of any contracting party and make appropriate recommendations.

PART IV*

TRADE AND DEVELOPMENT

Article XXXVI

Principles and Objectives

1.* The contracting parties,

(*a*) recalling that the basic objectives of this Agreement include the raising of standards of living and the progressive development of the economies of all contracting parties, and considering that the attainment of these objectives is particularly urgent for less-developed contracting parties;

(*b*) considering that export earnings of the less-developed contracting parties can play a vital part in their economic development and that the extent of this contribution depends on the prices paid by the less-developed contracting parties for essential imports, the volume of their exports, and the prices received for these exports;

(*c*) noting, that there is a wide gap between standards of living in less-developed countries and in other countries;

(*d*) recognizing that individual and joint action is essential to further the development of the economies of less-developed contracting parties and to bring about a rapid advance in the standards of living in these countries;

(*e*) recognizing that international trade as a means of achieving economic and social advancement should be governed by such rules and procedures - and measures in conformity with such rules and procedures - as are consistent with the objectives set forth in this Article;

(*f*) noting that the CONTRACTING PARTIES may enable less-developed contracting parties to use special measures to promote their trade and development;

agree as follows.

2. There is need for a rapid and sustained expansion of the export earnings of the less-developed contracting parties.

3. There is need for positive efforts designed to ensure that less-developed contracting parties secure a share in the growth in international trade commensurate with the needs of their economic development.

4. Given the continued dependence of many less-developed contracting parties on the exportation of a limited range of primary products,* there is need to provide in the largest possible measure more favourable and acceptable conditions of access to world markets for these products, and wherever appropriate to devise measures designed to stabilize and improve conditions of world markets in these products, including in particular measures designed to attain stable, equitable and remunerative prices, thus permitting an expansion of world trade and demand and a dynamic and steady growth of the real export earnings of these countries so as to provide them with expanding resources for their economic development.

5. The rapid expansion of the economies of the less-developed contracting parties will be facilitated by a diversification* of the structure of their economies and the avoidance of an excessive dependence on the export of primary products. There is, therefore, need for increased access in the largest possible measure to markets under favourable conditions for processed and manufactured products currently or potentially of particular export interest to less-developed contracting parties.

6. Because of the chronic deficiency in the export proceeds and other foreign exchange earnings of less-developed contracting parties, there are important inter-relationships between trade and financial assistance to development. There is, therefore, need for close and continuing collaboration between the CONTRACTING PARTIES and the international lending agencies so that they can contribute most effectively to alleviating the burdens these less-developed contracting parties assume in the interest of their economic development.

7. There is need for appropriate collaboration between the CONTRACTING PARTIES, other intergovernmental bodies and the organs and agencies of the United Nations system, whose activities relate to the trade and economic development of less-developed countries.

8. The developed contracting parties do not expect reciprocity for commitments made by them in trade negotiations to reduce or remove tariffs and other barriers to the trade of less-developed contracting parties.*

9. The adoption of measures to give effect to these principles and objectives shall be a matter of conscious and purposeful effort on the part of the contracting parties both individually and jointly.

Article XXXVII

Commitments

1. The developed contracting parties shall to the fullest extent possible - that is, except when compelling reasons, which may include legal reasons, make it impossible - give effect to the following provisions:

(*a*) accord high priority to the reduction and elimination of barriers to products currently or potentially of particular export interest to less-developed contracting parties, including customs duties and other restrictions which differentiate unreasonably between such products in their primary and in their processed forms;*

(*b*) refrain from introducing, or increasing the incidence of, customs duties or non-tariff import barriers on products currently or potentially of particular export interest to less-developed contracting parties; and

(*c*) (i) refrain from imposing new fiscal measures, and

(ii) in any adjustments of fiscal policy accord high priority to the reduction and elimination of fiscal measures, which would hamper, or which hamper, significantly the growth of consumption of primary products, in raw or processed form, wholly or mainly produced in the territories of less-developed contracting parties, and which are applied specifically to those products.

2. (*a*) Whenever it is considered that effect is not being given to any of the provisions of subparagraph (*a*), (*b*) or (*c*) of paragraph 1, the matter shall be reported to the CONTRACTING PARTIES either by the contracting party not so giving effect to the relevant provisions or by any other interested contracting party.

(*b*) (i) The CONTRACTING PARTIES shall, if requested so to do by any interested contracting party, and without prejudice to any bilateral consultations that may be undertaken, consult with the contracting party concerned and all interested contracting parties with respect to the matter with a view to reaching solutions satisfactory to all contracting parties concerned in order to further the objectives set forth in Article XXXVI. In the course of these consultations, the reasons given in cases where effect was not being given to the provisions of subparagraph (*a*), (*b*) or (*c*) of paragraph 1 shall be examined.

(ii) As the implementation of the provisions of subparagraph (*a*), (*b*) or (*c*) of paragraph 1 by individual contracting parties may in some cases be more readily achieved where action is taken jointly with other developed contracting parties, such consultation might, where appropriate, be directed towards this end.

(iii) The consultations by the CONTRACTING PARTIES might also, in appropriate cases, be directed towards agreement on joint action designed to further the objectives of this Agreement as envisaged in paragraph 1 of Article XXV.

3. The developed contracting parties shall:

(*a*) make every effort, in cases where a government directly or indirectly determines the resale price of products wholly or mainly produced in the territories of less-developed contracting parties, to maintain trade margins at equitable levels;

(*b*) give active consideration to the adoption of other measures* designed to provide greater scope for the development of imports from less-developed contracting parties and collaborate in appropriate international action to this end;

(*c*) have special regard to the trade interests of less-developed contracting parties when considering the application of other measures permitted under this Agreement to meet particular problems and explore all possibilities of constructive remedies before applying such measures where they would affect essential interests of those contracting parties.

4. Less-developed contracting parties agree to take appropriate action in implementation of the provisions of Part IV for the benefit of the trade of other less-developed contracting parties, in so

far as such action is consistent with their individual present and future development, financial and trade needs taking into account past trade developments as well as the trade interests of less-developed contracting parties as a whole.

5. In the implementation of the commitments set forth in paragraph 1 to 4 each contracting party shall afford to any other interested contracting party or contracting parties full and prompt opportunity for consultations under the normal procedures of this Agreement with respect to any matter or difficulty which may arise.

Article XXXVIII

Joint Action

1. The contracting parties shall collaborate jointly, with the framework of this Agreement and elsewhere, as appropriate, to further the objectives set forth in Article XXXVI.

2. In particular, the CONTRACTING PARTIES shall:

(*a*) where appropriate, take action, including action through international arrangements, to provide improved and acceptable conditions of access to world markets for primary products of particular interest to less-developed contracting parties and to devise measures designed to stabilize and improve conditions of world markets in these products including measures designed to attain stable, equitable and remunerative prices for exports of such products;

(*b*) seek appropriate collaboration in matters of trade and development policy with the United Nations and its organs and agencies, including any institutions that may be created on the basis of recommendations by the United Nations Conference on Trade and Development;

(*c*) collaborate in analysing the development plans and policies of individual less-developed contracting parties and in examining trade and aid relationships with a view to devising concrete measures to promote the development of export potential and to facilitate access to export markets for the products of the industries thus developed and, in this connection, seek appropriate collaboration with governments and international organizations, and in particular with organizations having competence in relation to financial assistance for economic development, in systematic studies of trade and aid relationships in individual less-developed contracting parties aimed at obtaining a clear analysis of export potential, market prospects and any further action that may be required;

(*d*) keep under continuous review the development of world trade with special reference to the rate of growth of the trade of less-developed contracting parties and make such recommendations to contracting parties as may, in the circumstances, be deemed appropriate;

(*e*) collaborate in seeking feasible methods to expand trade for the purpose of economic development, through international harmonization and adjustment of national policies and regulations, through technical and commercial standards affecting production, transportation and marketing, and through export promotion by the establishment of facilities for the increased flow of trade information and the development of market research; and

(*f*) establish such institutional arrangements as may be necessary to further the objectives set forth in Article XXXVI and to give effect to the provision of this Part.

General Agreement on Trade in Services

GENERAL AGREEMENT ON TRADE IN SERVICES

Members,

Recognizing the growing importance of trade in services for the growth and development of the world economy;

Wishing to establish a multilateral framework of principles and rules for trade in services with a view to the expansion of such trade under conditions of transparency and progressive liberalization and as a means of promoting the economic growth of all trading partners and the development of developing countries;

Desiring the early achievement of progressively higher levels of liberalization of trade in services through successive rounds of multilateral negotiations aimed at promoting the interests of all participants on a mutually advantageous basis and at securing an overall balance of rights and obligations, while giving due respect to national policy objectives;

Recognizing the right of Members to regulate, and to introduce new regulations, on the supply of services within their territories in order to meet national policy objectives and, given asymmetries existing with respect to the degree of development of services regulations in different countries, the particular need of developing countries to exercise this right;

Desiring to facilitate the increasing participation of developing countries in trade in services and the expansion of their service exports including, *inter alia,* through the strengthening of their domestic services capacity and its efficiency and competitiveness;

Taking particular account of the serious difficulty of the least-developed countries in view of their special economic situation and their development, trade and financial needs;

Hereby *agree* as follows:

PART I

SCOPE AND DEFINITION

Article I

Scope and Definition

1. This Agreement applies to measures by Members affecting trade in services.

2. For the purposes of this Agreement, trade in services is defined as the supply of a service:

   (a) from the territory of one Member into the territory of any other Member;

   (b) in the territory of one Member to the service consumer of any other Member;

   (c) by a service supplier of one Member, through commercial presence in the territory of any other Member;

   (d) by a service supplier of one Member, through presence of natural persons of a Member in the territory of any other Member.

3. For the purposes of this Agreement:

   (a) "measures by Members" means measures taken by:

      (i) central, regional or local governments and authorities; and

      (ii) non-governmental bodies in the exercise of powers delegated by central, regional or local governments or authorities;

   In fulfilling its obligations and commitments under the Agreement, each Member shall take such reasonable measures as may be available to it to ensure their observance by regional and local governments and authorities and non-governmental bodies within its territory;

   (b) "services" includes any service in any sector except services supplied in the exercise of governmental authority;

   (c) "a service supplied in the exercise of governmental authority" means any service which is supplied neither on a commercial basis, nor in competition with one or more service suppliers.

PART II

GENERAL OBLIGATIONS AND DISCIPLINES

Article II

Most-Favoured-Nation Treatment

1. With respect to any measure covered by this Agreement, each Member shall accord immediately and unconditionally to services and service suppliers of any other Member treatment no less favourable than that it accords to like services and service suppliers of any other country.

2. A Member may maintain a measure inconsistent with paragraph 1 provided that such a measure is listed in, and meets the conditions of, the Annex on Article II Exemptions.

3. The provisions of this Agreement shall not be so construed as to prevent any Member from conferring or according advantages to adjacent countries in order to facilitate exchanges limited to contiguous frontier zones of services that are both locally produced and consumed.

Article III

Transparency

1. Each Member shall publish promptly and, except in emergency situations, at the latest by the time of their entry into force, all relevant measures of general application which pertain to or affect the operation of this Agreement. International agreements pertaining to or affecting trade in services to which a Member is a signatory shall also be published.

2. Where publication as referred to in paragraph 1 is not practicable, such information shall be made otherwise publicly available.

3. Each Member shall promptly and at least annually inform the Council for Trade in Services of the introduction of any new, or any changes to existing, laws, regulations or administrative guidelines which significantly affect trade in services covered by its specific commitments under this Agreement.

4. Each Member shall respond promptly to all requests by any other Member for specific information on any of its measures of general application or international agreements within the meaning of paragraph 1. Each Member shall also establish one or more enquiry points to provide specific information to other Members, upon request, on all such matters as well as those subject to the notification requirement in paragraph 3. Such enquiry points shall be established within two years from the date of entry into force of the Agreement Establishing the WTO (referred to in this Agreement as the "WTO Agreement"). Appropriate flexibility with respect to the time-limit within which such enquiry points are to be established may be agreed upon for individual developing country Members. Enquiry points need not be depositories of laws and regulations.

5. Any Member may notify to the Council for Trade in Services any measure, taken by any other Member, which it considers affects the operation of this Agreement.

Article III bis

Disclosure of Confidential Information

Nothing in this Agreement shall require any Member to provide confidential information, the disclosure of which would impede law enforcement, or otherwise be contrary to the public interest, or which would prejudice legitimate commercial interests of particular enterprises, public or private.

Article IV

Increasing Participation of Developing Countries

1. The increasing participation of developing country Members in world trade shall be facilitated through negotiated specific commitments, by different Members pursuant to Parts III and IV of this Agreement, relating to:

(a) the strengthening of their domestic services capacity and its efficiency and competitiveness, *inter alia* through access to technology on a commercial basis;

(b) the improvement of their access to distribution channels and information networks; and

(c) the liberalization of market access in sectors and modes of supply of export interest to them.

2. Developed country Members, and to the extent possible other Members, shall establish contact points within two years from the date of entry into force of the WTO Agreement to facilitate the access of developing country Members' service suppliers to information, related to their respective markets, concerning:

(a) commercial and technical aspects of the supply of services;

(b) registration, recognition and obtaining of professional qualifications; and

(c) the availability of services technology.

3. Special priority shall be given to the least-developed country Members in the implementation of paragraphs 1 and 2. Particular account shall be taken of the serious difficulty of the least-developed countries in accepting negotiated specific commitments in view of their special economic situation and their development, trade and financial needs.

Article V

Economic Integration

1. This Agreement shall not prevent any of its Members from being a party to or entering into an agreement liberalizing trade in services between or among the parties to such an agreement, provided that such an agreement:

(a) has substantial sectoral coverage[1], and

(b) provides for the absence or elimination of substantially all discrimination, in the sense of Article XVII, between or among the parties, in the sectors covered under subparagraph (a), through:

(i) elimination of existing discriminatory measures, and/or

(ii) prohibition of new or more discriminatory measures,

either at the entry into force of that agreement or on the basis of a reasonable time-frame, except for measures permitted under Articles XI, XII, XIV and XIV bis.

2. In evaluating whether the conditions under paragraph 1(b) are met, consideration may be given to the relationship of the agreement to a wider process of economic integration or trade liberalization among the countries concerned.

---

1 This condition is understood in terms of number of sectors, volume of trade affected and modes of supply. In order to meet this condition, agreements should not provide for the a priori exclusion of any mode of supply.

3. (a) Where developing countries are parties to an agreement of the type referred to in paragraph 1, flexibility shall be provided for regarding the conditions set out in paragraph 1, particularly with reference to subparagraph (b) thereof, in accordance with the level of development of the countries concerned, both overall and in individual sectors and subsectors.

(b) Notwithstanding paragraph 6, in the case of an agreement of the type referred to in paragraph 1 involving only developing countries, more favourable treatment may be granted to juridical persons owned or controlled by natural persons of the parties to such an agreement.

4. Any agreement referred to in paragraph 1 shall be designed to facilitate trade between the parties to the agreement and shall not in respect of any Member outside the agreement raise the overall level of barriers to trade in services within the respective sectors or subsectors compared to the level applicable prior to such an agreement.

5. If, in the conclusion, enlargement or any significant modification of any agreement under paragraph 1, a Member intends to withdraw or modify a specific commitment inconsistently with the terms and conditions set out in its Schedule, it shall provide at least 90 days advance notice of such modification or withdrawal and the procedure set forth in paragraphs 2, 3 and 4 of Article XXI shall apply.

6. A service supplier of any other Member that is a juridical person constituted under the laws of a party to an agreement referred to in paragraph 1 shall be entitled to treatment granted under such agreement, provided that it engages in substantive business operations in the territory of the parties to such agreement.

7. (a) Members which are parties to any agreement referred to in paragraph 1 shall promptly notify any such agreement and any enlargement or any significant modification of that agreement to the Council for Trade in Services. They shall also make available to the Council such relevant information as may be requested by it. The Council may establish a working party to examine such an agreement or enlargement or modification of that agreement and to report to the Council on its consistency with this Article.

(b) Members which are parties to any agreement referred to in paragraph 1 which is implemented on the basis of a time-frame shall report periodically to the Council for Trade in Services on its implementation. The Council may establish a working party to examine such reports if it deems such a working party necessary.

(c) Based on the reports of the working parties referred to in subparagraphs (a) and (b), the Council may make recommendations to the parties as it deems appropriate.

8. A Member which is a party to any agreement referred to in paragraph 1 may not seek compensation for trade benefits that may accrue to any other Member from such agreement.

Article V bis

Labour Markets Integration Agreements

This Agreement shall not prevent any of its Members from being a party to an agreement establishing full integration[2] of the labour markets between or among the parties to such an agreement, provided that such an agreement:

---

2 Typically, such integration provides citizens of the parties concerned with a right of free entry to the employment markets of the parties and includes measures concerning conditions of pay, other conditions of employment and social benefits.

(a) exempts citizens of parties to the agreement from requirements concerning residency and work permits;

(b) is notified to the Council for Trade in Services.

Article VI

Domestic Regulation

1. In sectors where specific commitments are undertaken, each Member shall ensure that all measures of general application affecting trade in services are administered in a reasonable, objective and impartial manner.

2. (a) Each Member shall maintain or institute as soon as practicable judicial, arbitral or administrative tribunals or procedures which provide, at the request of an affected service supplier, for the prompt review of, and where justified, appropriate remedies for, administrative decisions affecting trade in services. Where such procedures are not independent of the agency entrusted with the administrative decision concerned, the Member shall ensure that the procedures in fact provide for an objective and impartial review.

(b) The provisions of subparagraph (a) shall not be construed to require a Member to institute such tribunals or procedures where this would be inconsistent with its constitutional structure or the nature of its legal system.

3. Where authorization is required for the supply of a service on which a specific commitment has been made, the competent authorities of a Member shall, within a reasonable period of time after the submission of an application considered complete under domestic laws and regulations, inform the applicant of the decision concerning the application. At the request of the applicant, the competent authorities of the Member shall provide, without undue delay, information concerning the status of the application.

4. With a view to ensuring that measures relating to qualification requirements and procedures, technical standards and licensing requirements do not constitute unnecessary barriers to trade in services, the Council for Trade in Services shall, through appropriate bodies it may establish, develop any necessary disciplines. Such disciplines shall aim to ensure that such requirements are, *inter alia*:

(a) based on objective and transparent criteria, such as competence and the ability to supply the service;

(b) not more burdensome than necessary to ensure the quality of the service;

(c) in the case of licensing procedures, not in themselves a restriction on the supply of the service.

5. (a) In sectors in which a Member has undertaken specific commitments, pending the entry into force of disciplines developed in these sectors pursuant to paragraph 4, the Member shall not apply licensing and qualification requirements and technical standards that nullify or impair such specific commitments in a manner which:

(i) does not comply with the criteria outlined in subparagraphs 4(a), (b) or (c); and

(ii) could not reasonably have been expected of that Member at the time the specific commitments in those sectors were made.

(b) In determining whether a Member is in conformity with the obligation under paragraph 5(a), account shall be taken of international standards of relevant international organizations[3] applied by that Member.

6. In sectors where specific commitments regarding professional services are undertaken, each Member shall provide for adequate procedures to verify the competence of professionals of any other Member.

Article VII

Recognition

1. For the purposes of the fulfilment, in whole or in part, of its standards or criteria for the authorization, licensing or certification of services suppliers, and subject to the requirements of paragraph 3, a Member may recognize the education or experience obtained, requirements met, or licenses or certifications granted in a particular country. Such recognition, which may be achieved through harmonization or otherwise, may be based upon an agreement or arrangement with the country concerned or may be accorded autonomously.

2. A Member that is a party to an agreement or arrangement of the type referred to in paragraph 1, whether existing or future, shall afford adequate opportunity for other interested Members to negotiate their accession to such an agreement or arrangement or to negotiate comparable ones with it. Where a Member accords recognition autonomously, it shall afford adequate opportunity for any other Member to demonstrate that education, experience, licenses, or certifications obtained or requirements met in that other Member' territory should be recognized.

3. A Member shall not accord recognition in a manner which would constitute a means of discrimination between countries in the application of its standards or criteria for the authorization, licensing or certification of services suppliers, or a disguised restriction on trade in services.

4. Each Member shall:

(a) within 12 months from the date on which the WTO Agreement takes effect for it, inform the Council for Trade in Services of its existing recognition measures and state whether such measures are based on agreements or arrangements of the type referred to in paragraph 1;

(b) promptly inform the Council for Trade in Services as far in advance as possible of the opening of negotiations on an agreement or arrangement of the type referred to in paragraph 1 in order to provide adequate opportunity to any other Member to indicate their interest in participating in the negotiations before they enter a substantive phase;

(c) promptly inform the Council for Trade in Services when it adopts new recognition measures or significantly modifies existing ones and state whether the measures are based on an agreement or arrangement of the type referred to in paragraph 1.

5. Wherever appropriate, recognition should be based on multilaterally agreed criteria. In appropriate cases, Members shall work in cooperation with relevant intergovernmental and non-governmental organizations towards the establishment and adoption of common international

---

3 The term "relevant international organizations" refers to international bodies whose membership is open to the relevant bodies of at least all Members of the WTO.

standards and criteria for recognition and common international standards for the practice of relevant services trades and professions.

Article VIII

Monopolies and Exclusive Service Suppliers

1. Each Member shall ensure that any monopoly supplier of a service in its territory does not, in the supply of the monopoly service in the relevant market, act in a manner inconsistent with that Member' obligations under Article II and specific commitments.

2. Where a Member' monopoly supplier competes, either directly or through an affiliated company, in the supply of a service outside the scope of its monopoly rights and which is subject to that Member' specific commitments, the Member shall ensure that such a supplier does not abuse its monopoly position to act in its territory in a manner inconsistent with such commitments.

3. The Council for Trade in Services may, at the request of a Member which has a reason to believe that a monopoly supplier of a service of any other Member is acting in a manner inconsistent with paragraph 1 or 2, request the Member establishing, maintaining or authorizing such supplier to provide specific information concerning the relevant operations.

4. If, after the date of entry into force of the WTO Agreement, a Member grants monopoly rights regarding the supply of a service covered by its specific commitments, that Member shall notify the Council for Trade in Services no later than three months before the intended implementation of the grant of monopoly rights and the provisions of paragraphs 2, 3 and 4 of Article XXI shall apply.

5. The provisions of this Article shall also apply to cases of exclusive service suppliers, where a Member, formally or in effect, (*a*) authorizes or establishes a small number of service suppliers and (*b*) substantially prevents competition among those suppliers in its territory.

Article IX

Business Practices

1. Members recognize that certain business practices of service suppliers, other than those falling under Article VIII, may restrain competition and thereby restrict trade in services.

2. Each Member shall, at the request of any other Member, enter into consultations with a view to eliminating practices referred to in paragraph 1. The Member addressed shall accord full and sympathetic consideration to such a request and shall cooperate through the supply of publicly available non-confidential information of relevance to the matter in question. The Member addressed shall also provide other information available to the requesting Member, subject to its domestic law and to the conclusion of satisfactory agreement concerning the safeguarding of its confidentiality by the requesting Member.

Article X

Emergency Safeguard Measures

1. There shall be multilateral negotiations on the question of emergency safeguard measures based on the principle of non-discrimination. The results of such negotiations shall enter into effect on a date not later than three years from the date of entry into force of the WTO Agreement.

2. In the period before the entry into effect of the results of the negotiations referred to in paragraph 1, any Member may, notwithstanding the provisions of paragraph 1 of Article XXI, notify the Council on Trade in Services of its intention to modify or withdraw a specific commitment after a period of one year from the date on which the commitment enters into force; provided that the Member shows cause to the Council that the modification or withdrawal cannot await the lapse of the three-year period provided for in paragraph 1 of Article XXI.

3. The provisions of paragraph 2 shall cease to apply three years after the date of entry into force of the WTO Agreement.

Article XI

Payments and Transfers

1. Except under the circumstances envisaged in Article XII, a Member shall not apply restrictions on international transfers and payments for current transactions relating to its specific commitments.

2. Nothing in this Agreement shall affect the rights and obligations of the members of the International Monetary Fund under the Articles of Agreement of the Fund, including the use of exchange actions which are in conformity with the Articles of Agreement, provided that a Member shall not impose restrictions on any capital transactions inconsistently with its specific commitments regarding such transactions, except under Article XII or at the request of the Fund.

Article XII

Restrictions to Safeguard the Balance of Payments

1. In the event of serious balance-of-payments and external financial difficulties or threat thereof, a Member may adopt or maintain restrictions on trade in services on which it has undertaken specific commitments, including on payments or transfers for transactions related to such commitments. It is recognized that particular pressures on the balance of payments of a Member in the process of economic development or economic transition may necessitate the use of restrictions to ensure, *inter alia*, the maintenance of a level of financial reserves adequate for the implementation of its programme of economic development or economic transition.

2. The restrictions referred to in paragraph 1:

(a) shall not discriminate among Members;

(b) shall be consistent with the Articles of Agreement of the International Monetary Fund;

(c) shall avoid unnecessary damage to the commercial, economic and financial interests of any other Member;

(d) shall not exceed those necessary to deal with the circumstances described in paragraph 1;

(e) shall be temporary and be phased out progressively as the situation specified in paragraph 1 improves.

3. In determining the incidence of such restrictions, Members may give priority to the supply of services which are more essential to their economic or development programmes. However, such restrictions shall not be adopted or maintained for the purpose of protecting a particular service sector.

4. Any restrictions adopted or maintained under paragraph 1, or any changes therein, shall be promptly notified to the General Council.

5. (a) Members applying the provisions of this Article shall consult promptly with the Committee on Balance-of-Payments Restrictions on restrictions adopted under this Article.

(b) The Ministerial Conference shall establish procedures[4] for periodic consultations with the objective of enabling such recommendations to be made to the Member concerned as it may deem appropriate.

(c) Such consultations shall assess the balance-of-payment situation of the Member concerned and the restrictions adopted or maintained under this Article, taking into account, *inter alia*, such factors as:

(i) the nature and extent of the balance-of-payments and the external financial difficulties;

(ii) the external economic and trading environment of the consulting Member;

(iii) alternative corrective measures which may be available.

(d) The consultations shall address the compliance of any restrictions with paragraph 2, in particular the progressive phaseout of restrictions in accordance with paragraph 2(e).

(e) In such consultations, all findings of statistical and other facts presented by the International Monetary Fund relating to foreign exchange, monetary reserves and balance of payments, shall be accepted and conclusions shall be based on the assessment by the Fund of the balance-of-payments and the external financial situation of the consulting Member.

6. If a Member which is not a member of the International Monetary Fund wishes to apply the provisions of this Article, the Ministerial Conference shall establish a review procedure and any other procedures necessary.

Article XIII

Government Procurement

1. Articles II, XVI and XVII shall not apply to laws, regulations or requirements governing the procurement by governmental agencies of services purchased for governmental purposes and not with a view to commercial resale or with a view to use in the supply of services for commercial sale.

2. There shall be multilateral negotiations on government procurement in services under this Agreement within two years from the date of entry into force of the WTO Agreement.

Article XIV

General Exceptions

Subject to the requirement that such measures are not applied in a manner which would constitute a means of arbitrary or unjustifiable discrimination between countries where like

---

4 It is understood that the procedures under paragraph 5 shall be the same as the GATT 1994 procedures.

conditions prevail, or a disguised restriction on trade in services, nothing in this Agreement shall be construed to prevent the adoption or enforcement by any Member of measures:

(a) necessary to protect public morals or to maintain public order;[5]

(b) necessary to protect human, animal or plant life or health;

(c) necessary to secure compliance with laws or regulations which are not inconsistent with the provisions of this Agreement including those relating to:

(i) the prevention of deceptive and fraudulent practices or to deal with the effects of a default on services contracts;

(ii) the protection of the privacy of individuals in relation to the processing and dissemination of personal data and the protection of confidentiality of individual records and accounts;

(iii) safety;

(d) inconsistent with Article XVII, provided that the difference in treatment is aimed at ensuring the equitable or effective[6] imposition or collection of direct taxes in respect of services or service suppliers of other Members;

(e) inconsistent with Article II, provided that the difference in treatment is the result of an agreement on the avoidance of double taxation or provisions on the avoidance of double taxation in any other international agreement or arrangement by which the Member is bound.

Article XIV bis

Security Exceptions

1. Nothing in this Agreement shall be construed:

(a) to require any Member to furnish any information, the disclosure of which it considers contrary to its essential security interests; or

---

5 The public order exception may be invoked only where a genuine and sufficiently serious threat is posed to one of the fundamental interests of society.

6 Measures that are aimed at ensuring the equitable or effective imposition or collection of direct taxes include measures taken by a Member under its taxation system which:

(i) apply to non-resident service suppliers in recognition of the fact that the tax obligation of non-residents is determined with respect to taxable items sourced or located in the Member's territory; or

(ii) apply to non-residents in order to ensure the imposition or collection of taxes in the Member's territory; or

(iii) apply to non-residents or residents in order to prevent the avoidance or evasion of taxes, including compliance measures; or

(iv) apply to consumers of services supplied in or from the territory of another Member in order to ensure the imposition or collection of taxes on such consumers derived from sources in the Member's territory; or

(v) distinguish service suppliers subject to tax on worldwide taxable items from other service suppliers, in recognition of the difference in the nature of the tax base between them; or

(vi) determine, allocate or apportion income, profit, gain, loss, deduction or credit of resident persons or branches, or between related persons or branches of the same person, in order to safeguard the Member's tax base.

Tax terms or concepts in paragraph (d) of Article XIV and in this footnote are determined according to tax definitions and concepts, or equivalent or similar definitions and concepts, under the domestic law of the Member taking the measure.

(b) to prevent any Member from taking any action which it considers necessary for the protection of its essential security interests:

(i) relating to the supply of services as carried out directly or indirectly for the purpose of provisioning a military establishment;

(ii) relating to fissionable and fusionable materials or the materials from which they are derived;

(iii) taken in time of war or other emergency in international relations; or

(c) to prevent any Member from taking any action in pursuance of its obligations under the United Nations Charter for the maintenance of international peace and security.

2. The Council for Trade in Services shall be informed to the fullest extent possible of measures taken under paragraphs 1(b) and (c) and of their termination.

Article XV

Subsidies

1. Members recognize that, in certain circumstances, subsidies may have distortive effects on trade in services. Members shall enter into negotiations with a view to developing the necessary multilateral disciplines to avoid such trade-distortive effects.[7] The negotiations shall also address the appropriateness of countervailing procedures. Such negotiations shall recognize the role of subsidies in relation to the development programmes of developing countries and take into account the needs of Members, particularly developing country Members, for flexibility in this area. For the purpose of such negotiations, Members shall exchange information concerning all subsidies related to trade in services that they provide to their domestic service suppliers.

2. Any Member which considers that it is adversely affected by a subsidy of another Member may request consultations with that Member on such matters. Such requests shall be accorded sympathetic consideration.

PART III

SPECIFIC COMMITMENTS

Article XVI

Market Access

1. With respect to market access through the modes of supply identified in Article I, each Member shall accord services and service suppliers of any other Member treatment no less favourable than that provided for under the terms, limitations and conditions agreed and specified in its Schedule.[8]

---

7 A future work programme shall determine how, and in what time-frame, negotiations on such multilateral disciplines will be conducted.

8 If a Member undertakes a market-access commitment in relation to the supply of a service through the mode of supply referred to in subparagraph 2(a) of Article I and if the cross-border movement of capital is an essential part of the service itself, that Member is thereby committed to allow such movement of capital. If a Member undertakes a market-access commitment in relation to the supply of a service through the mode of supply referred to in subparagraph 2(c) of Article I, it is thereby committed to allow related transfers of capital into its territory.

2. In sectors where market-access commitments are undertaken, the measures which a Member shall not maintain or adopt either on the basis of a regional subdivision or on the basis of its entire territory, unless otherwise specified in its Schedule, are defined as:

(a) limitations on the number of service suppliers whether in the form of numerical quotas, monopolies, exclusive service suppliers or the requirements of an economic needs test;

(b) limitations on the total value of service transactions or assets in the form of numerical quotas or the requirement of an economic needs test;

(c) limitations on the total number of service operations or on the total quantity of service output expressed in terms of designated numerical units in the form of quotas or the requirement of an economic needs test;[9]

(d) limitations on the total number of natural persons that may be employed in a particular service sector or that a service supplier may employ and who are necessary for, and directly related to, the supply of a specific service in the form of numerical quotas or the requirement of an economic needs test;

(e) measures which restrict or require specific types of legal entity or joint venture through which a service supplier may supply a service; and

(f) limitations on the participation of foreign capital in terms of maximum percentage limit on foreign shareholding or the total value of individual or aggregate foreign investment.

Article XVII

National Treatment

1. In the sectors inscribed in its Schedule, and subject to any conditions and qualifications set out therein, each Member shall accord to services and service suppliers of any other Member, in respect of all measures affecting the supply of services, treatment no less favourable than that it accords to its own like services and service suppliers.[10]

2. A Member may meet the requirement of paragraph 1 by according to services and service suppliers of any other Member, either formally identical treatment or formally different treatment to that it accords to its own like services and service suppliers.

3. Formally identical or formally different treatment shall be considered to be less favourable if it modifies the conditions of competition in favour of services or service suppliers of the Member compared to like services or service suppliers of any other Member.

Article XVIII

Additional Commitments

Members may negotiate commitments with respect to measures affecting trade in services not subject to scheduling under Articles XVI or XVII, including those regarding qualifications, standards or licensing matters. Such commitments shall be inscribed in a Member' Schedule.

---

9 Subparagraph 2(c) does not cover measures of a Member which limit inputs for the supply of services.

10 Specific commitments assumed under this Article shall not be construed to require any Member to compensate for any inherent competitive disadvantages which result from the foreign character of the relevant services or service suppliers.

PART IV

PROGRESSIVE LIBERALIZATION

Article XIX

Negotiation of Specific Commitments

1. In pursuance of the objectives of this Agreement, Members shall enter into successive rounds of negotiations, beginning not later than five years from the date of entry into force of the WTO Agreement and periodically thereafter, with a view to achieving a progressively higher level of liberalization. Such negotiations shall be directed to the reduction or elimination of the adverse effects on trade in services of measures as a means of providing effective market access. This process shall take place with a view to promoting the interests of all participants on a mutually advantageous basis and to securing an overall balance of rights and obligations.

2. The process of liberalization shall take place with due respect for national policy objectives and the level of development of individual Members, both overall and in individual sectors. There shall be appropriate flexibility for individual developing country Members for opening fewer sectors, liberalizing fewer types of transactions, progressively extending market access in line with their development situation and, when making access to their markets available to foreign service suppliers, attaching to such access conditions aimed at achieving the objectives referred to in Article IV.

3. For each round, negotiating guidelines and procedures shall be established. For the purposes of establishing such guidelines, the Council for Trade in Services shall carry out an assessment of trade in services in overall terms and on a sectoral basis with reference to the objectives of this Agreement, including those set out in paragraph 1 of Article IV. Negotiating guidelines shall establish modalities for the treatment of liberalization undertaken autonomously by Members since previous negotiations, as well as for the special treatment for least-developed country Members under the provisions of paragraph 3 of Article IV.

4. The process of progressive liberalization shall be advanced in each such round through bilateral, plurilateral or multilateral negotiations directed towards increasing the general level of specific commitments undertaken by Members under this Agreement.

Article XX

Schedules of Specific Commitments

1. Each Member shall set out in a schedule the specific commitments it undertakes under Part III of this Agreement. With respect to sectors where such commitments are undertaken, each Schedule shall specify:

(a) terms, limitations and conditions on market access;

(b) conditions and qualifications on national treatment;

(c) undertakings relating to additional commitments;

(d) where appropriate the time-frame for implementation of such commitments; and

(e) the date of entry into force of such commitments.

2. Measures inconsistent with both Articles XVI and XVII shall be inscribed in the column relating to Article XVI. In this case the inscription will be considered to provide a condition or qualification to Article XVII as well.

3. Schedules of specific commitments shall be annexed to this Agreement and shall form an integral part thereof.

Article XXI

Modification of Schedules

1. (a) A Member (referred to in this Article as the "modifying Member") may modify or withdraw any commitment in its Schedule, at any time after three years have elapsed from the date on which that commitment entered into force, in accordance with the provisions of this Article.

   (b) A modifying Member shall notify its intent to modify or withdraw a commitment pursuant to this Article to the Council for Trade in Services no later than three months before the intended date of implementation of the modification or withdrawal.

2. (a) At the request of any Member the benefits of which under this Agreement may be affected (referred to in this Article as an "affected Member") by a proposed modification or withdrawal notified under subparagraph 1(b), the modifying Member shall enter into negotiations with a view to reaching agreement on any necessary compensatory adjustment. In such negotiations and agreement, the Members concerned shall endeavour to maintain a general level of mutually advantageous commitments not less favourable to trade than that provided for in Schedules of specific commitments prior to such negotiations.

   (b) Compensatory adjustments shall be made on a most-favoured-nation basis.

3. (a) If agreement is not reached between the modifying Member and any affected Member before the end of the period provided for negotiations, such affected Member may refer the matter to arbitration. Any affected Member that wishes to enforce a right that it may have to compensation must participate in the arbitration.

   (b) If no affected Member has requested arbitration, the modifying Member shall be free to implement the proposed modification or withdrawal.

4. (a) The modifying Member may not modify or withdraw its commitment until it has made compensatory adjustments in conformity with the findings of the arbitration.

   (b) If the modifying Member implements its proposed modification or withdrawal and does not comply with the findings of the arbitration, any affected Member that participated in the arbitration may modify or withdraw substantially equivalent benefits in conformity with those findings. Notwithstanding Article II, such a modification or withdrawal may be implemented solely with respect to the modifying Member.

5. The Council for Trade in Services shall establish procedures for rectification or modification of Schedules. Any Member which has modified or withdrawn scheduled commitments under this Article shall modify its Schedule according to such procedures.

PART V

INSTITUTIONAL PROVISIONS

Article XXII

Consultation

1. Each Member shall accord sympathetic consideration to, and shall afford adequate opportunity for, consultation regarding such representations as may be made by any other Member with respect to any matter affecting the operation of this Agreement. The Dispute Settlement Understanding (DSU) shall apply to such consultations.

2. The Council for Trade in Services or the Dispute Settlement Body (DSB) may, at the request of a Member, consult with any Member or Members in respect of any matter for which it has not been possible to find a satisfactory solution through consultation under paragraph 1.

3. A Member may not invoke Article XVII, either under this Article or Article XXIII, with respect to a measure of another Member that falls within the scope of an international agreement between them relating to the avoidance of double taxation. In case of disagreement between Members as to whether a measure falls within the scope of such an agreement between them, it shall be open to either Member to bring this matter before the Council for Trade in Services.[11] The Council shall refer the matter to arbitration. The decision of the arbitrator shall be final and binding on the Members.

Article XXIII

Dispute Settlement and Enforcement

1. If any Member should consider that any other Member fails to carry out its obligations or specific commitments under this Agreement, it may with a view to reaching a mutually satisfactory resolution of the matter have recourse to the DSU.

2. If the DSB considers that the circumstances are serious enough to justify such action, it may authorize a Member or Members to suspend the application to any other Member or Members of obligations and specific commitments in accordance with Article 22 of the DSU.

3. If any Member considers that any benefit it could reasonably have expected to accrue to it under a specific commitment of another Member under Part III of this Agreement is being nullified or impaired as a result of the application of any measure which does not conflict with the provisions of this Agreement, it may have recourse to the DSU. If the measure is determined by the DSB to have nullified or impaired such a benefit, the Member affected shall be entitled to a mutually satisfactory adjustment on the basis of paragraph 2 of Article XXI, which may include the modification or withdrawal of the measure. In the event an agreement cannot be reached between the Members concerned, Article 22 of the DSU shall apply.

---

11 With respect to agreements on the avoidance of double taxation which exist on the date of entry into force of the WTO Agreement, such a matter may be brought before the Council for Trade in Services only with the consent of both parties to such an agreement.

Article XXIV

Council for Trade in Services

1. The Council for Trade in Services shall carry out such functions as may be assigned to it to facilitate the operation of this Agreement and further its objectives. The Council may establish such subsidiary bodies as it considers appropriate for the effective discharge of its functions.

2. The Council and, unless the Council decides otherwise, its subsidiary bodies shall be open to participation by representatives of all Members.

3. The Chairman of the Council shall be elected by the Members.

Article XXV

Technical Cooperation

1. Service suppliers of Members which are in need of such assistance shall have access to the services of contact points referred to in paragraph 2 of Article IV.

2. Technical assistance to developing countries shall be provided at the multilateral level by the Secretariat and shall be decided upon by the Council for Trade in Services.

Article XXVI

Relationship with Other International Organizations

The General Council shall make appropriate arrangements for consultation and cooperation with the United Nations and its specialized agencies as well as with other intergovernmental organizations concerned with services.

PART VI

FINAL PROVISIONS

Article XXVII

Denial of Benefits

A Member may deny the benefits of this Agreement:

(a) to the supply of a service, if it establishes that the service is supplied from or in the territory of a non-Member or of a Member to which the denying Member does not apply the WTO Agreement;

(b) in the case of the supply of a maritime transport service, if it establishes that the service is supplied:

(i) by a vessel registered under the laws of a non-Member or of a Member to which the denying Member does not apply the WTO Agreement, and

(ii) by a person which operates and/or uses the vessel in whole or in part but which is of a non-Member or of a Member to which the denying Member does not apply the WTO Agreement;

(c) to a service supplier that is a juridical person, if it establishes that it is not a service supplier of another Member, or that it is a service supplier of a Member to which the denying Member does not apply the WTO Agreement.

Article XXVIII

Definitions

For the purpose of this Agreement:

(a) "measure" means any measure by a Member, whether in the form of a law, regulation, rule, procedure, decision, administrative action, or any other form;

(b) "supply of a service" includes the production, distribution, marketing, sale and delivery of a service;

(c) "measures by Members affecting trade in services" include measures in respect of

(i) the purchase, payment or use of a service;

(ii) the access to and use of, in connection with the supply of a service, services which are required by those Members to be offered to the public generally;

(iii) the presence, including commercial presence, of persons of a Member for the supply of a service in the territory of another Member;

(d) "commercial presence" means any type of business or professional establishment, including through

(i) the constitution, acquisition or maintenance of a juridical person, or

(ii) the creation or maintenance of a branch or a representative office,

within the territory of a Member for the purpose of supplying a service;

(e) "sector" of a service means,

(i) with reference to a specific commitment, one or more, or all, subsectors of that service, as specified in a Member' Schedule,

(ii) otherwise, the whole of that service sector, including all of its subsectors;

(f) "service of another Member" means a service which is supplied,

(i) from or in the territory of that other Member, or in the case of maritime transport, by a vessel registered under the laws of that other Member, or by a person of that other Member which supplies the service through the operation of a vessel and/or its use in whole or in part; or

(ii) in the case of the supply of a service through commercial presence or through the presence of natural persons, by a service supplier of that other Member;

(g) "service supplier" means any person that supplies a service;[12]

(h) "monopoly supplier of a service" means any person, public or private, which in the relevant market of the territory of a Member is authorized or established formally or in effect by that Member as the sole supplier of that service;

(i) "service consumer" means any person that receives or uses a service;

(j) "person" means either a natural person or a juridical person;

(k) "natural person of another Member" means a natural person who resides in the territory of that other Member or any other Member, and who under the law of that other Member:

(i) is a national of that other Member; or

(ii) has the right of permanent residence in that other Member, in the case of a Member which:

1. does not have nationals; or

2. accords substantially the same treatment to its permanent residents as it does to its nationals in respect of measures affecting trade in services, as notified in its acceptance of or accession to the WTO Agreement, provided that no Member is obligated to accord to such permanent residents treatment more favourable than would be accorded by that other Member to such permanent residents. Such notification shall include the assurance to assume, with respect to those permanent residents, in accordance with its laws and regulations, the same responsibilities that other Member bears with respect to its nationals;

(l) "juridical person" means any legal entity duly constituted or otherwise organized under applicable law, whether for profit or otherwise, and whether privately-owned or governmentally-owned, including any corporation, trust, partnership, joint venture, sole proprietorship or association;

(m) "juridical person of another Member" means a juridical person which is either:

(i) constituted or otherwise organized under the law of that other Member, and is engaged in substantive business operations in the territory of that Member or any other Member; or

12 Where the service is not supplied directly by a juridical person but through other forms of commercial presence such as a branch or a representative office, the service supplier (i.e. the juridical person) shall, nonetheless, through such presence be accorded the treatment provided for service suppliers under the Agreement. Such treatment shall be extended to the presence through which the service is supplied and need not be extended to any other parts of the supplier located outside the territory where the service is supplied.

(ii) in the case of the supply of a service through commercial presence, owned or controlled by:

1. natural persons of that Member; or

2. juridical persons of that other Member identified under subparagraph (i);

(n) a juridical person is:

(i) "owned" by persons of a Member if more than 50 per cent of the equity interest in it is beneficially owned by persons of that Member;

(ii) "controlled" by persons of a Member if such persons have the power to name a majority of its directors or otherwise to legally direct its actions;

(iii) "affiliated" with another person when it controls, or is controlled by, that other person; or when it and the other person are both controlled by the same person;

(o) "direct taxes" comprise all taxes on total income, on total capital or on elements of income or of capital, including taxes on gains from the alienation of property, taxes on estates, inheritances and gifts, and taxes on the total amounts of wages or salaries paid by enterprises, as well as taxes on capital appreciation.

Article XXIX

Annexes

The Annexes to this Agreement are an integral part of this Agreement.

ANNEX ON ARTICLE II EXEMPTIONS

Scope

1. This Annex specifies the conditions under which a Member, at the entry into force of this Agreement, is exempted from its obligations under paragraph 1 of Article II.

2. Any new exemptions applied for after the date of entry into force of the WTO Agreement shall be dealt with under paragraph 3 of Article IX of that Agreement.

Review

3. The Council for Trade in Services shall review all exemptions granted for a period of more than 5 years. The first such review shall take place no more than 5 years after the entry into force of the WTO Agreement.

4. The Council for Trade in Services in a review shall:

(a) examine whether the conditions which created the need for the exemption still prevail; and

(b) determine the date of any further review.

Termination

5. The exemption of a Member from its obligations under paragraph 1 of Article II of the Agreement with respect to a particular measure terminates on the date provided for in the exemption.

6. In principle, such exemptions should not exceed a period of 10 years. In any event, they shall be subject to negotiation in subsequent trade liberalizing rounds.

7. A Member shall notify the Council for Trade in Services at the termination of the exemption period that the inconsistent measure has been brought into conformity with paragraph 1 of Article II of the Agreement.

Lists of Article II Exemptions

[The agreed lists of exemptions under paragraph 2 of Article II will be annexed here in the treaty copy of the WTO Agreement.]

ANNEX ON MOVEMENT OF NATURAL PERSONS SUPPLYING SERVICES UNDER THE AGREEMENT

1. This Annex applies to measures affecting natural persons who are service suppliers of a Member, and natural persons of a Member who are employed by a service supplier of a Member, in respect of the supply of a service.

2. The Agreement shall not apply to measures affecting natural persons seeking access to the employment market of a Member, nor shall it apply to measures regarding citizenship, residence or employment on a permanent basis.

3. In accordance with Parts III and IV of the Agreement, Members may negotiate specific commitments applying to the movement of all categories of natural persons supplying services under the Agreement. Natural persons covered by a specific commitment shall be allowed to supply the service in accordance with the terms of that commitment.

4. The Agreement shall not prevent a Member from applying measures to regulate the entry of natural persons into, or their temporary stay in, its territory, including those measures necessary to protect the integrity of, and to ensure the orderly movement of natural persons across, its borders, provided that such measures are not applied in such a manner as to nullify or impair the benefits accruing to any Member under the terms of a specific commitment.[13]

ANNEX ON AIR TRANSPORT SERVICES

1. This Annex applies to measures affecting trade in air transport services, whether scheduled or non-scheduled, and ancillary services. It is confirmed that any specific commitment or obligation assumed under this Agreement shall not reduce or affect a Member' obligations under bilateral or multilateral agreements that are in effect on the date of entry into force of the WTO Agreement.

2. The Agreement, including its dispute settlement procedures, shall not apply to measures affecting:

(a) traffic rights, however granted; or

(b) services directly related to the exercise of traffic rights,

except as provided in paragraph 3 of this Annex.

---

13 The sole fact of requiring a visa for natural persons of certain Members and not for those of others shall not be regarded as nullifying or impairing benefits under a specific commitment.

3. The Agreement shall apply to measures affecting:

(a) aircraft repair and maintenance services;

(b) the selling and marketing of air transport services;

(c) computer reservation system (CRS) services.

4. The dispute settlement procedures of the Agreement may be invoked only where obligations or specific commitments have been assumed by the concerned Members and where dispute settlement procedures in bilateral and other multilateral agreements or arrangements have been exhausted.

5. The Council for Trade in Services shall review periodically, and at least every five years, developments in the air transport sector and the operation of this Annex with a view to considering the possible further application of the Agreement in this sector.

6. Definitions:

(a) "Aircraft repair and maintenance services" mean such activities when undertaken on an aircraft or a part thereof while it is withdrawn from service and do not include so-called line maintenance.

(b) "Selling and marketing of air transport services" mean opportunities for the air carrier concerned to sell and market freely its air transport services including all aspects of marketing such as market research, advertising and distribution. These activities do not include the pricing of air transport services nor the applicable conditions.

(c) "Computer reservation system (CRS) services" mean services provided by computerised systems that contain information about air carriers' schedules, availability, fares and fare rules, through which reservations can be made or tickets may be issued.

(d) "Traffic rights" mean the right for scheduled and non-scheduled services to operate and/or to carry passengers, cargo and mail for remuneration or hire from, to, within, or over the territory of a Member, including points to be served, routes to be operated, types of traffic to be carried, capacity to be provided, tariffs to be charged and their conditions, and criteria for designation of airlines, including such criteria as number, ownership, and control.

ANNEX ON FINANCIAL SERVICES

1. *Scope and Definition*

(a) This Annex applies to measures affecting the supply of financial services. Reference to the supply of a financial service in this Annex shall mean the supply of a service as defined in paragraph 2 of Article I of the Agreement.

(b) For the purposes of subparagraph 3(b) of Article I of the Agreement, "services supplied in the exercise of governmental authority" means the following:

(i) activities conducted by a central bank or monetary authority or by any other public entity in pursuit of monetary or exchange rate policies;

(ii) activities forming part of a statutory system of social security or public retirement plans; and

(iii) other activities conducted by a public entity for the account or with the guarantee or using the financial resources of the Government.

(c) For the purposes of subparagraph 3(b) of Article I of the Agreement, if a Member allows any of the activities referred to in subparagraphs (b)(ii) or (b)(iii) of this paragraph to be conducted by its financial service suppliers in competition with a public entity or a financial service supplier, "services" shall include such activities.

(d) Subparagraph 3(c) of Article I of the Agreement shall not apply to services covered by this Annex.

2. *Domestic Regulation*

(a) Notwithstanding any other provisions of the Agreement, a Member shall not be prevented from taking measures for prudential reasons, including for the protection of investors, depositors, policy holders or persons to whom a fiduciary duty is owed by a financial service supplier, or to ensure the integrity and stability of the financial system. Where such measures do not conform with the provisions of the Agreement, they shall not be used as a means of avoiding the Member' commitments or obligations under the Agreement.

(b) Nothing in the Agreement shall be construed to require a Member to disclose information relating to the affairs and accounts of individual customers or any confidential or proprietary information in the possession of public entities.

3. *Recognition*

(a) A Member may recognize prudential measures of any other country in determining how the Member' measures relating to financial services shall be applied. Such recognition, which may be achieved through harmonization or otherwise, may be based upon an agreement or arrangement with the country concerned or may be accorded autonomously.

(b) A Member that is a party to such an agreement or arrangement referred to in subparagraph (a), whether future or existing, shall afford adequate opportunity for other interested Members to negotiate their accession to such agreements or arrangements, or to negotiate comparable ones with it, under circumstances in which there would be equivalent regulation, oversight, implementation of such regulation, and, if appropriate, procedures concerning the sharing of information between the parties to the agreement or arrangement. Where a Member accords recognition autonomously, it shall afford adequate opportunity for any other Member to demonstrate that such circumstances exist.

(c) Where a Member is contemplating according recognition to prudential measures of any other country, paragraph 4(b) of Article VII shall not apply.

4. *Dispute Settlement*

Panels for disputes on prudential issues and other financial matters shall have the necessary expertise relevant to the specific financial service under dispute.

5. *Definitions*

For the purposes of this Annex:

(a) A financial service is any service of a financial nature offered by a financial service supplier of a Member. Financial services include all insurance and insurance-related services, and all banking and other financial services (excluding insurance). Financial services include the following activities:

Insurance and insurance-related services

(i) Direct insurance (including co-insurance):

(A) life

(B) non-life

(ii) Reinsurance and retrocession;

(iii) Insurance intermediation, such as brokerage and agency;

(iv) Services auxiliary to insurance, such as consultancy, actuarial, risk assessment and claim settlement services.

Banking and other financial services (excluding insurance)

(v) Acceptance of deposits and other repayable funds from the public;

(vi) Lending of all types, including consumer credit, mortgage credit, factoring and financing of commercial transaction;

(vii) Financial leasing;

(viii) All payment and money transmission services, including credit, charge and debit cards, travellers cheques and bankers drafts;

(ix) Guarantees and commitments;

(x) Trading for own account or for account of customers, whether on an exchange, in an over-the-counter market or otherwise, the following:

(A) money market instruments (including cheques, bills, certificates of deposits);

(B) foreign exchange;

(C) derivative products including, but not limited to, futures and options;

(D) exchange rate and interest rate instruments, including products such as swaps, forward rate agreements;

(E) transferable securities;

(F) other negotiable instruments and financial assets, including bullion.

(xi) Participation in issues of all kinds of securities, including underwriting and placement as agent (whether publicly or privately) and provision of services related to such issues;

(xii) Money broking;

(xiii) Asset management, such as cash or portfolio management, all forms of collective investment management, pension fund management, custodial, depository and trust services;

(xiv) Settlement and clearing services for financial assets, including securities, derivative products, and other negotiable instruments;

(xv) Provision and transfer of financial information, and financial data processing and related software by suppliers of other financial services;

(xvi) Advisory, intermediation and other auxiliary financial services on all the activities listed in subparagraphs (v) through (xv), including credit reference and analysis, investment and portfolio research and advice, advice on acquisitions and on corporate restructuring and strategy.

(b) A financial service supplier means any natural or juridical person of a Member wishing to supply or supplying financial services but the term "financial service supplier" does not include a public entity.

(c) "Public entity" means:

(i) a government, a central bank or a monetary authority, of a Member, or an entity owned or controlled by a Member, that is principally engaged in carrying out governmental functions or activities for governmental purposes, not including an entity principally engaged in supplying financial services on commercial terms; or

(ii) a private entity, performing functions normally performed by a central bank or monetary authority, when exercising those functions.

SECOND ANNEX ON FINANCIAL SERVICES

1. Notwithstanding Article II of the Agreement and paragraphs 1 and 2 of the Annex on Article II Exemptions, a Member may, during a period of 60 days beginning four months after the date of entry into force of the WTO Agreement, list in that Annex measures relating to financial services which are inconsistent with paragraph 1 of Article II of the Agreement.

2. Notwithstanding Article XXI of the Agreement, a Member may, during a period of 60 days beginning four months after the date of entry into force of the WTO Agreement, improve, modify or withdraw all or part of the specific commitments on financial services inscribed in its Schedule.

3. The Council for Trade in Services shall establish any procedures necessary for the application of paragraphs 1 and 2.

ANNEX ON NEGOTIATIONS ON MARITIME TRANSPORT SERVICES

1. Article II and the Annex on Article II Exemptions, including the requirement to list in the Annex any measure inconsistent with most-favoured-nation treatment that a Member will maintain, shall enter into force for international shipping, auxiliary services and access to and use of port facilities only on:

(a) the implementation date to be determined under paragraph 4 of the Ministerial Decision on Negotiations on Maritime Transport Services; or,

(b) should the negotiations not succeed, the date of the final report of the Negotiating Group on Maritime Transport Services provided for in that Decision.

2. Paragraph 1 shall not apply to any specific commitment on maritime transport services which is inscribed in a Member' Schedule.

3. From the conclusion of the negotiations referred to in paragraph 1, and before the implementation date, a Member may improve, modify or withdraw all or part of its specific commitments in this sector without offering compensation, notwithstanding the provisions of Article XXI.

ANNEX ON TELECOMMUNICATIONS

1. *Objectives*

Recognizing the specificities of the telecommunications services sector and, in particular, its dual role as a distinct sector of economic activity and as the underlying transport means for other economic activities, the Members have agreed to the following Annex with the objective of elaborating upon the provisions of the Agreement with respect to measures affecting access to and use of public telecommunications transport networks and services. Accordingly, this Annex provides notes and supplementary provisions to the Agreement.

2. *Scope*

(a) This Annex shall apply to all measures of a Member that affect access to and use of public telecommunications transport networks and services.[14]

(b) This Annex shall not apply to measures affecting the cable or broadcast distribution of radio or television programming.

(c) Nothing in this Annex shall be construed:

(i) to require a Member to authorize a service supplier of any other Member to establish, construct, acquire, lease, operate, or supply telecommunications transport networks or services, other than as provided for in its Schedule; or

(ii) to require a Member (or to require a Member to oblige service suppliers under its jurisdiction) to establish, construct, acquire, lease, operate or supply telecommunications transport networks or services not offered to the public generally.

3. *Definitions*

For the purposes of this Annex:

(a) "Telecommunications" means the transmission and reception of signals by any electromagnetic means.

(b) "Public telecommunications transport service" means any telecommunications transport service required, explicitly or in effect, by a Member to be offered to the public

14 This paragraph is understood to mean that each Member shall ensure that the obligations of this Annex are applied with respect to suppliers of public telecommunications transport networks and services by whatever measures are necessary.

generally. Such services may include, *inter alia*, telegraph, telephone, telex, and data transmission typically involving the real-time transmission of customer-supplied information between two or more points without any end-to-end change in the form or content of the customer' information.

(c) "Public telecommunications transport network" means the public telecommunications infrastructure which permits telecommunications between and among defined network termination points.

(d) "Intra-corporate communications" means telecommunications through which a company communicates within the company or with or among its subsidiaries, branches and, subject to a Member' domestic laws and regulations, affiliates. For these purposes, "subsidiaries", "branches" and, where applicable, "affiliates" shall be as defined by each Member. "Intra-corporate communications" in this Annex excludes commercial or non-commercial services that are supplied to companies that are not related subsidiaries, branches or affiliates, or that are offered to customers or potential customers.

(e) Any reference to a paragraph or subparagraph of this Annex includes all subdivisions thereof.

4. *Transparency*

In the application of Article III of the Agreement, each Member shall ensure that relevant information on conditions affecting access to and use of public telecommunications transport networks and services is publicly available, including: tariffs and other terms and conditions of service; specifications of technical interfaces with such networks and services; information on bodies responsible for the preparation and adoption of standards affecting such access and use; conditions applying to attachment of terminal or other equipment; and notifications, registration or licensing requirements, if any.

5. *Access to and use of Public Telecommunications Transport Networks and Services*

(a) Each Member shall ensure that any service supplier of any other Member is accorded access to and use of public telecommunications transport networks and services on reasonable and non-discriminatory terms and conditions, for the supply of a service included in its Schedule. This obligation shall be applied, *inter alia*, through paragraphs (b) through (f).[15]

(b) Each Member shall ensure that service suppliers of any other Member have access to and use of any public telecommunications transport network or service offered within or across the border of that Member, including private leased circuits, and to this end shall ensure, subject to paragraphs (e) and (f), that such suppliers are permitted:

(i) to purchase or lease and attach terminal or other equipment which interfaces with the network and which is necessary to supply a supplier' services;

(ii) to interconnect private leased or owned circuits with public telecommunications transport networks and services or with circuits leased or owned by another service supplier; and

---

15 The term "non-discriminatory" is understood to refer to most-favoured-nation and national treatment as defined in the Agreement, as well as to reflect sector-specific usage of the term to mean "terms and conditions no less favourable than those accorded to any other user of like public telecommunications transport networks or services under like circumstances".

(iii) to use operating protocols of the service supplier' choice in the supply of any service, other than as necessary to ensure the availability of telecommunications transport networks and services to the public generally.

(c) Each Member shall ensure that service suppliers of any other Member may use public telecommunications transport networks and services for the movement of information within and across borders, including for intra-corporate communications of such service suppliers, and for access to information contained in data bases or otherwise stored in machine-readable form in the territory of any Member. Any new or amended measures of a Member significantly affecting such use shall be notified and shall be subject to consultation, in accordance with relevant provisions of the Agreement.

(d) Notwithstanding the preceding paragraph, a Member may take such measures as are necessary to ensure the security and confidentiality of messages, subject to the requirement that such measures are not applied in a manner which would constitute a means of arbitrary or unjustifiable discrimination or a disguised restriction on trade in services.

(e) Each Member shall ensure that no condition is imposed on access to and use of public telecommunications transport networks and services other than as necessary:

(i) to safeguard the public service responsibilities of suppliers of public telecommunications transport networks and services, in particular their ability to make their networks or services available to the public generally;

(ii) to protect the technical integrity of public telecommunications transport networks or services; or

(iii) to ensure that service suppliers of any other Member do not supply services unless permitted pursuant to commitments in the Member' Schedule.

(f) Provided that they satisfy the criteria set out in paragraph (e), conditions for access to and use of public telecommunications transport networks and services may include:

(i) restrictions on resale or shared use of such services;

(ii) a requirement to use specified technical interfaces, including interface protocols, for inter-connection with such networks and services;

(iii) requirements, where necessary, for the inter-operability of such services and to encourage the achievement of the goals set out in paragraph 7(a);

(iv) type approval of terminal or other equipment which interfaces with the network and technical requirements relating to the attachment of such equipment to such networks;

(v) restrictions on inter-connection of private leased or owned circuits with such networks or services or with circuits leased or owned by another service supplier; or

(vi) notification, registration and licensing.

(g) Notwithstanding the preceding paragraphs of this section, a developing country Member may, consistent with its level of development, place reasonable conditions on access to and use of public telecommunications transport networks and services necessary to strengthen its domestic telecommunications infrastructure and service capacity and to increase its participation in international trade in telecommunications services. Such conditions shall be specified in the Member' Schedule.

6. *Technical Cooperation*

(a) Members recognize that an efficient, advanced telecommunications infrastructure in countries, particularly developing countries, is essential to the expansion of their trade in services. To this end, Members endorse and encourage the participation, to the fullest extent practicable, of developed and developing countries and their suppliers of public telecommunications transport networks and services and other entities in the development programmes of international and regional organizations, including the International Telecommunication Union, the United Nations Development Programme, and the International Bank for Reconstruction and Development.

(b) Members shall encourage and support telecommunications cooperation among developing countries at the international, regional and sub-regional levels.

(c) In cooperation with relevant international organizations, Members shall make available, where practicable, to developing countries information with respect to telecommunications services and developments in telecommunications and information technology to assist in strengthening their domestic telecommunications services sector.

(d) Members shall give special consideration to opportunities for the least-developed countries to encourage foreign suppliers of telecommunications services to assist in the transfer of technology, training and other activities that support the development of their telecommunications infrastructure and expansion of their telecommunications services trade.

7. *Relation to International Organizations and Agreements*

(a) Members recognize the importance of international standards for global compatibility and inter-operability of telecommunication networks and services and undertake to promote such standards through the work of relevant international bodies, including the International Telecommunication Union and the International Organization for Standardization.

(b) Members recognize the role played by intergovernmental and non-governmental organizations and agreements in ensuring the efficient operation of domestic and global telecommunications services, in particular the International Telecommunication Union. Members shall make appropriate arrangements, where relevant, for consultation with such organizations on matters arising from the implementation of this Annex.

ANNEX ON NEGOTIATIONS ON BASIC TELECOMMUNICATIONS

1. Article II and the Annex on Article II Exemptions, including the requirement to list in the Annex any measure inconsistent with most-favoured-nation treatment that a Member will maintain, shall enter into force for basic telecommunications only on:

(a) the implementation date to be determined under paragraph 5 of the Ministerial Decision on Negotiations on Basic Telecommunications; or,

(b) should the negotiations not succeed, the date of the final report of the Negotiating Group on Basic Telecommunications provided for in that Decision.

2. Paragraph 1 shall not apply to any specific commitment on basic telecommunications which is inscribed in a Member' Schedule.

Agreement on Trade-Related Aspects of Intellectual Property Rights

AGREEMENT ON TRADE-RELATED ASPECTS OF INTELLECTUAL PROPERTY RIGHTS

Members,

Desiring to reduce distortions and impediments to international trade, and taking into account the need to promote effective and adequate protection of intellectual property rights, and to ensure that measures and procedures to enforce intellectual property rights do not themselves become barriers to legitimate trade;

Recognizing, to this end, the need for new rules and disciplines concerning:

(a) the applicability of the basic principles of GATT 1994 and of relevant international intellectual property agreements or conventions;

(b) the provision of adequate standards and principles concerning the availability, scope and use of trade-related intellectual property rights;

(c) the provision of effective and appropriate means for the enforcement of trade-related intellectual property rights, taking into account differences in national legal systems;

(d) the provision of effective and expeditious procedures for the multilateral prevention and settlement of disputes between governments; and

(e) transitional arrangements aiming at the fullest participation in the results of the negotiations;

Recognizing the need for a multilateral framework of principles, rules and disciplines dealing with international trade in counterfeit goods;

Recognizing that intellectual property rights are private rights;

Recognizing the underlying public policy objectives of national systems for the protection of intellectual property, including developmental and technological objectives;

Recognizing also the special needs of the least-developed country Members in respect of maximum flexibility in the domestic implementation of laws and regulations in order to enable them to create a sound and viable technological base;

Emphasizing the importance of reducing tensions by reaching strengthened commitments to resolve disputes on trade-related intellectual property issues through multilateral procedures;

Desiring to establish a mutually supportive relationship between the WTO and the World Intellectual Property Organization (referred to in this Agreement as "WIPO") as well as other relevant international organizations;

Hereby agree as follows:

PART I

GENERAL PROVISIONS AND BASIC PRINCIPLES

Article 1

Nature and Scope of Obligations

1. Members shall give effect to the provisions of this Agreement. Members may, but shall not be obliged to, implement in their law more extensive protection than is required by this Agreement, provided that such protection does not contravene the provisions of this Agreement. Members shall be free to determine the appropriate method of implementing the provisions of this Agreement within their own legal system and practice.

2. For the purposes of this Agreement, the term "intellectual property" refers to all categories of intellectual property that are the subject of Sections 1 through 7 of Part II.

3. Members shall accord the treatment provided for in this Agreement to the nationals of other Members.[1] In respect of the relevant intellectual property right, the nationals of other Members shall be understood as those natural or legal persons that would meet the criteria for eligibility for protection provided for in the Paris Convention (1967), the Berne Convention (1971), the Rome Convention and the Treaty on Intellectual Property in Respect of Integrated Circuits, were all Members of the WTO members of those conventions.[2] Any Member availing itself of the possibilities provided in paragraph 3 of Article 5 or paragraph 2 of Article 6 of the Rome Convention shall make a notification as foreseen in those provisions to the Council for Trade-Related Aspects of Intellectual Property Rights (the "Council for TRIPS").

Article 2

Intellectual Property Conventions

1. In respect of Parts II, III and IV of this Agreement, Members shall comply with Articles 1 through 12, and Article 19, of the Paris Convention (1967).

2. Nothing in Parts I to IV of this Agreement shall derogate from existing obligations that Members may have to each other under the Paris Convention, the Berne Convention, the Rome Convention and the Treaty on Intellectual Property in Respect of Integrated Circuits.

Article 3

National Treatment

1. Each Member shall accord to the nationals of other Members treatment no less favourable than that it accords to its own nationals with regard to the protection[3] of intellectual property, subject to the exceptions already provided in, respectively, the Paris Convention (1967), the Berne Convention (1971), the Rome Convention or the Treaty on Intellectual Property in Respect of Integrated Circuits. In respect of performers, producers of phonograms and broadcasting organizations, this obligation only applies in respect of the rights provided under this Agreement. Any Member availing itself of the possibilities provided in Article 6 of the Berne Convention (1971) or paragraph 1(b) of Article 16 of the Rome Convention shall make a notification as foreseen in those provisions to the Council for TRIPS.

2. Members may avail themselves of the exceptions permitted under paragraph 1 in relation to judicial and administrative procedures, including the designation of an address for service or the appointment of an agent within the jurisdiction of a Member, only where such exceptions are necessary to secure compliance with laws and regulations which are not inconsistent with the

---

1 When "nationals" are referred to in this Agreement, they shall be deemed, in the case of a separate customs territory Member of the WTO, to mean persons, natural or legal, who are domiciled or who have a real and effective industrial or commercial establishment in that customs territory.

2 In this Agreement, "Paris Convention" refers to the Paris Convention for the Protection of Industrial Property; "Paris Convention (1967)" refers to the Stockholm Act of this Convention of 14 July 1967. "Berne Convention" refers to the Berne Convention for the Protection of Literary and Artistic Works; "Berne Convention (1971)" refers to the Paris Act of this Convention of 24 July 1971. "Rome Convention" refers to the International Convention for the Protection of Performers, Producers of Phonograms and Broadcasting Organizations, adopted at Rome on 26 October 1961. "Treaty on Intellectual Property in Respect of Integrated Circuits" (IPIC Treaty) refers to the Treaty on Intellectual Property in Respect of Integrated Circuits, adopted at Washington on 26 May 1989. "WTO Agreement" refers to the Agreement Establishing the WTO.

3 For the purposes of Articles 3 and 4, "protection" shall include matters affecting the availability, acquisition, scope, maintenance and enforcement of intellectual property rights as well as those matters affecting the use of intellectual property rights specifically addressed in this Agreement.

provisions of this Agreement and where such practices are not applied in a manner which would constitute a disguised restriction on trade.

Article 4

Most-Favoured-Nation Treatment

With regard to the protection of intellectual property, any advantage, favour, privilege or immunity granted by a Member to the nationals of any other country shall be accorded immediately and unconditionally to the nationals of all other Members. Exempted from this obligation are any advantage, favour, privilege or immunity accorded by a Member:

(a) deriving from international agreements on judicial assistance or law enforcement of a general nature and not particularly confined to the protection of intellectual property;

(b) granted in accordance with the provisions of the Berne Convention (1971) or the Rome Convention authorizing that the treatment accorded be a function not of national treatment but of the treatment accorded in another country;

(c) in respect of the rights of performers, producers of phonograms and broadcasting organizations not provided under this Agreement;

(d) deriving from international agreements related to the protection of intellectual property which entered into force prior to the entry into force of the WTO Agreement, provided that such agreements are notified to the Council for TRIPS and do not constitute an arbitrary or unjustifiable discrimination against nationals of other Members.

Article 5

Multilateral Agreements on Acquisition or Maintenance of Protection

The obligations under Articles 3 and 4 do not apply to procedures provided in multilateral agreements concluded under the auspices of WIPO relating to the acquisition or maintenance of intellectual property rights.

Article 6

Exhaustion

For the purposes of dispute settlement under this Agreement, subject to the provisions of Articles 3 and 4 nothing in this Agreement shall be used to address the issue of the exhaustion of intellectual property rights.

Article 7

Objectives

The protection and enforcement of intellectual property rights should contribute to the promotion of technological innovation and to the transfer and dissemination of technology, to the mutual advantage of producers and users of technological knowledge and in a manner conducive to social and economic welfare, and to a balance of rights and obligations.

Article 8

Principles

1. Members may, in formulating or amending their laws and regulations, adopt measures necessary to protect public health and nutrition, and to promote the public interest in sectors of vital importance to their socio-economic and technological development, provided that such measures are consistent with the provisions of this Agreement.

2. Appropriate measures, provided that they are consistent with the provisions of this Agreement, may be needed to prevent the abuse of intellectual property rights by right holders or the resort to practices which unreasonably restrain trade or adversely affect the international transfer of technology.

PART II

STANDARDS CONCERNING THE AVAILABILITY, SCOPE AND USE OF INTELLECTUAL PROPERTY RIGHTS

SECTION 1: COPYRIGHT AND RELATED RIGHTS

Article 9

Relation to the Berne Convention

1. Members shall comply with Articles 1 through 21 of the Berne Convention (1971) and the Appendix thereto. However, Members shall not have rights or obligations under this Agreement in respect of the rights conferred under Article 6*bis* of that Convention or of the rights derived therefrom.

2. Copyright protection shall extend to expressions and not to ideas, procedures, methods of operation or mathematical concepts as such.

Article 10

Computer Programs and Compilations of Data

1. Computer programs, whether in source or object code, shall be protected as literary works under the Berne Convention (1971).

2. Compilations of data or other material, whether in machine readable or other form, which by reason of the selection or arrangement of their contents constitute intellectual creations shall be protected as such. Such protection, which shall not extend to the data or material itself, shall be without prejudice to any copyright subsisting in the data or material itself.

Article 11

Rental Rights

In respect of at least computer programs and cinematographic works, a Member shall provide authors and their successors in title the right to authorize or to prohibit the commercial rental to the public of originals or copies of their copyright works. A Member shall be excepted from this obligation in respect of cinematographic works unless such rental has led to widespread copying of such works which is materially impairing the exclusive right of reproduction conferred in that Member on authors and their successors in title. In respect of computer programs, this obligation does not apply to rentals where the program itself is not the essential object of the rental.

Article 12

Term of Protection

Whenever the term of protection of a work, other than a photographic work or a work of applied art, is calculated on a basis other than the life of a natural person, such term shall be no less than 50 years from the end of the calendar year of authorized publication, or, failing such authorized publication within 50 years from the making of the work, 50 years from the end of the calendar year of making.

Article 13

Limitations and Exceptions

Members shall confine limitations or exceptions to exclusive rights to certain special cases which do not conflict with a normal exploitation of the work and do not unreasonably prejudice the legitimate interests of the right holder.

Article 14

Protection of Performers, Producers of Phonograms (Sound Recordings) and Broadcasting Organizations

1. In respect of a fixation of their performance on a phonogram, performers shall have the possibility of preventing the following acts when undertaken without their authorization: the fixation of their unfixed performance and the reproduction of such fixation. Performers shall also have the possibility of preventing the following acts when undertaken without their authorization: the broadcasting by wireless means and the communication to the public of their live performance.

2. Producers of phonograms shall enjoy the right to authorize or prohibit the direct or indirect reproduction of their phonograms.

3. Broadcasting organizations shall have the right to prohibit the following acts when undertaken without their authorization: the fixation, the reproduction of fixations, and the rebroadcasting by wireless means of broadcasts, as well as the communication to the public of television broadcasts of the same. Where Members do not grant such rights to broadcasting organizations, they shall provide owners of copyright in the subject matter of broadcasts with the possibility of preventing the above acts, subject to the provisions of the Berne Convention (1971).

4. The provisions of Article 11 in respect of computer programs shall apply *mutatis mutandis* to producers of phonograms and any other right holders in phonograms as determined in a Member's law. If on 15 April 1994 a Member has in force a system of equitable remuneration of right holders in respect of the rental of phonograms, it may maintain such system provided that the commercial rental of phonograms is not giving rise to the material impairment of the exclusive rights of reproduction of right holders.

5. The term of the protection available under this Agreement to performers and producers of phonograms shall last at least until the end of a period of 50 years computed from the end of the calendar year in which the fixation was made or the performance took place. The term of

protection granted pursuant to paragraph 3 shall last for at least 20 years from the end of the calendar year in which the broadcast took place.

6. Any Member may, in relation to the rights conferred under paragraphs 1, 2 and 3, provide for conditions, limitations, exceptions and reservations to the extent permitted by the Rome Convention. However, the provisions of Article 18 of the Berne Convention (1971) shall also apply, *mutatis mutandis*, to the rights of performers and producers of phonograms in phonograms.

SECTION 2: TRADEMARKS

Article 15

Protectable Subject Matter

1. Any sign, or any combination of signs, capable of distinguishing the goods or services of one undertaking from those of other undertakings, shall be capable of constituting a trademark. Such signs, in particular words including personal names, letters, numerals, figurative elements and combinations of colours as well as any combination of such signs, shall be eligible for registration as trademarks. Where signs are not inherently capable of distinguishing the relevant goods or services, Members may make registrability depend on distinctiveness acquired through use. Members may require, as a condition of registration, that signs be visually perceptible.

2. Paragraph 1 shall not be understood to prevent a Member from denying registration of a trademark on other grounds, provided that they do not derogate from the provisions of the Paris Convention (1967).

3. Members may make registrability depend on use. However, actual use of a trademark shall not be a condition for filing an application for registration. An application shall not be refused solely on the ground that intended use has not taken place before the expiry of a period of three years from the date of application.

4. The nature of the goods or services to which a trademark is to be applied shall in no case form an obstacle to registration of the trademark.

5. Members shall publish each trademark either before it is registered or promptly after it is registered and shall afford a reasonable opportunity for petitions to cancel the registration. In addition, Members may afford an opportunity for the registration of a trademark to be opposed.

Article 16

Rights Conferred

1. The owner of a registered trademark shall have the exclusive right to prevent all third parties not having the owner's consent from using in the course of trade identical or similar signs for goods or services which are identical or similar to those in respect of which the trademark is registered where such use would result in a likelihood of confusion. In case of the use of an identical sign for identical goods or services, a likelihood of confusion shall be presumed. The rights described above shall not prejudice any existing prior rights, nor shall they affect the possibility of Members making rights available on the basis of use.

2. Article 6*bis* of the Paris Convention (1967) shall apply, *mutatis mutandis*, to services. In determining whether a trademark is well-known, Members shall take account of the knowledge of the trademark in the relevant sector of the public, including knowledge in the Member concerned which has been obtained as a result of the promotion of the trademark.

3. Article *6bis* of the Paris Convention (1967) shall apply, *mutatis mutandis*, to goods or services which are not similar to those in respect of which a trademark is registered, provided that use of that trademark in relation to those goods or services would indicate a connection between those goods or services and the owner of the registered trademark and provided that the interests of the owner of the registered trademark are likely to be damaged by such use.

Article 17

Exceptions

Members may provide limited exceptions to the rights conferred by a trademark, such as fair use of descriptive terms, provided that such exceptions take account of the legitimate interests of the owner of the trademark and of third parties.

Article 18

Term of Protection

Initial registration, and each renewal of registration, of a trademark shall be for a term of no less than seven years. The registration of a trademark shall be renewable indefinitely.

Article 19

Requirement of Use

1. If use is required to maintain a registration, the registration may be cancelled only after an uninterrupted period of at least three years of non-use, unless valid reasons based on the existence of obstacles to such use are shown by the trademark owner. Circumstances arising independently of the will of the owner of the trademark which constitute an obstacle to the use of the trademark, such as import restrictions on or other government requirements for goods or services protected by the trademark, shall be recognized as valid reasons for non-use.

2. When subject to the control of its owner, use of a trademark by another person shall be recognized as use of the trademark for the purpose of maintaining the registration.

Article 20

Other Requirements

The use of a trademark in the course of trade shall not be unjustifiably encumbered by special requirements, such as use with another trademark, use in a special form or use in a manner detrimental to its capability to distinguish the goods or services of one undertaking from those of other undertakings. This will not preclude a requirement prescribing the use of the trademark identifying the undertaking producing the goods or services along with, but without linking it to, the trademark distinguishing the specific goods or services in question of that undertaking.

Article 21

Licensing and Assignment

Members may determine conditions on the licensing and assignment of trademarks, it being understood that the compulsory licensing of trademarks shall not be permitted and that the owner of a registered trademark shall have the right to assign the trademark with or without the transfer of the business to which the trademark belongs.

SECTION 3: GEOGRAPHICAL INDICATIONS

Article 22

Protection of Geographical Indications

1. Geographical indications are, for the purposes of this Agreement, indications which identify a good as originating in the territory of a Member, or a region or locality in that territory, where a given quality, reputation or other characteristic of the good is essentially attributable to its geographical origin.

2. In respect of geographical indications, Members shall provide the legal means for interested parties to prevent:

(a) the use of any means in the designation or presentation of a good that indicates or suggests that the good in question originates in a geographical area other than the true place of origin in a manner which misleads the public as to the geographical origin of the good;

(b) any use which constitutes an act of unfair competition within the meaning of Article 10 *bis* of the Paris Convention (1967).

3. A Member shall, *ex officio* if its legislation so permits or at the request of an interested party, refuse or invalidate the registration of a trademark which contains or consists of a geographical indication with respect to goods not originating in the territory indicated, if use of the indication in the trademark for such goods in that Member is of such a nature as to mislead the public as to the true place of origin.

4. The protection under paragraphs 1, 2 and 3 shall be applicable against a geographical indication which, although literally true as to the territory, region or locality in which the goods originate, falsely represents to the public that the goods originate in another territory.

Article 23

Additional Protection for Geographical Indications for Wines and Spirits

1. Each Member shall provide the legal means for interested parties to prevent use of a geographical indication identifying wines for wines not originating in the place indicated by the geographical indication in question or identifying spirits for spirits not originating in the place indicated by the geographical indication in question, even where the true origin of the goods is indicated or the geographical indication is used in translation or accompanied by expressions such as "kind", "type", "style", "imitation" or the like.[4]

2. The registration of a trademark for wines which contains or consists of a geographical indication identifying wines or for spirits which contains or consists of a geographical indication identifying spirits shall be refused or invalidated, *ex officio* if a Member's legislation so permits or at the request of an interested party, with respect to such wines or spirits not having this origin.

3. In the case of homonymous geographical indications for wines, protection shall be accorded to each indication, subject to the provisions of paragraph 4 of Article 22. Each Member shall

---

4 Notwithstanding the first sentence of Article 42, Members may, with respect to these obligations, instead provide for enforcement by administrative action.

determine the practical conditions under which the homonymous indications in question will be differentiated from each other, taking into account the need to ensure equitable treatment of the producers concerned and that consumers are not misled.

4. In order to facilitate the protection of geographical indications for wines, negotiations shall be undertaken in the Council for TRIPS concerning the establishment of a multilateral system of notification and registration of geographical indications for wines eligible for protection in those Members participating in the system.

Article 24

International Negotiations; Exceptions

1. Members agree to enter into negotiations aimed at increasing the protection of individual geographical indications under Article 23. The provisions of paragraphs 4 through 8 below shall not be used by a Member to refuse to conduct negotiations or to conclude bilateral or multilateral agreements. In the context of such negotiations, Members shall be willing to consider the continued applicability of these provisions to individual geographical indications whose use was the subject of such negotiations.

2. The Council for TRIPS shall keep under review the application of the provisions of this Section; the first such review shall take place within two years of the entry into force of the WTO Agreement. Any matter affecting the compliance with the obligations under these provisions may be drawn to the attention of the Council, which, at the request of a Member, shall consult with any Member or Members in respect of such matter in respect of which it has not been possible to find a satisfactory solution through bilateral or plurilateral consultations between the Members concerned. The Council shall take such action as may be agreed to facilitate the operation and further the objectives of this Section.

3. In implementing this Section, a Member shall not diminish the protection of geographical indications that existed in that Member immediately prior to the date of entry into force of the WTO Agreement.

4. Nothing in this Section shall require a Member to prevent continued and similar use of a particular geographical indication of another Member identifying wines or spirits in connection with goods or services by any of its nationals or domiciliaries who have used that geographical indication in a continuous manner with regard to the same or related goods or services in the territory of that Member either (*a*) for at least 10 years preceding 15 April 1994 or (*b*) in good faith preceding that date.

5. Where a trademark has been applied for or registered in good faith, or where rights to a trademark have been acquired through use in good faith either:

(a) before the date of application of these provisions in that Member as defined in Part VI; or

(b) before the geographical indication is protected in its country of origin;

measures adopted to implement this Section shall not prejudice eligibility for or the validity of the registration of a trademark, or the right to use a trademark, on the basis that such a trademark is identical with, or similar to, a geographical indication.

6. Nothing in this Section shall require a Member to apply its provisions in respect of a geographical indication of any other Member with respect to goods or services for which the

relevant indication is identical with the term customary in common language as the common name for such goods or services in the territory of that Member. Nothing in this Section shall require a Member to apply its provisions in respect of a geographical indication of any other Member with respect to products of the vine for which the relevant indication is identical with the customary name of a grape variety existing in the territory of that Member as of the date of entry into force of the WTO Agreement.

7. A Member may provide that any request made under this Section in connection with the use or registration of a trademark must be presented within five years after the adverse use of the protected indication has become generally known in that Member or after the date of registration of the trademark in that Member provided that the trademark has been published by that date, if such date is earlier than the date on which the adverse use became generally known in that Member, provided that the geographical indication is not used or registered in bad faith.

8. The provisions of this Section shall in no way prejudice the right of any person to use, in the course of trade, that person's name or the name of that person's predecessor in business, except where such name is used in such a manner as to mislead the public.

9. There shall be no obligation under this Agreement to protect geographical indications which are not or cease to be protected in their country of origin, or which have fallen into disuse in that country.

SECTION 4: INDUSTRIAL DESIGNS

Article 25

Requirements for Protection

1. Members shall provide for the protection of independently created industrial designs that are new or original. Members may provide that designs are not new or original if they do not significantly differ from known designs or combinations of known design features. Members may provide that such protection shall not extend to designs dictated essentially by technical or functional considerations.

2. Each Member shall ensure that requirements for securing protection for textile designs, in particular in regard to any cost, examination or publication, do not unreasonably impair the opportunity to seek and obtain such protection. Members shall be free to meet this obligation through industrial design law or through copyright law.

Article 26

Protection

1. The owner of a protected industrial design shall have the right to prevent third parties not having the owner's consent from making, selling or importing articles bearing or embodying a design which is a copy, or substantially a copy, of the protected design, when such acts are undertaken for commercial purposes.

2. Members may provide limited exceptions to the protection of industrial designs, provided that such exceptions do not unreasonably conflict with the normal exploitation of protected industrial designs and do not unreasonably prejudice the legitimate interests of the owner of the protected design, taking account of the legitimate interests of third parties.

3. The duration of protection available shall amount to at least 10 years.

SECTION 5: PATENTS

Article 27

Patentable Subject Matter

1. Subject to the provisions of paragraphs 2 and 3, patents shall be available for any inventions, whether products or processes, in all fields of technology, provided that they are new, involve an inventive step and are capable of industrial application.[5] Subject to paragraph 4 of Article 65, paragraph 8 of Article 70 and paragraph 3 of this Article, patents shall be available and patent rights enjoyable without discrimination as to the place of invention, the field of technology and whether products are imported or locally produced.

2. Members may exclude from patentability inventions, the prevention within their territory of the commercial exploitation of which is necessary to protect *ordre public* or morality, including to protect human, animal or plant life or health or to avoid serious prejudice to the environment, provided that such exclusion is not made merely because the exploitation is prohibited by their law.

3. Members may also exclude from patentability:

(a) diagnostic, therapeutic and surgical methods for the treatment of humans or animals;

(b) plants and animals other than micro-organisms, and essentially biological processes for the production of plants or animals other than non-biological and microbiological processes. However, Members shall provide for the protection of plant varieties either by patents or by an effective *sui generis* system or by any combination thereof. The provisions of this subparagraph shall be reviewed four years after the date of entry into force of the WTO Agreement.

Article 28

Rights Conferred

1. A patent shall confer on its owner the following exclusive rights:

(a) where the subject matter of a patent is a product, to prevent third parties not having the owner's consent from the acts of: making, using, offering for sale, selling, or importing[6] for these purposes that product;

(b) where the subject matter of a patent is a process, to prevent third parties not having the owner's consent from the act of using the process, and from the acts of: using, offering for sale, selling, or importing for these purposes at least the product obtained directly by that process.

2. Patent owners shall also have the right to assign, or transfer by succession, the patent and to conclude licensing contracts.

---

5 For the purposes of this Article, the terms "inventive step" and "capable of industrial application" may be deemed by a Member to be synonymous with the terms "non-obvious" and "useful" respectively.

6 This right, like all other rights conferred under this Agreement in respect of the use, sale, importation or other distribution of goods, is subject to the provisions of Article 6.

Article 29

Conditions on Patent Applicants

1. Members shall require that an applicant for a patent shall disclose the invention in a manner sufficiently clear and complete for the invention to be carried out by a person skilled in the art and may require the applicant to indicate the best mode for carrying out the invention known to the inventor at the filing date or, where priority is claimed, at the priority date of the application.

2. Members may require an applicant for a patent to provide information concerning the applicant's corresponding foreign applications and grants.

Article 30

Exceptions to Rights Conferred

Members may provide limited exceptions to the exclusive rights conferred by a patent, provided that such exceptions do not unreasonably conflict with a normal exploitation of the patent and do not unreasonably prejudice the legitimate interests of the patent owner, taking account of the legitimate interests of third parties.

Article 31

Other Use Without Authorization of the Right Holder

Where the law of a Member allows for other use[7] of the subject matter of a patent without the authorization of the right holder, including use by the government or third parties authorized by the government, the following provisions shall be respected:

(a) authorization of such use shall be considered on its individual merits;

(b) such use may only be permitted if, prior to such use, the proposed user has made efforts to obtain authorization from the right holder on reasonable commercial terms and conditions and that such efforts have not been successful within a reasonable period of time. This requirement may be waived by a Member in the case of a national emergency or other circumstances of extreme urgency or in cases of public non-commercial use. In situations of national emergency or other circumstances of extreme urgency, the right holder shall, nevertheless, be notified as soon as reasonably practicable. In the case of public non-commercial use, where the government or contractor, without making a patent search, knows or has demonstrable grounds to know that a valid patent is or will be used by or for the government, the right holder shall be informed promptly;

(c) the scope and duration of such use shall be limited to the purpose for which it was authorized, and in the case of semi-conductor technology shall only be for public non-commercial use or to remedy a practice determined after judicial or administrative process to be anti-competitive;

(d) such use shall be non-exclusive;

(e) such use shall be non-assignable, except with that part of the enterprise or goodwill which enjoys such use;

---

7 "Other use" refers to use other than that allowed under Article 30.

(f) any such use shall be authorized predominantly for the supply of the domestic market of the Member authorizing such use;

(g) authorization for such use shall be liable, subject to adequate protection of the legitimate interests of the persons so authorized, to be terminated if and when the circumstances which led to it cease to exist and are unlikely to recur. The competent authority shall have the authority to review, upon motivated request, the continued existence of these circumstances;

(h) the right holder shall be paid adequate remuneration in the circumstances of each case, taking into account the economic value of the authorization;

(i) the legal validity of any decision relating to the authorization of such use shall be subject to judicial review or other independent review by a distinct higher authority in that Member;

(j) any decision relating to the remuneration provided in respect of such use shall be subject to judicial review or other independent review by a distinct higher authority in that Member;

(k) Members are not obliged to apply the conditions set forth in subparagraphs (b) and (f) where such use is permitted to remedy a practice determined after judicial or administrative process to be anti-competitive. The need to correct anti-competitive practices may be taken into account in determining the amount of remuneration in such cases. Competent authorities shall have the authority to refuse termination of authorization if and when the conditions which led to such authorization are likely to recur;

(l) where such use is authorized to permit the exploitation of a patent ("the second patent") which cannot be exploited without infringing another patent ("the first patent"), the following additional conditions shall apply:

   (i) the invention claimed in the second patent shall involve an important technical advance of considerable economic significance in relation to the invention claimed in the first patent;

   (ii) the owner of the first patent shall be entitled to a cross-licence on reasonable terms to use the invention claimed in the second patent; and

   (iii) the use authorized in respect of the first patent shall be non-assignable except with the assignment of the second patent.

Article 32

Revocation/Forfeiture

An opportunity for judicial review of any decision to revoke or forfeit a patent shall be available.

Article 33

Term of Protection

The term of protection available shall not end before the expiration of a period of twenty years counted from the filing date.[8]

---

8 It is understood that those Members which do not have a system of original grant may provide that the term of protection shall be computed from the filing date in the system of original grant.

Article 34

Process Patents: Burden of Proof

1. For the purposes of civil proceedings in respect of the infringement of the rights of the owner referred to in paragraph 1(b) of Article 28, if the subject matter of a patent is a process for obtaining a product, the judicial authorities shall have the authority to order the defendant to prove that the process to obtain an identical product is different from the patented process. Therefore, Members shall provide, in at least one of the following circumstances, that any identical product when produced without the consent of the patent owner shall, in the absence of proof to the contrary, be deemed to have been obtained by the patented process:

(a) if the product obtained by the patented process is new;

(b) if there is a substantial likelihood that the identical product was made by the process and the owner of the patent has been unable through reasonable efforts to determine the process actually used.

2. Any Member shall be free to provide that the burden of proof indicated in paragraph 1 shall be on the alleged infringer only if the condition referred to in subparagraph (a) is fulfilled or only if the condition referred to in subparagraph (b) is fulfilled.

3. In the adduction of proof to the contrary, the legitimate interests of defendants in protecting their manufacturing and business secrets shall be taken into account.

SECTION 6: LAYOUT-DESIGNS (TOPOGRAPHIES) OF INTEGRATED CIRCUITS

Article 35

Relation to the IPIC Treaty

Members agree to provide protection to the layout-designs (topographies) of integrated circuits (referred to in this Agreement as "layout-designs") in accordance with Articles 2 through 7 (other than paragraph 3 of Article 6), Article 12 and paragraph 3 of Article 16 of the Treaty on Intellectual Property in Respect of Integrated Circuits and, in addition, to comply with the following provisions.

Article 36

Scope of the Protection

Subject to the provisions of paragraph 1 of Article 37, Members shall consider unlawful the following acts if performed without the authorization of the right holder:[9] importing, selling, or otherwise distributing for commercial purposes a protected layout-design, an integrated circuit in which a protected layout-design is incorporated, or an article incorporating such an integrated circuit only in so far as it continues to contain an unlawfully reproduced layout-design.

---

9 The term "right holder" in this Section shall be understood as having the same meaning as the term "holder of the right" in the IPIC Treaty.

Article 37

Acts Not Requiring the Authorization of the Right Holder

1. Notwithstanding Article 36, no Member shall consider unlawful the performance of any of the acts referred to in that Article in respect of an integrated circuit incorporating an unlawfully reproduced layout-design or any article incorporating such an integrated circuit where the person performing or ordering such acts did not know and had no reasonable ground to know, when acquiring the integrated circuit or article incorporating such an integrated circuit, that it incorporated an unlawfully reproduced layout-design. Members shall provide that, after the time that such person has received sufficient notice that the layout-design was unlawfully reproduced, that person may perform any of the acts with respect to the stock on hand or ordered before such time, but shall be liable to pay to the right holder a sum equivalent to a reasonable royalty such as would be payable under a freely negotiated licence in respect of such a layout-design.

2. The conditions set out in subparagraphs (a) through (k) of Article 31 shall apply *mutatis mutandis* in the event of any non-voluntary licensing of a layout-design or of its use by or for the government without the authorization of the right holder.

Article 38

Term of Protection

1. In Members requiring registration as a condition of protection, the term of protection of layout-designs shall not end before the expiration of a period of 10 years counted from the date of filing an application for registration or from the first commercial exploitation wherever in the world it occurs.

2. In Members not requiring registration as a condition for protection, layout-designs shall be protected for a term of no less than 10 years from the date of the first commercial exploitation wherever in the world it occurs.

3. Notwithstanding paragraphs 1 and 2, a Member may provide that protection shall lapse 15 years after the creation of the layout-design.

SECTION 7: PROTECTION OF UNDISCLOSED INFORMATION

Article 39

1. In the course of ensuring effective protection against unfair competition as provided in Article 10*bis* of the Paris Convention (1967), Members shall protect undisclosed information in accordance with paragraph 2 and data submitted to governments or governmental agencies in accordance with paragraph 3.

2. Natural and legal persons shall have the possibility of preventing information lawfully within their control from being disclosed to, acquired by, or used by others without their consent in a manner contrary to honest commercial practices[10] so long as such information:

---

10 For the purpose of this provision, "a manner contrary to honest commercial practices" shall mean at least practices such as breach of contract, breach of confidence and inducement to breach, and includes the acquisition of undisclosed information by third parties who knew, or were grossly negligent in failing to know, that such practices were involved in the acquisition.

(a) is secret in the sense that it is not, as a body or in the precise configuration and assembly of its components, generally known among or readily accessible to persons within the circles that normally deal with the kind of information in question;

(b) has commercial value because it is secret; and

(c) has been subject to reasonable steps under the circumstances, by the person lawfully in control of the information, to keep it secret.

3. Members, when requiring, as a condition of approving the marketing of pharmaceutical or of agricultural chemical products which utilize new chemical entities, the submission of undisclosed test or other data, the origination of which involves a considerable effort, shall protect such data against unfair commercial use. In addition, Members shall protect such data against disclosure, except where necessary to protect the public, or unless steps are taken to ensure that the data are protected against unfair commercial use.

SECTION 8: CONTROL OF ANTI-COMPETITIVE PRACTICES IN CONTRACTUAL LICENCES

Article 40

1. Members agree that some licensing practices or conditions pertaining to intellectual property rights which restrain competition may have adverse effects on trade and may impede the transfer and dissemination of technology.

2. Nothing in this Agreement shall prevent Members from specifying in their legislation licensing practices or conditions that may in particular cases constitute an abuse of intellectual property rights having an adverse effect on competition in the relevant market. As provided above, a Member may adopt, consistently with the other provisions of this Agreement, appropriate measures to prevent or control such practices, which may include for example exclusive grantback conditions, conditions preventing challenges to validity and coercive package licensing, in the light of the relevant laws and regulations of that Member.

3. Each Member shall enter, upon request, into consultations with any other Member which has cause to believe that an intellectual property right owner that is a national or domiciliary of the Member to which the request for consultations has been addressed is undertaking practices in violation of the requesting Member's laws and regulations on the subject matter of this Section, and which wishes to secure compliance with such legislation, without prejudice to any action under the law and to the full freedom of an ultimate decision of either Member. The Member addressed shall accord full and sympathetic consideration to, and shall afford adequate opportunity for, consultations with the requesting Member, and shall cooperate through supply of publicly available non-confidential information of relevance to the matter in question and of other information available to the Member, subject to domestic law and to the conclusion of mutually satisfactory agreements concerning the safeguarding of its confidentiality by the requesting Member.

4. A Member whose nationals or domiciliaries are subject to proceedings in another Member concerning alleged violation of that other Member's laws and regulations on the subject matter of this Section shall, upon request, be granted an opportunity for consultations by the other Member under the same conditions as those foreseen in paragraph 3.

PART III

ENFORCEMENT OF INTELLECTUAL PROPERTY RIGHTS

SECTION 1: GENERAL OBLIGATIONS

Article 41

1. Members shall ensure that enforcement procedures as specified in this Part are available under their law so as to permit effective action against any act of infringement of intellectual property rights covered by this Agreement, including expeditious remedies to prevent infringements and remedies which constitute a deterrent to further infringements. These procedures shall be applied in such a manner as to avoid the creation of barriers to legitimate trade and to provide for safeguards against their abuse.

2. Procedures concerning the enforcement of intellectual property rights shall be fair and equitable. They shall not be unnecessarily complicated or costly, or entail unreasonable time-limits or unwarranted delays.

3. Decisions on the merits of a case shall preferably be in writing and reasoned. They shall be made available at least to the parties to the proceeding without undue delay. Decisions on the merits of a case shall be based only on evidence in respect of which parties were offered the opportunity to be heard.

4. Parties to a proceeding shall have an opportunity for review by a judicial authority of final administrative decisions and, subject to jurisdictional provisions in a Member's law concerning the importance of a case, of at least the legal aspects of initial judicial decisions on the merits of a case. However, there shall be no obligation to provide an opportunity for review of acquittals in criminal cases.

5. It is understood that this Part does not create any obligation to put in place a judicial system for the enforcement of intellectual property rights distinct from that for the enforcement of law in general, nor does it affect the capacity of Members to enforce their law in general. Nothing in this Part creates any obligation with respect to the distribution of resources as between enforcement of intellectual property rights and the enforcement of law in general.

SECTION 2: CIVIL AND ADMINISTRATIVE PROCEDURES AND REMEDIES

Article 42

Fair and Equitable Procedures

Members shall make available to right holders[11] civil judicial procedures concerning the enforcement of any intellectual property right covered by this Agreement. Defendants shall have the right to written notice which is timely and contains sufficient detail, including the basis of the claims. Parties shall be allowed to be represented by independent legal counsel, and procedures shall not impose overly burdensome requirements concerning mandatory personal appearances. All parties to such procedures shall be duly entitled to substantiate their claims and to present all relevant evidence. The procedure shall provide a means to identify and protect confidential information, unless this would be contrary to existing constitutional requirements.

---

11 For the purpose of this Part, the term "right holder" includes federations and associations having legal standing to assert such rights.

Article 43

Evidence

1. The judicial authorities shall have the authority, where a party has presented reasonably available evidence sufficient to support its claims and has specified evidence relevant to substantiation of its claims which lies in the control of the opposing party, to order that this evidence be produced by the opposing party, subject in appropriate cases to conditions which ensure the protection of confidential information.

2. In cases in which a party to a proceeding voluntarily and without good reason refuses access to, or otherwise does not provide necessary information within a reasonable period, or significantly impedes a procedure relating to an enforcement action, a Member may accord judicial authorities the authority to make preliminary and final determinations, affirmative or negative, on the basis of the information presented to them, including the complaint or the allegation presented by the party adversely affected by the denial of access to information, subject to providing the parties an opportunity to be heard on the allegations or evidence.

Article 44

Injunctions

1. The judicial authorities shall have the authority to order a party to desist from an infringement, *inter alia* to prevent the entry into the channels of commerce in their jurisdiction of imported goods that involve the infringement of an intellectual property right, immediately after customs clearance of such goods. Members are not obliged to accord such authority in respect of protected subject matter acquired or ordered by a person prior to knowing or having reasonable grounds to know that dealing in such subject matter would entail the infringement of an intellectual property right.

2. Notwithstanding the other provisions of this Part and provided that the provisions of Part II specifically addressing use by governments, or by third parties authorized by a government, without the authorization of the right holder are complied with, Members may limit the remedies available against such use to payment of remuneration in accordance with subparagraph (h) of Article 31. In other cases, the remedies under this Part shall apply or, where these remedies are inconsistent with a Member's law, declaratory judgments and adequate compensation shall be available.

Article 45

Damages

1. The judicial authorities shall have the authority to order the infringer to pay the right holder damages adequate to compensate for the injury the right holder has suffered because of an infringement of that person's intellectual property right by an infringer who knowingly, or with reasonable grounds to know, engaged in infringing activity.

2. The judicial authorities shall also have the authority to order the infringer to pay the right holder expenses, which may include appropriate attorney's fees. In appropriate cases, Members may authorize the judicial authorities to order recovery of profits and/or payment of pre-established damages even where the infringer did not knowingly, or with reasonable grounds to know, engage in infringing activity.

Article 46

Other Remedies

In order to create an effective deterrent to infringement, the judicial authorities shall have the authority to order that goods that they have found to be infringing be, without compensation of any sort, disposed of outside the channels of commerce in such a manner as to avoid any harm caused to the right holder, or, unless this would be contrary to existing constitutional requirements, destroyed. The judicial authorities shall also have the authority to order that materials and implements the predominant use of which has been in the creation of the infringing goods be, without compensation of any sort, disposed of outside the channels of commerce in such a manner as to minimize the risks of further infringements. In considering such requests, the need for proportionality between the seriousness of the infringement and the remedies ordered as well as the interests of third parties shall be taken into account. In regard to counterfeit trademark goods, the simple removal of the trademark unlawfully affixed shall not be sufficient, other than in exceptional cases, to permit release of the goods into the channels of commerce.

Article 47

Right of Information

Members may provide that the judicial authorities shall have the authority, unless this would be out of proportion to the seriousness of the infringement, to order the infringer to inform the right holder of the identity of third persons involved in the production and distribution of the infringing goods or services and of their channels of distribution.

Article 48

Indemnification of the Defendant

1. The judicial authorities shall have the authority to order a party at whose request measures were taken and who has abused enforcement procedures to provide to a party wrongfully enjoined or restrained adequate compensation for the injury suffered because of such abuse. The judicial authorities shall also have the authority to order the applicant to pay the defendant expenses, which may include appropriate attorney's fees.

2. In respect of the administration of any law pertaining to the protection or enforcement of intellectual property rights, Members shall only exempt both public authorities and officials from liability to appropriate remedial measures where actions are taken or intended in good faith in the course of the administration of that law.

Article 49

Administrative Procedures

To the extent that any civil remedy can be ordered as a result of administrative procedures on the merits of a case, such procedures shall conform to principles equivalent in substance to those set forth in this Section.

SECTION 3: PROVISIONAL MEASURES

Article 50

1. The judicial authorities shall have the authority to order prompt and effective provisional measures:

(a) to prevent an infringement of any intellectual property right from occurring, and in particular to prevent the entry into the channels of commerce in their jurisdiction of goods, including imported goods immediately after customs clearance;

(b) to preserve relevant evidence in regard to the alleged infringement.

2. The judicial authorities shall have the authority to adopt provisional measures *inaudita altera parte* where appropriate, in particular where any delay is likely to cause irreparable harm to the right holder, or where there is a demonstrable risk of evidence being destroyed.

3. The judicial authorities shall have the authority to require the applicant to provide any reasonably available evidence in order to satisfy themselves with a sufficient degree of certainty that the applicant is the right holder and that the applicant's right is being infringed or that such infringement is imminent, and to order the applicant to provide a security or equivalent assurance sufficient to protect the defendant and to prevent abuse.

4. Where provisional measures have been adopted *inaudita altera parte*, the parties affected shall be given notice, without delay after the execution of the measures at the latest. A review, including a right to be heard, shall take place upon request of the defendant with a view to deciding, within a reasonable period after the notification of the measures, whether these measures shall be modified, revoked or confirmed.

5. The applicant may be required to supply other information necessary for the identification of the goods concerned by the authority that will execute the provisional measures.

6. Without prejudice to paragraph 4, provisional measures taken on the basis of paragraphs 1 and 2 shall, upon request by the defendant, be revoked or otherwise cease to have effect, if proceedings leading to a decision on the merits of the case are not initiated within a reasonable period, to be determined by the judicial authority ordering the measures where a Member's law so permits or, in the absence of such a determination, not to exceed 20 working days or 31 calendar days, whichever is the longer.

7. Where the provisional measures are revoked or where they lapse due to any act or omission by the applicant, or where it is subsequently found that there has been no infringement or threat of infringement of an intellectual property right, the judicial authorities shall have the authority to order the applicant, upon request of the defendant, to provide the defendant appropriate compensation for any injury caused by these measures.

8. To the extent that any provisional measure can be ordered as a result of administrative procedures, such procedures shall conform to principles equivalent in substance to those set forth in this Section.

SECTION 4: SPECIAL REQUIREMENTS RELATED TO BORDER MEASURES[12]

Article 51

Suspension of Release by Customs Authorities

Members shall, in conformity with the provisions set out below, adopt procedures[13] to enable a right holder, who has valid grounds for suspecting that the importation of counterfeit

12 Where a Member has dismantled substantially all controls over movement of goods across its border with another Member with which it forms part of a customs union, it shall not be required to apply the provisions of this Section at that border.

13 It is understood that there shall be no obligation to apply such procedures to imports of goods put on the market in another country by or with the consent of the right holder, or to goods in transit.

trademark or pirated copyright goods[14] may take place, to lodge an application in writing with competent authorities, administrative or judicial, for the suspension by the customs authorities of the release into free circulation of such goods. Members may enable such an application to be made in respect of goods which involve other infringements of intellectual property rights, provided that the requirements of this Section are met. Members may also provide for corresponding procedures concerning the suspension by the customs authorities of the release of infringing goods destined for exportation from their territories.

Article 52

Application

Any right holder initiating the procedures under Article 51 shall be required to provide adequate evidence to satisfy the competent authorities that, under the laws of the country of importation, there is *prima facie* an infringement of the right holder's intellectual property right and to supply a sufficiently detailed description of the goods to make them readily recognizable by the customs authorities. The competent authorities shall inform the applicant within a reasonable period whether they have accepted the application and, where determined by the competent authorities, the period for which the customs authorities will take action.

Article 53

Security or Equivalent Assurance

1. The competent authorities shall have the authority to require an applicant to provide a security or equivalent assurance sufficient to protect the defendant and the competent authorities and to prevent abuse. Such security or equivalent assurance shall not unreasonably deter recourse to these procedures.

2. Where pursuant to an application under this Section the release of goods involving industrial designs, patents, layout-designs or undisclosed information into free circulation has been suspended by customs authorities on the basis of a decision other than by a judicial or other independent authority, and the period provided for in Article 55 has expired without the granting of provisional relief by the duly empowered authority, and provided that all other conditions for importation have been complied with, the owner, importer, or consignee of such goods shall be entitled to their release on the posting of a security in an amount sufficient to protect the right holder for any infringement. Payment of such security shall not prejudice any other remedy available to the right holder, it being understood that the security shall be released if the right holder fails to pursue the right of action within a reasonable period of time.

---

14 For the purposes of this Agreement:

(a) "counterfeit trademark goods" shall mean any goods, including packaging, bearing without authorization a trademark which is identical to the trademark validly registered in respect of such goods, or which cannot be distinguished in its essential aspects from such a trademark, and which thereby infringes the rights of the owner of the trademark in question under the law of the country of importation;

(b) "pirated copyright goods" shall mean any goods which are copies made without the consent of the right holder or person duly authorized by the right holder in the country of production and which are made directly or indirectly from an article where the making of that copy would have constituted an infringement of a copyright or a related right under the law of the country of importation.

Article 54

Notice of Suspension

The importer and the applicant shall be promptly notified of the suspension of the release of goods according to Article 51.

Article 55

Duration of Suspension

If, within a period not exceeding 10 working days after the applicant has been served notice of the suspension, the customs authorities have not been informed that proceedings leading to a decision on the merits of the case have been initiated by a party other than the defendant, or that the duly empowered authority has taken provisional measures prolonging the suspension of the release of the goods, the goods shall be released, provided that all other conditions for importation or exportation have been complied with; in appropriate cases, this time-limit may be extended by another 10 working days. If proceedings leading to a decision on the merits of the case have been initiated, a review, including a right to be heard, shall take place upon request of the defendant with a view to deciding, within a reasonable period, whether these measures shall be modified, revoked or confirmed. Notwithstanding the above, where the suspension of the release of goods is carried out or continued in accordance with a provisional judicial measure, the provisions of paragraph 6 of Article 50 shall apply.

Article 56

Indemnification of the Importer and of the Owner of the Goods

Relevant authorities shall have the authority to order the applicant to pay the importer, the consignee and the owner of the goods appropriate compensation for any injury caused to them through the wrongful detention of goods or through the detention of goods released pursuant to Article 55.

Article 57

Right of Inspection and Information

Without prejudice to the protection of confidential information, Members shall provide the competent authorities the authority to give the right holder sufficient opportunity to have any goods detained by the customs authorities inspected in order to substantiate the right holder's claims. The competent authorities shall also have authority to give the importer an equivalent opportunity to have any such goods inspected. Where a positive determination has been made on the merits of a case, Members may provide the competent authorities the authority to inform the right holder of the names and addresses of the consignor, the importer and the consignee and of the quantity of the goods in question.

Article 58

Ex Officio Action

Where Members require competent authorities to act upon their own initiative and to suspend the release of goods in respect of which they have acquired *prima facie* evidence that an intellectual property right is being infringed:

(a) the competent authorities may at any time seek from the right holder any information that may assist them to exercise these powers;

(b) the importer and the right holder shall be promptly notified of the suspension. Where the importer has lodged an appeal against the suspension with the competent authorities, the suspension shall be subject to the conditions, *mutatis mutandis*, set out at Article 55;

(c) Members shall only exempt both public authorities and officials from liability to appropriate remedial measures where actions are taken or intended in good faith.

Article 59

Remedies

Without prejudice to other rights of action open to the right holder and subject to the right of the defendant to seek review by a judicial authority, competent authorities shall have the authority to order the destruction or disposal of infringing goods in accordance with the principles set out in Article 46. In regard to counterfeit trademark goods, the authorities shall not allow the re-exportation of the infringing goods in an unaltered state or subject them to a different customs procedure, other than in exceptional circumstances.

Article 60

De Minimis Imports

Members may exclude from the application of the above provisions small quantities of goods of a non-commercial nature contained in travellers' personal luggage or sent in small consignments.

SECTION 5: CRIMINAL PROCEDURES

Article 61

Members shall provide for criminal procedures and penalties to be applied at least in cases of wilful trademark counterfeiting or copyright piracy on a commercial scale. Remedies available shall include imprisonment and/or monetary fines sufficient to provide a deterrent, consistently with the level of penalties applied for crimes of a corresponding gravity. In appropriate cases, remedies available shall also include the seizure, forfeiture and destruction of the infringing goods and of any materials and implements the predominant use of which has been in the commission of the offence. Members may provide for criminal procedures and penalties to be applied in other cases of infringement of intellectual property rights, in particular where they are committed wilfully and on a commercial scale.

PART IV

ACQUISITION AND MAINTENANCE OF INTELLECTUAL PROPERTY RIGHTS AND RELATED *INTER-PARTES* PROCEDURES

Article 62

1. Members may require, as a condition of the acquisition or maintenance of the intellectual property rights provided for under Sections 2 through 6 of Part II, compliance with reasonable

procedures and formalities. Such procedures and formalities shall be consistent with the provisions of this Agreement.

2. Where the acquisition of an intellectual property right is subject to the right being granted or registered, Members shall ensure that the procedures for grant or registration, subject to compliance with the substantive conditions for acquisition of the right, permit the granting or registration of the right within a reasonable period of time so as to avoid unwarranted curtailment of the period of protection.

3. Article 4 of the Paris Convention (1967) shall apply *mutatis mutandis* to service marks.

4. Procedures concerning the acquisition or maintenance of intellectual property rights and, where a Member's law provides for such procedures, administrative revocation and *inter partes* procedures such as opposition, revocation and cancellation, shall be governed by the general principles set out in paragraphs 2 and 3 of Article 41.

5. Final administrative decisions in any of the procedures referred to under paragraph 4 shall be subject to review by a judicial or quasi-judicial authority. However, there shall be no obligation to provide an opportunity for such review of decisions in cases of unsuccessful opposition or administrative revocation, provided that the grounds for such procedures can be the subject of invalidation procedures.

PART V

DISPUTE PREVENTION AND SETTLEMENT

Article 63

Transparency

1. Laws and regulations, and final judicial decisions and administrative rulings of general application, made effective by a Member pertaining to the subject matter of this Agreement (the availability, scope, acquisition, enforcement and prevention of the abuse of intellectual property rights) shall be published, or where such publication is not practicable made publicly available, in a national language, in such a manner as to enable governments and right holders to become acquainted with them. Agreements concerning the subject matter of this Agreement which are in force between the government or a governmental agency of a Member and the government or a governmental agency of another Member shall also be published.

2. Members shall notify the laws and regulations referred to in paragraph 1 to the Council for TRIPS in order to assist that Council in its review of the operation of this Agreement. The Council shall attempt to minimize the burden on Members in carrying out this obligation and may decide to waive the obligation to notify such laws and regulations directly to the Council if consultations with WIPO on the establishment of a common register containing these laws and regulations are successful. The Council shall also consider in this connection any action required regarding notifications pursuant to the obligations under this Agreement stemming from the provisions of Article 6*ter* of the Paris Convention (1967).

3. Each Member shall be prepared to supply, in response to a written request from another Member, information of the sort referred to in paragraph 1. A Member, having reason to believe that a specific judicial decision or administrative ruling or bilateral agreement in the area of intellectual property rights affects its rights under this Agreement, may also request in writing to be given access to or be informed in sufficient detail of such specific judicial decisions or administrative rulings or bilateral agreements.

4. Nothing in paragraphs 1, 2 and 3 shall require Members to disclose confidential information which would impede law enforcement or otherwise be contrary to the public interest or would prejudice the legitimate commercial interests of particular enterprises, public or private.

Article 64

Dispute Settlement

1. The provisions of Articles XXII and XXIII of GATT 1994 as elaborated and applied by the Dispute Settlement Understanding shall apply to consultations and the settlement of disputes under this Agreement except as otherwise specifically provided herein.

2. Subparagraphs 1(b) and 1(c) of Article XXIII of GATT 1994 shall not apply to the settlement of disputes under this Agreement for a period of five years from the date of entry into force of the WTO Agreement.

3. During the time period referred to in paragraph 2, the Council for TRIPS shall examine the scope and modalities for complaints of the type provided for under subparagraphs 1(b) and 1(c) of Article XXIII of GATT 1994 made pursuant to this Agreement, and submit its recommendations to the Ministerial Conference for approval. Any decision of the Ministerial Conference to approve such recommendations or to extend the period in paragraph 2 shall be made only by consensus, and approved recommendations shall be effective for all Members without further formal acceptance process.

PART VI

TRANSITIONAL ARRANGEMENTS

Article 65

Transitional Arrangements

1. Subject to the provisions of paragraphs 2, 3 and 4, no Member shall be obliged to apply the provisions of this Agreement before the expiry of a general period of one year following the date of entry into force of the WTO Agreement.

2. A developing country Member is entitled to delay for a further period of four years the date of application, as defined in paragraph 1, of the provisions of this Agreement other than Articles 3, 4 and 5.

3. Any other Member which is in the process of transformation from a centrally-planned into a market, free-enterprise economy and which is undertaking structural reform of its intellectual property system and facing special problems in the preparation and implementation of intellectual property laws and regulations, may also benefit from a period of delay as foreseen in paragraph 2.

4. To the extent that a developing country Member is obliged by this Agreement to extend product patent protection to areas of technology not so protectable in its territory on the general date of application of this Agreement for that Member, as defined in paragraph 2, it may delay the application of the provisions on product patents of Section 5 of Part II to such areas of technology for an additional period of five years.

5. A Member availing itself of a transitional period under paragraphs 1, 2, 3 or 4 shall ensure that any changes in its laws, regulations and practice made during that period do not result in a lesser degree of consistency with the provisions of this Agreement.

Article 66

Least-Developed Country Members

1. In view of the special needs and requirements of least-developed country Members, their economic, financial and administrative constraints, and their need for flexibility to create a viable technological base, such Members shall not be required to apply the provisions of this Agreement, other than Articles 3, 4 and 5, for a period of 10 years from the date of application as defined under paragraph 1 of Article 65. The Council for TRIPS shall, upon duly motivated request by a least-developed country Member, accord extensions of this period.

2. Developed country Members shall provide incentives to enterprises and institutions in their territories for the purpose of promoting and encouraging technology transfer to least-developed country Members in order to enable them to create a sound and viable technological base.

Article 67

Technical Cooperation

In order to facilitate the implementation of this Agreement, developed country Members shall provide, on request and on mutually agreed terms and conditions, technical and financial cooperation in favour of developing and least-developed country Members. Such cooperation shall include assistance in the preparation of laws and regulations on the protection and enforcement of intellectual property rights as well as on the prevention of their abuse, and shall include support regarding the establishment or reinforcement of domestic offices and agencies relevant to these matters, including the training of personnel.

PART VII

INSTITUTIONAL ARRANGEMENTS; FINAL PROVISIONS

Article 68

Council for Trade-Related Aspects of Intellectual Property Rights

The Council for TRIPS shall monitor the operation of this Agreement and, in particular, Members' compliance with their obligations hereunder, and shall afford Members the opportunity of consulting on matters relating to the trade-related aspects of intellectual property rights. It shall carry out such other responsibilities as assigned to it by the Members, and it shall, in particular, provide any assistance requested by them in the context of dispute settlement procedures. In carrying out its functions, the Council for TRIPS may consult with and seek information from any source it deems appropriate. In consultation with WIPO, the Council shall seek to establish, within one year of its first meeting, appropriate arrangements for cooperation with bodies of that Organization.

Article 69

International Cooperation

Members agree to cooperate with each other with a view to eliminating international trade in goods infringing intellectual property rights. For this purpose, they shall establish and notify contact points in their administrations and be ready to exchange information on trade in infringing goods. They shall, in particular, promote the exchange of information and cooperation between customs authorities with regard to trade in counterfeit trademark goods and pirated copyright goods.

Article 70

Protection of Existing Subject Matter

1. This Agreement does not give rise to obligations in respect of acts which occurred before the date of application of the Agreement for the Member in question.

2. Except as otherwise provided for in this Agreement, this Agreement gives rise to obligations in respect of all subject matter existing at the date of application of this Agreement for the Member in question, and which is protected in that Member on the said date, or which meets or comes subsequently to meet the criteria for protection under the terms of this Agreement. In respect of this paragraph and paragraphs 3 and 4, copyright obligations with respect to existing works shall be solely determined under Article 18 of the Berne Convention (1971), and obligations with respect to the rights of producers of phonograms and performers in existing phonograms shall be determined solely under Article 18 of the Berne Convention (1971) as made applicable under paragraph 6 of Article 14 of this Agreement.

3. There shall be no obligation to restore protection to subject matter which on the date of application of this Agreement for the Member in question has fallen into the public domain.

4. In respect of any acts in respect of specific objects embodying protected subject matter which become infringing under the terms of legislation in conformity with this Agreement, and which were commenced, or in respect of which a significant investment was made, before the date of acceptance of the WTO Agreement by that Member, any Member may provide for a limitation of the remedies available to the right holder as to the continued performance of such acts after the date of application of this Agreement for that Member. In such cases the Member shall, however, at least provide for the payment of equitable remuneration.

5. A Member is not obliged to apply the provisions of Article 11 and of paragraph 4 of Article 14 with respect to originals or copies purchased prior to the date of application of this Agreement for that Member.

6. Members shall not be required to apply Article 31, or the requirement in paragraph 1 of Article 27 that patent rights shall be enjoyable without discrimination as to the field of technology, to use without the authorization of the right holder where authorization for such use was granted by the government before the date this Agreement became known.

7. In the case of intellectual property rights for which protection is conditional upon registration, applications for protection which are pending on the date of application of this Agreement for the Member in question shall be permitted to be amended to claim any enhanced protection provided under the provisions of this Agreement. Such amendments shall not include new matter.

8. Where a Member does not make available as of the date of entry into force of the WTO Agreement patent protection for pharmaceutical and agricultural chemical products commensurate with its obligations under Article 27, that Member shall:

(a) notwithstanding the provisions of Part VI, provide as from the date of entry into force of the WTO Agreement a means by which applications for patents for such inventions can be filed;

(b) apply to these applications, as of the date of application of this Agreement, the criteria for patentability as laid down in this Agreement as if those criteria were being applied on the date of filing in that Member or, where priority is available and claimed, the priority date of the application; and

(c) provide patent protection in accordance with this Agreement as from the grant of the patent and for the remainder of the patent term, counted from the filing date in accordance with Article 33 of this Agreement, for those of these applications that meet the criteria for protection referred to in subparagraph (b).

9. Where a product is the subject of a patent application in a Member in accordance with paragraph 8(a), exclusive marketing rights shall be granted, notwithstanding the provisions of Part VI, for a period of five years after obtaining marketing approval in that Member or until a product patent is granted or rejected in that Member, whichever period is shorter, provided that, subsequent to the entry into force of the WTO Agreement, a patent application has been filed and a patent granted for that product in another Member and marketing approval obtained in such other Member.

Article 71

Review and Amendment

1. The Council for TRIPS shall review the implementation of this Agreement after the expiration of the transitional period referred to in paragraph 2 of Article 65. The Council shall, having regard to the experience gained in its implementation, review it two years after that date, and at identical intervals thereafter. The Council may also undertake reviews in the light of any relevant new developments which might warrant modification or amendment of this Agreement.

2. Amendments merely serving the purpose of adjusting to higher levels of protection of intellectual property rights achieved, and in force, in other multilateral agreements and accepted under those agreements by all Members of the WTO may be referred to the Ministerial Conference for action in accordance with paragraph 6 of Article X of the WTO Agreement on the basis of a consensus proposal from the Council for TRIPS.

Article 72

Reservations

Reservations may not be entered in respect of any of the provisions of this Agreement without the consent of the other Members.

Article 73

Security Exceptions

Nothing in this Agreement shall be construed:

(a) to require a Member to furnish any information the disclosure of which it considers contrary to its essential security interests; or

(b) to prevent a Member from taking any action which it considers necessary for the protection of its essential security interests;

(i) relating to fissionable materials or the materials from which they are derived;

(ii) relating to the traffic in arms, ammunition and implements of war and to such traffic in other goods and materials as is carried on directly or indirectly for the purpose of supplying a military establishment;

(iii) taken in time of war or other emergency in international relations; or

(c) to prevent a Member from taking any action in pursuance of its obligations under the United Nations Charter for the maintenance of international peace and security.

Understanding on Rules and Procedures Governing the Settlement of Disputes

Members hereby *agree* as follows:

Article 1

Coverage and Application

1. The rules and procedures of this Understanding shall apply to disputes brought pursuant to the consultation and dispute settlement provisions of the agreements listed in Appendix 1 to this Understanding (referred to in this Understanding as the "covered agreements"). The rules and procedures of this Understanding shall also apply to consultations and the settlement of disputes between Members concerning their rights and obligations under the provisions of the Agreement Establishing the World Trade Organization (referred to in this Understanding as the "WTO Agreement") and of this Understanding taken in isolation or in combination with any other covered agreement.

2. The rules and procedures of this Understanding shall apply subject to such special or additional rules and procedures on dispute settlement contained in the covered agreements as are identified in Appendix 2 to this Understanding. To the extent that there is a difference between the rules and procedures of this Understanding and the special or additional rules and procedures set forth in Appendix 2, the special or additional rules and procedures in Appendix 2 shall prevail. In disputes involving rules and procedures under more than one covered agreement, if there is a conflict between special or additional rules and procedures of such agreements under review, and where the parties to the dispute cannot agree on rules and procedures within 20 days of the establishment of the panel, the Chairman of the Dispute Settlement Body provided for in paragraph 1 of Article 2 (referred to in this Understanding as the "DSB"), in consultation with the parties to the dispute, shall determine the rules and procedures to be followed within 10 days after a request by either Member. The Chairman shall be guided by the principle that special or additional rules and procedures should be used where possible, and the rules and procedures set out in this Understanding should be used to the extent necessary to avoid conflict.

Article 2

Administration

1. The Dispute Settlement Body is hereby established to administer these rules and procedures and, except as otherwise provided in a covered agreement, the consultation and dispute settlement provisions of the covered agreements. Accordingly, the DSB shall have the authority to establish panels, adopt panel and Appellate Body reports, maintain surveillance of

implementation of rulings and recommendations, and authorize suspension of concessions and other obligations under the covered agreements. With respect to disputes arising under a covered agreement which is a Plurilateral Trade Agreement, the term "Member" as used herein shall refer only to those Members that are parties to the relevant Plurilateral Trade Agreement. Where the DSB administers the dispute settlement provisions of a Plurilateral Trade Agreement, only those Members that are parties to that Agreement may participate in decisions or actions taken by the DSB with respect to that dispute.

2. The DSB shall inform the relevant WTO Councils and Committees of any developments in disputes related to provisions of the respective covered agreements.

3. The DSB shall meet as often as necessary to carry out its functions within the time-frames provided in this Understanding.

4. Where the rules and procedures of this Understanding provide for the DSB to take a decision, it shall do so by consensus.[1]

Article 3

General Provisions

1. Members affirm their adherence to the principles for the management of disputes heretofore applied under Articles XXII and XXIII of GATT 1947, and the rules and procedures as further elaborated and modified herein.

2. The dispute settlement system of the WTO is a central element in providing security and predictability to the multilateral trading system. The Members recognize that it serves to preserve the rights and obligations of Members under the covered agreements, and to clarify the existing provisions of those agreements in accordance with customary rules of interpretation of public international law. Recommendations and rulings of the DSB cannot add to or diminish the rights and obligations provided in the covered agreements.

3. The prompt settlement of situations in which a Member considers that any benefits accruing to it directly or indirectly under the covered agreements are being impaired by measures taken by another Member is essential to the effective functioning of the WTO and the maintenance of a proper balance between the rights and obligations of Members.

4. Recommendations or rulings made by the DSB shall be aimed at achieving a satisfactory settlement of the matter in accordance with the rights and obligations under this Understanding and under the covered agreements.

5. All solutions to matters formally raised under the consultation and dispute settlement provisions of the covered agreements, including arbitration awards, shall be consistent with those agreements and shall not nullify or impair benefits accruing to any Member under those agreements, nor impede the attainment of any objective of those agreements.

6. Mutually agreed solutions to matters formally raised under the consultation and dispute settlement provisions of the covered agreements shall be notified to the DSB and the relevant Councils and Committees, where any Member may raise any point relating thereto.

---

1 The DSB shall be deemed to have decided by consensus on a matter submitted for its consideration, if no Member, present at the meeting of the DSB when the decision is taken, formally objects to the proposed decision.

7. Before bringing a case, a Member shall exercise its judgement as to whether action under these procedures would be fruitful. The aim of the dispute settlement mechanism is to secure a positive solution to a dispute. A solution mutually acceptable to the parties to a dispute and consistent with the covered agreements is clearly to be preferred. In the absence of a mutually agreed solution, the first objective of the dispute settlement mechanism is usually to secure the withdrawal of the measures concerned if these are found to be inconsistent with the provisions of any of the covered agreements. The provision of compensation should be resorted to only if the immediate withdrawal of the measure is impracticable and as a temporary measure pending the withdrawal of the measure which is inconsistent with a covered agreement. The last resort which this Understanding provides to the Member invoking the dispute settlement procedures is the possibility of suspending the application of concessions or other obligations under the covered agreements on a discriminatory basis vis-à-vis the other Member, subject to authorization by the DSB of such measures.

8. In cases where there is an infringement of the obligations assumed under a covered agreement, the action is considered *prima facie* to constitute a case of nullification or impairment. This means that there is normally a presumption that a breach of the rules has an adverse impact on other Members parties to that covered agreement, and in such cases, it shall be up to the Member against whom the complaint has been brought to rebut the charge.

9. The provisions of this Understanding are without prejudice to the rights of Members to seek authoritative interpretation of provisions of a covered agreement through decision-making under the WTO Agreement or a covered agreement which is a Plurilateral Trade Agreement.

10. It is understood that requests for conciliation and the use of the dispute settlement procedures should not be intended or considered as contentious acts and that, if a dispute arises, all Members will engage in these procedures in good faith in an effort to resolve the dispute. It is also understood that complaints and counter-complaints in regard to distinct matters should not be linked.

11. This Understanding shall be applied only with respect to new requests for consultations under the consultation provisions of the covered agreements made on or after the date of entry into force of the WTO Agreement. With respect to disputes for which the request for consultations was made under GATT 1947 or under any other predecessor agreement to the covered agreements before the date of entry into force of the WTO Agreement, the relevant dispute settlement rules and procedures in effect immediately prior to the date of entry into force of the WTO Agreement shall continue to apply.[2]

12. Notwithstanding paragraph 11, if a complaint based on any of the covered agreements is brought by a developing country Member against a developed country Member, the complaining party shall have the right to invoke, as an alternative to the provisions contained in Articles 4, 5, 6 and 12 of this Understanding, the corresponding provisions of the Decision of 5 April 1966 (BISD 14S/18), except that where the Panel considers that the time-frame provided for in paragraph 7 of that Decision is insufficient to provide its report and with the agreement of the complaining party, that time-frame may be extended. To the extent that there is a difference between the rules and procedures of Articles 4, 5, 6 and 12 and the corresponding rules and procedures of the Decision, the latter shall prevail.

Article 4

Consultations

1. Members affirm their resolve to strengthen and improve the effectiveness of the consultation procedures employed by Members.

---

2 This paragraph shall also be applied to disputes on which panel reports have not been adopted or fully implemented.

2. Each Member undertakes to accord sympathetic consideration to and afford adequate opportunity for consultation regarding any representations made by another Member concerning measures affecting the operation of any covered agreement taken within the territory of the former.[3]

3. If a request for consultations is made pursuant to a covered agreement, the Member to which the request is made shall, unless otherwise mutually agreed, reply to the request within 10 days after the date of its receipt and shall enter into consultations in good faith within a period of no more than 30 days after the date of receipt of the request, with a view to reaching a mutually satisfactory solution. If the Member does not respond within 10 days after the date of receipt of the request, or does not enter into consultations within a period of no more than 30 days, or a period otherwise mutually agreed, after the date of receipt of the request, then the Member that requested the holding of consultations may proceed directly to request the establishment of a panel.

4. All such requests for consultations shall be notified to the DSB and the relevant Councils and Committees by the Member which requests consultations. Any request for consultations shall be submitted in writing and shall give the reasons for the request, including identification of the measures at issue and an indication of the legal basis for the complaint.

5. In the course of consultations in accordance with the provisions of a covered agreement, before resorting to further action under this Understanding, Members should attempt to obtain satisfactory adjustment of the matter.

6. Consultations shall be confidential, and without prejudice to the rights of any Member in any further proceedings.

7. If the consultations fail to settle a dispute within 60 days after the date of receipt of the request for consultations, the complaining party may request the establishment of a panel. The complaining party may request a panel during the 60-day period if the consulting parties jointly consider that consultations have failed to settle the dispute.

8. In cases of urgency, including those which concern perishable goods, Members shall enter into consultations within a period of no more than 10 days after the date of receipt of the request. If the consultations have failed to settle the dispute within a period of 20 days after the date of receipt of the request, the complaining party may request the establishment of a panel.

9. In cases of urgency, including those which concern perishable goods, the parties to the dispute, panels and the Appellate Body shall make every effort to accelerate the proceedings to the greatest extent possible.

10. During consultations Members should give special attention to the particular problems and interests of developing country Members.

11. Whenever a Member other than the consulting Members considers that it has a substantial trade interest in consultations being held pursuant to paragraph 1 of Article XXII of GATT 1994, paragraph 1 of Article XXII of GATS, or the corresponding provisions in other covered agreements[4], such Member may notify the consulting Members and the DSB, within 10 days after

---

3 Where the provisions of any other covered agreement concerning measures taken by regional or local governments or authorities within the territory of a Member contain provisions different from the provisions of this paragraph, the provisions of such other covered agreement shall prevail.

4 The corresponding consultation provisions in the covered agreements are listed hereunder: Agreement on Agriculture, Article 19; Agreement on the Application of Sanitary and Phytosanitary Measures, paragraph 1 of Article 11; Agreement on Textiles and Clothing, paragraph 4 of Article 8; Agreement on Technical Barriers to Trade, paragraph 1 of Article 14; Agreement on Trade-Related Investment Measures, Article 8; Agreement on Implementation of Article VI of GATT 1994, paragraph 2 of Article 17;

the date of the circulation of the request for consultations under said Article, of its desire to be joined in the consultations. Such Member shall be joined in the consultations, provided that the Member to which the request for consultations was addressed agrees that the claim of substantial interest is well-founded. In that event they shall so inform the DSB. If the request to be joined in the consultations is not accepted, the applicant Member shall be free to request consultations under paragraph 1 of Article XXII or paragraph 1 of Article XXIII of GATT 1994, paragraph 1 of Article XXII or paragraph 1 of Article XXIII of GATS, or the corresponding provisions in other covered agreements.

Article 5

Good Offices, Conciliation and Mediation

1. Good offices, conciliation and mediation are procedures that are undertaken voluntarily if the parties to the dispute so agree.

2. Proceedings involving good offices, conciliation and mediation, and in particular positions taken by the parties to the dispute during these proceedings, shall be confidential, and without prejudice to the rights of either party in any further proceedings under these procedures.

3. Good offices, conciliation or mediation may be requested at any time by any party to a dispute. They may begin at any time and be terminated at any time. Once procedures for good offices, conciliation or mediation are terminated, a complaining party may then proceed with a request for the establishment of a panel.

4. When good offices, conciliation or mediation are entered into within 60 days after the date of receipt of a request for consultations, the complaining party must allow a period of 60 days after the date of receipt of the request for consultations before requesting the establishment of a panel. The complaining party may request the establishment of a panel during the 60-day period if the parties to the dispute jointly consider that the good offices, conciliation or mediation process has failed to settle the dispute.

5. If the parties to a dispute agree, procedures for good offices, conciliation or mediation may continue while the panel process proceeds.

6. The Director-General may, acting in an *ex officio* capacity, offer good offices, conciliation or mediation with the view to assisting Members to settle a dispute.

Article 6

Establishment of Panels

1. If the complaining party so requests, a panel shall be established at the latest at the DSB meeting following that at which the request first appears as an item on the DSB's agenda, unless at that meeting the DSB decides by consensus not to establish a panel.[5]

Agreement on Implementation of Article VII of GATT 1994, paragraph 2 of Article 19; Agreement on Preshipment Inspection, Article 7; Agreement on Rules of Origin, Article 7; Agreement on Import Licensing Procedures, Article 6; Agreement on Subsidies and Countervailing Measures, Article 30; Agreement on Safeguards, Article 14; Agreement on Trade-Related Aspects of Intellectual Property Rights, Article 64.1; and any corresponding consultation provisions in Plurilateral Trade Agreements as determined by the competent bodies of each Agreement and as notified to the DSB.

5 If the complaining party so requests, a meeting of the DSB shall be convened for this purpose within 15 days of the request, provided that at least 10 days' advance notice of the meeting is given.

2. The request for the establishment of a panel shall be made in writing. It shall indicate whether consultations were held, identify the specific measures at issue and provide a brief summary of the legal basis of the complaint sufficient to present the problem clearly. In case the applicant requests the establishment of a panel with other than standard terms of reference, the written request shall include the proposed text of special terms of reference.

Article 7

Terms of Reference of Panels

1. Panels shall have the following terms of reference unless the parties to the dispute agree otherwise within 20 days from the establishment of the panel:

> "To examine, in the light of the relevant provisions in (name of the covered agreement(s) cited by the parties to the dispute), the matter referred to the DSB by (name of party) in document . . . and to make such findings as will assist the DSB in making the recommendations or in giving the rulings provided for in that/those agreement(s)."

2. Panels shall address the relevant provisions in any covered agreement or agreements cited by the parties to the dispute.

3. In establishing a panel, the DSB may authorize its Chairman to draw up the terms of reference of the panel in consultation with the parties to the dispute, subject to the provisions of paragraph 1. The terms of reference thus drawn up shall be circulated to all Members. If other than standard terms of reference are agreed upon, any Member may raise any point relating thereto in the DSB.

Article 8

Composition of Panels

1. Panels shall be composed of well-qualified governmental and/or non-governmental individuals, including persons who have served on or presented a case to a panel, served as a representative of a Member or of a contracting party to GATT 1947 or as a representative to the Council or Committee of any covered agreement or its predecessor agreement, or in the Secretariat, taught or published on international trade law or policy, or served as a senior trade policy official of a Member.

2. Panel members should be selected with a view to ensuring the independence of the members, a sufficiently diverse background and a wide spectrum of experience.

3. Citizens of Members whose governments[6] are parties to the dispute or third parties as defined in paragraph 2 of Article 10 shall not serve on a panel concerned with that dispute, unless the parties to the dispute agree otherwise.

4. To assist in the selection of panelists, the Secretariat shall maintain an indicative list of governmental and non-governmental individuals possessing the qualifications outlined in paragraph 1, from which panelists may be drawn as appropriate. That list shall include the roster of non-governmental panelists established on 30 November 1984 (BISD 31S/9), and other rosters and indicative lists established under any of the covered agreements, and shall retain the names of persons on those rosters and indicative lists at the time of entry into force of the

---

6 In the case where customs unions or common markets are parties to a dispute, this provision applies to citizens of all member countries of the customs unions or common markets.

WTO Agreement. Members may periodically suggest names of governmental and non-governmental individuals for inclusion on the indicative list, providing relevant information on their knowledge of international trade and of the sectors or subject matter of the covered agreements, and those names shall be added to the list upon approval by the DSB. For each of the individuals on the list, the list shall indicate specific areas of experience or expertise of the individuals in the sectors or subject matter of the covered agreements.

5. Panels shall be composed of three panelists unless the parties to the dispute agree, within 10 days from the establishment of the panel, to a panel composed of five panelists. Members shall be informed promptly of the composition of the panel.

6. The Secretariat shall propose nominations for the panel to the parties to the dispute. The parties to the dispute shall not oppose nominations except for compelling reasons.

7. If there is no agreement on the panelists within 20 days after the date of the establishment of a panel, at the request of either party, the Director-General, in consultation with the Chairman of the DSB and the Chairman of the relevant Council or Committee, shall determine the composition of the panel by appointing the panelists whom the Director-General considers most appropriate in accordance with any relevant special or additional rules or procedures of the covered agreement or covered agreements which are at issue in the dispute, after consulting with the parties to the dispute. The Chairman of the DSB shall inform the Members of the composition of the panel thus formed no later than 10 days after the date the Chairman receives such a request.

8. Members shall undertake, as a general rule, to permit their officials to serve as panelists.

9. Panelists shall serve in their individual capacities and not as government representatives, nor as representatives of any organization. Members shall therefore not give them instructions nor seek to influence them as individuals with regard to matters before a panel.

10. When a dispute is between a developing country Member and a developed country Member the panel shall, if the developing country Member so requests, include at least one panelist from a developing country Member.

11. Panelists' expenses, including travel and subsistence allowance, shall be met from the WTO budget in accordance with criteria to be adopted by the General Council, based on recommendations of the Committee on Budget, Finance and Administration.

Article 9

Procedures for Multiple Complainants

1. Where more than one Member requests the establishment of a panel related to the same matter, a single panel may be established to examine these complaints taking into account the rights of all Members concerned. A single panel should be established to examine such complaints whenever feasible.

2. The single panel shall organize its examination and present its findings to the DSB in such a manner that the rights which the parties to the dispute would have enjoyed had separate panels examined the complaints are in no way impaired. If one of the parties to the dispute so requests, the panel shall submit separate reports on the dispute concerned. The written submissions by each of the complainants shall be made available to the other complainants, and each complainant shall have the right to be present when any one of the other complainants presents its views to the panel.

3. If more than one panel is established to examine the complaints related to the same matter, to the greatest extent possible the same persons shall serve as panelists on each of the separate panels and the timetable for the panel process in such disputes shall be harmonized.

Article 10

Third Parties

1. The interests of the parties to a dispute and those of other Members under a covered agreement at issue in the dispute shall be fully taken into account during the panel process.

2. Any Member having a substantial interest in a matter before a panel and having notified its interest to the DSB (referred to in this Understanding as a "third party") shall have an opportunity to be heard by the panel and to make written submissions to the panel. These submissions shall also be given to the parties to the dispute and shall be reflected in the panel report.

3. Third parties shall receive the submissions of the parties to the dispute to the first meeting of the panel.

4. If a third party considers that a measure already the subject of a panel proceeding nullifies or impairs benefits accruing to it under any covered agreement, that Member may have recourse to normal dispute settlement procedures under this Understanding. Such a dispute shall be referred to the original panel wherever possible.

Article 11

Function of Panels

The function of panels is to assist the DSB in discharging its responsibilities under this Understanding and the covered agreements. Accordingly, a panel should make an objective assessment of the matter before it, including an objective assessment of the facts of the case and the applicability of and conformity with the relevant covered agreements, and make such other findings as will assist the DSB in making the recommendations or in giving the rulings provided for in the covered agreements. Panels should consult regularly with the parties to the dispute and give them adequate opportunity to develop a mutually satisfactory solution.

Article 12

Panel Procedures

1. Panels shall follow the Working Procedures in Appendix 3 unless the panel decides otherwise after consulting the parties to the dispute.

2. Panel procedures should provide sufficient flexibility so as to ensure high-quality panel reports, while not unduly delaying the panel process.

3. After consulting the parties to the dispute, the panelists shall, as soon as practicable and whenever possible within one week after the composition and terms of reference of the panel have been agreed upon, fix the timetable for the panel process, taking into account the provisions of paragraph 9 of Article 4, if relevant.

4. In determining the timetable for the panel process, the panel shall provide sufficient time for the parties to the dispute to prepare their submissions.

5. Panels should set precise deadlines for written submissions by the parties and the parties should respect those deadlines.

6. Each party to the dispute shall deposit its written submissions with the Secretariat for immediate transmission to the panel and to the other party or parties to the dispute. The complaining party shall submit its first submission in advance of the responding party's first submission unless the panel decides, in fixing the timetable referred to in paragraph 3 and after consultations with the parties to the dispute, that the parties should submit their first submissions simultaneously. When there are sequential arrangements for the deposit of first submissions, the panel shall establish a firm time-period for receipt of the responding party's submission. Any subsequent written submissions shall be submitted simultaneously.

7. Where the parties to the dispute have failed to develop a mutually satisfactory solution, the panel shall submit its findings in the form of a written report to the DSB. In such cases, the report of a panel shall set out the findings of fact, the applicability of relevant provisions and the basic rationale behind any findings and recommendations that it makes. Where a settlement of the matter among the parties to the dispute has been found, the report of the panel shall be confined to a brief description of the case and to reporting that a solution has been reached.

8. In order to make the procedures more efficient, the period in which the panel shall conduct its examination, from the date that the composition and terms of reference of the panel have been agreed upon until the date the final report is issued to the parties to the dispute, shall, as a general rule, not exceed six months. In cases of urgency, including those relating to perishable goods, the panel shall aim to issue its report to the parties to the dispute within three months.

9. When the panel considers that it cannot issue its report within six months, or within three months in cases of urgency, it shall inform the DSB in writing of the reasons for the delay together with an estimate of the period within which it will issue its report. In no case should the period from the establishment of the panel to the circulation of the report to the Members exceed nine months.

10. In the context of consultations involving a measure taken by a developing country Member, the parties may agree to extend the periods established in paragraphs 7 and 8 of Article 4. If, after the relevant period has elapsed, the consulting parties cannot agree that the consultations have concluded, the Chairman of the DSB shall decide, after consultation with the parties, whether to extend the relevant period and, if so, for how long. In addition, in examining a complaint against a developing country Member, the panel shall accord sufficient time for the developing country Member to prepare and present its argumentation. The provisions of paragraph 1 of Article 20 and paragraph 4 of Article 21 are not affected by any action pursuant to this paragraph.

11. Where one or more of the parties is a developing country Member, the panel's report shall explicitly indicate the form in which account has been taken of relevant provisions on differential and more-favourable treatment for developing country Members that form part of the covered agreements which have been raised by the developing country Member in the course of the dispute settlement procedures.

12. The panel may suspend its work at any time at the request of the complaining party for a period not to exceed 12 months. In the event of such a suspension, the time-frames set out in paragraphs 8 and 9 of this Article, paragraph 1 of Article 20, and paragraph 4 of Article 21 shall be extended by the amount of time that the work was suspended. If the work of the panel has been suspended for more than 12 months, the authority for establishment of the panel shall lapse.

Article 13

Right to Seek Information

1. Each panel shall have the right to seek information and technical advice from any individual or body which it deems appropriate. However, before a panel seeks such information or advice from any individual or body within the jurisdiction of a Member it shall inform the authorities of that Member. A Member should respond promptly and fully to any request by a panel for such information as the panel considers necessary and appropriate. Confidential information which is provided shall not be revealed without formal authorization from the individual, body, or authorities of the Member providing the information.

2. Panels may seek information from any relevant source and may consult experts to obtain their opinion on certain aspects of the matter. With respect to a factual issue concerning a scientific or other technical matter raised by a party to a dispute, a panel may request an advisory report in writing from an expert review group. Rules for the establishment of such a group and its procedures are set forth in Appendix 4.

Article 14

Confidentiality

1. Panel deliberations shall be confidential.

2. The reports of panels shall be drafted without the presence of the parties to the dispute in the light of the information provided and the statements made.

3. Opinions expressed in the panel report by individual panelists shall be anonymous.

Article 15

Interim Review Stage

1. Following the consideration of rebuttal submissions and oral arguments, the panel shall issue the descriptive (factual and argument) sections of its draft report to the parties to the dispute. Within a period of time set by the panel, the parties shall submit their comments in writing.

2. Following the expiration of the set period of time for receipt of comments from the parties to the dispute, the panel shall issue an interim report to the parties, including both the descriptive sections and the panel's findings and conclusions. Within a period of time set by the panel, a party may submit a written request for the panel to review precise aspects of the interim report prior to circulation of the final report to the Members. At the request of a party, the panel shall hold a further meeting with the parties on the issues identified in the written comments. If no comments are received from any party within the comment period, the interim report shall be considered the final panel report and circulated promptly to the Members.

3. The findings of the final panel report shall include a discussion of the arguments made at the interim review stage. The interim review stage shall be conducted within the time-period set out in paragraph 8 of Article 12.

Article 16

Adoption of Panel Reports

1. In order to provide sufficient time for the Members to consider panel reports, the reports shall not be considered for adoption by the DSB until 20 days after the date they have been circulated to the Members.

2. Members having objections to a panel report shall give written reasons to explain their objections for circulation at least 10 days prior to the DSB meeting at which the panel report will be considered.

3. The parties to a dispute shall have the right to participate fully in the consideration of the panel report by the DSB, and their views shall be fully recorded.

4. Within 60 days after the date of circulation of a panel report to the Members, the report shall be adopted at a DSB meeting[7] unless a party to the dispute formally notifies the DSB of its decision to appeal or the DSB decides by consensus not to adopt the report. If a party has notified its decision to appeal, the report by the panel shall not be considered for adoption by the DSB until after completion of the appeal. This adoption procedure is without prejudice to the right of Members to express their views on a panel report.

Article 17

Appellate Review

Standing Appellate Body

1. A standing Appellate Body shall be established by the DSB. The Appellate Body shall hear appeals from panel cases. It shall be composed of seven persons, three of whom shall serve on any one case. Persons serving on the Appellate Body shall serve in rotation. Such rotation shall be determined in the working procedures of the Appellate Body.

2. The DSB shall appoint persons to serve on the Appellate Body for a four-year term, and each person may be reappointed once. However, the terms of three of the seven persons appointed immediately after the entry into force of the WTO Agreement shall expire at the end of two years, to be determined by lot. Vacancies shall be filled as they arise. A person appointed to replace a person whose term of office has not expired shall hold office for the remainder of the predecessor's term.

3. The Appellate Body shall comprise persons of recognized authority, with demonstrated expertise in law, international trade and the subject matter of the covered agreements generally. They shall be unaffiliated with any government. The Appellate Body membership shall be broadly representative of membership in the WTO. All persons serving on the Appellate Body shall be available at all times and on short notice, and shall stay abreast of dispute settlement activities and other relevant activities of the WTO. They shall not participate in the consideration of any disputes that would create a direct or indirect conflict of interest.

4. Only parties to the dispute, not third parties, may appeal a panel report. Third parties which have notified the DSB of a substantial interest in the matter pursuant to paragraph 2 of Article 10 may make written submissions to, and be given an opportunity to be heard by, the Appellate Body.

---

7 If a meeting of the DSB is not scheduled within this period at a time that enables the requirements of paragraphs 1 and 4 of Article 16 to be met, a meeting of the DSB shall be held for this purpose.

5. As a general rule, the proceedings shall not exceed 60 days from the date a party to the dispute formally notifies its decision to appeal to the date the Appellate Body circulates its report. In fixing its timetable the Appellate Body shall take into account the provisions of paragraph 9 of Article 4, if relevant. When the Appellate Body considers that it cannot provide its report within 60 days, it shall inform the DSB in writing of the reasons for the delay together with an estimate of the period within which it will submit its report. In no case shall the proceedings exceed 90 days.

6. An appeal shall be limited to issues of law covered in the panel report and legal interpretations developed by the panel.

7. The Appellate Body shall be provided with appropriate administrative and legal support as it requires.

8. The expenses of persons serving on the Appellate Body, including travel and subsistence allowance, shall be met from the WTO budget in accordance with criteria to be adopted by the General Council, based on recommendations of the Committee on Budget, Finance and Administration.

Procedures for Appellate Review

9. Working procedures shall be drawn up by the Appellate Body in consultation with the Chairman of the DSB and the Director-General, and communicated to the Members for their information.

10. The proceedings of the Appellate Body shall be confidential. The reports of the Appellate Body shall be drafted without the presence of the parties to the dispute and in the light of the information provided and the statements made.

11. Opinions expressed in the Appellate Body report by individuals serving on the Appellate Body shall be anonymous.

12. The Appellate Body shall address each of the issues raised in accordance with paragraph 6 during the appellate proceeding.

13. The Appellate Body may uphold, modify or reverse the legal findings and conclusions of the panel.

Adoption of Appellate Body Reports

14. An Appellate Body report shall be adopted by the DSB and unconditionally accepted by the parties to the dispute unless the DSB decides by consensus not to adopt the Appellate Body report within 30 days following its circulation to the Members.[8] This adoption procedure is without prejudice to the right of Members to express their views on an Appellate Body report.

Article 18

Communications with the Panel or Appellate Body

1. There shall be no *ex parte* communications with the panel or Appellate Body concerning matters under consideration by the panel or Appellate Body.

---

8 If a meeting of the DSB is not scheduled during this period, such a meeting of the DSB shall be held for this purpose.

2. Written submissions to the panel or the Appellate Body shall be treated as confidential, but shall be made available to the parties to the dispute. Nothing in this Understanding shall preclude a party to a dispute from disclosing statements of its own positions to the public. Members shall treat as confidential information submitted by another Member to the panel or the Appellate Body which that Member has designated as confidential. A party to a dispute shall also, upon request of a Member, provide a non-confidential summary of the information contained in its written submissions that could be disclosed to the public.

Article 19

Panel and Appellate Body Recommendations

1. Where a panel or the Appellate Body concludes that a measure is inconsistent with a covered agreement, it shall recommend that the Member concerned[9] bring the measure into conformity with that agreement.[10] In addition to its recommendations, the panel or Appellate Body may suggest ways in which the Member concerned could implement the recommendations.

2. In accordance with paragraph 2 of Article 3, in their findings and recommendations, the panel and Appellate Body cannot add to or diminish the rights and obligations provided in the covered agreements.

Article 20

Time-frame for DSB Decisions

Unless otherwise agreed to by the parties to the dispute, the period from the date of establishment of the panel by the DSB until the date the DSB considers the panel or appellate report for adoption shall as a general rule not exceed nine months where the panel report is not appealed or 12 months where the report is appealed. Where either the panel or the Appellate Body has acted, pursuant to paragraph 9 of Article 12 or paragraph 5 of Article 17, to extend the time for providing its report, the additional time taken shall be added to the above periods.

Article 21

Surveillance of Implementation of Recommendations and Rulings

1. Prompt compliance with recommendations or rulings of the DSB is essential in order to ensure effective resolution of disputes to the benefit of all Members.

2. Particular attention should be paid to matters affecting the interests of developing country Members with respect to measures which have been subject to dispute settlement.

3. At a DSB meeting held within 30 days[11] after the date of adoption of the panel or Appellate Body report, the Member concerned shall inform the DSB of its intentions in respect of implementation of the recommendations and rulings of the DSB. If it is impracticable to comply immediately with the recommendations and rulings, the Member concerned shall have a reasonable period of time in which to do so. The reasonable period of time shall be:

---

9 The "Member concerned" is the party to the dispute to which the panel or Appellate Body recommendations are directed.

10 With respect to recommendations in cases not involving a violation of GATT 1994 or any other covered agreement, see Article 26.

11 If a meeting of the DSB is not scheduled during this period, such a meeting of the DSB shall be held for this purpose.

(a) the period of time proposed by the Member concerned, provided that such period is approved by the DSB; or, in the absence of such approval,

(b) a period of time mutually agreed by the parties to the dispute within 45 days after the date of adoption of the recommendations and rulings; or, in the absence of such agreement,

(c) a period of time determined through binding arbitration within 90 days after the date of adoption of the recommendations and rulings.[12] In such arbitration, a guideline for the arbitrator[13] should be that the reasonable period of time to implement panel or Appellate Body recommendations should not exceed 15 months from the date of adoption of a panel or Appellate Body report. However, that time may be shorter or longer, depending upon the particular circumstances.

4. Except where the panel or the Appellate Body has extended, pursuant to paragraph 9 of Article 12 or paragraph 5 of Article 17, the time of providing its report, the period from the date of establishment of the panel by the DSB until the date of determination of the reasonable period of time shall not exceed 15 months unless the parties to the dispute agree otherwise. Where either the panel or the Appellate Body has acted to extend the time of providing its report, the additional time taken shall be added to the 15-month period; provided that unless the parties to the dispute agree that there are exceptional circumstances, the total time shall not exceed 18 months.

5. Where there is disagreement as to the existence or consistency with a covered agreement of measures taken to comply with the recommendations and rulings such dispute shall be decided through recourse to these dispute settlement procedures, including wherever possible resort to the original panel. The panel shall circulate its report within 90 days after the date of referral of the matter to it. When the panel considers that it cannot provide its report within this time frame, it shall inform the DSB in writing of the reasons for the delay together with an estimate of the period within which it will submit its report.

6. The DSB shall keep under surveillance the implementation of adopted recommendations or rulings. The issue of implementation of the recommendations or rulings may be raised at the DSB by any Member at any time following their adoption. Unless the DSB decides otherwise, the issue of implementation of the recommendations or rulings shall be placed on the agenda of the DSB meeting after six months following the date of establishment of the reasonable period of time pursuant to paragraph 3 and shall remain on the DSB's agenda until the issue is resolved. At least 10 days prior to each such DSB meeting, the Member concerned shall provide the DSB with a status report in writing of its progress in the implementation of the recommendations or rulings.

7. If the matter is one which has been raised by a developing country Member, the DSB shall consider what further action it might take which would be appropriate to the circumstances.

8. If the case is one brought by a developing country Member, in considering what appropriate action might be taken, the DSB shall take into account not only the trade coverage of measures complained of, but also their impact on the economy of developing country Members concerned.

---

12 If the parties cannot agree on an arbitrator within ten days after referring the matter to arbitration, the arbitrator shall be appointed by the Director-General within ten days, after consulting the parties.

13 The expression "arbitrator" shall be interpreted as referring either to an individual or a group.

Article 22

Compensation and the Suspension of Concessions

1. Compensation and the suspension of concessions or other obligations are temporary measures available in the event that the recommendations and rulings are not implemented within a reasonable period of time. However, neither compensation nor the suspension of concessions or other obligations is preferred to full implementation of a recommendation to bring a measure into conformity with the covered agreements. Compensation is voluntary and, if granted, shall be consistent with the covered agreements.

2. If the Member concerned fails to bring the measure found to be inconsistent with a covered agreement into compliance therewith or otherwise comply with the recommendations and rulings within the reasonable period of time determined pursuant to paragraph 3 of Article 21, such Member shall, if so requested, and no later than the expiry of the reasonable period of time, enter into negotiations with any party having invoked the dispute settlement procedures, with a view to developing mutually acceptable compensation. If no satisfactory compensation has been agreed within 20 days after the date of expiry of the reasonable period of time, any party having invoked the dispute settlement procedures may request authorization from the DSB to suspend the application to the Member concerned of concessions or other obligations under the covered agreements.

3. In considering what concessions or other obligations to suspend, the complaining party shall apply the following principles and procedures:

(a) the general principle is that the complaining party should first seek to suspend concessions or other obligations with respect to the same sector(s) as that in which the panel or Appellate Body has found a violation or other nullification or impairment;

(b) if that party considers that it is not practicable or effective to suspend concessions or other obligations with respect to the same sector(s), it may seek to suspend concessions or other obligations in other sectors under the same agreement;

(c) if that party considers that it is not practicable or effective to suspend concessions or other obligations with respect to other sectors under the same agreement, and that the circumstances are serious enough, it may seek to suspend concessions or other obligations under another covered agreement;

(d) in applying the above principles, that party shall take into account:

(i) the trade in the sector or under the agreement under which the panel or Appellate Body has found a violation or other nullification or impairment, and the importance of such trade to that party;

(ii) the broader economic elements related to the nullification or impairment and the broader economic consequences of the suspension of concessions or other obligations;

(e) if that party decides to request authorization to suspend concessions or other obligations pursuant to subparagraphs (b) or (c), it shall state the reasons therefor in its request. At the same time as the request is forwarded to the DSB, it also shall be forwarded to the relevant Councils and also, in the case of a request pursuant to subparagraph (b), the relevant sectoral bodies;

(f) for purposes of this paragraph, "sector" means:

(i) with respect to goods, all goods;

(ii) with respect to services, a principal sector as identified in the current "Services Sectoral Classification List" which identifies such sectors;[14]

(iii) with respect to trade-related intellectual property rights, each of the categories of intellectual property rights covered in Section 1, or Section 2, or Section 3, or Section 4, or Section 5, or Section 6, or Section 7 of Part II, or the obligations under Part III, or Part IV of the Agreement on TRIPS;

(g) for purposes of this paragraph, "agreement" means:

(i) with respect to goods, the agreements listed in Annex 1A of the WTO Agreement, taken as a whole as well as the Plurilateral Trade Agreements in so far as the relevant parties to the dispute are parties to these agreements;

(ii) with respect to services, the GATS;

(iii) with respect to intellectual property rights, the Agreement on TRIPS.

4. The level of the suspension of concessions or other obligations authorized by the DSB shall be equivalent to the level of the nullification or impairment.

5. The DSB shall not authorize suspension of concessions or other obligations if a covered agreement prohibits such suspension.

6. When the situation described in paragraph 2 occurs, the DSB, upon request, shall grant authorization to suspend concessions or other obligations within 30 days of the expiry of the reasonable period of time unless the DSB decides by consensus to reject the request. However, if the Member concerned objects to the level of suspension proposed, or claims that the principles and procedures set forth in paragraph 3 have not been followed where a complaining party has requested authorization to suspend concessions or other obligations pursuant to paragraph 3(b) or (c), the matter shall be referred to arbitration. Such arbitration shall be carried out by the original panel, if members are available, or by an arbitrator[15] appointed by the Director-General and shall be completed within 60 days after the date of expiry of the reasonable period of time. Concessions or other obligations shall not be suspended during the course of the arbitration.

7. The arbitrator[16] acting pursuant to paragraph 6 shall not examine the nature of the concessions or other obligations to be suspended but shall determine whether the level of such suspension is equivalent to the level of nullification or impairment. The arbitrator may also determine if the proposed suspension of concessions or other obligations is allowed under the covered agreement. However, if the matter referred to arbitration includes a claim that the principles and procedures set forth in paragraph 3 have not been followed, the arbitrator shall examine that claim. In the event the arbitrator determines that those principles and procedures have not been followed, the complaining party shall apply them consistent with paragraph 3. The parties shall accept the arbitrator's decision as final and the parties concerned shall not seek a second arbitration. The DSB shall be informed promptly of the decision of the arbitrator and shall upon request, grant authorization to suspend concessions or other obligations where the request is consistent with the decision of the arbitrator, unless the DSB decides by consensus to reject the request.

---

14 The list in document MTN.GNS/W/120 identifies eleven sectors.

15 The expression"arbitrator" shall be interpreted as referring either to an individual or a group.

16 The expression "arbitrator" shall be interpreted as referring either to an individual or a group or to the members of the original panel when serving in the capacity of arbitrator.

8. The suspension of concessions or other obligations shall be temporary and shall only be applied until such time as the measure found to be inconsistent with a covered agreement has been removed, or the Member that must implement recommendations or rulings provides a solution to the nullification or impairment of benefits, or a mutually satisfactory solution is reached. In accordance with paragraph 6 of Article 21, the DSB shall continue to keep under surveillance the implementation of adopted recommendations or rulings, including those cases where compensation has been provided or concessions or other obligations have been suspended but the recommendations to bring a measure into conformity with the covered agreements have not been implemented.

9. The dispute settlement provisions of the covered agreements may be invoked in respect of measures affecting their observance taken by regional or local governments or authorities within the territory of a Member. When the DSB has ruled that a provision of a covered agreement has not been observed, the responsible Member shall take such reasonable measures as may be available to it to ensure its observance. The provisions of the covered agreements and this Understanding relating to compensation and suspension of concessions or other obligations apply in cases where it has not been possible to secure such observance.[17]

Article 23

Strengthening of the Multilateral System

1. When Members seek the redress of a violation of obligations or other nullification or impairment of benefits under the covered agreements or an impediment to the attainment of any objective of the covered agreements, they shall have recourse to, and abide by, the rules and procedures of this Understanding.

2. In such cases, Members shall:

(a) not make a determination to the effect that a violation has occurred, that benefits have been nullified or impaired or that the attainment of any objective of the covered agreements has been impeded, except through recourse to dispute settlement in accordance with the rules and procedures of this Understanding, and shall make any such determination consistent with the findings contained in the panel or Appellate Body report adopted by the DSB or an arbitration award rendered under this Understanding;

(b) follow the procedures set forth in Article 21 to determine the reasonable period of time for the Member concerned to implement the recommendations and rulings; and

(c) follow the procedures set forth in Article 22 to determine the level of suspension of concessions or other obligations and obtain DSB authorization in accordance with those procedures before suspending concessions or other obligations under the covered agreements in response to the failure of the Member concerned to implement the recommendations and rulings within that reasonable period of time.

---

17 Where the provisions of any covered agreement concerning measures taken by regional or local governments or authorities within the territory of a Member contain provisions different from the provisions of this paragraph, the provisions of such covered agreement shall prevail.

Article 24

Special Procedures Involving Least-Developed Country Members

1. At all stages of the determination of the causes of a dispute and of dispute settlement procedures involving a least-developed country Member, particular consideration shall be given to the special situation of least-developed country Members. In this regard, Members shall exercise due restraint in raising matters under these procedures involving a least-developed country Member. If nullification or impairment is found to result from a measure taken by a least-developed country Member, complaining parties shall exercise due restraint in asking for compensation or seeking authorization to suspend the application of concessions or other obligations pursuant to these procedures.

2. In dispute settlement cases involving a least-developed country Member, where a satisfactory solution has not been found in the course of consultations the Director-General or the Chairman of the DSB shall, upon request by a least-developed country Member offer their good offices, conciliation and mediation with a view to assisting the parties to settle the dispute, before a request for a panel is made. The Director-General or the Chairman of the DSB, in providing the above assistance, may consult any source which either deems appropriate.

Article 25

Arbitration

1. Expeditious arbitration within the WTO as an alternative means of dispute settlement can facilitate the solution of certain disputes that concern issues that are clearly defined by both parties.

2. Except as otherwise provided in this Understanding, resort to arbitration shall be subject to mutual agreement of the parties which shall agree on the procedures to be followed. Agreements to resort to arbitration shall be notified to all Members sufficiently in advance of the actual commencement of the arbitration process.

3. Other Members may become party to an arbitration proceeding only upon the agreement of the parties which have agreed to have recourse to arbitration. The parties to the proceeding shall agree to abide by the arbitration award. Arbitration awards shall be notified to the DSB and the Council or Committee of any relevant agreement where any Member may raise any point relating thereto.

4. Articles 21 and 22 of this Understanding shall apply *mutatis mutandis* to arbitration awards.

Article 26

1. Non-Violation Complaints of the Type Described in Paragraph 1(b) of Article XXIII of GATT 1994

Where the provisions of paragraph 1(b) of Article XXIII of GATT 1994 are applicable to a covered agreement, a panel or the Appellate Body may only make rulings and recommendations where a party to the dispute considers that any benefit accruing to it directly or indirectly under the relevant covered agreement is being nullified or impaired or the attainment of any objective of that Agreement is being impeded as a result of the application by a Member of any measure, whether or not it conflicts with the provisions of that Agreement. Where and to the extent that such party considers and a panel or the Appellate Body determines that a case concerns a measure that does not conflict with the provisions of a covered agreement to which the provisions of paragraph 1(b) of Article XXIII of GATT 1994 are applicable, the procedures in this Understanding shall apply, subject to the following:

(a) the complaining party shall present a detailed justification in support of any complaint relating to a measure which does not conflict with the relevant covered agreement;

(b) where a measure has been found to nullify or impair benefits under, or impede the attainment of objectives, of the relevant covered agreement without violation thereof, there is no obligation to withdraw the measure. However, in such cases, the panel or the Appellate Body shall recommend that the Member concerned make a mutually satisfactory adjustment;

(c) notwithstanding the provisions of Article 21, the arbitration provided for in paragraph 3 of Article 21, upon request of either party, may include a determination of the level of benefits which have been nullified or impaired, and may also suggest ways and means of reaching a mutually satisfactory adjustment; such suggestions shall not be binding upon the parties to the dispute;

(d) notwithstanding the provisions of paragraph 1 of Article 22, compensation may be part of a mutually satisfactory adjustment as final settlement of the dispute.

2. *Complaints of the Type Described in Paragraph 1(c) of Article XXIII of GATT 1994*

Where the provisions of paragraph 1(c) of Article XXIII of GATT 1994 are applicable to a covered agreement, a panel may only make rulings and recommendations where a party considers that any benefit accruing to it directly or indirectly under the relevant covered agreement is being nullified or impaired or the attainment of any objective of that Agreement is being impeded as a result of the existence of any situation other than those to which the provisions of paragraphs 1(a) and 1(b) of Article XXIII of GATT 1994 are applicable. Where and to the extent that such party considers and a panel determines that the matter is covered by this paragraph, the procedures of this Understanding shall apply only up to and including the point in the proceedings where the panel report has been circulated to the Members. The dispute settlement rules and procedures contained in the Decision of 12 April 1989 (BISD 36S/61-67) shall apply to consideration for adoption, and surveillance and implementation of recommendations and rulings. The following shall also apply:

(a) the complaining party shall present a detailed justification in support of any argument made with respect to issues covered under this paragraph;

(b) in cases involving matters covered by this paragraph, if a panel finds that cases also involve dispute settlement matters other than those covered by this paragraph, the panel shall circulate a report to the DSB addressing any such matters and a separate report on matters falling under this paragraph.

Article 27

Responsibilities of the Secretariat

1. The Secretariat shall have the responsibility of assisting panels, especially on the legal, historical and procedural aspects of the matters dealt with, and of providing secretarial and technical support.

2. While the Secretariat assists Members in respect of dispute settlement at their request, there may also be a need to provide additional legal advice and assistance in respect of dispute

settlement to developing country Members. To this end, the Secretariat shall make available a qualified legal expert from the WTO technical cooperation services to any developing country Member which so requests. This expert shall assist the developing country Member in a manner ensuring the continued impartiality of the Secretariat.

3. The Secretariat shall conduct special training courses for interested Members concerning these dispute settlement procedures and practices so as to enable Members' experts to be better informed in this regard.

Index